American Furniture

AMERICAN FURNITURE 2007

Edited by Luke Beckerdite

THE CHIPSTONE FOUNDATION

Milwaukee

CHIPSTONE FOUNDATION BOARD OF DIRECTORS
Edward S. Cooke Jr.
Charles Hummel
Ted Kellner
Peter M. Kenny
W. David Knox II   *Chairman and* CEO
John S. McGregor
Jonathan Prown   *Executive Director*
Alison Stone
Stanley Stone III
Allen M. Taylor   *Vice President*

EDITOR
Luke Beckerdite

BOOK AND EXHIBITION REVIEW EDITOR
Gerald W. R. Ward

EDITORIAL ADVISORY BOARD
Glenn Adamson, *Director of Graduate Studies, Victoria & Albert Museum*
David Barquist, *Curator of American Decorative Arts, Philadelphia Museum of Art*
Wendy Cooper, *Curator of Furniture, Winterthur Museum*
Leroy Graves, *Upholstery Conservator, Colonial Williamsburg Foundation*
Robert A. Leath, *Vice President, Collections & Research, Old Salem Museums & Gardens*
Alan Miller, *Conservator and Independent Furniture Consultant, Quakertown, Pennsylvania*
Sumpter Priddy III, *Decorative Arts Scholar and Dealer, Virginia*
Robert F. Trent, *Independent Furniture Consultant, Wilmington, Delaware*
Gerald W. R. Ward, *Katharine Lane Weems Senior Curator of Decorative Arts and Sculpture, Art of the Americas, Museum of Fine Arts, Boston*
Philip Zea, *Executive Director, Historic Deerfield*

Cover Illustration: Detail of a sideboard table with carving attributed to John Pollard, Philadelphia, Pennsylvania, 1765–1770. (Courtesy Metropolitan Museum of Art, John Stewart Kennedy Fund, 1918 [18.110.27]; photo, Gavin Ashworth.)

Design: Wynne Patterson, Pittsfield, VT
Copyediting: Fronia Simpson, Bennington, VT
Typesetting: Aardvark Type, Hartford, CT
Printing: Meridian Printing, East Greenwich, RI

Published by the Chipstone Foundation, 7820 North Club Circle, Milwaukee, WI 53217
Distributed by Antique Collectors' Club, Ltd., Easthampton, MA, and Woodbridge, Suffolk, UK
Distributed to the Trade by National Book Network, Inc.

© 2007 by the Chipstone Foundation
All rights reserved
Printed in the United States of America   5 4 3 2 1
ISSN 1069-4188
ISBN 0-9767344-1-9

Contents

Editorial Statement *Luke Beckerdite*	VII
Benjamin Randolph Revisited *Andrew Brunk*	2
American Board-Seated Turned Chairs, 1640–1740 *Robert F. Trent and John D. Alexander*	83
From Apprentice to Master: The Life and Career of Philadelphia Cabinetmaker George G. Wright *Clark Pearce, Catherine Ebert, and Alexandra Alevizatos Kirtley*	110
Early American Furniture Makers' Marks *Philip D. Zimmerman*	132
Reading Japanned Furniture *Ethan W. Lasser*	167
The Written Evidence of Furniture Repairs and Alterations: How Original Is "All Original"? *Nancy Goyne Evans*	191
Book Reviews	251
Recent Writing on American Furniture: A Bibliography *Gerald W. R. Ward*	271
Index	281

Editorial Statement

American Furniture is an interdisciplinary journal dedicated to advancing knowledge of furniture made or used in the Americas from the seventeenth century to the present. Authors are encouraged to submit articles on any aspect of furniture history, essays on conservation and historic technology, reproductions or transcripts of documents, annotated photographs of new furniture discoveries, and book and exhibition reviews. References for compiling an annual bibliography also are welcome.

Manuscripts must be typed, double-spaced, illustrated with black-and-white prints or transparencies, and prepared in accordance with the *Chicago Manual of Style*. Computer disk copy is requested but not required. The Chipstone Foundation will offer significant honoraria for manuscripts accepted for publication and reimburse authors for all photography approved in writing by the editor. Low resolution digital images are not acceptable.

Luke Beckerdite

American Furniture

Figure 1 Charles Willson Peale, *Benjamin Randolph,* Philadelphia, Pennsylvania, 1775–1780. Watercolor on ivory. 1¼" x 1". (Courtesy, Philadelphia Museum of Art; gift of Mr. and Mrs. Timothy Johnes Westbrook, 1990.)

Andrew Brunk

Benjamin Randolph Revisited

▼ BENJAMIN RANDOLPH (fig. 1) was the proprietor of one of the most successful cabinetmaking shops in Philadelphia during the 1760s and 1770s. That period witnessed the arrival of highly skilled immigrant carvers from Britain, the establishment of nonimportation agreements, and the building and furnishing of many grand houses by the city's elite. Randolph's surviving account book and receipt book reveal that he enjoyed the patronage of merchants, professionals, politicians, and prosperous tradesmen. The output of his shop was prodigious, and the purchases documented in his account book suggest that Randolph produced some of the most sophisticated and expensive furniture made in Philadelphia. Yet, despite his apparent prominence and the significant amount of documentation pertaining to his career, only a handful of objects have been convincingly linked to Randolph's shop.[1]

The objective of this article is to summarize previous scholarship on Randolph and place it in the context of his account book and receipt book. A complete name index for the accounts has been compiled to aid scholars in applying this documentary evidence (see App. 1, 2). In addition to identifying Randolph's patrons, his account book and receipt book provide information about his workforce, shop practices, and business dealings with other woodworkers. These documents also shed light on the complex and interconnected network of Philadelphia cabinetmakers and related tradesmen during the third quarter of the eighteenth century.

Randolph was born in 1737 and died in 1792. Although the names of his parents are not known, his lineage can be traced to the Fitz-Randolph family of New Jersey and Pennsylvania. Benjamin subsequently dropped the prefix from his name, abandoned his Quaker roots, and became an active member of St. Paul's Episcopal Church in Philadelphia. He married Anna Bromwich in 1762 and began renting quarters from joiner John Jones by May of the following year. In November 1763 Benjamin and Anna inherited a large sum of money from her father's estate. Two years later the couple moved into a house owned by William Milnor on Arch Street.[2]

In 1767 Randolph purchased the shop of Quaker carpenter Thomas Shoemaker on Chestnut Street and began advertising cabinet and chair work at the Sign of the Golden Eagle. Two years later, Randolph built a large shop and house on a town lot owned by James Hamilton, to whom he paid ground rent. Randolph remained in business at that location until he joined the Revolutionary War effort. In 1778 he sold his tools and remaining stock and retired to New Jersey. He died in 1791 and was buried at St. Paul's.[3]

Inconclusive Documents and Tantalizing Clues

The primary sources for information about Randolph's shop and business are his receipt book, account book, and miscellaneous papers in public and private collections. His receipt book is 229 pages long, arranged chronologically, and covers the years 1763 to 1777 (see App. 2). The entries record Randolph's purchases and transactions with other Philadelphians, but most simply read "Received of Benjamin Randolph" and designate the amount in local currency. More informative is the account book—a bound, folio-size volume documenting transactions from October 1, 1768, through 1787. Several of the entries from 1768 are continued from an earlier account book, the location of which is unknown. Most of the pages in the surviving book are clearly numbered and indexed. The left side of the page lists the purchase or what was taken from the shop (i.e., cash, stock, lumber, unspecified goods),

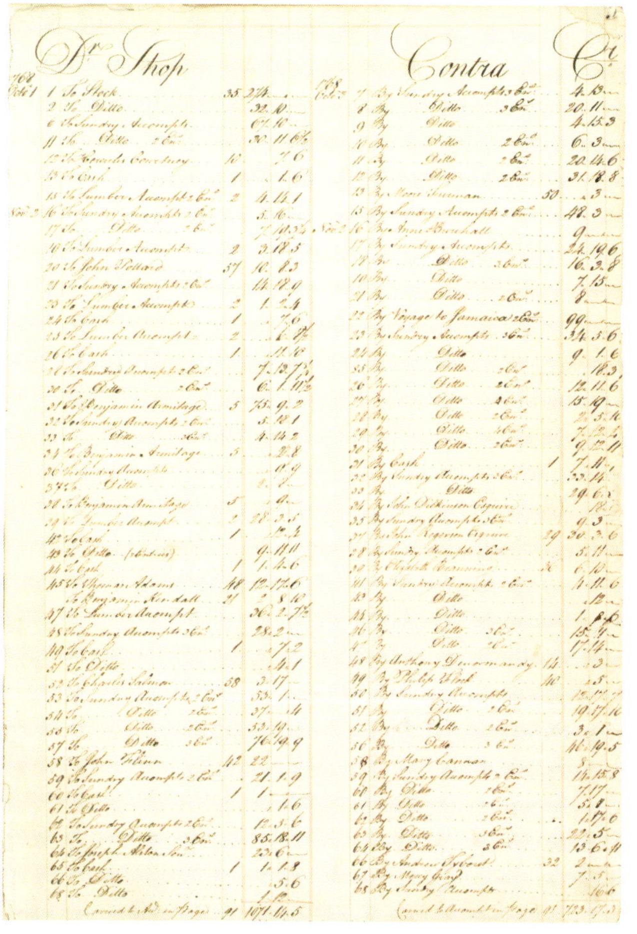

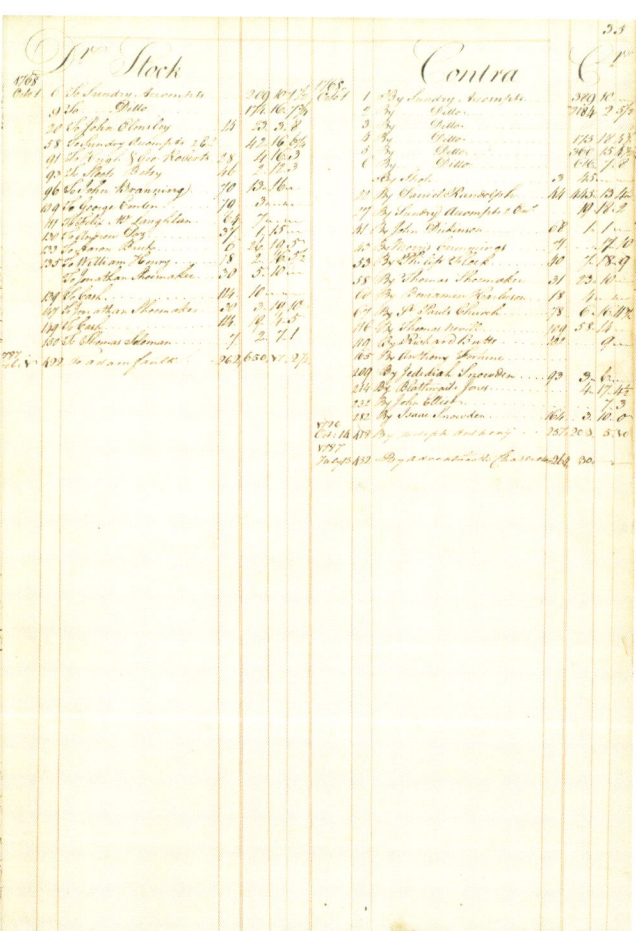

Figure 2 Page 3 from Benjamin Randolph's account book. (Courtesy, Manuscripts and Archives Division, New York Public Library, Astor, Lenox and Tilden Foundations.)

Figure 3 Page 35 from Benjamin Randolph's account book. (Courtesy, Manuscripts and Archives Division, New York Public Library, Astor, Lenox and Tilden Foundations.)

while the right side, designated "contra," indicates how the client paid (i.e., cash, sundries, "to shop," stock). Other pages set aside for general accounting include such headings as "Shop" (fig. 2), "Stock" (fig. 3), "Expense" (fig. 4), and "Sawmill." Regrettably, several pages are missing from the book. The index, which was compiled at a later date, does not list pages 2, 5, 6, 11–14, 111–22, and 127–38. What remains, however, is the most complete record of any cabinet shop active in Philadelphia during this period.[4]

4   ANDREW BRUNK

Because entries in Randolph's account book are not specific, one cannot assume that every individual who paid him received furniture. Moreover, many of the entries record payments by Randolph for lumber, sundries, rent, work performed by employees, and investments in his many financial concerns. The accounts that do refer to furniture are identified by the phrases "to shop" and "to stock." The former may refer to commission orders, whereas the latter may refer to finished goods for inventory or furniture that Randolph purchased from other cabinetmakers for retail.

Few of Randolph's employees are identified by profession, but their role in his shop can be confirmed or inferred by the way certain accounts are written or by other supporting documentation. Several cabinetmakers other than those employed by Randolph are also mentioned, some of whom purchased lumber, stock, unspecified goods, or services. The inde-

Figure 4 Page 43 from Benjamin Randolph's account book. (Courtesy, Manuscripts and Archives Division, New York Public Library, Astor, Lenox and Tilden Foundations.)

pendent cabinetmakers who purchased stock may have been acquiring furniture for resale or to satisfy orders within their respective shops.

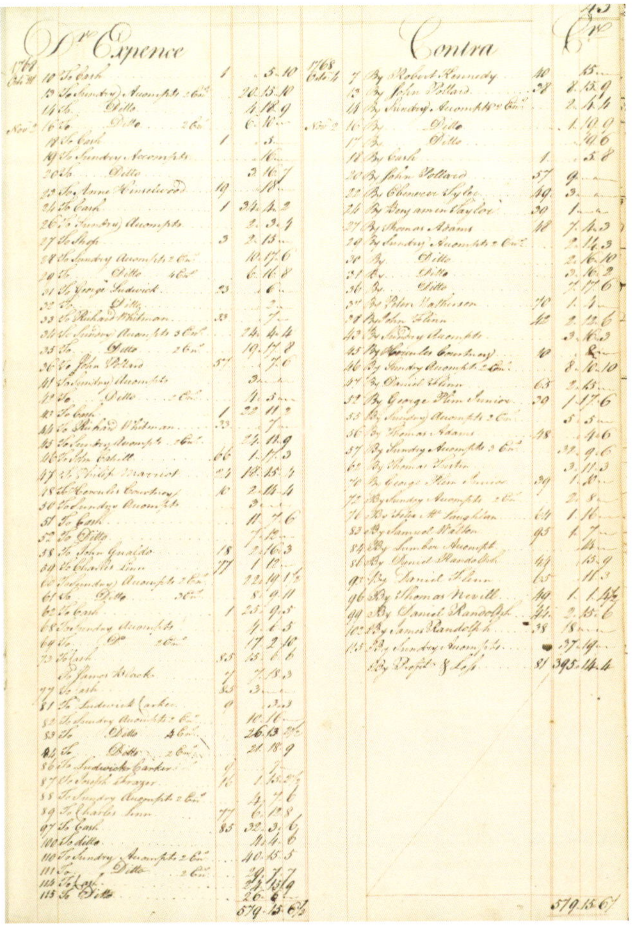

Hercules Courtenay and John Pollard were among the most important artisans in Randolph's shop. Courtenay had served his apprenticeship with renowned London carver and designer Thomas Johnson, whose publications *One Hundred and Fifty New Designs* (1758, 1761) and *A New Book of Ornaments* (1762) included some of the most advanced designs in the British rococo style. Although the identity of Pollard's master remains unknown, the carving attributed to the Philadelphia émigré suggests that his training was comparable to that of Courtenay.[5]

The earliest reference to Courtenay in Philadelphia is his signature on the Nonimportation Agreement of 1765, but he may have come to the colonies earlier under an indenture with Randolph. On December 23, 1766, Randolph paid Jacob Chrysler £3.16.6 on Courtenay's account. The following July, tailor Joseph Graisbury charged Randolph sixteen shillings for making Courtenay a "barygane coat." If Courtenay was an indentured servant, his term probably expired by May 19, 1768, when he married Mary Shute. In the August 7, 1769, issue of the *Pennsylvania Gazette*, Courtenay advertised "all Manner of Carving and Gilding in the newest Taste, at his house between Chestnut and Walnut on Front Street."[6]

The trusses, center tablet, and frieze appliqués on a chimneypiece from the parlor of Samuel Powel's town house are the earliest carved details documented to Courtenay (figs. 5, 6). Between August and October 1770, Powel paid the carver a total of £60 for work in his "dwelling house." These carved components indicate that Courtenay was extremely proficient and capable of working in the latest taste. The center tablet depicts Aesop's fable "The Dog and the Meat." Courtenay probably became acquainted with allegorical imagery during his apprenticeship in London. Thomas Johnson incorporated illustrations of Aesop's fables in designs for architectural tablets and friezes published in *One Hundred and Fifty New Designs*.[7]

Although Randolph's account book contains numerous references to Courtenay, Pollard received more credits and appears to have been the cabinetmaker's principal carver during the late 1760s and early 1770s. Like Courtenay, Pollard eventually established his own shop. On February 22, 1773, the *Pennsylvania Gazette* reported that Pollard and his partner Richard Butts could provide "all manner of carving" at the Sign of the Chinese Shield. Other immigrant carvers are mentioned in Randolph's account and receipt books, but there is little evidence that they consistently worked in his shop.[8]

No documented carving by Pollard is known, but strong circumstantial evidence suggests that he worked on some of the most important Philadelphia furniture and architectural woodwork in the rococo style. He almost certainly carved the remarkable scroll-foot sideboard table that descended in the family of John and Elizabeth (Lloyd) Cadwalader (see fig. 45) and furnished most of the architectural ornament for parlors from the Stamper-Blackwell House in Philadelphia and the Ringgold House in Chestertown, Maryland (figs. 7, 8). Both interiors have details taken from Johnson's *A New Book of Ornaments* (figs. 9, 10).[9]

Occupational tax records suggest that Randolph had a very profitable business. The only other Philadelphia cabinetmakers with comparable assessments were Thomas Affleck and George Claypoole. Much of Randolph's financial success appears to have come from investments in privateers, venture cargo, and "vendue" purchases, which are the largest transactions recorded in his account book. While most of Randolph's

Figure 5 Chimneypiece from the Samuel Powel House, Philadelphia, Pennsylvania, 1770. (Courtesy, Philadelphia Museum of Art; photo, Gavin Ashworth.)

Figure 6 Detail of the center tablet of the chimneypiece illustrated in fig. 5. (Photo, Gavin Ashworth).

Figure 7 Chimneypiece from the Thomas Ringgold House, Chestertown, Maryland, ca. 1770. (Courtesy, Baltimore Museum of Art.)

Figure 8 Detail of the frieze appliqué over a door from the Thomas Ringgold House. (Photo, Gavin Ashworth.)

Figure 9 Detail of the frieze appliqué on the chimneypiece illustrated in fig. 7. (Photo, Gavin Ashworth.)

Figure 10 Design for a frieze appliqué illustrated on pl. 2 in Thomas Johnson's *A New Book of Ornaments* (1762). (Courtesy, Victoria & Albert Museum.)

clients spent less than £100 pounds in total (£10 was sufficient to purchase a significant piece of furniture), he paid £20,438.5.4 for goods at vendue on October 12, 1778, then spent the extraordinary sum of £105,770.15.5 outfitting the brig *Argo* as a "privateer." The means by which Randolph financed such ventures remains a mystery, but his account book contains numerous references to ships and cargo assembled for export. Randolph's account book does not describe the various lots of cargo, but many of his shipments probably included lumber. Randolph's brother owned a sawmill, called Speedwell, in which Randolph ultimately became a partner, and numerous transactions in the account book refer to lumber. The lumber exported by Randolph probably included mahogany as well as indigenous woods, and some may have been shipped to England. In 1765 Randolph

Figure 11 Benjamin Randolph, side chair, Philadelphia, Pennsylvania, ca. 1770. Mahogany. H. 38 1/8", W. 23 3/4", D. 19". (Courtesy, Museum of Fine Arts, Boston, M. and M. Karolik Collection, © 2000, all rights reserved.)

purchased 19,000 board feet of lumber from David Tryon. Although some scholars have cited that purchase as evidence that Randolph was involved in house carpentry, it is more likely that the lumber was intended as venture cargo. Destinations mentioned in his account book include London, Honduras, Jamaica, and Charleston, South Carolina, and many export entries mention the Philadelphia mercantile firm Willing and Morris. Some shipments may have included finished furniture, but only a handful of documents support that theory. In 1767 Randolph billed George Croghan for furniture "for yourself" as well as other pieces "to go abroad." The cabinetmaker furnished packing cases for each piece intended for export. They may have been destined for a foreign port as venture cargo or for one of Croghan's residences in this country.[10]

The account book of Philadelphia carpenter Thomas Neville supports the theory that Randolph enjoyed considerable success. During the 1760s and 1770s Neville oversaw the construction of houses for Captain John McPherson, the Cadwaladers, and other members of Philadelphia's elite. The carpenter's accounts record transactions with Randolph from December 1765 to February 1773. The most extensive charges were for work "in the best manner" installed in the cabinetmaker's new house in 1769 and 1770. Among the architectural components provided by Neville were "77 yards 4 feet 2 ins. of Bilection wainscot," "2 sets of Pillaster fluted with proper bases & Ionic Capitals, Ovilas round the chimney & mantle broak over truss's," "Ramp rails of mahogany, ½ rails, open pilasters & plinths against ye wall," and "20 feet 8 ins. of moulding to form a Tabernacle frame finished with a Scrool like a Pediment & 8 knees Ovila round the chimney & 2 trusses." Clearly, Randolph's house was commensurate to a gentleman of means.[11]

While Cadwalader and McPherson usually paid Neville in cash, Randolph settled his debt with money, lumber, and "sundries." In 1769 Neville credited Randolph's account £8.4.10 for an easy chair and £1.10 for "Carving a pare of brackets for a dormer window." In November of the following year, Neville billed Randolph for "Preparing 2 Ionic caps for carving" and in a separate entry recorded that three pounds of his debt to workman William Stephenson had been settled with a dressing table from Randolph's shop. On March 26, 1771, Neville credited John Derry £15 for "the Workmanship of Benjamin Randolph's frontis-Piece Door" and indicated that payment consisted of "a desk had of Benjamin Randolph." Five months later, Neville credited Randolph's account for "½ dozen mahogany chairs" and "2 clock cases delivered to William Huston."[12]

Documentation and Attribution: A Sliding Scale
The only objects bearing Randolph's label are a card table and a small group of seating furniture; however, all of these pieces can be used as benchmarks for attributing other work to his shop. The construction of the labeled side chair shown in figure 11 matches that of an unlabeled armchair (fig. 12), and both objects have knee carving by the same hand (figs. 13, 14). Based on these commonalities, it would be reasonable to assume that the armchair is also a

Figure 12 Armchair attributed to the shop of Benjamin Randolph, Philadelphia, Pennsylvania, ca. 1770. Mahogany. H. 37⅝", W. 24¾" (seat), D. 19¾" (seat). (Private collection; photo, Joe Kindig Antiques.)

Figure 13 Detail of the knee carving on the side chair illustrated in fig. 11.

Figure 14 Detail of the knee carving on the armchair illustrated in fig. 12.

product of Randolph's shop. When comparing different forms, additional evidence is often required to support attribution. The tea table illustrated in figure 15 serves as a case in point. Its knee carving (fig. 16) is similar to that on the preceding chairs, but there are no structural parallels between the table and the seating forms. The table can, however, be attributed to Randolph by

Figure 15 Tea table attributed to the shop of Benjamin Randolph, Philadelphia, Pennsylvania, 1765–1775. Mahogany. Dimensions not recorded. (Private collection; photo, Joe Kindig Antiques.)

Figure 16 Detail of the knee carving on the tea table illustrated in fig. 15.

factoring in other pertinent information. Its feet are attributed to Hercules Courtenay based on their similarity to those on the card table illustrated in figure 17, and the card table is attributed to Courtenay based on its knee acanthus (fig. 18), which matches that on his documented mantel trusses from the parlor of Samuel Powel's house (figs. 5, 19). In sum, the tea table has carving by two artisans known to have worked for Randolph; thus, the preponderance of evidence suggests that the table is from his shop.[13]

Figure 17   Card table with carving attributed to Hercules Courtenay, Philadelphia, Pennsylvania, 1765–1775. Mahogany with unidentified secondary woods. Dimensions not recorded. (Private collection; photo, Mack Coffey.)

Figure 18   Detail of the knee carving on the card table illustrated in fig. 17.

Several pieces of Philadelphia furniture have histories associated with Randolph patrons, but attributions based solely on provenance are highly conjectural, since consumers typically patronized more than one shop. Moreover, most of the entries in Randolph's account book are not descriptive, and cost only hints at the type of work his shop may have performed for a given patron. A plausible representation of Randolph's production can be posited, however, through formal analysis of objects associated with his clients and comparison of those pieces with furniture bearing his label. If a significant number of unmarked objects associated with Randolph's clients have unifying structural, stylistic, and ornamental details, it would be reasonable to assume that they are products of his shop.

The cabriole-leg high chest illustrated in figure 20 bears the signature of Philadelphia cabinetmaker Isaac Barnet and a partially legible date that may be 1766 (fig. 21). Barnet's name first appears in Randolph's account book on

Figure 19 Detail of the right mantle truss of the chimneypiece illustrated in fig. 5. (Photo, Gavin Ashworth.)

Figure 20 High chest attributed to the shop of Benjamin Randolph, Philadelphia, Pennsylvania, 1765–1770. Mahogany with poplar, yellow pine, and cedar. H. 89⅞", W. 46⅛", D. 23⅝". (Courtesy, Nelson-Atkins Museum of Art.)

Figure 21 Detail of the inscription on the high chest illustrated in fig. 20.

Figure 22 Detail of the carving on the lower shell drawer of the high chest illustrated in fig. 20.

Figure 23 Detail of the knee carving on the high chest illustrated in fig. 20.

May 5, 1770, and there are fifteen subsequent entries totaling £39.6 for work identified by the phrase "by shop" and "contra" recorded on March 9, 1771.[14]

The carving on the high chest is clearly by two different hands. All of the work on the upper case and the shell and appliqués on the center bottom drawer (fig. 22) are attributed to an anonymous artisan know today as the "Garvan high chest carver." Research by Luke Beckerdite and Alan Miller suggests that this carver probably trained in Philadelphia and worked from the early to mid-1750s to the late 1760s. Nearly all of the case pieces carved by him are constructed in the same distinctive manner, which suggests that he was part of the workforce of a large cabinet shop rather than an independent tradesman. In contrast, the carving on the knees and skirt of the high chest (fig. 23) has affinities with work attributed to John Pollard. Barnet's signature and date suggest that the high chest was made in Randolph's shop shortly after Pollard arrived. The earliest reference to Pollard in Philadelphia is a December 1765 entry in Randolph's receipt book.[15]

Figure 24 Base of a high chest with carving attributed to John Pollard, Philadelphia, Pennsylvania, 1765–1775. Mahogany with yellow pine, sweet gum, and white cedar. H. 38", W. 45 5/8", D. 22 13/16". (Courtesy, Diplomatic Reception Rooms, U.S. Department of State.)

Figure 25 Detail of the carving on the center drawer of the high chest base illustrated in fig. 24.

The construction of the high chest and the design and execution of the carving on its base link it to several other important Philadelphia case pieces, including a high chest base (figs. 24, 25) and a dressing table (Museum of Fine Arts, Boston) possibly made en suite. Whereas all three of these objects may have come from the same cabinet shop, other case pieces with carving attributed to Pollard display significantly different construction techniques. He undoubtedly worked for several cabinetmakers and chair makers after establishing his own business in 1773.

Figure 26 James Smither, trade card of Benjamin Randolph, Philadelphia, Pennsylvania, 1769. Engraving on paper. 7" x 9". (Courtesy, Library Company of Philadelphia.) The desk-and-bookcase at the bottom center was copied from an engraving in Thomas Chippendale's *Gentleman and Cabinet-Maker's Director* (see fig. 27). No other contemporary reproduction of that image in Philadelphia is known.

While the high chest illustrated in figure 20 suggests that Randolph's shop produced traditional Philadelphia forms, the furniture depicted on his trade card (fig. 26) attests to his familiarity with the latest British fashions. The desk-and-bookcase directly above the cartouche at the bottom was copied from plate 108 in the third edition of Thomas Chippendale's *Gentleman and Cabinet-Maker's Director* (1762) (fig. 27). The same *Director* engraving inspired the lower case design of a monumental desk-and-bookcase (fig. 28) that art historian Robert C. Smith attributed to Randolph in a 1971 article entitled "A Philadelphia Desk-and-Bookcase from Chippendale's *Director*."[16]

Subsequent scholars have questioned Smith's attribution because he based his argument almost entirely on the imagery of Randolph's trade card and failed to reconcile the fact that several Philadelphia cabinetmakers had access to Chippendale's *Director* (the Library Company of Philadelphia had a copy of the 1754 edition). Although few have challenged the circa 1770 date that Smith later assigned to the piece, the integral pediment and Palladian design of the upper case suggest that the piece was made at least five years earlier. Most Philadelphia desk-and-bookcases and chest-on-chests from the

Figure 27 Design for a desk-and-bookcase illustrated on plate 108 in the third edition of Thomas Chippendale's *Gentleman and Cabinet-Maker's Director* (1762) This design appeared on pl. 78 in the first (1754) and second (1755) editions.

Figure 28 Desk-and-bookcase attributed to the shop of Benjamin Randolph, Philadelphia, Pennsylvania, ca. 1765. Mahogany with yellow pine, white cedar, poplar, and white oak. H. 114¼", W. 53¾", D. 26⅞". (Collection of Mrs. George M. Kaufman; photo, Dirk Bakker.) The lower case of this desk-and-bookcase was derived from a design in Thomas Chippendale's *Gentleman and Cabinet-Maker's Director* (see fig. 27). The only other Philadelphia case piece with details corresponding to that design is a desk-and-bookcase (see fig. 31) with feet like those on the example shown here.

19 BENJAMIN RANDOLPH REVISITED

Figure 29 Detail of the carving on the left door adjacent to the lower drawers of the desk-and-bookcase illustrated in fig. 28. (Photo, Gavin Ashworth.)

1770s have removable pediments. Similarly, the interiors of Philadelphia desks from the 1770s are typically quite severe, whereas the writing compartment of the desk-and-bookcase illustrated in figure 28 has boldly shaped serpentine drawers, a mirrored prospect door, and pilaster-fronted document drawers. Furthermore, all of the ornament on the desk-and-bookcase is by the Garvan high chest carver, whose career appears to have ended by the late 1760s (fig. 29).[17]

Although Smith's attribution of the desk-and-bookcase to Randolph was a bit premature, evidence suggests that the art historian may have been correct. A bill of sale from Randolph to George Croghan documents the cabinetmaker's production of very expensive furniture by 1765. At £30, the desk-and-bookcase commissioned by Croghan (fig. 30) cost more than twice as much as the most expensive example listed in James Humphreys Jr.'s *Prices of Cabinet and Chair Work*, published in Philadelphia in 1772. Although the entry for desk-and-bookcases included various options, the most expensive standardized model described in the price book cost £13 and had "doors . . . without glazing" and "carved work not to exceed 25s." To reach a cost of £30, Croghan's desk almost certainly had mirrored doors and elaborate carving. Given the probable date of the desk-and-bookcase and the extravagance of Croghan's purchase, one is tempted to speculate that the desk-and-bookcase illustrated in figure 28 may be the very one made for Croghan.[18]

Figure 30 Bill from Benjamin Randolph to George Croghan. (Courtesy, Historical Society of Pennsylvania, Cadwalader Collection.)

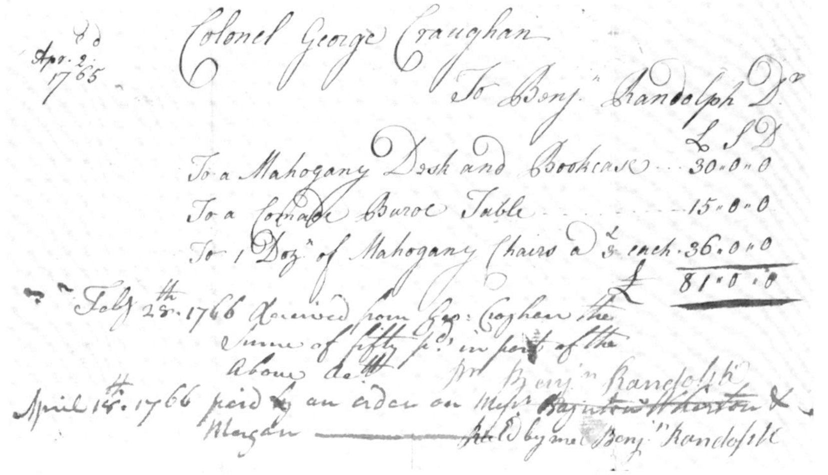

Croghan's wealth and prominence peaked during the years covered by Randolph's bills. As Deputy Agent of Indian Affairs, he negotiated important peace treaties while speculating on land and profiting from trade networks made accessible through his position. He counted members of the illustrious Penn, Gratz, and Wharton families among his friends and business associates, and maintained houses in New York and Carlisle and Fort Pitt, Pennsylvania, where he was stationed.[19]

While neither Croghan's name nor that of the mercantile firm that represented him during his residence at Fort Pitt appear in Randolph's account book, itemized bills provide evidence of other furniture forms made in the cabinetmaker's shop during the mid-1760s. No Philadelphia bracket clocks from that period are known, but Randolph's shop clearly produced examples with such sculptural details as "cerebim head[s] carved." At £15, Croghan's "comade [commode] bureau table" must have been comparable to his desk-and-bookcase in form, materials, and ornament. One Philadelphia bureau table of commode, or serpentine, form is known, but it appears to date from the 1770s.[20]

Another desk-and-bookcase (fig. 31) with even stronger connections to Randolph supports the theory that his shop produced the example shown in figure 28. The former object's integral pitch pediment, carved door moldings, mirrored door panels (now replaced with wood), and carved ogee-bracket feet represent later iterations of details found on the latter. The feet on these two pieces are nearly identical in design but were carved by different hands (figs. 32, 33). The carving on the prospect door and drawers in the writing compartment of the desk-and-bookcase illustrated in figure 31 is similar to that on the knees of a card table bearing Randolph's label (figs. 34–36). With its fine acanthus leaves and thin, precisely carved scrolls, the desk is among the most delicate work associated with Pollard.

Figure 31 Desk-and-bookcase attributed to the shop of Benjamin Randolph with carving attributed to John Pollard, Philadelphia, Pennsylvania, ca. 1770. Mahogany with tulip poplar and white cedar. H. 98½", W. 46", D. 25½". (Private collection; photo, Gavin Ashworth.)

Figure 32 Detail of the left front foot of the desk-and-bookcase illustrated in fig. 28. (Photo, Gavin Ashworth.)

Figure 33 Detail of the left front foot of the desk-and-bookcase illustrated in fig. 31. (Photo, Gavin Ashworth.)

Figure 34 Detail showing the carving on the prospect door and flanking drawers in the writing compartment of the desk-and-bookcase illustrated in fig. 31. (Photo, Gavin Ashworth.)

Figure 35 Benjamin Randolph, card table, Philadelphia, Pennsylvania, 1765–1775. Mahogany with white oak and poplar. H. 28¾", W. 33¼", D. 16". (Courtesy, Winterthur Museum.)

Figure 36 Detail of the knee carving on the card table illustrated in fig. 35.

The top drawer of the desk section is inscribed "Nancy Emlen" and dated 1771, two years before the carver began working as an independent tradesman. Members of the Emlen family were among Randolph's most important patrons. George Emlen Jr. had accounts totaling £262. 10s. and is the most likely person to have commissioned the desk-and-bookcase illustrated in figure 31. His daughter Ann went by the nickname of Nancy and may have been responsible for the inscription on the desk. She would have been sixteen years old in 1771. On May 13 of that year Randolph debited "Miss Sally Emlen" £38.12, and four days later he received payment in cash. Her relationship to Nancy Emlen is not known, nor is the specific nature of her purchase.[21]

A high chest that reputedly descended in the family of William Turner of Philadelphia may also be a product of Randolph's shop (fig. 37). Several transactions between the two men are recorded in the cabinetmaker's account book between October 1765 and September 1773. On June 29, 1767, Turner married Mary King. Sixteen months later, he purchased "stock" from Randolph valued at £36.10.10. Given the fact that this entry appears to have been continued from an earlier account, it is possible that Turner commissioned the high chest shortly after his wedding.[22]

The carving on the high chest is closely allied with that on the Emlen desk-and-bookcase, labeled card table, and other furniture and architectural work associated with Pollard. Although the designs of their knee carving differ, the acanthus leaves on the chest (fig. 38) and table (fig. 36) have mirror-image turns as they approach the ankle. The tympanum appliqué on the

Figure 37 High chest attributed to the shop of Benjamin Randolph, Philadelphia, Pennsylvania, ca. 1770. Mahogany with poplar, yellow pine, white oak, and white cedar. H. 90¼", W. 45⅝", D. 25½". (Courtesy, Winterthur Museum.)

Figure 38 Detail of the knee carving on the high chest illustrated in fig. 37.

Figure 39 Detail of the tympanum appliqué of the high chest illustrated in fig. 37.

Figure 40 Detail of the garland to the right of the chimneypiece illustrated in fig. 7. (Photo, Gavin Ashworth.)

chest (fig. 39) bears an even stronger resemblance to the carving from the Ringgold and Stamper-Blackwell parlors. Elements of the naturalistic festoon interwoven between the scrolls and Chinese columns of the appliqué are repeated on the garlands flanking both chimneypieces (fig. 40).

Provenance, patronage, and workmanship also support the theory that the pillar-and-claw tea table illustrated in figure 41 was made in Randolph's shop. Family tradition and lineage suggest that the table's original owner was Quaker merchant and patriot Clement Biddle. On March 6, 1775, he

Figure 41 Tea table attributed to the shop of Benjamin Randolph, Philadelphia, Pennsylvania, ca. 1775. Mahogany. H. 29½", diam. of top: 35". (Private collection; photo, Christie's.)

Figure 42 Page 181 from Benjamin Randolph's account book. (Courtesy, Manuscripts and Archives Division, New York Public Library, Astor, Lenox and Tilden Foundations.)

Figure 43 Detail of the knee carving on the tea table illustrated in fig. 41.

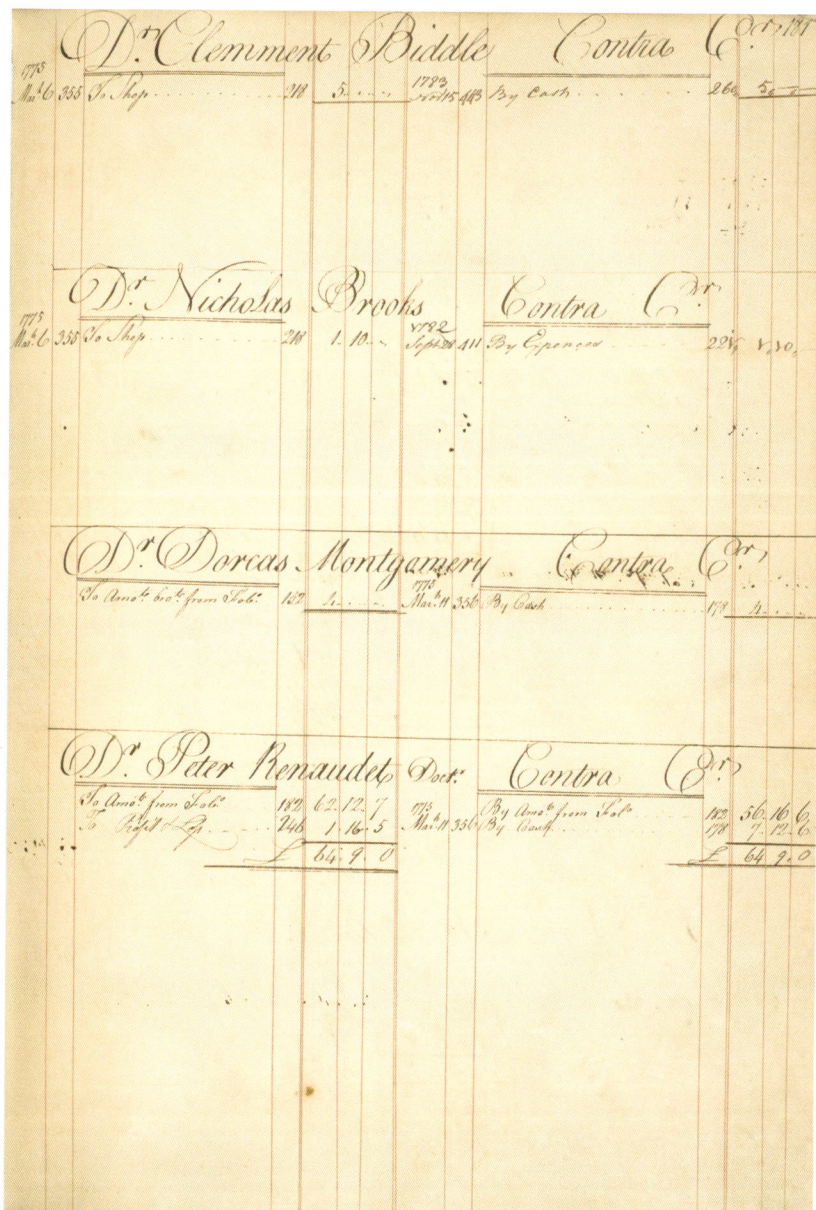

made a single purchase from Randolph totaling £5 (fig. 42). That amount appears to have been the going rate for a table like the one that descended in Biddle's family. In 1769 Philadelphia cabinetmaker James Gillingham charged £5 for "1 mahog. Tea Table Scalloped Claw feet and leaves on knees." The Philadelphia price book published three years later assigned a value of £5.15 to a tea table with claw feet, leaves on the knees, a scalloped top, and a carved pillar. While there were other furniture forms that cost the same amount, the timing and value of Biddle's purchase suggest that it was the table shown in figure 41. Furthermore, the carving on the knees and pillar is attributed to Pollard (fig. 43). Although he had opened his own shop by 1773, Pollard continued to receive sizable payments from Randolph as late as August 1775.[23]

Vanguard of the Avant-Garde

A small group of objects associated with Randolph and Pollard represent the most stylistically advanced rococo furniture produced in colonial America. The easy chair illustrated in figure 44 descended in the family of Randolph's second wife, Mary Wilkinson Fenimore, and was probably made in his shop during the mid- to late 1760s. The carving is attributed to

Figure 44 Easy chair attributed to the shop of Benjamin Randolph with carving attributed to John Pollard, Philadelphia, Pennsylvania, 1765–1775. Mahogany with white oak. H. 45¼", W. 24⅜", D. 27¹⁵⁄₁₆". (Courtesy, Philadelphia Museum of Art, purchased with museum funds, 1929.)

Pollard based on technical and stylistic parallels with other work, particularly that on the Cadwalader sideboard table (figs. 45, 46) and architectural components from the Ringgold and Stamper-Blackwell parlors (fig. 46).[24]

With its mahogany arm faces, applied carved rails, and hairy-paw feet, the design of the easy chair is unique among known Philadelphia examples. The mask on the front rail is an urban British detail likely introduced by either Pollard or Courtenay. As one might expect, the earliest work associated with these artisans shows the strongest reliance on English design. By the late 1760s both carvers had begun assimilating details of the Philadelphia vernacular.[25]

Figure 45 Sideboard table attributed to the shop of Benjamin Randolph with carving attributed to John Pollard, Philadelphia, Pennsylvania, 1765–1770. Mahogany with yellow pine and walnut. H. 32 3/8", W. 48", D. 23 1/4". (Courtesy, Metropolitan Museum of Art, John Stewart Kennedy Fund, 1918 [18.110.27]; photo, Gavin Ashworth.)

During the 1760s and 1770s Randolph maintained accounts with several Philadelphia upholsterers, including Plunkett Fleeson, Samuel How, Thomas Lawrence, William Martin, John Webster, and John Read. Much of the cabinetmaker's business went to Fleeson, whose shop at the "Sign of the Easy Chair on Chestnut Street above 3rd Street" was just a few steps away. In March 1767 Fleeson charged George Croghan five pounds for upholstering "2 mahogany French chair frames," which were most likely not the "pair [of] mahogany armchairs" Randolph had sold Croghan a month earlier.[26]

Figure 46 Details showing from top to bottom the carving on a side rail of the easy chair illustrated in fig. 44; the side rail of the sideboard table illustrated in fig. 45; and the left frieze appliqué below the mantle of the chimneypiece from the Stamper-Blackwell parlor.

The Cadwalader sideboard table (fig. 45) is the most elaborately carved object that can be linked to Randolph's shop. Its basic form and the reclining figure in the center were taken from a design for a pier glass and table illustrated on plate 152 of Chippendale's *Gentleman and Cabinet-Maker's Director* (1762) (fig. 47). John Cadwalader's waste book notes that on October 10, 1769, he reimbursed his brother Lambert £94.15 for "B. Randolph[s] acct for Furniture" and £30 for "2 marble Slabs etc. had of C. Coxe." Randolph's account book contains only passing mention of John Cadwalader and his brother and agent Lambert, but the entry corresponding to the

Figure 47 Design for a pier glass and table illustrated on pl. 152 in the third edition of Thomas Chippendale's *Gentleman and Cabinet-Maker's Director* (1762). (Courtesy, Winterthur Museum.)

£94.15 purchase was probably on one of the pages removed from that document. Luke Beckerdite, Leroy Graves, and Alan Miller have speculated that the table dates from the mid- to late 1760s, because its design and carving show no concession to prevailing Philadelphia styles. If they are correct, then the table is almost certainly from Randolph's shop. His account book suggests that Pollard was a full-time employee during that period. The carver received £180.24 for work performed between November 1768 and September 1769. The last payment occurred only ten days before the entry in Cadwalader's waste book.[27]

Although it is impossible to determine the cost of the sideboard table, the £94.15 payment to Randolph may have been sufficient for both its carved frame and a set of commode-seat side chairs that descended in the Cadwalader family (fig. 48). This seating appears to have been completed by September 1, 1770, when Charles Willson Peale received payment in full for his portrait of Lambert Cadwalader, depicted with his hand resting on one of the chairs (fig. 49). That date indicates that the chairs were the genesis of a much larger suite of furniture with related carving designs that John and Elizabeth Cadwalader commissioned from Philadelphia cabinetmaker Thomas Affleck later in the year.[28]

Figure 48 Side chair, attributed to the shop of Benjamin Randolph, Philadelphia, Pennsylvania, ca. 1769. Mahogany with white cedar. H. 36¾", W. 21¾" (seat), D. 17⅞" (seat). (Chipstone Foundation; photo, Hans Lorenz.)

Figure 49 Charles Willson Peale, *Lambert Cadwalader*, Philadelphia, Pennsylvania, 1770. 50" x 40". (Courtesy, Philadelphia Museum of Art, purchased for the Cadwalader Collection with funds contributed by the Mabel Pew Myrin Trust and the gift of an anonymous donor.)

The splats of the Cadwalader chairs may have been inspired by designs for "Ribband Back Chairs" illustrated on plate 15 in the third edition of Chippendale's *Director* (1762). As Beckerdite and Graves have noted, the acanthus leaves on the rails and knees are by the same hand that carved the side chairs bearing Randolph's label (figs. 13, 50). Because aspects of the carving on Cadwalader's seating also relate to that associated with both Pollard and Courtenay, the aforementioned scholars believe that the commode-seat chairs were produced in Randolph's shop and probably accounted for the £94.15 expenditure recorded in John Cadwalader's waste book.[29]

A chair that descended in the family of Randolph's second wife (fig. 51) also supports the theory that his shop produced the commode-seat examples (fig. 48). All of these chairs have rear stiles with acanthus leaves similar to those on trusses that Courtenay carved for the mantel in Samuel Powel's parlor (figs. 5, 52, 53). With its scroll feet and carved seat rails, the chair illustrated in figure 51 conforms to contemporary London taste more closely than its paw-foot counterparts (fig. 48).

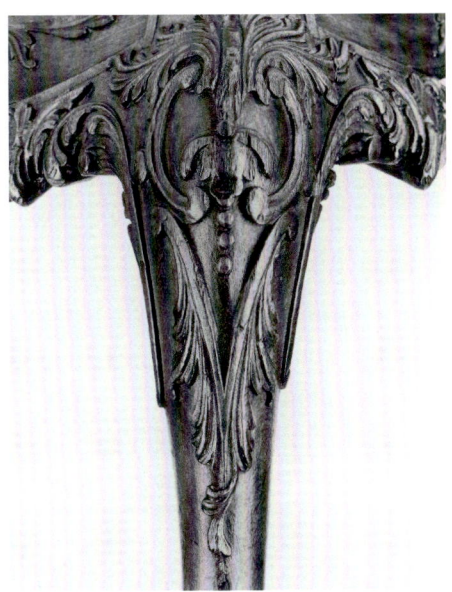

Figure 50 Detail of the knee carving on the side chair illustrated in fig. 48.

Figure 51 Side chair attributed to the shop of Benjamin Randolph, Philadelphia, Pennsylvania, 1765–1770. Mahogany. H. 37½", W. 24½", D. 21". (Courtesy, Philadelphia Museum of Art; photo, Gavin Ashworth.)

Figure 52 Detail of the carving on the left stile of the side chair illustrated in fig. 48

Figure 53 Detail of the carving on the left stile of the side chair illustrated in fig. 51. (Photo, Gavin Ashworth.)

Figure 54 Side chair attributed to the shop of Benjamin Randolph, Philadelphia, Pennsylvania, 1765–1770. Mahogany with tulip poplar. H. 41½", W. 27", D. 15½". (Courtesy, Colonial Williamsburg Foundation; photo, Hans Lorenz.)

Because they shared the same history of descent, Samuel Woodhouse speculated that the chairs illustrated in figures 48, 51, and 54 were samples that Randolph kept on display at his shop. Although that theory is refuted by roman numerals on certain examples (indicating their number in a set), these extraordinary seating forms are important in connecting other work to Randolph's shop. The knee carving on the chair illustrated in figure 54 is closely related to that on a pair of card tables and a set of side chairs with trapezoidal seat frames (figs. 55–57) owned by John and Elizabeth Cadwalader. Like the couple's commode-seat chairs (fig. 48), this suite is not identified in any known bills or accounts.[30]

Figure 55 Detail of the knee carving on the side chair illustrated in fig. 54.

Figure 56 Side chair attributed to the shop of Benjamin Randolph, Philadelphia, Pennsylvania, ca. 1770. Mahogany with unidentified secondary woods. Dimensions not recorded. . (Courtesy, Philadelphia Museum of Art, purchased with the Fiske Kimball Fund, the John T. Morris Fund, and funds contributed by Marguerite and Gerry Lenfest, the Richard Chilton Foundation, H. Richard Dietrich Jr., Robert L. McNeil Jr., Fitz Eugene Dixon Jr., Mrs. E. Newbold Smith, Charlene Sussel, Anne H. and Frederick Vogel III, Andrew M. Rouse, and Dr. and Mrs. Robert E. Booth, 2003.)

Figure 57 Detail of the knee carving on the side chair illustrated in fig. 56. (Photo, Gavin Ashworth.)

The backs of the trapezoidal-frame chairs match those on two elaborate side chairs from a set of at least eight (fig. 58). As Philip Zimmerman has noted, the backs of all these examples have comparable husk and acanthus ornament that appears to have been laid out using the same pattern. The carving on the knees and seat rails of the chairs represented by figure 58 is attributed to Pollard based on its relationship to architectural work in the Ringgold and Stamper-Blackwell parlors (figs. 8, 9, 59, 60). The front and side rails are made of oak and have mahogany laminates below. This two-part structure has an experimental quality recalling the construction of the easy chair illustrated in figure 44.

Although the strength of individual attributions advanced for the avant-garde furniture mentioned above varies, when considered as a group the design, construction, carving, and provenances of these objects strongly suggest that all are products of Randolph's shop. His account book and surviving bills and receipts indicate that he maintained a workforce capable of

Figure 58 Side chair attributed to the shop of Benjamin Randolph with carving attributed to John Pollard, Philadelphia, Pennsylvania, ca. 1770. Mahogany with white oak. H. 36¾", W. (seat) 23", D. (seat) 19⅛". The feet are restored. (Courtesy, Metropolitan Museum of Art, Rogers Fund, 1908 [08.51.10]; photo, Gavin Ashworth.)

Figure 59 Detail showing the knee carving on the chair illustrated in fig. 58. (Photo, Gavin Ashworth.)

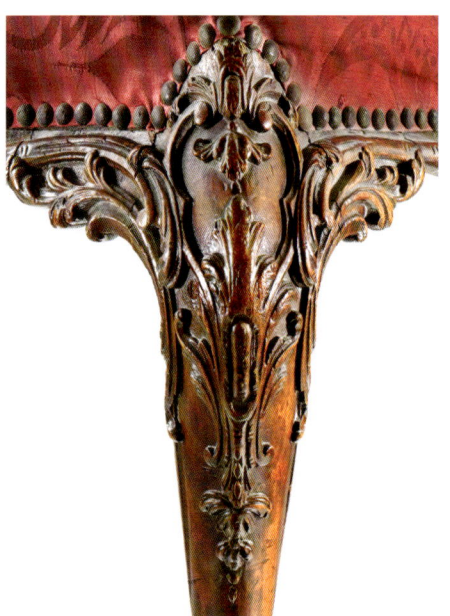

Figure 60 Detail of the door frieze illustrated in fig. 8. (Photo, Gavin Ashworth.)

manufacturing furniture in the latest London styles as well as pieces reflecting more traditional Philadelphia tastes. As the side chair illustrated in figure 61 suggests, he also offered furniture at a variety of price points ranging from astonishingly expensive objects like the desk-and-bookcase commissioned by George Croghan to simple forms suitable for export. The

Figure 61 Benjamin Randolph, side chair, Philadelphia, Pennsylvania, ca. 1770. Mahogany with white cedar. H. 37", W. 22⅝", D. 19½". (Courtesy, Yale University Art Gallery.) This chair has Randolph's label on a seat rail.

ability to accommodate a wide variety of tastes and budgets was key to Randolph's success as a cabinetmaker.

Insights into Randolph's shop can be inferred from omissions in the account book as well. A tea table in the collection of the Philadelphia Museum of Art has been previously attributed to Randolph with reasonable assurance based in a bill of sale documenting Vincent Loockerman's £38.8 purchase on October 26, 1774. However, current scholarship suggests that the carving is by Nicholas Bernard and Martin Jugiez, and the account book indicates that Bernard and Jugiez had no significant connection to the shop.

Loockerman clearly patronized Randolph's shop, but his purchase probably did not include this table. Loockerman, like most other wealthy Philadelphia consumers, purchased furniture from numerous shops.³¹

1. Beatrice B. Garvan discovered Randolph's folio account book for the years 1768–1787 in the New York Public Library, catalogued as "Philadelphia Merchant's Account Book." Among the many illustrious names that appear in Randolph's accounts are those of George and Martha Washington, Thomas Jefferson, and John Penn. George paid the cabinetmaker for Martha's lodging during the spring and summer of 1776 ("Sundry bills pd. by Mrs. Washington at Philadelphia," 1776, George Washington Papers, 5th ser., vol. 24: "Vouchers and receipted accounts," Library of Congress). Jefferson also stayed with Randolph when he arrived in Philadelphia in July 1775, and again when he returned the following May. During his stay, Jefferson purchased from Randolph the lap desk on which he drafted the Declaration of Independence. According to Jefferson, "[the desk] . . . was made from a drawing of his own, by Ben. Randall, cabinetmaker of Philadelphia with whom he first lodged on his arrival in that city" (Susan Stein, *The Worlds of Thomas Jefferson* [New York: Harry N. Abrams, 1993], pp. 364–65).

2. Several men named Benjamin Fitz-Randolph were born in eastern Pennsylvania and New Jersey between 1721 and 1737. The marriage and working dates of the man who is the subject of this article suggest that he was born ca. 1737. Building on the work of Samuel Woodhouse Jr. and other scholars, Beatrice B. Garvan developed a concise but thorough biography of the cabinetmaker (Beatrice B. Garvan, "Benjamin Randolph," in *Philadelphia: Three Centuries of American Art* [Philadelphia: Philadelphia Museum of Art, 1976], pp. 110–11; Samuel Woodhouse Jr., "Benjamin Randolph of Philadelphia," *Antiques* 11, no. 5 [May 1927]: 336–71; and Samuel Woodhouse Jr., "More about Benjamin Randolph," *Antiques* 17, no. 1 [January 1930]: 21–25). The account book records that John Penn made a single purchase from Randolph's shop, spending £10 on September 30, 1773, and paying for his purchase in cash on October 9 of that year. Penn left Philadelphia for London in 1771 but returned in 1773, and was appointed governor on August 30. A sofa with John Penn provenance, now at Cliveden of the National Trust, corresponds to the description of the sofa costing that amount in James Humphrey's *Prices of Cabinet and Chair Work* but has traditionally been attributed to cabinetmaker Thomas Affleck.

3. Randolph's shop was adjacent to property owned by joiner Henry Mitchell (Garvan, "Benjamin Randolph," pp. 110–11). Randolph advertised the sale of his tools and remaining stock in the November 10, 1778, issue of the *Pennsylvania Packett*.

4. William Macpherson Hornor Jr. alluded to the existence of "original manuscript account books and a receipt book" as the basis for attributing furniture to Thomas Affleck in his *Blue Book Philadelphia Furniture* (Philadelphia: by the author, 1935), p. 73. The receipt book may have been the one maintained by Affleck's patron David Deschler now in the Marion Carson Collection, Manuscript Division, Library of Congress.

5. For more on Courtenay and Pollard, see Beatrice B. Garvan, "Hercules Courtenay" and "John Pollard," in *Three Centuries of American Art,* pp. 111–12; Luke Beckerdite, "Philadelphia Carving Shops, Part III: Hercules Courtenay and His School," *Antiques* 131, no. 5 (May 1987): 1044–63; and Luke Beckerdite and Leroy Graves, "New Insights on John Cadwalader's Commode-Seat Side Chairs," in *American Furniture,* edited by Luke Beckerdite (Hanover, N.H.: University Press of New England for the Chipstone Foundation, 2000), pp. 152–60. For Courtenay's apprenticeship to Johnson, see Morrison H. Heckscher, *American Furniture in the Metropolitan Museum of Art, vol. 2, Late Colonial Period: The Queen Anne and Chippendale Styles* (New York: Random House for the Metropolitan Museum of Art, 1985), p. 25. Randolph's account book also mentions James Reynolds, a British-trained carver who immigrated in 1766. Reynolds was credited £8 under Andrew Doz's account with Randolph in 1769. Ten years later, the carver received a £6.14 credit on Randolph's shop page. Although Reynolds had limited interaction with Randolph's shop, he received considerable patronage from Philadelphia cabinetmaker Thomas Affleck. For more on Reynolds, see Luke Beckerdite, "Philadelphia Carving Shops, Part I: James Reynolds," *Antiques* 125, no. 5 (May 1985): 1120–33. The prolific carving partnership of Nicholas Bernard and Martin Jugiez is conspicuously absent from Randolph's account book. The cabinetmaker's receipt book contains one reference to their carving firm, but there is no evidence that Bernard and Jugiez did work for Randolph. For more on

their carving firm, see Luke Beckerdite, "Philadelphia Carving Shops, Part II: Bernard and Jugiez," *Antiques* 128, no. 3 (September 1985): 498–513; and Luke Beckerdite and Alan Miller, "A Table's Tale: Craft, Art, and Opportunity in Eighteenth-Century Philadelphia," *American Furniture,* edited by Luke Beckerdite (Hanover, N.H.: University Press of New England for the Chipstone Foundation, 2004), pp. 2–45. The only other carvers mentioned in Randolph's account book are Bryan Wilkinson, Richard Butts, and James Wilson. For more on Wilkinson, see Beckerdite and Miller, "A Table's Tale," p. 5. On February 22, 1773, the *Philadelphia Packett* reported that "[John] Pollard and [Richard] Butts [would] . . . undertake . . . all manner of Carving in the House, Cabinet, Coach, and Ship way (Alfred Coxe Prime, comp., *The Arts and Crafts in Philadelphia, Maryland, and South Carolina, 1721–1785: Gleanings from Newspapers,* 2 vols. [1929; reprint, New York: Da Capo Press, 1969], 1: 224). Randolph's account book refers to Wilson on pages 1, 44, and 56 in 1768. Six years earlier, Philadelphia cabinetmaker George Claypoole paid Wilson for "carving 8 table feet" during the period 1753–1758 (James Wilson to George Claypoole, April 1762, box 2, folder 15, Marion Carson Collection, Manuscript Division, Library of Congress). It is difficult to assess the role Randolph played in the day-to-day operation of his shop. Period documents usually refer to him as a cabinetmaker, but when he signed a deed book in 1781 he identified himself as a carver and gilder (Woodhouse, "Benjamin Randolph of Philadelphia," p. 35). Regrettably, it is impossible to determine whether Randolph actually worked as a carver and gilder or contracted it to independent specialists. The names of other carvers likely appear in the account book, but they are as yet unidentified.

6. Garvan, "Hercules Courtenay," p. 112; Beckerdite, "Philadelphia Carving Shops, Part III," pp. 1044–46; and Beckerdite and Graves, "New Insights," p. 156.

7. Samuel Powel Ledger, 1760–1793, p. 129, Library Company of Philadelphia, as cited in Beckerdite, "Philadelphia Carving Shops, Part III," p. 1048. For more on the use of Aesop's fables as design sources, see Richard H. Randall Jr., "Designs for Philadelphia Carvers," in *American Furniture,* edited by Luke Beckerdite (Hanover, N.H.: University Press of New England for the Chipstone Foundation, 1996), pp. 57–62. Aesop's fable "The Dog and the Meat" also appears on the front of a ten-plate stove marked "H. W Stiegel / 1769 / Elizabeth Furnace." The patterns for the plates of the stove were undoubtedly carved by Courtenay.

8. Beckerdite and Graves, "New Insights," pp. 152–60. Pollard was listed as a joiner in the Proprietary Tax in 1769. The apparent error in describing his trade probably stems from the fact that he was working for Randolph in that year (Garvan, "John Pollard," p. 114).

9. Beckerdite and Graves, "New Insights," pp. 153, 156–58. Randolph's account book contains an August 5, 1771, debit entry under Ringgold's name, "To Shop £23.6.6" (p. 144). The carving attributions presented in this article are largely based on research by Luke Beckerdite and Alan Miller.

10. For 1785 occupational tax figures, see Hornor, *Blue Book,* pp. 317–21. Randolph's expenses for outfitting the *Argo* are listed in his account book, pp. 245, 247. Garvan cited Randolph's purchase of large parcels of lumber as evidence that he engaged in house joinery. (Garvan, "Benjamin Randolph," p. 111). Although his shop clearly did architectural carving, Randolph's lumber purchases were most likely intended for resale. For Randolph's bill to Croghan, see Historical Society of Pennsylvania, Cadwalader Collection, Series IV, Box 2, Folder 6. Croghan had several residences, and during this period was moving from Pennsylvania to New York. The furnishings may have been intended for his new home on Otsego Lake, New York, but he did not leave for Otsego until 1769, and then it was to supervise construction. The distinction between "for yourself" and "to go abroad" suggests that the furniture was destined for a foreign port, perhaps as venture cargo. See Albert T. Volwiler, "George Croghan and the Development of Central New York, 1763–1800," *Quarterly Journal of the New York State Historical Association* [*New York History*] 4, no. 1 (January 1923): 21–40.

11. Thomas Neville Account Book, NA 733 W47 MF, pp. 164–70, University of Pennsylvania Library, Philadelphia. The author thanks Alexandra Kirtley for bringing the account book to his attention. Randolph and Neville clearly disagreed about their accounts. On February 27, 1773, Neville credited Randolph "the Ballence of his Acct. as Alo'd by the Court & jury in ye 3rd of this instant 180.19.9" (p. 184).

12. Ibid., pp. 135, 134, 172, 178, 180. Stephenson and Derry do not appear in Randolph's account book, as they were presumably recorded on Neville's account.

13. For more on the labeled Randolph side chairs, see Philip D. Zimmerman, "Labeled Randolph Chairs Rediscovered," in *American Furniture,* edited by Luke Beckerdite (Hanover,

N.H.: University Press of New England for the Chipstone Foundation, 1998), pp. 81–99. An armchair sold by C. L. Prickett and Sons was probably made in Randolph's shop and reputedly descended with a bill of sale. It is illustrated and discussed in *Antiques* 60, no. 3 (September 1951): 178–79. The article refers to a May 5, 1767, bill from Randolph for "an armed chair" valued at £4.11 that "[came] down in the family with [the chair]." In comparison, George Croghan paid Randolph £5 each for a pair of armchairs that same year (Martha H. Willoughby, "Discoveries from the Field: Randolph Chairs?" *Catalogue of Antiques and Fine Art* 5, no. 1 [Spring 2004]: 150–51). Another chair bearing Randolph's label is from a set that reputedly descended from Robert Kennedy of Washington's Crossing, New Jersey. Randolph's account book mentions a Robert Kennedy, but only in connection to minor lumber and "sundry" accounts (Randolph Account Book, pp. 40, 43, 218). If Kennedy was the first owner of these chairs, the set probably predates the account book. Randolph may have begun referring to his shop and Chestnut Street address on labels in 1767. The label on this chair reads: "All Sorts of Cabinet and Chairwork Made and Sold by Benjn. Randolph at the Sign of the Golden Ball in Chestnut Street Philadelphia" (Christie's, *Important Americana*, New York, October 21, 1989, lot 402). The chairs with the Kennedy history differ considerably from the majority of seating documented and attributed to Randolph's shop and are the only examples with shells on the knees and this splat design. Kennedy's chairs may have been made by another furniture maker, then labeled by Randolph and retailed through his shop. With its many references to other cabinetmakers and chair makers, Randolph's account book suggests this possibility. He used furniture as payment for goods and services provided by Thomas Neville (Neville Account Book, pp. 134–35).

14. Randolph Account Book, p. 124. Barnet may have served his apprenticeship in Randolph's shop and continued to work as a journeyman after his term ended. If so, that could explain why Barnet's name appears on the high chest, which clearly predates the entry for Barnet in Randolph's account book. There would have been no reason for Randolph to record an apprentice's name, since young men in training typically received no payment. Barnet may have begun working as a journeyman in 1770, and he received most of his payments in cash. On March 14, 1771, he received £1.15.9 "in full of all accounts"(Benjamin Randolph Receipt Book, p. 139).

15. Randolph's shop was producing high chests by 1766. In September of that year, Randolph charged Isaac Zane £22 for a mahogany high chest and matching dressing table (Receipt from Benjamin Randolph to Isaac Zane, Box 3, Folder 30, Marion Carson Collection, Manuscript Division, Library of Congress). Randolph Receipt Book, p. 57.

16. Robert C. Smith, "A Philadelphia Desk-and-Bookcase from Chippendale's Director," *Antiques* 107, no. 1 (January 1973): 129–35. On November 10, 1778, the *Pennsylvania Packett* reported: "To be SOLD at Public Vendue, On Thursday the nineteenth instant, at the Ware Room of Benjamin Randolph, in Chesnut street, A QUANTITY of Carvers and Cabinet makers Tools, consisting of planes, saws, gouges, chisels, work benches, &c. &c. with a variety of carved mahogany brackets, figures, carved and gilt girandoles, with sundry other furniture of different kinds, and a small quantity of mahogany." The reference to "figures" suggests that Randolph's shop produced sculptural busts like the one on the desk-and-bookcase illustrated in figure 28.

17. Smith, "A Philadelphia Desk-and-Bookcase." The author thanks Luke Beckerdite and Alan Miller for their thoughts on the working dates of the Garvan high chest carver and the changes in his style over time.

18. The Humphreys price book is in the Philadelphia Museum of Art. The early history of the desk-and-bookcase illustrated in figure 28 is opaque and provides no links to George Croghan. The only owner identified to date was Rev. Edward Craig Mitchell (1836–1911) of Philadelphia and St. Paul, Minnesota (J. Michael Flanigan, *American Furniture from the Kaufman Collection* [Washington, D.C.: National Gallery of Art, 1986], pp. 90–93).

19. Volwiler, "George Croghan and the Development of Central New York," pp. 21–40.

20. Hornor, *Blue Book*, p. 96, pl. 116. The 1772 price book lists a "commode dressing table, with four long drawers" valued at £11 and a "Bureau Table" with prospect door and quarter columns valued at £8.10. For a desk with a commode front and slant lid, see Parke Bernet Galleries, *Property of the Estate of the Late Reginald M. Lewis*, New York, March 24 and 25, 1961, lot 246.

21. For George Emlen Jr.'s purchases, see Randolph Account Book, pp. 15, 38, 178, 218, 228. Sarah Emlen's purchases totaled £92.6 (ibid., pp. 124, 154, 247). For Sally Emlen's purchases, see ibid., p. 143. Randolph records Pollard's presence in the shop throughout this period,

including several times in 1771, with accounts for £70.17 listed on the shop page under the date October 14, 1771 (p. 153).

22. Randolph Account Book, p. 31. Turner paid for his purchases with "sundries" in 1773. There is uncertainty about the exact line of descent. Alternative accounts of the history indicate that William Turner married either Mary King or Sarah King. The probable line of descent is as follows: William Turner to his daughter Abby Ann Turner (unmarried) to her niece Abby Ann King Turner (second wife of Rev. Peter Van Pelt) to Edward and Ellen Van Pelt. The chest was purchased by Howard Reifsnyder in 1921, then acquired at his sale by Henry Francis du Pont in 1929.

23. Randolph Account Book, p. 181. Biddle married his second wife, Rebekah Cornell, in 1774. For the provenance of the Biddle tea table, see Christie's, *Important American Furniture, Silver, Prints, Folk Art, and Decorative Arts,* New York, January 18–19, 2001, lot 119. Harold E. Gillingham, "Benjamin Lehman, a Germantown Cabinetmaker," *Pennsylvania Magazine of History and Biography* 54 (1930): fig. 2, as cited in Morrison H. Heckscher and Leslie Green Bowman, *American Rococo, 1750–1775: Elegance in Ornament* (New York: Metropolitan Museum of Art and Harry N. Abrams, 1992), p. 196. Randolph Account Book, p. 207.

24. The easy chair illustrated in figure 44 is one of six so-called sample chairs identified by Samuel Woodhouse Jr. who attributes them to Randolph in Woodhouse, "Benjamin Randolph of Philadelphia," pp. 33–38.

25. This easy chair is the only American example with hairy-paw back feet.

26. The 1772 Philadelphia price book indicates that a mahogany easy chair with "claw feet and leaves on knees" cost £3.5 indicating that the easy chair for which Thomas Neville credited Randolph £8.4.10 in 1769 was probably already upholstered (Neville Account Book, p. 135).

27. For more on the attribution of the pier table to Pollard and its derivation from the *Director* engraving, see Beckerdite and Graves, "New Insights," pp. 156–60. Nicholas B. Wainwright, *Colonial Grandeur in Philadelphia: The House and Furnishings of General John Cadwalader* (Philadelphia: Historical Society of Pennsylvania, 1964), p. 22. According to Wainwright, Randolph furnished £252.16.1 worth of architectural carving for John and Elizabeth Cadwalader's town house (pp. 20–21).

28. For more the attribution of the commode-seat chairs to Randolph, see Beckerdite and Graves, "New Insights," pp. 152–61. According to the two scholars:

> The saddle-seat chairs were clearly part of a unified decorative scheme that included the suite made by Affleck and that extended to the architectural carving and fabrics used in each of Cadwalader's principal rooms. Bills pertaining to the textile furnishings in Cadwalader's house shed light on the probable number, upholstery, and placement of the saddle-seat chairs. On October 18, 1770, Philadelphia upholsterer Plunkett Fleeson charged Cadwalader £13.13 for "covering thirty-two chairs over rail finish'd in canvis." The following January, the upholsterer made seventy-six Saxon blue French check cases with blue and white fringe for these chairs and others that Cadwalader had either purchased or inherited from his father-in-law. The commode-seat chairs were subsequently fitted with covers made of blue and yellow silk damask that Cadwalader ordered from London merchants Rushton & Beachcroft. In January 1772, Philadelphia upholsterer John Webster billed Cadwalader £18.7.10 for making the curtains for four windows and for upholstering twenty chairs and three sofas with these fabrics. A subsequent entry in Cadwalader's Waste Book provides additional information on Webster's work, noting that the payment was for "Curtains in [the] front & back Rooms, Covers to Settees & Covers to Chairs in front & back Rooms." The curtains and covers in the front room were blue and the ones in the back parlor were yellow to match the colors of each room's walls and Wilton carpets. An "Inventory of Contents Remaining in [the] Cadwalader House" taken in 1786 lists two blue damask window curtains, a blue damask settee cover, ten blue damask chair covers, two yellow silk damask window curtains, ten yellow silk damask chair bottoms, and "1 cover of a settee for d" (the bills from Fleeson, Webster, and Rushton & Beachcroft [the London merchants who provided the silk fabrics, fringe, and tape] are reproduced in Wainwright, *Colonial Grandeur,* pp. 40–41, 59, 61). Cadwalader owned a second suite of furniture with hairy paw feet and straight rails (see fig. 56). The chairs and matching card tables in the second suite may have sat in the small front parlor, which had green walls. Assuming that there were twelve chairs in this suite and twenty saddle-seat chairs, that would account for the thirty-two that Fleeson covered over the rail. Although chair "bottoms" could be interpreted as slip seats, this term probably referred to slipcovers. The use of two terms in the inventory may result from its having been taken by John Cadwalader's sister

Rebecca and his brother-in-law Samuel Meredeth. Three copies of the inventory survive, and they vary slightly. The 1786 inventory also lists one mahogany dining table, one marble slab [table], and one card table in the "small front parlor," one marble slab [table], one card table and ten mahogany chairs, in the "back parlor," one large settee, one small settee, one card table, ten mahogany chairs in the "front parlor," one small settee in the "entry" on the second floor, six mahogany chairs with chintz "furniture" in the "back chamber" on the second floor, six mahogany "carpet bottom" chairs in the "front chamber" on the second floor, two old chairs and six mahogany chairs in the "front room" on the third floor" and two green covers for card tables, 1onelarge easy chair, and ten old mahogany chairs "many broke" in the front garret on the third floor. (p. 161)

29. Beckerdite and Graves, "New Insights," pp. 153–59.

30. Woodhouse, "Benjamin Randolph of Philadelphia," pp. 33–38. Beckerdite and Graves have speculated that the card tables and chairs with trapezoidal seats may have been used in the small front parlor of the Cadwaladers' house (see n. 28 above). For a different viewpoint on the Cadwalader furniture, see Phillip Zimmerman, "A Methodological Study in the Identification of Some Important Philadelphia Chippendale Furniture," *Winterthur Portfolio* 13 (1979): 193–208. The matching card tables from the suite including the side chair shown in fig. 56 are in the Winterthur Museum and in the Philadelphia Museum of Art.

31. Beatrice B. Garvan, cat. no. 101 in *Three Centuries of American Art*, pp. 127–28. Randolph Account Book, p. 211. Loockerman paid for his purchase in cash on November 26, 1774. For more on Bernard and Jugiez, see Beckerdite, "Philadelphia Carving Shops, Part II: Bernard and Jugiez"; and Beckerdite and Miller, "A Table's Tale."

Appendix 1

The following is a complete index for Randolph's account book at the New York Public Library, catalogued as a Philadelphia Merchant's Account Book, 1768–1787. While Randolph's handwriting is generally, though not always, legible, he used many different spellings for the same name. Names that appear in parentheses after the principal name are variations that are thought to refer to the same person. When the correct spelling of a name is known, that version is used in the index, with Randolph's variations given in parentheses. The date ranges for account book entries are meant as guidelines but often do not reflect the actual period of activity within the shop. Randolph sold his tools and stock in 1778, but many accounts stayed open for years while remaining inactive, and dates in the 1780s typically refer to Randolph's transactions with his sawmill Speedwell or to idle accounts that were finally being closed in the book. Often Randolph listed a specific date and then subsequent entries for the same client were left undated, and sometimes these undated entries appear to have extended for years. Thus, the dates referenced in the index refer to the first and last date explicitly noted. A loose quarto page with a list of names is inserted into the front of the folio, and names appearing on this page are indexed on page one, though the original folio page one is missing. The page is undated, and its exact context is not clear.

Name	Pages	Date Ranges
Abbott, John	171, 223	1773–1782
Adams, Thomas	3, 29, 33, 43, 48	1768–1769
Affleck, Thomas	126, 138	1770
Allen, Isaac	107	1770
Allen, James, Esq.	141	1771
Alston, Joseph	36, 76, 85, 86	1768–1770
Alston, Joseph, Jr.	1, 84, 227	1769–1775
Alston, Joseph, Sr.	1, 3, 8, 151, 180	1768–1773
Anderson, Henry	218, 236, 247	1776–1779
Anderson, Joseph (Joseph H.)	78, 90, 246	1769–1779
Anthony, Hewes?	247, 250	1786
Anthony, Joseph	35, 257, 260	1786–1787
Argo, brig	245, 247	1779–1787
Armitage, Benjamin	3, 58, 163, 167, 252	1768–1785
Bache, Richard	62, 190	1770–1774
Bacon, Daniel	258	1786

Name	Pages	Years
Bagnal, Samuel	157, 166	1772–1773
Bailey, John	7	1768
Baion?, Daniel	250	1786
Baker, William	36, 93, 126, 144, 163, 179, 246	1768–1779
Ball, William	221, 226	1775
Barclay, Thomas	162	1772
Barnes, Lambert	7	1768
Barnett, Isaac (Barnet)	124	1770–1771
Barrett, Timothy (Barut)	149, 198, 205	1771–1775
Barrow, Joseph	162	1772–1773
Barrow, Samuel	1, 144, 246	1773–1779
Bartram, George	62, 144, 165, 178	1770–1774
Bartram, Robert	165	1772–1773
Batchelor, Edward	38, 50	1768–1771
Bayard, Dr. James	92	1769–1770
Bayard, John	152	1771
Beck, John	8, 144, 265	1768–1787
Bell, Henry	202, 218	1774–1779
Benezet, Daniel	80	1769
Berberie, Peter	242	1776
Berry, Abley	221, 231	1777–1779
Betsy, sloop	1	
Biddle, Clement	181	1775–1783
Biggs, Peter	1, 151	1771
Binks, Christopher	238, 248	1776–1779
Bird, Mark (Burd?)	58, 154, 162, 246	1771–1779
Bishop, William	237, 247, 250	1776–1786
Black, James	7, 43, 85	1768–1769
Blair, Rev. Samuel	208	1774–1775
Bland, Major	231, 247	1777–1779
Bloomfield and Atkins	218, 229	1775–1776
Bloomfield, Joseph	249	1784–1787
Bloomfield, Thomas	247, 250	1786
Bolden & Starr	1	
Bond, Dr. Phineas	61	1768
Bond, Thomas	8, 23, 85	1768–1769
Bonham, Abraham	144	1773
Bonham, Ephraim	155, 183	1772–1776
Boucher, Francis	149	1771
Bradford, William	81	1769
Branning, Elizabeth	3, 36, 144, 179	1768–1780
Branning, John (Brann, Branin)	1, 35, 88, 156, 169, 177, 218, 246	1774–1776
Branning, Joseph (Brannin, Branin)	47, 180	1768–1779
Branson, Day	151, 246	1771–1779
Branson, Jacob	193	1774
Bridges, Robert	8, 45	1768
Bringhurst, James	1	
Bringhurst, John	204	1774–1782

Broderick, Richard (Brodrick)	144, 194, 213, 214, 246	1774–1779
Bromall, Thomas (Bromel)	179, 234, 247	1775–1779
Brooks, David	1, 4, 154	1768–1771
Brooks, Nicholas	181	1775–1782
Brooks, William	169, 247	1773–1779
Brown, John	218, 232	1775–1779
Brown, Margaret	1, 37, 55, 144, 160, 161, 169, 221	1768–1779
Brown, Nicholas	1	
Bruk, Aaron	35	1768
Bunting, William B.	186	1773–1775
Burchall, Anne (Burchill, Burchalt)	1, 3, 55, 81	1768–1769
Burchalt, John	189	1773–1787
Burd, Mark (Bird?)	158	1772–1773
Butts, Richard	1, 32, 35, 247	1768–1778
Byrne, James	151	1771
Cadwalader, J. and L.	18, 36, 49	1768
Cadwalader, John	1, 4, 18	1768
Cadwalader, Lambert	18	1768
Cahill, John	1, 43	1768
Calla, J. W.?	144	1774
Canell, Samuel	260	1787
Caner, Michael	263, 270	1787
Cannan, Jonathan	203	1774–1776
Cannon, Mary	3, 83	1768–1769
Carker, Ludwick (Barker, Lodewick)	9, 46, 221, 154	1768–1782
Carman, John (Carnan)	221, 240	1776
Carsen, Robert	62	1770
Cartwright, Shackerly	9, 81	1768–1769
Cash, Thomas (and estate of)	125, 144, 158, 221	1771–1779
Chambers, David	9	1768
Charles & Petit	250	1786
Charleston, adventure to	35, 248, 260, 263, 264	1786–1787
Chevalier, John and Peter (Shevalier)	243, 247	1777–1779
Chevalier, Peter	206	1774–1775
Chryster, Jacob (Christer)	193	1774–1775
Cisle?, Charles	254, 260	1785–1787
Clarke, Capt. John	49, 54	1768
Claypoole, George	10	1768
Claypoole, James	1	
Clifford, John	247, 250, 255, 260, 263, 271	1786–1787
Clime, Andrew?	144	1774
Cline, Hannah	48, 179, 213	1775–1779
Cline, John	144, 213	1774–1775
Clowe, James	246	1779
Clymer, Baltis	1, 36, 81, 88, 144	1768–1771
Coates, Isaac	1, 94, 223	1769–1775
Coats, William	202	1774
Cobb, Thomas	221	1779

Cockshot, John	1, 267	1787
Coker, Thomas	81	1769
Collins, Abraham	158	1772
Collins, Edmund	250	1785
Collins, Edward	251	1785–1786
Collins, Capt. Robert	144, 158	1772–1774
Committee of Safety	234	1776
Condy, Benjamin	157	1772–1773
Conover, Peter	87	1769
Conrad, John	1, 221	1782
Cook, Jonathan	1	
Cook, Jos. & Co.	254	1785–1787
Cook, Nathan	139, 247	1771–1782
Coombe, Thomas	78, 246	1770–1779
Coradine, Thomas	1, 184	1773–1774
Coufman, Jacob	269	1787
Courtenay, Hercules	3, 10, 43, 81, 91	1768–1769
Coward, John (Cowardly)	1, 93, 179	1771–1779
Cowell, Capt. Samuel (Covell)	179, 185	1773–1777
Crackit, Anne	197, 247	1774–1779
Craig, Andrew	217	1774
Craig, William	58, 144, 163, 182	1771–1787
Crane, Richard (Crain)	36, 81	1768–1769
Crawford & Thompson	143	1771
Cresson, Jeremiah (Crisson)	54, 156	1770–1775
Cribs, John	153	1771
Cromfield, Joseph B.	247	1785
Cross, Peter	1, 93	1769
Cullen, Thomas	151, 174	1773–1775
Cummings, Morris	35	1768
Curry, Robert	228	1776–1787
Davids, John	250, 261	1786
Davidson, William	161, 165, 170, 180	1772–1774
Davis, Polly	148	1771
Davis, Capt. William	81, 146, 153	1769–1771
Dawson & Snowden	260, 269	1787
Dawson, David	259	1786–1787
Dawson, William	61	1768
Dayman, Frances (Daymon)	178, 179, 209, 210	1774–1777
Deakin, John	49	1768
Deakin, Robert (Deaking)	49, 52, 53, 55, 78, 80, 81, 85,	1768–1769
Dean, Joseph	162	1772
Dearnalle?, Alverino	246	1779
Delano?, Thomas	1	
Delong, Peter	221	1775
Denormandie, Anthony	3, 81, 218	1768–1779
Denormandie, Doctor	249, 268	1785–1787
Deshong, Harry	236	1776

Deshong, Peter	144, 200	1774–1776
Devine, Mrs.	217	1775
Dickinson, John	1, 3, 35, 81, 247	1768–1782
Dobson, Thomas	260, 265	1787
Donal, Grace	189	1774
Donnell, Nathaniel (Donnel, Donnald)	54, 144, 153, 156, 187, 221, 224	1771–1776
Donnells, Alverin	15	1775
Douglass, Alexander	171	1773–1774
Dowal, Grace (Dowall)	180, 246	1774–1779
Doz, Andrew	35, 37	1768–1769
Duncan, Ann	228	1776
Duncan, Elliot	1	
Duncan, James	144, 156	1771–1773
Dunlap and Claypoole	107	1773
Dunlap, John	259	1786
Easton, Robert	205, 218, 222	1769–1779
Egerly, Lawrence	1	
Eldridge, Abraham	179, 243	1778–1779
Elliot, John	1, 35, 126, 138	1768–1776
Elmsley, John	35	1768
Emanuel, Josiah	21	1768
Emlen, Caleb	1	
Emlen, George, Jr.	15, 38, 178, 218, 228	1768–1775
Emlen, George, Sr.	15, 35, 79	1768–1769
Emlen, Miss Sally	143	1771
Emlen, Sarah	1, 124, 154, 247	1771–1779
Evans, David	15	1768
Evans, Samuel	222	1777
Faries, James	141	1771
Faulk, Adam (Faulke)	35, 248, 260, 262	1768–1787
Fearis, John	223	1775
Fishbauger, Simon	263	1787
Fisher, Samuel	16, 109, 144, 145, 233	1768–1787
Fisher, Thomas	164, 223	1775
Fitzbaugh, Simon	264	1787
Fitzgerald, Thomas	250, 253, 256, 263,	1786–1787
Fitz-Randolph, S.	260, 264	1787
Fiz, John?	212, 218	1775
Fleeson, Plunkett	16, 81, 108, 219, 239	1768–1787
Fling, John (Flinn?)	1, 42	1768–1770
Flinn, Daniel	1, 37, 43, 85, 179	1768–1779
Flock, Philip (Flockly)	1, 3, 27, 35, 40, 88, 89	1768–1769
Flower, Samuel	17	1768
Footman, Moore?	1	
Footman, Peter	144, 150, 154, 160, 180, 200, 247	1771–1779
Footman, Richard	184	1773
Forster, Moses	1, 15	1768
Fort, Madame	247	1786

Fortune, Anthony	1, 35, 84, 144, 221, 247	1768–1782
Fowell, John	126	1770
Fox, Joseph	170, 246	1773–1779
Frances, Philip	158	1772
Frances, Turbutt, Esq. (Turbitt)	162, 247	1772–1779
Frazer, Joseph	1, 16, 43, 45, 47, 81	1768–1771
Fuller, Benjamin	84, 86	1769
Fulton, James	15, 81, 209	1768–1774
Furmann, Moore	50	1768
Fustain, Thomas (Tristin?)	1, 4, 247	1768–1779
Fustian, John (Fustain)	56, 153, 160, 172	1771–1776
Galloway, Joseph	77, 91	1769
Gamber, John	270	1787
Gardner, John	246	1779
Gebler, George	221	1775
Gebler, Godfrey (Gabler, Geller, Gibler, Gobler)	144, 163, 182, 213, 218, 221, 238, 247, 253	1773–1787
Genchman, John	1	
Gibbons, Abel	1, 246	1779
Gibson, John, Esq.	146	1771–1777
Gill, John	17, 154	1768–1773
Granger, Henry	30, 81, 139, 143, 144, 153, 154, 159, 170, 246	1768–1779
Grasbury, Joseph	17	1768
Grass, Peter	93	1771
Gratz, Michael, Esq. (Gatz, Gatts)	4, 17, 85, 144, 154, 197	1768–1774
Gray, Mercy (Mary?)	1, 3, 87, 247	1768–1779
Gregg, David	86	1769
Gribble, Andrew	155, 223	1772–1775
Griffin, Samuel	54, 207	1774–1776
Grigson, Thomas (Grigeston)	220, 248	1776–1779
Grinny?, Henry	179	1777
Gross, Peter	145, 246	1771–1779
Gualdo, John (Giovanni)	18, 43, 81	1768–1769
Gunther, George	270	1787
Gurney, Henry	230	1776–1777
Guyer, Casper (Geyer?)	170	1773
Haines, Ephraim	92	1769
Haines, Jonathan	1, 126, 247	1770–1779
Hale, Thomas	143	1771–1782
Hall & Sellers	231, 248	1777–1779
Hall, Phillip	196	1774–1775
Hall?, Thomas	247	1782
Hall, William	144, 162, 184	1773
Hallowell, Joseph	19	1768
Hamilton, Andrew	20	1768
Hamilton, William	81	1769
Hancock, Hugh	61, 62	1768–1769
Hanlin, John (Hanlon)	1, 8, 37, 57, 59, 108, 125, 218	1768–1779

Harbeson, Benjamin	18, 35, 47, 148, 201	1768–1776
Harminson, Jonathan	201	1774
Harris, George	218	1775
Harrison, Col. Benjamin	178, 179, 198, 209, 221, 226, 247	1774–1779
Harvey, William	176	1773
Haskins, George	1	
Hasslehurst, Isaac & Co.	267	1787
Haughton, John	232	1775–1782
Hawke, Capt.	83	1770
Hawkins, George	155, 246	1772?–1779
Hays, John	49, 51	1768–1769
Hays, Mary (Hayes)	1, 183, 221	1773–1779
Hays, Morris (Hayes)	1, 158, 183	1772–1773
Helmsley, William	49, 77, 85	1769
Hemmings, Benjamin (Hemmins)	123, 221	1775–1779
Hendrickson, William	44, 56	1768–1769
Henry, Hugh	19, 93, 248, 260, 266, 268	1768–1787
Henry, John	255	1785–1786
Henry, Samuel	250, 252, 253	1785–1787
Henry, William	18, 35, 171	1768–1773
Hertrog, Andrew (Hartrog)	144, 170, 218, 224, 230	1773–1782
Hewes & Anthony	258	1786–1787
Hewlings, William	156	1772
Hickinham, Amos	263	1787
Hicks, Charles	206	1774
Hill, Jonathan	144	1774
Hill, Robert	94	1769
Hillie, Jonothan	260, 263	1787
Hinselwood, Anne	19, 43, 81	1768–1769
Hiorn, William	1, 10, 85, 247	1768–1779
Hiselman?, John	250	1785
Hockenhull, John (Harkenhull)	139, 142, 144, 153, 160, 163, 170, 192, 218, 235	1771–1779
Hodge, Andrew	217	1775
Hodgkinson, Bathana	247, 253, 254	1785–1786
Hodgson, John	150, 155	1771–1772
Honduras, adventure to	93, 246	1769–1779
Hood, John	260, 262	1787
Hood, Thomas	157	1772
How, Samuel	1	
Howard, John	51, 52	1768–1770
Howell, Joshua	54	1768
Hudson, Susannah	1	
Hummingbird, schooner	244, 247	1779
Humphreys, James	18	1768
Humphreys, Joshua	142	1771
Humphreys, Whitehead	19	1768–1770
Hunt, John	37	1768

Jacobs, Elizabeth	20, 81	1768–1769
James & Drinker	80	1769
Jefferson, Thomas, Esq.	227	1775
Jeffries, Charles	228, 248	1775–1779
Jeffries, Samuel (Jeffreys)	216, 246	1774–1779
Jervis, John, Jr. (Jarvis?)	1, 52	1769
Jewell, Robert	80	1769–1770
Johns, Stephen	20, 56	1768–1770
Johns, Stephen, Jr.	156	1773–1777
Johns, Stephen, Sr.	1, 156	1773–1777
Johnston, John	21	1772
Johnston, Mary	61, 246	1768–1779
Johnston, Thomas (Johnson)	1, 107, 247	1769–1779
Jones, Blathwaite	35, 141	1768–1771
Jones, John	20, 81	1768–1769
Jones, William	84	1770
Josiah, Emanuel	46, 179	1768–1779
Josiah, Robert	172, 246	1773–1779
Keen, Matthias	81, 179	1769–1779
Keen, Reynold	53	1770–1772
Kelly, John	22, 81	1768–1769
Kendall, Benjamin	3, 21, 179	1768–1773
Kendall, Joseph	139	1771
Kennedy, Andrew	267	1787
Kennedy, George	179, 193, 221	1774–1778
Kennedy, Robert	40, 43, 218	1768–1779
Keppele, Henry (Cepple, Kepple, Jr.)	142, 144, 247	1771–1782
King, Daniel	21, 168, 171, 176	1768–1787
King, Joseph	22, 46	1768–1773
Kirk, Samuel	214	1776
Kizelman, Fredrik	251	1785
Lane, Isaac (Zane?)	34, 189	1768–1776
Lane, Jacob	1, 194	1774
Lane, Jonathan	39, 246	1779
Lasley, Peter	1, 32, 37, 63, 75, 85, 91, 144, 153, 161, 169, 198, 215, 218	1768–1779
Latemore, George	266	1787
Lawrence, John	22	1768–1773
Lawrence, Thomas	1, 22, 81	1768–1769
Lawrence, Thomas, Jr. (Esq.)	1, 8, 23, 44	1768–1773
Lea, Thomas	260, 263, 264	1787
Leacock, John	162	1772–1782
Leavy, Sampson	1	
Ledren, Joseph	23	1768
Library Company	212	1774
Lightfoot, James	210, 224, 225	1774–1775
Lillie, Nathaniel	203	1774–1775
Linn, Charles	43, 77, 81	1768–1770
Lloyd, Gilbert	163	1772

Lock, George (Loch)	23	1768
Lockerman, Vincent	211	1774
Lockwood, James and Co.	261	1787
London, adventure to	87, 246, 247	1769–1779
Long, Melchor	146, 246	1771–1779
Long, Walker	1	
Lowry, James	59, 94, 246	1769–1779
Ludwig, George (Ludwick)	23, 43	1768
Lukens, Jasper	1, 154, 172	1771–1773
Lunan, Alexander	53	1768
Macken, Thomas	25	1768–1770
Maddox, Abraham	1, 139, 147	1771
Maggs, Catherine (Maag)	156	1772
Maggs, Jacob (Maag)	218, 220	1775
Maggs, John (Magg, Muggs)	143, 156, 170, 174, 199, 214	1772–1776
Mangany?, Alexander	1	
Marcer, George (Mancer)	247, 257, 260, 268	1786–1787
Marchenton, Philip (Marchinton)	230, 247	1775–1779
Markoe, Abram	180	1773
Markoe, Uran	188	1773–1774
Marks, Levy	233	1775–1776
Marriot, Philip (Marriott)	1, 4, 24, 43, 62, 79, 81, 123, 145	1768–1772
Marshall, Benjamin	24	1768
Marshall, Charles	149	1772
Marshall, Christopher	174	1773
Marshall, Ralph	1, 15, 83	1769
Martin, William (Marton)	179, 185, 217, 247	1773–1779
Mason, Richard	25, 85	1768–1769
Masters, Elizabeth (Sally)	229, 246	1775–1779
Matherson, Peter	1, 43, 179	1768–1779
Matthews, Samuel	24, 81	1768–1769
Maxfield, John	173	1773
Mayse, James	89	1775
McAlister, Michael	194	1774–1775
McCaben, James	1	
McCall, Ann (widow)	193	1774
McCalla, John	173, 175, 219	1773–1787
McCraby, John	147	1771
McCubbin, James	25, 148	1768–1773
McCullogh, Hugh (McCullough)	18, 144, 171	1771–1773
McDonaugh	214	1774
McDowell, William	218, 243	1777–1787
McGuire, Matthew	148	1775
McKean, Thomas	178, 209	1774–1776
McKim, Thomas	25	1770
McLaughlan, Felix	35, 43	1768
McNeal, Bryan	246	1779
McPherson, Capt. John	81, 89, 94, 173, 178, 180, 206, 221, 247	1769–1779

McRane, Thomas	204	1775
Mears, John	179	1779
Melcher, Isaac	144, 191	1774
Meredith, Reese	1	
Meyer, Henry	263, 266	1787
Meyers, Jacob	255	1785–1787
Middleton, John	24, 81	1768–1769
Mifflin, Samuel, Esq.	160, 167	1772
Milenburg, Michael	82	1769
Milne, Edmund	53	1770
Mitchell, John	179, 230	1775–1777
Mitchell, Randle	50	1768
Mongomery, Alexander	93, 152, 154	1771–1774
Montgomery, Dorcas	152, 181	1771–1775
Montgomery, John and William	260, 269	1787
Moody, John	82, 139, 147, 180	1769–1773
Moore & Chestnut	26	1768
Moore, Joshua	25	1768
Moore, Capt. Thomas	26	1768
Moore, William	169	1773–1775
Morgeltright, Widow (Morgebright)	1, 77, 246	1769–1779
Morrell, James	24	1768
Morris, Anthony	1, 164	1772
Morris, John, Esq.	156	1772
Morris, Margaret	1, 56, 126	1770
Morris, Paul	1, 26, 27, 61, 62, 85	1768–1769
Morris, Robert	54, 86	1768–1777
Morton, William	218	1777
Mosley, George (Morsely)	1, 17, 41	1768–1770
Mount, Michael	32, 221, 247	1768–1780
Moyes, John (Moyse)	34, 153	1769–1771
Mullen, Joseph	256	1785
Mullen, Thomas (Mullan)	80	1769
Mullony, Capt. John	175	1773
Murgatroyd, Thomas	87	1769
Murray, Alexander	25	1768
Musgrove, Aaron	26	1768–1769
Needham, John	174, 246	1773–1779
Nevill, James	183	1773
Nevill, Thomas (Neville)	1, 15, 35, 43, 47, 49, 93, 109, 140, 223	1768–1775
Newlings, Abraham	254	1785
Nicola, Lewis	57	1769
Nixon, John	149, 154	1771–1774
Nolings, Michael	26, 81	1768–1769
Norton & West	267	1787
Noxon, Benjamin	16, 27, 81	1768–1769
Oakall, Widow	1, 246	1779
Olden, Benjamin	246	1779
Orr, James	246	1779

Orr, Robert	92	1769–1770
Osborne, Widow Jane	176, 246	1773–1787
Osborne, William	27, 81	1768–1769
Palmer, John	247, 252, 253, 260	1785–1787
Palmer, Thomas	247	1785
Paschall, Beulah	197	1774
Paschall, I. and J.	94	1771–1773
Paschall, Joseph (Spashall)	227, 250	1775–1786
Patterson, Thomas	27, 40, 250, 261, 263, 268	1768–1787
Paul, Richard	91	1769
Pearson, Ruth	236	1776
Pemberton, John	1, 27	1768–1773
Pemberton, Joseph	124, 178	1775
Pendleton, Edward	224, 244	1775–1779
Penn, John	177	1773
Peters, Reese	246	1779
Peters, Richard, Esq.	220	1776
Petit, Charles and Andrew	253, 258, 263	1786–1787
Phile, Dr. Frederick	172	1773
Philips, Thomas (Philyrs)	1, 144, 168	1771–1772
Physick, Edmund, Esq.	1, 110, 247	1769–1779
Piles, John	1, 93	1769
Pinkerton, John	15, 38	1768–1787
Pleasant, Samuel	78	1769–1775
Plim, George, Jr.	32, 39, 43	1768
Polk, Jonophat	253, 257	1786
Polk, Thomas	250	1786
Pollard, John	3, 18, 38, 43, 57, 77, 79, 93, 123, 144, 153, 207, 218	1768–1779
Poor, John (estate of)	170, 191, 208, 246	1773–1779
Porter, Alexander	142	1771
Potts, David	38, 81, 88	1769
Potts, John	1, 51, 153, 157	1771–1772
Power, John (estate of)	144	1774
Power, Thomas	218, 238	1776–1779
Prankard, John (Prankhard)	1, 160, 246	1772–1779
Preston, Rachael	242, 248	1777–1779
Preston, Robert	221	1777
Pringle, John	263, 265	1787
Pritchard, John	42	1768
Prowle, Lawrence	179, 221, 234	1776–1779
Pusey, William	221, 242	1777
Randle, Isaac	221	1776
Randolph, Daniel	4, 8, 43, 44, 47, 56, 88, 198, 205, 247	1768–1779
Randolph, Isaac	55, 56, 126, 221, 240	1768–1787
Randolph, James	38, 43, 179	1768–1779
Rawle, Benjamin	154, 163	1771–1772
Read, Charles, Esq.	247	1779

Read, John	211, 220	1774–1775
Read, Joseph, Esq.	154, 178	1771–1774
Read, Charles	144	1774
Reary, Jacob (Reavy)	1, 4, 109, 246	1768–1779
Recovery, brig	244, 248	1778–1779
Redman, Dr. John	28, 33, 144, 247	1768–1775
Redman, Joseph	27	1768–1775
Redwood, William	204	1775
Reed, Col. Joseph, Esq.	211, 237	1775–1777
Renaudet, Doctor (Renault)	144, 180, 181, 182, 246	1773–1779
Renshaw, Richard	9, 144	1772–1773
Reynolds, James	37, 218	1769–1779
Rich, John	1, 28	1768–1771
Richards, Daniel	246	1779
Richards, William	60	1768–1772
Richardson, John	152	1771
Richardson, Sarah	141	1771
Ringold, Thomas	110, 147	1771
Risk, Charles	172	1773
Rittenhouse, D. (Ritenhouse)	195	1774
Ritter, Jacob	218, 242	1776–1779
Roach, Capt. Thomas	86, 88, 213	1769–1774
Robenson, Daniel	221	1775
Roberdeau, Daniel (Roberdon)	28, 180	1768–1773
Roberts, Daniel	212, 216	1774–1775
Roberts, Hugh & Geo.	28, 35	1768–1769
Roberts, William	52, 88	1769
Robeson, Peter	28	1768–1770
Robin, Moses (Robins)	144, 153, 172, 178, 183	1771–1773
Robinson, Daniel	218	1779
Robinson, Henry	177, 195, 221	1773–1779
Robinson, William	81, 223	1769–1775
Rodman, Pierson	256, 268, 271	1785–1787
Rogerson, John, Esq. (Roberson)	1, 3, 28, 29, 55, 85, 90	1768–1772
Rogerson, Widow	218	1779
Ross, James and John	55	1768
Ross, John (estate of)	51, 91, 179	1769–1777
Ross, John, Jr.	175, 218	1773–1775
Rusk, David	147	1771
Russel, Jacob	269	1787
Ryan, Peter (Riyan)	218, 241	1777–1779
Salmon, Charles	3, 58, 81	1768–1769
Sandyford, Doctor	190	1774
Sartain, Capt. John (Sortain)	16, 47, 88, 93, 246	1768–1769, 1779
Saunders, Peter	210, 225	1774–1775
Savage, John (Savadge)	153	1771
Savage, Robert	153	1771
Savage, Thomas (Savadge)	30, 47, 84, 93, 170, 246	1768–1779
Savery, William (Savord, Savory)	1, 29, 53, 186, 218	1768–1779

Scull, John	139	1771
Searle, James	78	1769
Sears, Joseph (estate)	37, 179	1769?–1779
Sewell, Capt. Robert	232	1775
Sharrold, Josiah (Sharald)	31, 179	1768–1779
Shee, Bertles	1, 246	1779
Shepherd, Thomas	1	
Shepper, John	140, 145, 166, 173, 201, 218, 231	1771–1779
Sherman, John	29	1768
Shewell, Stephen	152	1771
Shippen, Joseph	211	1774
Shippen, Miss	1, 149	1771
Shippen, Dr. William	1, 208	1768–1776
Shippen, Dr. Wm., Jr. (Shippin)	30, 49, 123, 155, 218, 221	1768–1775
Shoemaker, Jonathan (John)	1, 30, 35, 143, 179, 218	1768–1777
Shoemaker, Philip	35	1768
Shoemaker, Thomas	31, 45, 82	1768–1775
Sill, Thomas	31	1768–1775
Silverman, Moore?	3	1768
Simmons, John	148	1771
Sisdal, Thomas	187	1773–1777
Smith, Daniel	221, 233, 248	1775–1779
Smith, James (J.)	250, 260, 261	1787
Smith, William	250, 252, 253	1785–1787
Smith, Dr. William Drewet	171	1770–1773
Smither, James (Smithers)	1, 31, 79, 123, 246	1768–1779
Snowden, Anthony	35	1768
Snowden, Isaac	1, 4, 18, 30, 35, 56, 81, 153, 164	1768–1773
Snowden, Jedediah	8, 19, 29, 31, 36, 93, 145, 149, 170, 173, 180, 198	1768–1775
Snowden, John	187	1773
Snowden, Miles	163	1772
Solomon, Charles	1	
Solomon, Thomas	7, 35	1768–1770
Souder, Charles	185	1773
Souder, Jacob	185	1773
Spashall?, Joseph	250	1786
St. Paul's Church	1, 35, 78, 81	1768–1771
Stangston?, George	219	1782
Stanlin, John	60	1768–1769
Sterling & Norcross	255	1785–1786
Steward, George	92	1769
Stilley, John	56, 144	1768–1787
Stockenmuller, Jacob	259	1786–1787
Stogdon, Abraham (Absm)	221, 250, 251	1785–1786
Stonemetz, Jacob (Stonemitz)	46, 179, 223	1775–1779
Stote, Thomas	223	1782

Stout, Capt. Joseph (estate of)	53, 186	1770–1773
Stoutage?, Andries	221	1782
Sweene, Colonel (Cornel)	184	1773
Taylor, Benjamin	1, 39, 43	1768
Taylor, John	160, 173	1772–1773
Thomas, Edward	32, 81	1768–1769
Thomas, Moses	32	1768
Thompson, Capt.	144	1771
Thompson, Charles	208	1774–1782
Thompson, Capt. George	216, 247	1774–1779
Thompson, Capt. James	1, 165	1772
Thompson, John	218	1779
Thompson, Thomas	32, 81	1768–1769
Tilghman, Francis J.	110	1771
Tilghman, James	87	1769
Tisdale, Thomas	218, 221	1777
Todd, John	1, 144	1771
Tomkins, Thomas	164	1772
Tomlinson, James	196	1774
Topham, Daniel	60	1768
Tristin & Marshall (Fustain?)	1	
Tristin, John	29, 38, 42, 93, 164, 196	1768–1771
Tristin, Rachel	182	1773–1775
Tristin, Thomas (see also Fustain)	43, 83	1768–1773
Trumble, Francis	60	1769
Tryon, David	8, 45, 46, 47	1768–1769
Turner, Joseph	1, 81, 144, 146, 149, 153, 168, 211	1769–1774
Turner, William	1, 31	1768–1773
Tybout, Andrew	3, 32, 142, 144, 205	1768–1777
Tyler, Ebenezer	1, 8, 29, 30, 43, 49, 50, 51, 60, 61	1768
Tyler, John	160, 173	1772–1773
United States	47, 231	1777
Vallance, Robert (Vollace)	93, 170, 175, 188, 213, 246	1771–1779
Vandike, James	206	1774
Van Lier, Doctor	250, 262	1787
Vanwinkle, Sarah (Vonwinkle)	142, 169	1772–1774
Vasse, Ambrose	266	1787
Vendue, goods purchased at	243	1778
Wade, Francis	1, 169	1772
Wagenar, John	260, 270	1787
Waggaman, Henry (Wageman)	1, 51, 247	1771–1779
Waggaman, John	142, 144	1771
Walker, Capt. George	34, 85	1768–1769
Walker, Margaret	1, 168	1772–1782
Walker, Robert	33, 110	1770–1772
Walker, Thomas	33, 110	1768–1770
Wallace, James	162, 246	1772–1779
Wallace, Josiah	249	1785–1786

Walton, Samuel	1, 39, 43, 81, 93, 144, 148, 157	1768–1772
Ware, David	212	1774–1775
Warner, William	34, 81	1768–1769
Washington, General	221, 226, 247	1775–1779
Wayne, Humphrey (Wayn)	32	1775
Webster, John	144, 221	1771–1779
Webster, Peletiah	202	1774
Welch, Capt. John	88	1769
Wescot, John	259, 263	1786–1787
West, Richard	246	1779
Wetherspoon, Dr. John	41	1775
Wheeler, Samuel	262	1787
White, John	186, 191, 195, 218	1773–1779
White, John, Jr.	221	1779
White, John, Sr.	190	1774–1779
White, Townsend & John	245, 247	1779
White, Townsend, Jr.	217	1774–1782
White, Townsend, Sr.	191	1774–1779
Whitehead, John	1	
Whitman, Richard	33, 43, 48, 144, 179	1768–1779
Wickenham, Amos	265, 268, 253	1787
Wikoff, Peter	110	1769
Wilkinson, Bryan	53, 78	1768–1772
Williams, Daniel	151, 174	1772–1775
Williams, Edward	200	1774
Williams, John	28, 33	1768–1769
Williams, John	1, 33	1768
Williams, Samuel	218	1777
Willing & Morris	51, 54, 90, 179, 207, 218	1768–1779
Willing, Richard	1, 44	1768
Willing, Thomas	1, 33	1768
Wilson, Henry (Willson)	83	1769–1776
Wilson, James (Willson)	1, 44, 56	1768
Wilson, Robert	1, 107, 247	1769–1779
Winney, John	1, 141, 246	1771–1779
Wittman, Nathaniel	204	1774
Wolley, Richard	1, 79	1770
Wood, John	1, 81, 149	1769–1771
Wood, Joseph	176, 247	1773–1779
Wood, Patrick	40, 81	1768–1769
Woodrow, William	172	1773
Woodville, John (Woolville)	221, 222, 247	1771–1779
Worrell	216	1774
Yard, Mrs.	218	1777
Yard, Sarah	179, 203, 221	1774–1777
Yarnal, Mary	182	1773–1775
Yates, Joseph (Yeats?)	1, 34	1768–1773
Young, John	34	1768
Young, John, Jr.	143, 221	1771–1779

Young, Nathaniel	167, 183	1772–1774
Young, Robert	246	1779
Zane, Isaac, Sr. (Lane?)	34, 189	1768–1776
Zankinger, Adam (Lantzinger?)	175, 180	1773–1782

Appendix 2

The following index is reprinted from an original created for the Randolph receipt book for the years 1763–1777 at the Winterthur Museum and Library. The entries in the receipt book are arranged chronologically and record purchases and transactions between Randolph and other Philadelphians.

Adams, Thomas	118
Allen, Charles Rober	154
Alston, Joseph	48
Alston, Zachariah?	150
Anderson, Henry	215
Anderson, Thomas	155
Andrews, Peter	198
Angell, Wm.	126
Anthony, Joseph	211
Appleby, Hanna	134
Appleby, William	133
Armitage, Benjamin	85, 103, 121, 143, 159
Ashmead, Jos.	4, 16, 45
Assheton, Thos.	41
Attmore & Peters	81, 93, 116
Bache, Richard	214
Bagnall, Samuel	167
Baker, George	124
Baker, George A.	211
Baker, Godfred	216, 221
Baker & Weiss	216, 221
Barg, Charles	179
Barnes, James	100
Barnett, Isaac	139
Bartram, George	105, 133
Bartram & Lennox	76
Bateman, Nehemiah	86
Bayard, Stephen	78
Bayney, George	136
Beagler, J (n° ?)	85
Beere, Mary	212
Behan, Wiliam	7, 12, 43, 90
Bell, Ann	58, 96

Benezet, Philip	59
Bennet, Jnº	4
Bernard, Nicholas	146
Betterton, Sarah	184
Bi[illegible], Peter	172
Binks, Christopher	214
Birchall, Jnº	213
Bishop, William	79
Bissell, Jn.º	35
Black, Andrew	209
Black, John	217
Blonshed, Peter (Blanchard)	137
Bohean, Sibey	159
Boucher, Frances	100
Boutcher, Samuel	180
Boys, Elias	26
Bramich, William	10a
Branin, John	79, 84, 93
Brice, Rebecca	84
Bridges, Robert	71
Bringhurst, James	73, 77, 171, 201
Bringhurst, John	200, 206
Bringhurst, Joseph	196
Britton, John	28
Britton, Jnº	159
Broderick, Richard	173
Brole, Lehr	120
Bromwick, William	19
Brooks, Nicholas (Broocks in one case)	112, 217
Brown, David	121
Brown, Elijah	156
Brown, James	182
Brown, John	48
Brumage	21
Brumage, Willm.	17
Buck, Aaron	129
Budd & Coates	10
Budd, Levi	18
Budden, (Capt.)	59
Bunbury, Robert	181
Bure, Jonathan	184
Burge?, Samuel	136
Burns, J.	205
Burns, Joseph	211
Burroughs, Jacob	22
Burt, William	178
Bussy, Moses	119

Byerly, Christopher	35
Call, Ebenezer	176
Calvert, Daniel	110
Cambell, John	209
Cannan, Mary	136
Carmichael, Alexander	213
Carruthers, Sam.[1]	33
Carson, Andrew	215
Carter, Thomas	56
Carter, William	163
Cartwright, Shackler	22, 27
Cash, Thomas	55
Cass, Peter	212
Ceiret, Bernart (Bernard)	129
Chance, sloop	132
Chamber, D.	31
Chapman, Hanah	176
Chevalier, John	223
Chevalier, Peter	223
Chrystler, Jacob	87
Clark, John	62, 115
Clark, Jn.º	170
Clark & Wetherill	191
Claypoole, George	155
Claypoole, James	14, 44, 76, 139, 145
Clifton, James	71
Climer, Boltas	87
Climer, Elizabeth	131
Cline, Hannah	170, 190, 196, 204, 206, 210, 218, 222, 224
Clow, James	141
Coe, Robt.	28
Coles, James	5, 10, 11
Commin?, Fritz	21
Connell, George	221
Cook, John	83
Corneals, Marey	111
Cornell, William (Connell?)	121
Cortenay, Harclus (Hercules Courtenay); *see* Courtenay, H.	
Couch, David	82
Courtenay, H. (Hercules Courtnay)	87, 119
Coward, Mr.	68
Coward, John	31, 53, 60, 66
Coyle, William	209
Coxe & Furman	95
Craess, John	151
Craig & Morrell	158
Craig, Andrew	210

Craig, William	66, 68
Cramer, Israel	55
Creemer, Cristan	66
Cressen, James	216
Cresson, Jeremiah	137
Cresson, John	116
Culp, Barbara	16
Daly, Mary	188
Davidson, William	164, 173, 197
Davis, Samuel	64
Dea[illegible], Henry	93
Deakin, Robt.	130
Delany, William	197
Devine, Susanna	157
Diana, ship	115
Dicas, Thomas	142
Dickinson, Cadr.	9, 44, 79, 103, 128
Dickinson, Mary	113
Doddridge, Mary	167
Donaldson, Joseph	211
Donnell, Nathaniel	152, 162, 175, 196, 216
Donnelly, Mary	192
Dorsius, John	112
Dowell, Wm.	23, 29
Doz, Andrew	60
Douglas, George	174
Drinker	211
Duell, John	104, 108
Duffield, Edward	106
Dunfield & Hendricksons	94
Dunlap, John	222
Easton, Ed. (Elnathan)	113
Easton, Robert	194
Eavenson, Thomas	102
Ekart, Adam (Akart)	6, 8, 91
Elliott, John, Jr.	212
Elmslie, John	10b, 35, 116
Elmley, John	83
England, Jane	46
Erwin, Rob	156
Evans, Peter	6
Everett, Jeremiah	105, 107
Evrate (Everett), Jermiih (Jeremiah), *see* Everett, Jeremiah	
Ewan, John	40
Ewing, Thos.	209
Farn, Thomas	56
Farns, John	39, 49

Fawcet, Nathan	42
Fawkes, Richard	46
Ferguson, Richard	149, 162, 164
Ferguson, Samuel	36
Field, Nichlus	49
Field, Nicholas	89
Figener, Andrew	225
Finley & Taylor	53
Fitzgerald, Thomas	210
Fitzrandolph, Isaac	219, 223
Fleming, Benjamin (Heming)	195
Fletcher, Jane	82
Fletcher, Robert	125
Flinn, Daniel	111, 117, 128
Flower, Jn.º	5
Folks, Stephen; *see* Foulk	
Footman, Peter	186
Forman, Aaron	90
Forman, Samuell	10b
Forsberg, Nichol	31
Forsythe, Andrew	67
Fortere, Thos.	12
Foulk, Stephen	48, 64 (as Folks), 78
Foulke, Judah	163
Foulke, Mary	196
Fowler?	206
Frank, George	24
Frailey, Jacob	220
Federick, Miles	199
Frinke?, Gottfried	4
Fry, Alexander	136
Fullerton, George	105, 155
Fullton, James	38
Fulton, James	108
Futtler, James	140
Garretson, Cornelious	137
Garrits, Lawrence	161
Gebler, Godfrey	224
Georgia Packet, brig	141
Gibbon, Abel	50, 89, 97, 117, 122
Gibbons, Joseph	76
Gibson, John	41
Gibson, William	56
Gilbert, Thomas	98
Gisbor & Hendrickson	94
Gitts, Mi^l (Michael)	97, 146
Glinn, John	158

Goebel, Andrew	187
Goldsmith, Maurice	102
Gollen, Samuel	227
Gordon, Capt. Harry	67
Gordon, Thomas	196, 200
Gosling, John	104, 108
Granger, Henry	32, 138, 140, 141
Granger, John	2
Gray, Mary	86
Gray, William	86
Greaves, Robert	88
Greer, Andw	21
Greig, David	125
Greiner, Jacob	216
Guy, Margaret	178
Guy, William	178
Gyger, George	108, 111
Hagerty, Paul	115
Haines, Ephraim	123
Haines, Jonathan	153
Haines, Mary	153
Halere, John	96
Hall, Jacob	62
Hall, Samuel	126
Hall & Sellers	221
Hall, William (Franklin & Hall?)	207
Hamilton, James	41, 151
Hamilton, William	208
Hammond, Chas.	224
Handlyn, John	144, 178, 192
Harper, Ebenaezer	61
Harper, Thomas	76
Harris, Fras	101
Harris, George	139, 141, 152, 156, 184
Harrison, Colonel Benjn.	210
Harrison, Thomas	68
Havaland, John (Haviland)	118
Hayes, John	135
Hazelton, Sarah	184
Heming, Benjamin (Fleming)	195?
Henderson, John	71
Hendricks, Abraham	106, 108, 147
Hendrickson, John	52
Henke, Gottfried	10a
Herbergre, Christopher	214
Herley, Mr.	182
Heron?, Ann	55

Hew, Robert	61
Hewes, Dan.¹	5, 25, 75
Hewes, Jonah	211
Hill, John	59
Hill, Robt.	122
Hobart & Pratt	50, 88
Hobart, Enoch	88
Hockenhull, John	208, 217
Hodge, McCulloch and Bayard	78
Hodgkinson, Peter	120
Hogeland, Benjamin	1
Hollingsworth, Levi	155
Hood?, John	34
Hopkinson, Francis	112, 120
Hornin(g), Catrena	22, 27
Hornor, Benjn,	27
Howard, John	119, 123, 166
Howard, Peter	101
Howard, Thos	119, 123
Howlan, Michael	94
Huff, Abby	179
Hull, John	140
Hume, James	171
Humphreys, Benjamin	137
Hutch, Zachariah	150
Jacobs, John	181
Jacobs, Jos.	16, 77
Jaffrey, Charles	184
James	211
Jarvis, John	140
Jenkins, James	204
Jenkins, Morgan	204
John[illegible], Jr.	99
Johnis, Stephan	40
Johnson, Curnell?, Jr.	138
Johnson, Lawrence	74
Johnson, Nichlos	30
Johnson, Nicholas	19
Johnson, Samuel	57
Johnston, Joseph	219
Jones, J.	70
Jones, Jehu	59, 72
Jones, John	3, 8, 10b, 11, 17, 21, 25, 27, 33, 35, 37, 56, 70
Jones, Lewis	207
Jones, Thomas	194
Joseph	68, 69
Joseph Hight & Company	165

Josiah, Emanuel	58, 85
Josiah, Robert	58, 85
Justin & Marshall	124, 128, 130
Kemble, Geo.	18
Kennedy, Geo.	1
Kennedy, Mary	88
Kessler, Jossam	75
Kineman, Susanah	220
King, Dan	205
Kinsey, Abraham	62, 151
Knorr, Fuller	130, 132, 135
Knowles, John	123
Knowles, Jnº	186
Lahea, Alener (Eleanor)	177
Landers, Cuthbert	192
Laught, Sebastian	171, 180
Lawrence, John, Jr.	149
Lawrence, Thos.	16, 74, 192
Laycock, John	185
Leacock, John	177, 207
Lee, Gershom	96
Lesley, Peter; *see* Leslie	
Leslie, Peter	207, 215, 218
Lewis (Esquire)	38
Lewis, Ellis	115
Lewis, John	176
Lewis, Robt.	115
Lewis, Squire	65
Ley, Hannah (Lees)	63
Lightfoot, James	195
Linn, Cliveley?	137
Lloyd, Robert	90
Lockerman, Mr.	182
Londers, George	94, 154
Londey, Daniel	154
Long, Malken	148
Longstreet, Daniel	106
Lorley, Peter	137
Lort, John	113
Losh?, George	26
Lounsburg?, Benjn.	53
Loxley, Abraham	197
MacLeane? & Stuart	43
Maddock, Abraham	152
Magg, John	218
Mags, John	109
Maguire, Matt	213

Major, Dan	95
Marple?, George	3
Marshall, Ralph	138, 153
Martin, William	149, 182, 184
Martin, John	102
Martin & Row	224
Martin, Wm.	2
Mason, Richard	183
Mathews, James	223
Mathews, William	149
Mathieson	117
McCalesters, Michael	181
MCall, Archd.	127, 132
McCarde?, John	42
MCrakin, Jn.º (Jonathan McCracken?)	10b
McKim, Tho.	22
McLane, Samuel	226
McLaughlan, Felix	133, 134
McWilliams, George	191
Mendenhall, Robt.	7, 36
Meredith?, Daniel	29
Meredith, Reese	149
Micham, Thomas	94
Middleton, Aaron	127, 158, 179
Middleton, Rebecca	24
Miencken, Morris	197
Mifflin	127
Mifflin, Samuel	155, 170
Miller, Alexander	200
Miller, Ann	14
Milne, Edward	130
Milnor, William	30, 32, 38, 41, 49, 62
Mitchie, Jn.º	224
M'Nilleam, John	15
Moore, William	162
More, John	84
More, Joseph	9
Morgan, John	65
Morris, Anthony	157
Morton, John	88
Morton, Samuel	88
Mosely, George	131, 154
Mount, Elizabeth	10b
Muirheld, Andrew (Morehead?)	114
Murgatroyd, Thos.	44
Musgrove, Jn.	100
Mushett, Thomas	183, 187

Nast & Browne	65
Neal, Mary	118
Neff, Thos.	13
Neille, Sarah	220
Nevill, Daniel	92
Newbold, Daniel	227
Nigloskan, Felix	114
Ogden & Hewes	10
Ogden, Joseph	161
Ogle, John	24, 32, 80
Oliphant, Hosea	81, 82
O'Neaill, Daniel	122, 126
On[e][illegible], Dan.[1]	199
Onger, Cristan	80
Ord, John	47, 109
Owen, Edward	101
Packer, Daniel	200
Palmer, Jacob	219
Palmer, John	219
Parr, William	62
Parrish, Isaac	17
Parsons, Sarah	172
Parsons, Seth	173
Paschall, Isaac	13, 110
Paschall, Joseph	13, 110
Peare, Richard	226
Pecock, Adoniga	79
Peirse, John	80
Pemberton, Charles	110
Pennsylvania Hospital	19
Peterson, Peter	42, 47, 52
Phides, S.?	130
Philp, James	99
Phipps, Stephen	214
Plesants, Samuel	110
Polard, John	67, 71
Pollard, John	57
Pollard, William	194
Potts, David	53, 92
Prankerd, John	157
Predmore, John	117
Preston, Rachel	1, 164
Pusey, William	199, 225
Pyusell, John	109
Quigley, Aaron	170
Randolph, Daniel	14, 55, 67, 68, 69, 72, 79, 100, 105, 114, 198, 227
Randolph, Daniel & Benjn.	105

Randolph, James	15, 120
Randolph, Stephen	73
Rayn, Petter (Peter)	225
Renaudet, Dr.	177
Rice, James	210
Richards, David	87
Richardson, Wm.	9
Rickhor, Adrian	153
Ridgway, Henry	129, 135
Ridgway, Solomon	129
Riley, Edwd.	205
Rings, Thomas	121
Rissett, Christian	98
Ritter, Jacob	211
Ritter, Wilhelm	119
Roadge, Thomas	74
Roberts, Edward	63, 64
Roberts, George	63
Roberts, Hugh	19, 63, 64
Robins?, Cornelius?	45
Robins, Esek	50
Robinson, Cornelius	39
Robinson, Daniel	191
Robinson, William, Jr.	161
Rock, William	75
Roo?, John	26
Rose, J. L.	81, 90
Rosen, David, Jr.	175
Ross, Dr.	161
Ross, John	150, 193
Rundle, Danl	44, 60
Rundle, Richard, Jr.	60
Rush, William	152
Rush, William, Jr.	152
Saltar, Jn.º	165
Saltar, Joseph	165
Sansom, Samuel, Jr.	148
Saunders, Peter	195
Savage, Thomas	20, 141, 143
"Scotch presperterean Church"	160
Scott, John	219
Scr[illegible], James	100
Seaton, Rebecca (Leaton)	20
Sewell, R.	16
Sewell, Rd.	74
Shaeos, William	67
Shafer, Borbuy	189

Sharp, William	92
Shearman, John	6
Shield & Bradford	131
Shiney, Lorrance	172
Shiney, Michael	172
Sho, William	65, 79
Shockelea, Albartus	5, 95, 98
Shoemaker, Geo.	38, 54
Shoemaker, Jacob, Jr.	70
Shoemaker, Jona.	10
Shoemaker, Thomas	95, 136, 143
Sims, Esek Robins (Robinson's)	97
Sitgreave, Wm.	28
Skillman, Thomas	46
Smith, Christopher	188
Smith, Daniel	148, 210
Smith, Isaac	43
Smith, James	39
Smith, Robert	70
Smith, Robert, Jr.	91
Smith, Thos.	6, 8, 57, 101, 226
Smith, William	86, 97, 104, 107, 161
Smith, William D.	189, 197
Snowden, Isaac	40
Sparhawk, John	220
Standley & Jacob	77
Stansbury, Joseph	168
Stapler & Smith	74, 80, 88, 106
Stause, George	120
Steward, George	124
Stewr, Samuel (Stewart or Steward)	63
Stille, John	73, 102, 225
Stone, William	89
Stonem(atz?), Daniel	212
Stonematz, Jacob	194
Story, E.	75
Stout & Stout	2
Stout, John	62
Stout, Joseph	67
Stretch, Peter	205
Sutton, Susanna	190
Swain, Samuel	194
Taggart?, Robt.	33
Tatnal, Robt.	27
Taylor, Benjamin	14, 118, 120, 121, 134
Taylor, George	47, 190
Taylor, Isaac	118

Taylor, Josiah	165
Taylor, Samuel	133
Taylor, Sarah	134
Thackwray, Francis (Thackeray?)	111
Thomson, George	185, 195
Thomson, Rebecca	171
Tiltinghart, Joseph	125
Tisson, Edward	23
Todd & Dickinson	109
Todd, John	191
Toland, John	65
Tomlisson, James	8
Tonlay, Nathaniel	120
Torrence, Charles	193, 201
Treczer, Joseph	112
Trimble, Jn.	36
Trimble, Joseph	199, 47
Trimble, Samuel	48
Trimble, Wm.	36, 47
Truman, Richard	185, 215
Trumble, Francis	5, 10b
Trumble, Joseph	10a
Tryon & Gordon	72
Tryon, David	52, 58, 91, 199
Tuley, Abraham	50
Turnbull, William	76, 174, 209
Turner, William	52, 107, 123
Tybout, James	11
Tyler, Ann	125
Uber, David	188
Urion?, Miles	2
Vallance, Robert	189
Vandike, Charles	49
Van Sciver, Jacob	81
Vanwinkle, Sarah	176
Varet, Richard	148
Vhares, William	14, 65, 67, 79
Wade, Francis	194
Walker, Margaret	208
Wall, John	64
Wallace, Joshua M.	127, 132
Walsh, John	144
Walton, Samuel	151, 153
Ward, Andrew	158
Watkins, Joseph	148
Watkins, Joseph, Jr.	147, 151, 155
Watkinson, William	128

Watts, Arthur	19
Webb, John	140
Webber, Thomas	198
Webster, John	150, 156, 160
Wells, Richard	188
Welpher, Frederick	204
Wetherill, Sam.[l]	11
White, Jn.[o]	174, 175
Whitelock, John	160
Wickersham, Robert	165, 166
Wikoff, Isaac	106
Wikoff, John	108
Wilkinson, Anthony	122
Williams, John	157
William(s), Sam.[l]	7
Williams, Samuel	181, 183
Willing, Morris & Co.	1, 126
Willis, Jon[a]	223
Wilson, Robert	132
Wilton, John	71
Winter, John	39, 61
Wood, Jos.	12
Wood, Sacheveral	163
Woodrow, Henry	20
Woodrow, William	178
Wynkoop, Abrm.	59
Yarnall, Mary	185
Yoricke, Daniel	109
York, Jonathan	180
Young, Ellenore	204
Zane, Joel	187
Zane, Jonathan	182
Zantzinger, Adam	174

Appendix 3

The following is a list of people who appear in Randolph's account books who are known or thought to be craftsmen. A few are identified by Randolph by profession, but most have been identified by using other sources, including Beatrice Garvan's biography of Randolph in *Philadelphia: Three Centuries of American Art,* Alfred Coxe Prime's compilation *The Arts and Crafts in Philadelphia, Maryland and South Carolina, 1721–1785: Gleanings from Newspapers,* and William Macpherson Hornor's *Blue Book Philadelphia Furniture.* Many others appear to have been in Randolph's employ based on how their accounts are written. Some were paid regular wages, while others appear to have been paid for subcontracted work. However, for many of the names in his accounts the nature of the business transacted is not known, and, as a result, the following list is likely incomplete.

Thomas Affleck	Presumably Randolph's competitor in the cabinetmaking trade, Affleck purchased lumber on July 7, 1770.
Joseph Alston Jr.	Alston was probably a journeyman, since he received wages from March 1769 through February 1770. His relationship to Joseph Sr. is not known.
Joseph Alston Sr.	Alston was probably a journeyman, since he received wages from late 1768 through December 1770.
Henry Anderson	Anderson probably worked as a journeyman, though briefly, since he received cash from the shop account between April and July 1776.
Samuel Bagnal	He appears to have drawn wages from May 1772 to March 1773.
William Baker	Randolph may have employed Baker briefly in 1768, but if the latter was a journeyman, his role in the shop was minor.
Isaac Barnet	Barnet was probably a cabinetmaker. He appears in the Occupational Tax Records in 1783 and 1786 (William Macpherson Hornor Jr., *Blue Book Philadelphia Furniture* [Philadelphia: By the author, 1935], p. 317). Between May 5, 1770, and March 9, 1771, Barnet received cash totaling £36.9. The payments were charged as "by shop."

John Branning	Branning was probably a sawyer, since references to him usually mention lumber.
Richard Butts	Butts appears to have been a carver or joiner, but he apparently did little work for Randolph. References to him are found under the date October 15, 1768, under the "contra" column for Benjamin Harbeson on December 5, 1768, and on Randolph's cash page in 1779. On February 22, 1773, the *Philadelphia Packett* reported that "[John] Pollard and [Richard] Butts [would] . . . undertake . . . all manner of Carving in the House, Cabinet, Coach, and Ship way" (Alfred Coxe Prime, comp., *The Arts and Crafts in Philadelphia, Maryland, and South Carolina, 1721–1785: Gleanings from Newspapers,* 2 vols. [1929; reprint, New York: Da Capo Press, 1969], 1: 224).
Shackerley Cartwright	An August 1, 1764, entry in Randolph's receipt book indicates that he paid Catermon Hornington for Cartwright's rent. Cartwright was probably an indentured servant. Randolph's account book described him as "runaway—save trouble."
Hercules Courtenay	He probably entered into an indenture agreement with Randolph to repay the cost of his voyage from England. Courtenay appears to have worked exclusively for Randolph from the time of his arrival in late 1766 until he opened his own shop in the summer of 1769. Courtenay continued to work for Randolph after completing his term. The cabinetmaker's account book records payments to Courtenay between October 1, 1768, and December 29, 1776.
Jeremiah Cresson	He was a joiner, but the account book references suggest he was selling small amounts of lumber to Randolph.
William Davidson	Davidson's trade is not known, but he was undoubtedly an employee of Randolph. The former drew cash from the shop between November 1772 and April 1774 and received payments "by shop." Davidson's name appears under the accounts of Andrew Hertrog and Peter Lasley.
Nathaniel Donnell	He appears to have been a merchant rather than a craftsman.
Robert Easton	Since between August 1774 and September 1775, he received payments "by shop" in both cash and "sundries," it is impossible to determine if he was an artisan or merchant.

Plunkett Fleeson	A prominent upholsterer, Fleeson did considerable business with Randolph between August 1769 and June 1776.
John Fling	He was probably a journeyman, since he received wages from October 1768 through 1770.
Philip Flock	His account with Randolph ran from 1768 to 1770. Flock received payments in cash, though often small amounts, as well as stock and lumber. John Pritchard and John McPherson appear under his account.
Peter Footman	Based on the amounts listed in his transactions with Randolph between May 1774 and March 1775, Footman was a minor figure in the shop.
John Fowell	Fowell received seven shillings sometime in July 1770, then repaid that amount on December 6, 1770. He made a speaker's chair for the statehouse and an orrery cabinet for David Rittenhouse (Hornor, *Blue Book*, pp. 74–76).
Henry Granger	He appears to have been an employee. Granger's name appears on the "shop" page for 1771, and the dates of his account run from July 6, 1772, to February 1774.
Jonathan Haines	He received payments in cash. A John Haines is listed as a joiner in 1742 in Prime, *The Arts and Crafts in Philadelphia*, 1: 169.
William Hamilton	He is mentioned once in the account book A cabinetmaker from Edinburgh named William Hamilton is listed in Prime, *The Arts and Crafts in Philadelphia*, 1: 169.
John Hanlin	Hanlin was a journeyman joiner who worked for Randolph from 1768 until the Revolution. See Beatrice B. Garvan, "Benjamin Randolph," in *Philadelphia: Three Centuries of American Art* (Philadelphia: Philadelphia Museum of Art, 1976), p. 111.
John Haughton	Haughton appears in numerous entries between 1775 and 1782, but he does not appear to have received a wage. He may have been an upholsterer and a relative of George Haughton who advertised in the *Pennsylvania Packett* on January 30, 1775 (Prime, *The Arts and Crafts in Philadelphia*, 1: 170).
Andrew Hertrog	He appears to have been a minor employee. Hertrog did not receive any cash payments, but his account ran from January 1773 to April 1775, and the contra column for the account mentions John Magg, William Davidson, Henry Granger, and Robert Vallance.

John Hockenhull	Hockenhull was a journeyman, receiving wages from February 1774 to December 1775. His name appears earlier in conjunction with those of other craftsmen, suggesting that Randolph hired him full-time in 1774. The shop page dated 1779 indicates that Hockenhull received £244.18.4, but the entry is not specific.
John Howard	Howard may have been a sailor, since his name appears with that of the ship *Diana*. He received cash payments between October 1768 and November 1770. The contra column for these payments includes the notations "adventure to London" and "by shop, etc."
John Jones	He was a joiner and Randolph's landlord. In October 1768 Jones bought stock from Randolph valued at £4.8.10.
Benjamin Kendall	Kendall was a joiner who did a small amount of business with Randolph between 1768 and 1773 (Garvan, "Benjamin Randolph," pp. 110–11).
Robert Kennedy	According to Prime, *The Arts and Crafts in Philadelphia,* pp. 33, 37, 221, Kennedy was a carver and frame maker. Kennedy's account runs from 1768 to 1775 and lists purchases of sundries and lumber. He appears on the shop and expense pages. On March 28, 1776, Randolph recorded that Kennedy took a "Mahogany Card Table."
Peter Lasley	Lasley was a joiner. He appears at the beginning of Randolph's account book and received wages until the Revolution. (Garvan, "Benjamin Randolph," p. 111).
Thomas Lawrence	Randolph referred to Lawrence as an upholsterer. In 1768 Lawrence received stock (presumably furniture) and paid in stock (presumably upholstery). Randolph's account book also mentions a Thomas Lawrence Jr. and a Thomas Lawrence Esq., presumably different people.
James Lightfoot	He received cash payments totaling £79.5.6 for unspecified "work" performed between October 1774 and September 1775.
Melchor Long	Long received cash "by shop" in 1771, but he was a minor employee.
Abraham Maddock	Maddock received several cash payments "by shop" in 1771.
John Maggs	Maggs was an apprentice and journeyman. A May 8, 1768, entry in Randolph's receipt book indicates that he paid Todd & Dickinson "thirteen shilling and ninepence which with one Sett of bed rail's is

	in full for teaching John Mags at Nightschool." Maggs probably attained journeyman status by 1772. His account with Randolph ran from that year until 1776. Maggs appears to have been most active between June 1773 and March 1774.
William Martin	Randolph referred to Martin as an "Upholder" and recorded transactions with him totaling £122.16.11 between November 1773 and July 1777. Randolph paid him £15 for work done for Vincent Loockerman's account on December 3, 1774.
Samuel Matthews	Matthews was a joiner who had a small account with Randolph from 1768 to 1769 (Arthur Liebundguth, "The Furniture-Making Crafts in Philadelphia, ca. 1730–1760" [master's thesis, University of Delaware, 1964], p. 27).
John Mears	He appears in a minor reference on a cash page. Prime, *The Arts and Crafts in Philadelphia*, 2: 226, refers to a joiner named John Mears.
John Moody	Moody had a substantial account with Randolph, and his name appears on a cash page along with those of craftsmen. At this time, it is impossible to determine if Moody was an artisan or a merchant.
Joshua Moore	He purchased stock valued at £12 from Randolph in 1768. A joiner named Joshua Moore worked in Philadelphia during the 1770s (Hornor, *Blue Book*, pp. 138, 143).
Paul Morris	Morris received wages for work done between November 1768 and September 1769.
John Moyse	Prime, *The Arts and Crafts in Philadelphia*, 1: 178, refers to a chair maker named John Moyse. His name appears on a shop page, but Moyse apparently did little work for Randolph. House joiner Thomas Neville credited Randolph's account £5.5 for "12 Rush Bottom Chairs had of John Mois" (Thomas Neville Account Book, NA 773 W47 MF, p. 175, University of Pennsylvania Library).
John Pollard	A London-trained carver, Pollard was one of the most important artisans in Randolph's shop. Pollard's name is mentioned in accounts from October 1, 1768, to February 1779.
Thomas Power	Power received a small cash payment "by shop," presumably for work performed between 1776 and 1777.
John Prankhard	He received cash "by shop," presumably for work performed between 1772 and 1773. John Tristin was mentioned in conjunction with Prankhard.
John Read	Prime, *The Arts and Crafts in Philadelphia*, 1: 228 refers to Read as an upholsterer, but his business

	with Randolph was minor and apparently limited to the years 1774–1775.
James Reynolds	Reynolds was a London carver who arrived in Philadelphia in 1766. His name appears under Andrew Doz's account in 1769 (£8) and 1779 and on the shop page for £6.14. Although an important carver, Reynolds appears to have played a very minor role in Randolph's shop.
Peter Saunders	He received cash payments and "sundries" between October 1774 and September 1775.
Thomas Savadge	Savage (or Savadge) was a sawyer who did a great deal of business with Randolph.
John Shepper	He received regular cash payments and appears to have been a full-time employee from 1771 to 1775.
Jonathan Shoemaker	Shoemaker was a cabinetmaker who purchased stock and lumber from Randolph. John Maggs, an apprentice and journeyman in Randolph's shop, is listed in the contra column of one entry pertaining to Shoemaker.
Thomas Shoemaker	Shoemaker was a carpenter who sold his shop to Randolph. The former tradesman subsequently purchased stock and lumber from Randolph and settled his debts by "sundry accounts."
James Smither	He engraved Randolph's trade card. Smither's account dated October 1768 indicates that he purchased stock and lumber valued at more than £21. Smither's name also appears under Pollard's account in 1770, suggesting a connection between the two craftsmen.
Isaac Snowden	Probably a relative of Jedediah Snowden, Isaac had an account with Randolph from 1768 to 1773.
Jedediah Snowden	Jedediah was a cabinetmaker and Windsor chairmaker whose account with Randolph covered the years 1768 to 1775.
John Tristin	He received cash from Randolph in late 1768 and was credited for stock valued at £16.7.4. Tristin apparently did a great deal of work for Randolph. The shop page indicates Randolph paid him at least £83.14. Tristin's name also appears under John Fling's account.
Thomas Tristin	Probably a relation of John, he had minor dealings with Randolph between 1769 and 1771. Certain entries refer to "New House" and "shop."
Francis Trumble	Trumble was a cabinetmaker and Windsor chairmaker. His account in 1768 refers to the purchase of lumber, and the contra column gives the amount £10.16 and refers to a "voyage to Jamaica."

	Randolph's receipt book records a purchase from Trumble in 1763 (Garvan, "Benjamin Randolph," p. 110).
Andrew Tybout	Randolph's account book has numerous entries for Tybout between 1768 and 1777, and he appears to have been paid wages from August 1774 to May 1777.
Robert Vallance	Vallance appears to have been a workman in the shop and received wages totaling £80.0.6 from July 1773 to December 1774.
Samuel Walton	There is only one minor reference to Walton, wherein he drew cash and was paid by shop. Prime, *The Arts and Crafts in Philadelphia*, 1: 184, refers to him as a cabinetmaker.
Bryan Wilkinson	Probably a carver, his name appears several times in Randolph's accounts. Wilkinson does not seem to have received a wage. His name first appears under the account of "Robert Deakin his Sales Ship Diana" on October 31, 1768. In August 1772 Wilkinson received payment "by New House," presumably for work done on Randolph's home.
John Williams	Randolph identified Williams as a carpenter. Williams purchased stock in 1768 and John Redman made the payment.
Samuel Williams	Williams received a credit for £20.16.9 on the shop page in July 1777. Prime, *The Arts and Crafts in Philadelphia*, 1: 186, refers to him as a joiner.
James Wilson	Probably a carver, he had some accounts noted in 1768, but his work in the shop may predate that period (see note 5).
Nathan Young	Young's account dated 1773 mentions a note for £20.8.9. The contra column has an entry for the same amount, and the adjacent reference to "shop" suggests that he settled his debt with work.

Appendix 4

Randolph records transactions involving numerous ships, captains, and ports, and sometimes records specifics such as "adventure to Charleston," though the contents of these shipments are never noted. The following compilation is meant to aid scholars in finding such references within the account book at the New York Public Library.

Date	Entry	Amount
1768	Capt. John Clarke, "Voyage to Jamaica"	£110.12.4
1768	Capt. John Clarke, "Voyage to Jamaica"	£110.12.4
1768–1769	John Deakin, ship *Diana*, "adventure to London"	£49.85
1768–1787	Adam Foulk, "to stock"	£650.17.12
1768–1770	John Howard, ship *Diana*	
1768–1779	Emanuel Josiah, sloop *Betsy*	
1768–1773	Joseph King, sloop *Betsy*	
1768–1777	Willing and Morris, including April 1769	£196
1768–1772	John Rogerson, major purchases recorded	
1768	John and James Ross, ship *Diana*	
1768–1769	David Tryon, sloop *Betsy*, sawmill mentioned	
1768	Ebenezer Tyler, "Voyage to Jamaica"	
1768–1772	Bryan Wilkinson, ship *Diana*	
1768–1779	Willing and Morris, ship *Diana*	
1769–1771	Capt. William Davis, large purchases "to shop"	
1769–1779	"Adventure to Honduras"	
1769–1779	"Adventure to London," *Penn's Pacquet*	
1769	Capt. John Welch, lumber accounts	
1770	Sloop *Betsy*	
1772–1774	Captain Robert Collins, "to shop"	
1773	Captain John Mullony, to shop	£3.10
1778–1789	Brig *Recovery*	£21,602.14.7
1778	"Vendue, Goods purchased"	£20,438.5.4
1779–1787	Brig *Argo*, "fitted out as a privateer"	£105,770.15.5
1779	Schooner *Hummingbird*	£2,793.14.5

*Robert F. Trent and
John D. Alexander*

American Board-Seated Turned Chairs, 1640–1740

▼ ONLY TWELVE AMERICAN board-seated turned chairs made before 1720 are known. The term "board-seated" refers to a thin, planed board, or panel, with feathered edges that engage grooves plowed in the inner edges of a chair's seat rungs or "lists." Sometimes the board is held in the front and rear seat rungs only, but in most surviving chairs, the seat board is held in all four rungs. The seat board is thick enough to be fairly rigid but thin enough to flex slightly under the sitter's weight; usually the optimum thickness at the center is about half an inch. In view of the fact that hundreds of early American turned chairs with vegetable fiber seats are known, it would seem that board-seated versions were infrequently made, and that special skills were required to produce them. This article will examine the board-seated genre within the context of traditional chair making and present theories about the European origins of various examples.[1]

Turned chairs with board seats occupied an anomalous position in the woodworking hierarchy. Although they may have been considered equal in status to simple joined chairs, most of the American turned chairs with board seats appear to have been preserved because of their historical associations rather than their aesthetics. Of the twelve known examples, three came down in the families of Pilgrim leaders, two belonged to influential seventeenth-century clerics (Rev. John Eliot [1604–1690] of Roxbury, Massachusetts, the minister who translated the Bible into the Algonquian language, and Rev. Cotton Mather [1662–1728] of Boston), and one reputedly descended in the prominent Fauntleroy and Lee families of Virginia.[2]

Board-seated chairs raise additional interpretative quandaries. Although they constitute a subset of turned chairs, the structural peculiarities of certain board-seated variants often deviate from accepted notions of traditional post-and-rung chair construction. Within the cohort of traditional seating, post-and-rung chairs included seating with shaved components (otherwise known as plain chairs) and seating with turned components. Both of these variants feature socket joints assembled by driving dry tenons into wet mortises. Before 1500 some chairs combined joinery, turning, shaved work, and latticework of the sort associated with casement frames, as seen in the drawing *Men Shoveling Chairs* (fig. 7). Board seats, therefore, may be a vestigial structure within the post-and-rung chair tradition, dating from a period when the boundaries between seating types were blurred.[3]

Figure 1 Great chair, England, 1300–1400. Materials and dimensions not recorded. (*Antiques* 32, no. 3 [September 1937]: 112–13.) The leather covers are later additions and many of the small components are replacements.

Figure 2 Side view of the chair illustrated in fig. 1.

Figure 3 Rear view of the chair illustrated in fig. 1.

Figure 4 Diagram showing the seat rail construction of the chair illustrated in fig. 1. The seat boards are thick and do not have feathered edges.

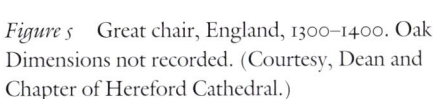

Figure 5 Great chair, England, 1300–1400. Oak. Dimensions not recorded. (Courtesy, Dean and Chapter of Hereford Cathedral.)

Early British Chairs

British woodworkers had produced board-seated turned chairs centuries before the first colonists settled in North America. The chair illustrated in figures 1–3 probably dates as early as the fourteenth century, having reputedly descended in the family of Scottish military leader William Wallace (d. 1305). The post diameters are large, the frame has suffered losses due to insect infestation, and some parts have been replaced. The side view (fig. 2) shows that the lowest surviving side rail into which the original plain spindles fit was not on the same level as the front and rear seat rails. While most of the spindles visible in the rear view (fig. 3) are replacements, they indicate that some arrangement of turnings was present in the back. The most important observation that can be gleaned from these images is that the seat boards were secured only in the front and rear seat rails and were, therefore, probably thick and inflexible (fig. 4).[4]

Wallace's chair strongly resembles a coeval English example referred to as "King Stephen's throne" (fig. 5). King Stephen reigned from 1135 to 1154, but most scholars date the chair 1300 to 1400. The most striking thing about this object is that it appears metallic. With their straight passages and small bands, the turned parts resemble cast metal tubes connected by rings or junctions. This was probably the maker's intent, because the prototypes for such chairs were bronze or ebony-and-ivory thrones, typically assembled from many small parts. According to some nineteenth-century antiquarians, "King Stephen's throne" retained traces of gilding and red paint, a color possibly intended to suggest polished bronze.[5]

All the principal joints of the chair illustrated in figure 5 are through-drilled. The board seat is composed of two heavy oak planks held in grooves in the front and rear seat rails. Neither of the side rails is at the same level as the seat boards. Surprisingly, the front and rear seat rails lack rectangular tenons, which would have prevented those rails from rotating in their mortises and releasing the seat boards. The maker may have felt that the thick seat boards were set deep enough in their grooves to resist rotation. That could explain why he apparently neglected to use trunnels (wooden pegs) to secure the seat rungs in their mortises.[6]

The chairs illustrated in figures 1–5 are important in understanding the chronology and development of board-seated furniture. Because they differ from turned seating depicted in Netherlandish paintings from the 1400s, the William Wallace, King Stephen, and associated chairs may represent index artifacts for a peculiarly English chair-making tradition. The "Bishop Ridley chair" at Pembroke College, Cambridge (fig. 6), appears to be in this

Figure 6 Great chair, probably London, 1540–1550. Elm. H. 46¼", W. 23½", D. 18⅝". (Courtesy, Pembroke College, Cambridge; photo, James Austin.) The rear feet are pieced, the lower back rail is replaced, the rear seat rail groove has split out, and two slats nailed underneath reinforce the seat boards. The seat boards are not held in the side seat rails. The front and rear seat rails are pegged, and all the mortises are through-bored. The crest rail originally had fifteen applied buttons.

same line of development. Nicholas Ridley (ca. 1500–1555) was a Reformation cleric allied with the radical Protestants Thomas Cranmer, archbishop of Canterbury, and Hugh Latimer, bishop of Worcester.[7]

Like King Stephen's throne, the Ripley chair has a board seat held in the front and rear seat rails and through-tenoned horizontal members, some of which are back-wedged. Accepting the chair as dating from the bishop's lifetime is somewhat problematic because of the reels and intermittent spherical turnings. This style of turning usually is thought to date from the 1660s, but the heavy finials and old-fashioned seat construction tend to support a sixteenth-century date.[8]

Early Dutch Chairs

Stools with a different type of board-seat construction are depicted in the fifteenth-century Netherlandish drawing *Men Shoveling Chairs (Scupstoel)* (fig. 7). This allegory of social unrest jumbles together chairs reserved for the elite with peasants' stools. Among the seating forms shown are stools with plank seats and stake feet, folding stools of the sort associated with church dignitaries, and a chair with shaved posts, a rush seat, and a joined back in-filled with latticework. The most important objects represented in the drawing are three-post, turned stools with board seats. To trap the seat board on all three sides, the rails of three-post stools had to be set at the same

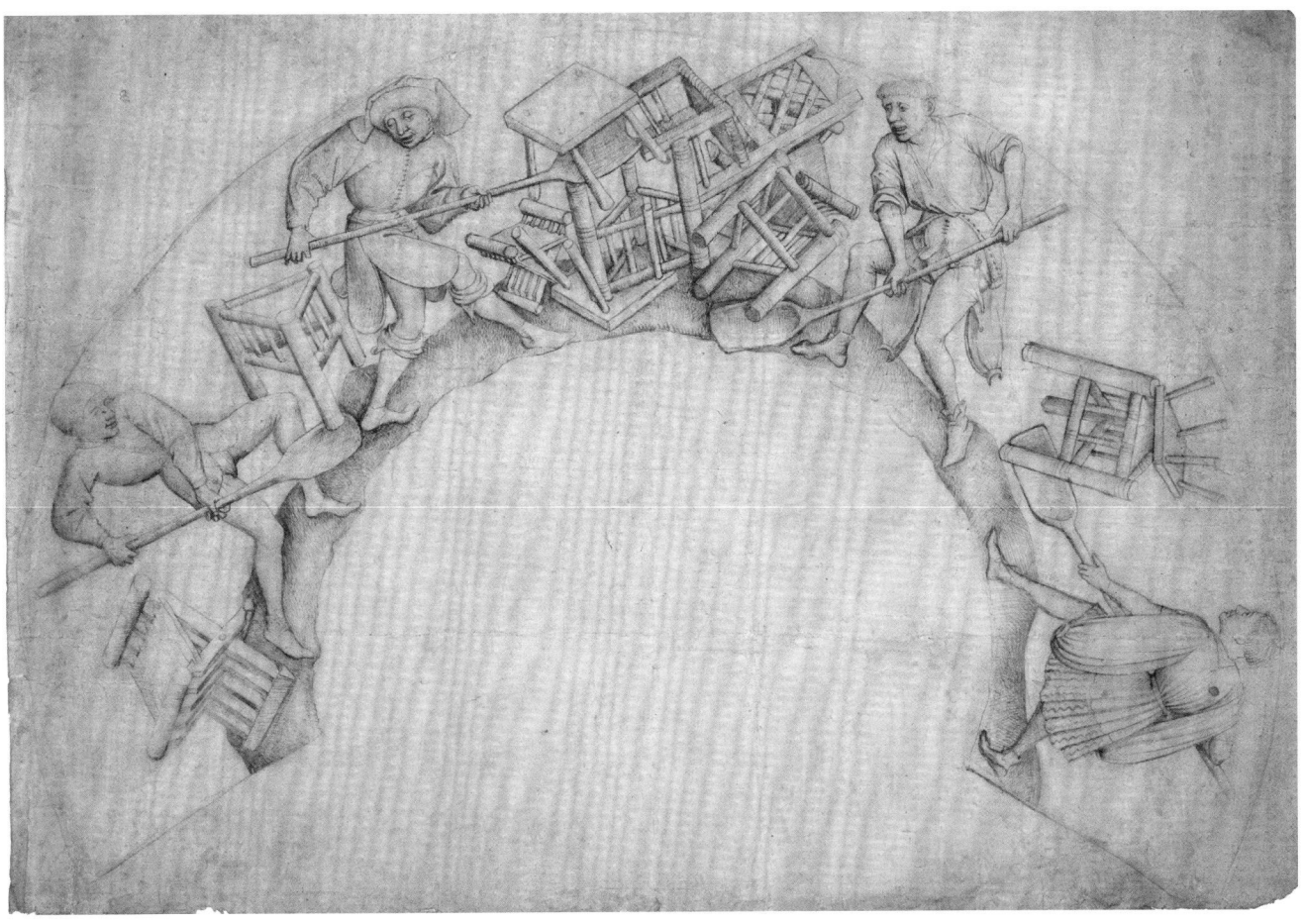

Figure 7 *Men Shoveling Chairs (Scupstoel)*, Circle of Rogier van der Weyden, Flemish, 1444–1450. Pen and brown ink over traces of black chalk. 11¹³⁄₁₆" x 16¾". (Courtesy, Metropolitan Museum of Art, Robert Lehman Collection, 1975 [1975.1.848]. Image © Metropolitan Museum of Art.)

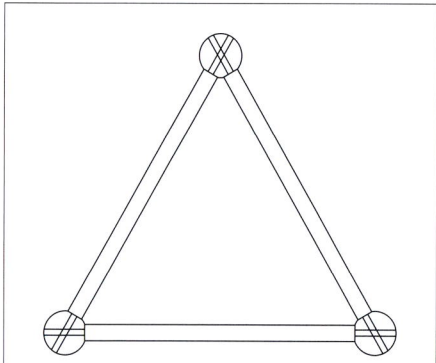

Figure 8 Diagram showing the placement of square and round tenons in the frame of a triangular stool.

Figure 9 Great chair, England or the Netherlands, 1500–1650. Possibly fruitwood and beech. H. 31", W. 24", D. 18". (Private collection; photo, National Trust, Northwest Region, Cumbria.)

level. This created a problem, because the tenons entering each post intersected with each other. Makers overcame this problem by using a round tenon at one end of each seat rail and a square tenon at the other end (fig. 8). On each post the smaller round tenon passed through the larger rectangular tenon, creating an interlocking joint. Usually, the round tenons were pinned to prevent them from withdrawing from their mortises. In addition to creating a stronger joint, the rectangular tenons prevented the seat rails from rotating under the weight of the sitter and causing the seat board to slip out of place.

To construct stools of this type, makers had to be precise when chopping and drilling their mortises. Assembling the frame also required considerable dexterity, since the maker had to rotate the frame while hammering each joint in sucession. If any tenon was driven much farther in than the other two, the entire structure would bind or one of the posts would split under the stress.

Although three-posted stools often appear in Netherlandish art, furniture historians have either ignored these seating forms or posited that they were

Figure 10 Great chair, South Africa, eighteenth century. Possibly stinkwood. H. 32", W. 23¾", D. 15½". (Private collection; photo, H. K. J. Roos.)

Figure 11 Great chair, South Africa, eighteenth-century. Possibly stinkwood. H. 31", W. 22¾", D. 15½". (Private collection; photo, H. K. J. Roos.)

the antecedents of chairs. Under that "evolutionary" model, the rear post of stools rose higher over time, eventually providing a backrest for the sitter. It is more likely that fully developed stools and chairs with extended back posts were made simultaneously. The chair shown in figure 9 has a horizontal crest curved to conform to the sitter's back and two diagonal struts that function as braces. On other examples, the crest has a deeper curve and extends farther forward to provide cantilevered armrests. The three-post format had advantages because it was stable on uneven floors.[9]

During the sixteenth and seventeenth centuries, armchairs were among the most comfortable and prestigious seating forms. Some provision for arms is seen in two eighteenth-century South African chairs based on Netherlandish examples made two centuries earlier (figs. 10, 11). The rear posts of these derivatives have paddlelike crests with diagonal struts, and the arms are continuous, bent slats that are pinned to the rear post and tenoned into the front posts. The abstract turnings of the posts, consisting of long, inswept collars, are similar to those on the chair illustrated in figure 9. That chair represents another variant within the tradition, having a broader crest, crooked struts worked with a draw shave, and turned arms. All these chairs (figs. 9–11) have blind joints at the seat rails, presumably with a rectangular tenon at one end of each seat rail and a round tenon at the other end.

Another early type of board-seated construction occurs on a chair with a straight turned crest braced with diagonal struts and turned arms that fall

Figure 12 Great chair, England, 1600–1650. Ash and possibly elm or yew. H. 35", W. 23", D. 17¾". (Private collection; photo, Robert J. Bitondi.) The side stretcher nearest the viewer is pulled up at the rear to such an extent that it is not parallel to the seat rail above it.

on a diagonal to extensions of the two front posts (fig. 12). This object displays a technically sophisticated version of the intersecting tenon system (figs. 13–15). The shoulders of the rectangular tenons are sawn at an angle to conform to the shape of the posts, and the round tenons are back-wedged, an alternative to pinning. The shaped shoulders also function as a redundant antirotation device. This precise execution and overconstruction is reminiscent of Germanic work of the period. After all, rectangular tenons without conforming shoulders would have held as well, and the seat board did not have to fit so tightly in the corners.

In this chair, the complexities inherent in assembling a three-post stool were multiplied. The maker had to work his way around the frame, gradually driving together three intersecting joints without causing any to bind while simultaneously joining the arms to the crest rail and the two front posts. Exactly how he accomplished this task is unclear, but the long,

Figure 13 Detail of the left front post of the chair illustrated in fig. 12. The small round tenon pierces the rectangular tenon and is back-wedged.

Figure 14 Detail of the left seat joint of the chair illustrated in fig. 12. The shoulders of the front seat rail are sawn on the bias to conform to the post. The seat board is extremely snug. On some chairs of this type, the corners of the seat board fit into a slight groove incised in the post.

tapered turnings at the front of the arms suggest that the maker began by assembling the entire back with its crest rail and diagonal struts (no mean feat in and of itself). He then could have driven the rear tenons of the arms completely into the crest rail and proceeded to assemble the seat frame and stretchers, while forcing the front tenons of the arms into the posts.

Plotting the locations of the stretchers was another problem. The maker of the chair illustrated in figure 12 set them at different heights. This provided structural integrity but denied bilateral symmetry. While both side stretchers enter their respective front posts at about the same level, they enter the rear post one above the other.

The Welsh Tradition

Most of the British board-seated, turned chairs that survive have histories of ownership in Wales. Some have seat frames constructed with rectangular tenons intersected by round tenons, whereas others have seat rails with intersecting large and small round tenons (fig. 15). Both types of joints appear in chairs that are virtually identical, so no chronological or developmental priority may be assigned to either variant.

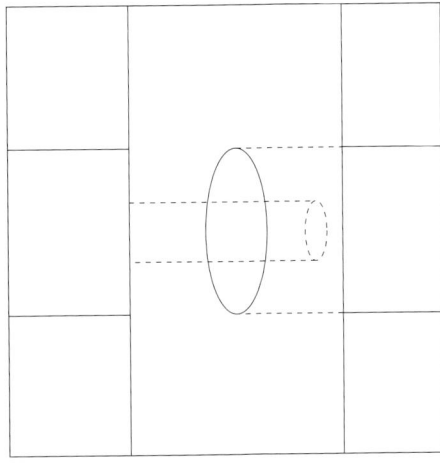

Figure 15 Diagram showing the seat rail joint of a board-seated chair with intersecting round tenons.

Figure 16 Great chair, Wales, 1550–1660. Woods not recorded. H. 39", W. 26", D. 21". (Courtesy, Museum of Welsh Life, St. Fagan's, Cardiff, Glamorgan; photo, Robert F. Trent.) The seat board is made in two pieces and the seat rails have a round tenon at one end and a rectangular tenon at the other.

Figure 17 Great chair, Wales, 1550–1650. Yew and oak. H. 38 1/8", W. 25 1/2", D. 20 1/2". (Courtesy, Museum of Welsh Life, St. Fagan's, Cardiff, Glamorgan; photo, Robert F. Trent.) The seat board is made in two pieces and the seat rails have a rectangular tenon at one end and a round tenon at the other. The shoulders of the rectangular tenons are cut on the bias to conform to the shape of the posts. Some of the applied finials and the left upper arm are replacements.

The chairs illustrated in figures 16 and 17 are relatively plain, having straight rear posts and heavy turned horizontal crest rails. Both have two arms set at different angles on each side and spindles between the seat rails and the stretchers. An important stylistic and structural detail is the use of turned ledges on the rear post, which serve as seats for the diagonal struts supporting the crest of each chair. The vigorous turnings, including the heavy urns on the front posts, are squarely in the mannerist design tradition, and it is difficult to believe that such objects could have been made in Wales much before 1560. These chairs also have applied buttons of various forms and punchwork in some moldings. They continue the practice of placing the three stretchers at different levels, without reference to bilateral symmetry. These chairs represent a standard model. Other versions feature complex superstructures that were labor-intensive, expensive options. The most elaborate chairs were preserved as relics of departed patriarchs and matriarchs.

The chair illustrated in figure 18 has a history of ownership in Ty'n-y-cymer, Glamorganshire. Its understructure is not all that different from those of the previous Welsh examples, but its crest is ornamented with a superimposed cage of interlocked posts, rails, and spindles. Connected to this cage are two lateral structures that resemble the wings or cheeks of early-eighteenth-century easy chairs. This elaborate framework may have been draped in winter. Features not previously encountered include gouge carving on the flanges of turnings and free rings made from the same piece of wood as the spindles they surround. The multiple bands on the posts and the crest rail

Figure 18 Great chair, Wales, 1550–1650. Elm and oak. H. 57¼", W. 28", D. 22¾". (Courtesy, Museum of Welsh Life, St. Fagan's, Cardiff, Glamorgan; photo, Robert F. Trent.) The seat board is made in two pieces and the seat rails have a large round tenon at one end and a small round tenon at the other. The arm joints and the entire back superstructure are extensively pinned. The turned buttons on the crest have round tenons that were shaved square before being forced into smaller, round mortises. The buttons are not pinned, which suggests that the crest rail retained considerable moisture at the time of manufacture and the maker expected the mortises to shrink around the tenons.

Figure 19 Great chair, Cornwall or Devon, England, 1550–1650. Ash. H. 45", W. 23⅞", D. 26½". (Courtesy, Church of St. Marnarch, Lanreath, Cornwall; photo, Robert F. Trent.) The seat is an incorrect replacement installed on top of the seat rails. The right seat rail is replaced.

appear on some of the chairs in *Men Shoveling Chairs* (fig. 7), suggesting a connection between this Welsh chair-making school and the late medieval Netherlandish tradition that preceded it; however, many of the other turnings are well-defined renaissance forms.

The extraordinarily complex fabrication and assembly problems posed by these Welsh chairs suggest that they may be earlier than some related stools. Although the chairs may have provided greater comfort, their backs forced the user to sit upright, leaving little room for relaxation. As long as the principal support for the back rail was an extension of the rear leg, this posture was difficult to avoid.

To create layback, makers began using a large horizontal rail immediately above the seat. This allowed them to set the back posts at an angle, providing additional comfort for the sitter. As the chair illustrated in figure 19 suggests, this design often made construction more complex. The maker of this example probably began by assembling the seat frame using the interlocking round-tenon system described above. Then he began driving the joints connecting the lower arms to the front posts and large horizontal rail, the diagonal struts to the low rear post and large horizontal rail, and the large horizontal rail to the low rear posts. The maker performed this work gradually and sequentially to keep the joints from binding. Having completed the undercarriage, he could begin installing the back. He drove the arms into the upper back posts, inserted the big back spindles into the frame, maneuvered the back posts and spindles into their mortises in the large horizontal rail, and forced the front tenons of the arms into their mortises in

Figure 20 Great chair, Wales, 1550–1650. Elm. H. 53 5/8", W. 33", D. 26 1/8". (Courtesy, Temple Newsam House, City of Leeds, Yorkshire; photo, Norman Taylor.)

the front posts. The high degree of skill required to bore the mortises of this chair accurately and to assemble its frame attest to the sophistication of the board-seat design tradition.[10]

The diagonal struts supporting the large crest rail of the armchair illustrated in figure 18 feature bilaterally symmetrical balusters with a thin reel at the waist, a turning sequence repeated on the lower back pillars of a related chair (fig. 20). Although the chair illustrated in figure 20 has two horizontal rails above the seat, its back is framed with a series of medium-weight spindles rather than two large outer posts. The two rails are nearly identical in size and diameter, and the superstructure with cheeks or wings is higher relative to the seat and the back than that of the chair in figure 18. The maker chose to retain a primary and secondary pair of arms, but he set one pair between the structural rail and the front posts and the other between the crest rail and the front posts. Consequently, both pairs of arms are set at the same angle. Embellishments on the chair illustrated in figure 20 include free rings, applied buttons, and gougework. With its pronounced urns and balusters, the turned ornament of this example has stronger renaissance overtones than that of the chair shown in figure 18.[11]

Three-post chairs with high superstructures tend to tip over if the sitter shifts too much weight to either side. At some point, makers introduced a four-post plan. A striking example of the latter form has a history of ownership in Tregib, Llandeilo, Carmarthenshire (fig. 21), and appears to be

Figure 21 Great chair, Wales, 1550–1650. Elm. H. 52⅞", W. 31¾", D. 25½". (Courtesy, Museum of Welsh Life, St. Fagan's, Cardiff, Glamorgan; photo, Robert F. Trent.) The upper and lower arm joints are pinned; the intermediate arms are not pinned. The left rear leg, seat rails, upper front stretcher, upper left arm, and seat board are replacements. The finials on the back posts are enlarged versions of the small, applied buttons on the top of the crest rail, and the footrest is a later addition.

Figure 22 Great chair, Wales, 1550–1650. Ash and oak. H. 44⅞", W. 30⅜", D. 22⅜". (Private collection; photo, George Fistrovich.) This object is part of a large group of almost identical chairs, including an example acquired for the president of Harvard College in the mid-eighteenth century.

from the same shop tradition that produced several three-post chairs (fig. 22) including one acquired in the 1750s for the president of Harvard University. Like all of the seating in this group, the chair illustrated in figure 21 has little layback despite having a low structural rail mounted just above the seat. The front posts of these chairs also lack pommels, or handgrips, a feature found on many other examples of board-seat furniture. The chair

Figure 23 Great chair, Cornwall, England, 1550–1650. Ash. H. 41", W. 25 3/8", D. 19 3/8". (Courtesy, Church of St. Marnarch, Lanreath, Cornwall; photo, Robert F. Trent.) The seat boards are incorrect replacements installed atop the seat rails, and the finials are restored.

illustrated in figure 21 deviates from the group in having a back framed with heavy outer posts rather than several medium-size spindles. The only renaissance turnings are the heavy urns on the front posts and a few minor ball-and-reel sequences.[12]

The simple but distinctive great chair illustrated in figure 23 was probably made for the church of St. Marnarch in Lanreath, Cornwall. Unlike most turned great chairs, this example has posts braced by stretchers set just below the seat rails rather than near the floor. The maker's use of extremely heavy stock for the posts may have been dictated by a concern for stability. The turnings of this chair relate directly to those on two similar American examples. Pertinent elements include the slightly indented ball turning on the front and rear posts and a barrel-like turning on the back spindles with indented ends and a central incised band.[13]

The Board-Seat Tradition in America
The American chairs that relate most closely to the St. Marnarch example represent the work of two different makers. One descended in the Foote family of Wethersfield, Connecticut (figs. 24, 25), and the other reputedly belonged to Jacob Strycker, a German who lived on western Long Island near New York (fig. 26). The earliest member of the Foote family was a turner named Nathaniel (ca. 1593–1644).[14]

At this time, it is impossible to determine if the makers of the Foote and Strycker chairs trained in the same regional tradition that produced the St. Marnarch chair and other related board-seat forms. The backs of the American examples have greater layback (fig. 25) than their British antecedents, and the turnings on the Foote and Strycker chairs are more conservative than those on the St. Marnarch chair, although still based almost entirely in the renaissance tradition.

Figure 24 Great chair, probably Wethersfield, Connecticut, or New York City, 1650–1700. Ash and oak. H. 41⅛", W. 26", D. 20". (Courtesy, Connecticut Historical Society, Hartford, Connecticut; photo, Robert J. Bitondi.)

Figure 25 Side view of the chair illustrated in fig. 24, showing the angle at which the back is set in the low structural bar.

Figure 26 Great chair, New York City, 1650–1700. Ash and oak. H. 39½", W. 24", D. 17". (Courtesy, Metropolitan Museum of Art, Rogers Fund, 1941 [41.111]; photo, Gavin Ashworth.) The seat board is a modern replacement.

Figure 27 Great chair, Connecticut or New York, 1650–1700. Maple and ash. H. 43½", W. 23" (front) and 17" (rear), D. 16". (Private collection; photo, Gavin Ashworth.)

A straight-post chair in the same style as the Foote and Strycker examples suggests how this board-seated tradition may have evolved in America (fig. 27). Although it has turned ornament similar to that on the preceding examples (figs. 24, 26), the chair illustrated in figure 27 does not have a horizontal back rail set just above the seat. This suggests that the same shops that made chairs with such rails also produced seating without them.[15]

The Plymouth Tradition

The most widely published American board-seat chairs were made in Plymouth, Massachusetts. One reputedly belonged to William Bradford (1589/90–1657) (fig. 28), one to William Brewster (1567–1644) (fig. 29), and one to Myles Standish (1584–1656) (fig. 30). Skeptics have decried these his-

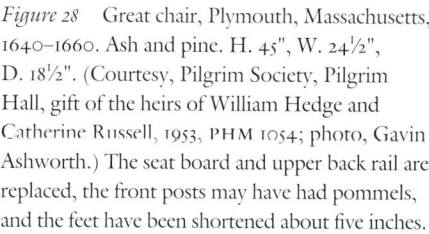

Figure 28 Great chair, Plymouth, Massachusetts, 1640–1660. Ash and pine. H. 45", W. 24½", D. 18½". (Courtesy, Pilgrim Society, Pilgrim Hall, gift of the heirs of William Hedge and Catherine Russell, 1953, PHM 1054; photo, Gavin Ashworth.) The seat board and upper back rail are replaced, the front posts may have had pommels, and the feet have been shortened about five inches.

Figure 29 Great chair, Plymouth, Massachusetts, 1640–1660. Ash. H. 45", W. 24", D. 18". (Courtesy, Pilgrim Society, Pilgrim Hall, gift of Daniel Brewster, 1838, PHM 942; photo, Gavin Ashworth.) Fragments of the pommels remain on the front posts. The top back rail, seat board, lower front stretcher, and five spindles are missing.

Figure 30 Great chair, Plymouth, Massachusetts, 1640–1660. Maple and ash. H. 39", W. 26", D. 17½". (Courtesy, Pilgrim Society, Pilgrim Hall, Museum purchase from Roger Bacon, 1967; photo, Gavin Ashworth.) The posts were replaced in the eighteenth century and the spindles replaced at a later date. Tradition maintains that the spindles under the arms came from pews from the 1682 meetinghouse in Hingham, Massachusetts.

tories for years, partly because other Pilgrim provenances have proven specious and partly because of the existence of replicas made over the years to satisfy the cult of ancestor worship surrounding the Pilgrims. Many Pilgrim descendants owned or own artifacts that reputedly arrived on the *Mayflower*, but most of these objects were first owned by later generations of the families in question. All of the chairs in the Plymouth group were once considered part of that ship's cargo, but their American woods refute that theory. The chairs may, however, represent the work of an immigrant craftsman. If that is true, then their histories of ownership by immigrant Pilgrim patriarchs are probably correct.

Several British and Netherlandish chairs can be interpreted as antecedents or cognates for the Bradford, Brewster, and Standish seating. The woodworking tradition encompassing the Plymouth chairs probably emanated from London, where Dutch influence was strong. The Ridley chair (fig. 6) suggests that turned chairs with board seats were being made in that city by the mid-1550s. A chair that reputedly belonged to Dutch humanist Desiderius Erasmus (ca. 1466–1536) supports that theory (fig. 31). He visited England repeatedly between 1499 and 1517 and was often the guest of Sir Thomas More (1478–1535). Presumably Erasmus obtained the chair during his unhappy residence as a lecturer at Cambridge from 1510 to 1514, or

Figure 31 Great chair, probably London or Cambridge, England, 1510–1514. Ash and pine. H. 49", W. 24⅝", D. 17". (Courtesy, Queen's College, Cambridge; photo, Reeve Photography.) The seat rails have a large rectangular tenon at one end and a small round tenon at the other. The upper back rail is an addition, the front stretcher is replaced, the feet have been pieced out, and the rear stretcher and six spindles under the front seat rail are missing.

perhaps earlier during one of his visits at More's house near London. The Erasmus chair is one of the few English four-post examples without a low structural back rail that can be associated with southeastern England.[16]

Another English chair has features rarely seen outside the Plymouth group (fig. 32). Its front and back posts are canted, but all of its horizontal components remain parallel to the floor (fig. 33). This design allowed the maker to produce layback without using a low structural back rail, but it did not provide the same level of comfort. The muscles of a sitter's back and legs

Figure 32 Great chair, England, 1550–1650. Ash and chestnut. H. 43⅛", W. 24½", D. 17½". (Private collection; photo, Robert J. Bitondi.) The seat board is replaced, the front posts may have had pommels, and the tip of the right finial is missing. The frame never had a lower rear stretcher. The seat construction is the rectangular tenon–small round tenon type.

Figure 33 Side view of the chair illustrated in fig. 32, showing the rake of the frame.

cannot relax as long as the seat remains level. A cushion at the front may have alleviated some tension by slightly elevating the sitter's legs. The vasiform turning vocabulary of this chair is closely related to that of the Plymouth examples and has almost no medieval antecedents.

Perhaps the most important cognate for the Plymouth group is a small side chair likely of Netherlandish origin or made by a Dutch turner who resided in London or another Channel port (fig. 34). Turned side chairs rarely survive, and those with board seats are exceptionally rare. The turnings on the chair illustrated in figure 34 are far more detailed and refined in concept and execution than those on the Plymouth chairs (figs. 28–30). The deeply incised accents and sharp-edged, elegant flanges (figs. 35, 36) are indices of high-quality work, where the turner was pushing his design to the limits of the material. Many of the thinner edges have chipped off, possibly

Figure 34 Side chair, the Netherlands or southeastern England, 1600–1650. Cherry. H. 30½", W. 17½", D. 14⅞". (Courtesy, Antiquarian & Landmarks Society, Hartford, Connecticut; photo, Robert J. Bitondi.) The seat board and left stretcher are replaced.

Figure 35 Detail of a spindle on the chair illustrated in fig. 34.

Figure 36 Detail of the left finial of the chair illustrated in fig. 34.

because the cherry became brittle with age—a characteristic of most fruitwoods. Dutch turners often made chairs of cherry, with the intention of painting them black to resemble ebony.[17]

The William Bradford chair (fig. 28) is the most intact example in the Plymouth group, and it has subtle refinements that are not immediately evident. The side rails of the seat are angled, dropping about one-half inch from front to back, but the front and rear posts are upright. When combined with the use of a cushion, this feature would have made the chair more comfortable than a comparable example with seat rails oriented parallel to the floor. The Bradford chair maker turned long tapered stops on the ends of his vasiform spindles so he could trim and fit them in a seamless fashion and turned the spindles in batches of five different heights based on their intended location in the frame. The Brewster and Standish chairs (figs. 29, 30) originally looked very much like the Bradford example. The latter chair is the only one retaining its original upper turned back rail.

All of the board-seated chairs in the Plymouth group have interlocking rectangular and round tenons where the seat rails join each post. The tops and bottoms of the mortises are rounded, suggesting that the maker used a brace fitted with a piercer to bore holes at each end and a mortising chisel to chop out the waste between. After turning the seat rails, he sawed the cheeks of the tenons to make the upper and lower edges conform,

Figure 37 Great chair, Plymouth, Massachusetts, 1660–1690. Maple and ash. H. 45³⁄₄", W. 24", D. 17½". (Private collection; photo, Gavin Ashworth.) This chair reputedly belonged to William Brewster's grandson, Benjamin Brewster (1633–1710), who moved from Plymouth to New London, Connecticut, in 1653 and then to Norwich, Connecticut, by 1662.

approximately, to the bored ends of the mortises. The maker of the English chair illustrated in figure 32 followed the same practice.

All of the Plymouth chairs appear to be from the same shop tradition, if not by the same hand. The turnings display minor variations, but that is to be expected in early seating of this caliber and complexity. The spindle profiles of the Bradford and Brewster chairs are virtually identical, a fact somewhat obscured by turnings on the latter example, which were shaved flat on their front faces at a later date.

The worn front stretcher of the Bradford chair provides evidence that all of the Plymouth examples were assembled using wet-and-dry construction. Both ends of the stretcher are almost perfect half-sections of the tenons secured in the mortises. The tenons have compression marks that match the spoon-bit kerfs of their mortises. These marks occurred as the wet posts dried, shrinking around the tenons. The tenons were probably dry and slightly oversized at the time of assembly.

A slat-back armchair (fig. 37) recently discovered by furniture scholar Donald P. White III is the only other example from this shop tradition, which is surprising considering the large number of surviving turned chairs made by Ephriam Tinkham (1649–1713) of nearby Middleborough. The slat-back armchair descended in the Brewster family of Plymouth and New London County, Connecticut, until the late eighteenth century, when a member of the Roach family of New London County acquired the piece. Not only does the slat-back chair have finials similar to those on the Bradford and Brewster examples, but it also retains its abbreviated pommels. The pommels on the Brewster chair are too fragmentary to determine if they resembled those on the slat-back example.[18]

The Boston Tradition
A chair with urn-and-flame finials (fig. 38) that match those on many other examples of Boston seating serves as an index for understanding the board-seat tradition in that city. This imposing object descended in the Tufts

Figure 38 Great chair, probably Boston, Massachusetts, 1640–1680. Ash and oak. H. 44¾", W. 23½", D. 15¾". (Courtesy, Metropolitan Museum of Art, bequest of Mrs. J. Insley Blair, 1951 [51.12.2]; photo, Gavin Ashworth.) This chair descended in the Tufts family of Medford, Massachusetts. The seat board and pommels are modern replacements.

Figure 39   Great chair, probably Boston, Massachusetts, 1650–1690. Ash and oak. H. 43½", W. 24", D. 17⅛". (Courtesy, Roxbury Latin School, Unitarian Universalist Church in America; photo, Gavin Ashworth.) Rev. Thaddeus Mason Harris (1768–1842) acquired this chair from a Roxbury, Massachusetts, family and gave it to the First Church in Dorchester, Massachusetts. The chair was subsequently transferred to the Unitarian Universalist Church in America and is currently at the Roxbury Latin School. The top back rail is replaced, and the posts are pieced out.

family of Medford, Massachusetts, about five miles northeast of Boston. One of the earliest turners active in Boston was Thomas Edsall (1588–1676), a London-trained craftsman who immigrated in 1635. Given his dominance of the turning trade over the following forty years, he may have introduced many of the ornamental details found on later Boston seating.[19]

The Tufts chair is obviously the product of a sophisticated, established tradition. Although its turnings differ from those of the Brewster, Bradford, and Standish chairs, the construction of the Tufts example shares several details with the Plymouth group. The maker turned his spindles in different heights, so that the proportions of the frame could be adjusted, and set the side rails of the seat at an angle to produce a slight fall from front to back.

A related Boston chair (fig. 39) reputedly belonged to Rev. John Eliot (1603–1690), the minister of the church in Roxbury, Massachusetts, who translated the Bible and other religious texts into the Algonquian language. Like the Tufts chair, Eliot's example has seat rail joints wherein a rectangular tenon is pierced by a round tenon, a board seat set in grooves on all four sides, and built-in seat fall. Despite these structural affinities, the Eliot chair is clearly by a different maker. It has two upper crest rails and only one stretcher at each side. The somewhat straight-sided turnings of the Eliot chair are repeated on a fragmentary example by the same maker (fig. 40).[20]

Figure 40 Great chair, probably Boston, Massachusetts, 1660–1690. Ash, maple, and oak. H. 41", W. 21½", D. 15¹⁄₁₆". (Courtesy, Historic New England, gift of Mary Thacher; photo, Gavin Ashworth.) The rear legs are pieced out below the seat, the spindles beneath the arms and the finials are replaced, and the front posts may be replaced.

Figure 41 Child's high chair, probably Boston, Massachusetts, 1660–1700. Maple and ash. H. 38⅝", W. 18¼", D. 14⅝". (Courtesy, American Antiquarian Society, gift of Mrs. Hannah Mather Crocker.) The seat board and a footboard are missing, the center front spindle is a replacement, and the top back rail may be replaced.

Figure 42 Child's high chair, Virginia, 1670–1710. Black walnut. H. 36½", W. 14¼", D. 11½". (Courtesy, Colonial Williamsburg Foundation; photo, Hans Lorenz.) This chair may have belonged to Hancock Lee (1653–1709) of Virginia. The seat board, footboard, and seat board are missing. Both right stretchers, both rear stretchers, both back spindles, and the lower back rail are replacements.

A high chair (fig. 41) that reputedly belonged to Rev. Increase Mather (1639–1723) of Boston also appears to be a product of that city's board-seat tradition. The seat board is missing, but the rails have grooves cut on the inside edges and join the posts in much the same manner as those on the Tufts and Eliot chairs (figs. 38, 39). Some question exists about the age of the top back rail, which is loose in its mortises. The long, tapered posts and spindles, accented only by fine score lines, seem austere, but the forms may have been dictated by considerations of hygiene. Apparently this battered or pylon format was common in high chairs. A similar design can be observed in the only known southern chair with a board seat (fig. 42).

A board-seated great chair associated with Rev. James Keith (1643–1719) of Bridgewater in Plymouth County (fig. 43) may have been made in Boston, but it has no known cognates. At first glance, the finials appear to be related to those of the Plymouth group, but the turnings differ in several

Figure 43 Great chair, probably Boston, Massachusetts, 1660–1700. Maple and ash. H. 41¾", W. 24", D. 19½". (Courtesy, Museum of Fine Arts, Boston, bequest of Charles Hitchcock Tyler.) The left back spindle and the front two inches of the seat are replaced, and the posts are pieced out at the bottom.

details. The Keith chair may date from the early eighteenth century and is, perhaps, the latest American example in the board-seat tradition.

The dating, technology, and stylistic progression of board-seated turned chairs is not entirely secure and requires far more research in European sources. Nevertheless, it is clear that the twelve American examples that survive have an ancient lineage. They may seem forbidding and cagelike to modern observers, but in their time, these chairs were regarded as throne-like enclosures that dignified their sitters and alluded to a tradition reaching back to the Assyrians if not the Egyptians.

ACKNOWLEDGMENTS

For assistance with this article, the authors thank Pauline Agius, James Austin, Peggy Baker, Gerry and Randy Bennett, Robert J. Bitondi, Kerry P. Brennan, Allan Breed, Rosalind Caird, Nancy Carlisle, Bill Cotton, Gerry Cotton, Richard Dearlove, J. Donovan, Peter Follansbee, the late Benno Forman, the late Christopher Gilbert, Tara Gleason, Donald Hare, Frank Kravic, Sandra Lackenby, Joshua Lane, Beverly Johnson Lucas, Richard C. Malley, Eddy Nicholson, Lionel Reynolds, Violet Riegel, Dr. Richard D. Ryder, Adrienne Sage, Erin Schleigh, Rev. L. J. Smith, Robert Blair St. George, Frances Gruber Stafford, Susan Stubbs, Michael Taviner, Roy Thompson, the Van Horne family, Donald P. White III, Sioned Williams, and Philip Zea.

1. For more on board-seated chairs, see Robert Blair St. George, "New England Turned Chairs of the Seventeenth Century: A Preliminary Survey," seminar paper, Winterthur Program in Early American Culture, 1978 (manuscript in the authors' possession); Benno M. Forman, *American Seating Furniture, 1630–1730* (New York: W. W. Norton, 1988), pp. 67–69; Victor Chinnery, *Oak Furniture: The British Tradition* (Woodbridge, Suffolk: Antique Collectors' Club, 1979), pp. 87–103; Robert F. Trent, "Wet and Dry: A Preview of the Great Turned Chairs Round-Up," *Western Reserve Antiques Show* 13 (1988): 56–59; and Robert F. Trent, "The Board-Seated Turned Chairs Project," *Regional Furniture* 4 (1990): 42–48.

2. The Brewster and Standish chairs have been at Pilgrim Hall since the the mid-nineteenth century. For the history of the Bradford chair, see Helen Comstock, "The Bradford and Churchill Chairs," *Antiques* 58, no. 5 (November 1955): 151. For the history of the Eliot chair, see *The Memorial History of Boston*, edited by Justin Winsor (Boston: James R. E. Osgood & Co., 1880), p. 415. The history of the Mather chair is published in Horace E. Mather, *Lineage of Rev. Richard Mather* (Hartford, Conn.: privately printed, 1890), p. 25. For more on the Lee chair, see Ronald L. Hurst and Jonathan Prown, *Southern Furniture, 1680–1830: The Colonial Williamsburg Collection* (New York: Harry Abrams for the Colonial Williamsburg Foundation, 1997), pp. 57–59.

3. For more on the construction of post-and-rung using wet and dry components, see John D. Alexander Jr., *Make a Chair from a Tree: An Introduction to Working Green Wood,* rev. and enl. ed. (1978; Mendham, N.J.: Astragal Press, 1994). DVDs of this book were issued in 1999 and 2006.

4. Netherlandish turned seating had a powerful influence on British chair-making traditions. Because few early chairs with original histories of ownership are in Dutch museums, much of the information about Netherlandish turned seating comes from period genre painting and prints. While the authors have speculated on the origins of the European chairs illustrated in this article, much more research is required to separate British and Dutch work with any degree of certainty. Many surviving board-seat chairs are in Wales and Cornwall, and some scholars have assumed that such examples were confined to the so-called Celtic Fringe. This article attributes several chairs to London, and the inference is strong that board-seat traditions originated in metropolitan centers in the Low Countries and in English ports, not in regional or folk sources.

5. For the history of thrones in England, see Clare Graham, *Ceremonial and Commemorative Chairs in Great Britain* (London: Victoria & Albert Museum, 1994). Green paint may have been used to simulate patinated bronze, white paint to simulate ivory, and black paint to simulate ebony.

6. For more on King Stephen's throne, see Penelope Eames, "Furniture in England, France, and the Netherlands from the Twelfth to the Fifteenth Century," in *Furniture History* 13 (1977): 192–94, pls. 54, 55; Chinnery, *Oak Furniture*, pp. 98–101; Julia W. Torrey, "Ancestors of the Turned Chair," *Antiques* 32, no. 3 (September 1937): 120–21; and Richard D. Ryder, "Four-Legged Turned Chairs," *Connoisseur* 191, no. 767 (January 1976): 48.

7. For Ridley's biography, see *The Dictionary of National Biography*, edited by Leslie Stephen and Sidney Lee, 22 vols. (London: Oxford University Press, 1937–1938), 16: 1172–76.

8. A descendant donated Ridley's chair to Pembroke College in 1928. The Ridley chair is illustrated and discussed in *An Inventory of the Historical Monuments in the City of Cambridge*, 2 vols. (London: Her Majesty's Stationery Office, 1959), 1: pl. 44, 2: pl. 154.

9. For more on English turned chairs made before 1700, see Chinnery, *Oak Furniture*, pp. 87–104; Richard D. Ryder, "Three-Legged Turned Chairs," *Connoisseur* 190, no. 766 (December 1975): 242–47, and Ryder, "Four-Legged Turned Chairs," pp. 44–49. Almost all other surveys of English seating are concerned with regional traditions that evolved during the eighteenth and nineteenth centuries.

10. Cross-sectional measurement of the components of many turned chairs indicates that makers relied on shrinkage to secure their joints. In general, components with mortises were green (wet) and those with tenons were seasoned (dry). Pins were required to construct chairs as complicated as the example illustrated in figure 18. On most seating of this genre, all of the joints on the low structural rail of the back and the tenons of primary and secondary arms are pinned.

11. Christopher Gilbert, *Furniture at Temple Newsam House and Lotherton Hall,* 3 vols. (Leeds: Leeds Art Collections Fund and W. S. Maney and Sons, 1998), 3: 576–78. The front seat rail of the chair illustrated in figure 20 has a large round tenon at each end, rather than

the more typical arrangement featuring a large tenon at one end and a small tenon at the other. The small, round tenons of the side rails pierce and lock the front ones. This tenon arrangement enabled the maker to drive the entire rear of the chair, including both pairs of arms, onto the front frame at once instead of assembling the seat frame, driving in the low structural rail and lower arms, and then driving in the crest rail and upper arms. It is remarkable that the former method was not used more often.

12. The Harvard president's chair has been published many times, notably in *New England Begins: The Seventeenth Century*, edited by Jonathan L. Fairbanks and Robert F. Trent, 3 vols. (Boston: Museum of Fine Arts, 1982), 3: 511–12. Related chairs are at the Museum of Welsh Life, St. Fagan's, Cardiff, England; at Bunratty Castle, County Clare, Ireland; and in several private collections.

13. One reason for thinking that this chair has always been in the church is the presence of a copy that may date from the eighteenth century. While many nineteenth-century copies of such chairs are known, this replica reflects traditional workmanship.

14. The provenance of the Foote chair is discussed in several articles cited above in n. 1. The Strycker chair is illustrated in Helen Comstock, *American Furniture: Seventeenth, Eighteenth, and Nineteenth Century Styles* (New York: Viking Press, 1962), pp. 30–31. This chair will also appear in Frances Gruber Safford, *American Furniture in the Metropolitan Museum of Art*, vol. 1, *Early Colonial Period: The Seventeenth-Century and William and Mary Styles* (New York: Metropolitan Museum of Art, forthcoming).

15. The Foote chair has been used as a prototype for several fakes. See Wallace Nutting, *Furniture of the Pilgrim Century, 1620–1720* (Framingham, Mass.: Old America Co., 1921), pp. 190, 205.

16. Victor Chinnery published a chair with a history of use by the president of the Placemen at the London City Cornmeter's Office, but the authors are not certain that the piece was made in England (Chinnery, *Oak Furniture*, p. 99). The Erasmus chair is illustrated in *An Inventory of the Historical Monuments in the City of Cambridge*, 1: pl. 44, 2: pl. 224.

17. This chair is illustrated in Sara Emerson Rolleston, *Historic Houses and Interiors in Southern Connecticut* (New York: Hastings House, 1976), p. 35. A walnut fake modeled on the Dutch chair and dating ca. 1950 is in the collection of Historic Deerfield.

18. For more on the Tinkham shop tradition, see Robert Blair St. George, "A Plymouth Area Chairmaking Tradition of the Late Seventeenth Century," *Middleborough Antiquarian* 19, no. 2 (December 1978): 3–11; and Robert F. Trent and Karin Goldstein, "Notes about New 'Tinkham' Chairs," *American Furniture*, edited by Luke Beckerdite (Hanover, N.H.: University Press of New England for the Chipstone Foundation, 1998), pp. 215–37.

19. For the Tufts chair, see Wallace Nutting, *Furniture of the Pilgrim Century* (1921, reprint; Framingham, Mass.: Old American Co., 1924), pp. 182–83. Edsall is documented in Benno M. Forman, "Boston Furniture Craftsmen, 1630–1730," MS, 1969 (copy in authors' possession).

20. The Eliot chair was published in *The Memorial History of Boston*, edited by Juston Winsor (Boston: James R. Osgood & Co., 1880), p. 415; *The Dorchester Book* (Boston: George H. Ellis, 1899), p. 17; Jane De Normandie, "John Eliot: The Apostle to the Indians," *West Roxbury Magazine* (Hudson, Mass.: E. F. Worcester Press, 1900), pp. 31–36; and Forman, *American Seating Furniture, 1630–1730*, p. 77. The authors thank Robert Blair St. George for these references.

Figure 1 George G. Wright, sideboard, Philadelphia, Pennsylvania, 1811. White pine with yellow poplar. H. 29½", W. 73", D. 23¼". (Courtesy, Philadelphia Museum of Art; photo, Gavin Ashworth.) The sideboard's kidney shape is similar to that of contemporary mahogany examples from Philadelphia. This example sat on top of a baseboard and would have been several inches higher than it stands presently. The associated panel was probably installed in the wall above a mirror surmounting the sideboard.

Clark Pearce, Catherine Ebert, and Alexandra Alevizatos Kirtley

From Apprentice to Master: The Life and Career of Philadelphia Cabinetmaker George G. Wright

▼ WHILE WORKING AS foreman for the cabinetmaking firm Joseph B. Barry & Son, George G. Wright (1780–1853) signed and dated the back of a paint-decorated sideboard (fig. 1) made for the dining room of William (1775–1826) and Mary (Wilcocks) Waln's (1781–1841) Philadelphia house. Other furniture forms marked by Wright include an iconic pier table commissioned by French-born merchant Louis Clapier (1764–1837) and a card table bearing the date 1813, the year that Wright left Barry's firm and established his own shop. These and other objects associated with Wright show how the contributions of apprentices, journeymen, and specialists contributed to the success of Philadelphia cabinet shops during the late eighteenth and early nineteenth centuries.[1]

Details pertaining to Wright's personal life are sketchy. He was born in Pennsylvania on July 31, 1780. Wright's parents, John and Sarah (Fleming), were married in Cambridge, Massachusetts, and later moved to Philadelphia, where John worked as an innkeeper. At the age of thirty-two, George married Elizabeth Robins (1781–1857) of Pennsylvania. They had five children, born between the years 1814 and 1823.[2]

Marriage may have prompted George to establish his own business. Between 1813 and 1817, he was listed at four Philadelphia locations: 196 Pine Street, 93 Bell's Court, 15 Branch Street, and Back 86 Spruce Street (fig. 2). By January 16, 1818, George and his family had moved to Pittsburgh,

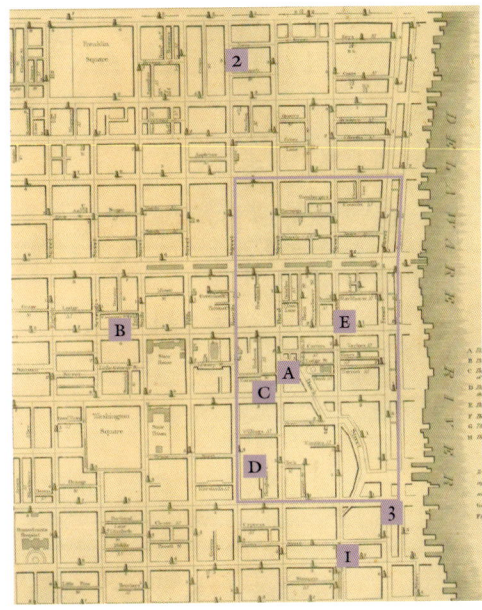

Figure 2 Detail of John A. Paxton's, *This New Map of the City of Philadelphia for the use of Firemen and others,* Philadelphia, Pennsylvania, ca. 1816. Engraving on paper. 13⅞" x 24⅛". (Courtesy, American Philosophical Society.) George Wright's shop locations are designated chronologically as 1–3. John Aitken's shop locations are designated chronologically as A and B, and Joseph Barry's as C–E. The box area shows where the French émigré community settled.

Pennsylvania, where he worked independently and in various partnerships until at least 1826. George and Elizabeth moved to Washington Township, in Brown County, Ohio, before 1845. George died there on August 5, 1853, and Elizabeth on November 22, 1857.[3]

Apprenticeship and Stylistic Development
Wright began serving his apprenticeship with Philadelphia cabinetmaker John Aitken (active c. 1787–1814) at age twenty-one, seven years later than customary. Given the fact that Wright's term was only four years (1801–1805), he may have previously served two years with another master. Born in Dalkeith, Scotland, Aitken probably trained in Edinburgh or London before immigrating to America in 1798. Two years later, the *Federal Gazette* reported that his "cabinet and chair manufactory" produced "chairs of various patterns, some of which are entirely new . . . and finished with an elegancy of stile peculiar to themselves [along with] . . . desks, bureaus, book cases, bedsteads, tea tables, card ditto and dining ditto etc." During the late 1790s Aitken entered into partnership with William Cocks, a British cabinetmaker who arrived in Philadelphia by 1790. In the August 5, 1797, issue of the *Federal Gazette,* their firm Cocks and Company boasted that their "long experience in London" would allow them to satisfy the demands of potential customers. Regrettably, little is known about either principal's career or work. George Washington's household accounts record the purchase of a pair of inlaid sideboards and a set of twenty-four square-back dining chairs with elliptically cornered tops from Aitken on February 21, 1797, and a tambour cylinder desk-and-bookcase the following month, but neither entry specifies whether the cabinetmaker was in partnership with Cocks at those dates.[4]

During his apprenticeship with Aitken, Wright would have learned to make many of the forms offered by his master's shop and become acquainted with the intricate network of furniture makers and specialists working in the city. Wright may have also met some of Aitken's patrons and business associates, some of whom were active in the venture cargo trade. In the January 13, 1800, issue of the *Federal Gazette,* Aitken reported that he had "removed the store to No. 79 Dock, near Third Street, lately occupied by Cocks & Co., where he has a large and general assortment of Cabinet Furniture suitable for the home and exportation trade."

The Journeyman Years
Much of the information on Wright's early career as a journeyman is derived from his inscription on the sideboard illustrated in figures 1 and 3: "Made for Mr. W. Waln, Corner of Seventh and Chestnut Streets By order / of Mr G. Bridport, By Geo G. Wright, whilst Foreman for Mr. J. B. Barry & Son / No 134 South Second Streets, October 18. 1811, one thousand eight hundred / and eleven." He must have worked for Barry much earlier in order to have earned the trust required of a foreman.

Born in Dublin, Ireland, Barry immigrated to Philadelphia before 1790. After partnering with Alexander Calder in 1794 and Lewis G. Affleck (son of cabinetmaker Thomas Affleck) in 1795, Barry established his own business

Figure 3 Detail of the inscription on the sideboard illustrated in fig. 1. (Photo, Gavin Ashworth.)

and began advertising furniture in the "newest London and French patterns." By the turn of the century, Barry enjoyed the patronage of many prominent clients. In 1800 Barry sold Thomas Jefferson's agent "J. Barnes" $193 worth of furniture, probably for the president's house in Washington, D.C. Although it is impossible to determine the size and scope of Barry's business or the number of tradesmen he employed, the 1811 Tax Assessment valued his shop and property at $21,000. By comparison, in 1809 the shop and property of John Aitken and Henry Connelly received valuations of $2,500 and $3,000 respectively. In addition to producing furniture, Barry imported and sold British and European goods. In the January 12, 1812, issue of the *Aurora General Advertiser,* Barry reported that during his recent "stay in London and Paris," he had "made some selections of the Most Fashionable and Elegant Articles in Their Line, which in addition to [his] . . . excellent stock on hand, forms a display of furniture well worth the attention of the respectable citizens of Philadelphia."[5]

During the time that Barry was abroad, Wright oversaw the day-to-day operations of his master's shop, which included the production of William and Mary Waln's sideboard and the mirror probably intended to hang above it (fig. 1). In 1805 the couple commissioned Benjamin Henry Latrobe (1764–1820) to design a house for their lot at the corner of Seventh and Chestnut streets. Construction began in late 1807, and the house was completed the following year (fig. 4). Like many of his British contemporaries, Latrobe was intimately involved with the furnishing of his buildings. The suite of painted furniture he designed for the Walns' drawing room (figs. 5–7) was intended to resonate with the finishes, fabrics, and interior architectural details of that space. Although the firm responsible for making the furniture remains unknown, the decoration has been convincingly attributed to immigrant British painter and architect George Bridport (1783–1819). The name of Philadelphia carpenter Thomas Wetherill (d. 1824) is written on the backboard of a pier table from the suite, but it is unlikely that he was the maker of the entire suite, which also included at least sixteen

Figure 4 A. C. Kern, *The Waln House—S. E. Cor. Chestnut & Seventh ST.*, Philadelphia, Pennsylvania, 1847. Watercolor and ink wash on paper. 11" x 15½". (Courtesy, Library Company of Philadelphia.)

Figure 5 Side chair designed by B. Henry Latrobe, Philadelphia, Pennsylvania, ca. 1808. Yellow poplar, oak, maple, and white pine; painted, gessoed, and gilded ornament. H. 34 1/2", W. 19 3/4", D. 19 1/2". (Courtesy, Philadelphia Museum of Art.)

Figure 6 Pier table designed by B. Henry Latrobe, Philadelphia, Pennsylvania, ca. 1808. Yellow poplar and white pine; painted, gessoed, and gilded ornament; silvered glass, pot metal, and yellow cut velvet. H. 41 1/2", W. 66", D. 23". (Courtesy, Philadelphia Museum of Art.) The backboard is inscribed "Thos: Wetherill." His uncle Samuel Wetherill was a paint manufacturer patronized by Latrobe and Bridport.

Figure 7 Card table designed by B. Henry Latrobe, Philadelphia, Pennsylvania, ca. 1808. Yellow poplar, maple, and white pine; painted, gessoed, and gilded ornament. H. 29½", W. 36", D. 17⅞". (Collection of Mrs. George M. Kaufman; photo, Gavin Ashworth.) This table is one of a pair. They are among the earliest American examples with swivel mechanisms for their tops.

side chairs, a pair of card tables, a window bench, and a Grecian sofa. The size of the suite suggests the involvement of a large cabinet- and chair-making shop. Joseph Barry & Sons is a likely candidate, since the suite dates circa 1808 and Bridport ordered the sideboard for the Walns' dining room from that firm three years later.[6]

The pier table illustrated in figure 8 was also made under Wright's supervision while Barry was in England and France. The initials "GW" are incised

Figure 8 Pier table made under George Wright's supervision by Joseph B. Barry & Son, Philadelphia, Pennsylvania, 1810–1813. Mahogany and satinwood, mahogany and burl veneers with poplar; gilt bronze mounts and cast brass moldings. H. 38⅝", W. 53⅞", D. 23⅞". (Courtesy, Metropolitan Museum of Art, Museum Purchase 1976; photo, Gavin Ashworth.) Like the pier table illustrated in fig. 6, this example was made without feet. This architectonic detail amplified the mass of both objects. Wright may have done everything but the carving.

Figure 9   Detail of George Wright's initials on the pier table illustrated in fig. 8. (Photo, Gavin Ashworth.)

Figure 10   Detail of George Wright's inscription "Jos B. Barry & Son" on the pier table illustrated in fig. 8. (Photo, Gavin Ashworth.)

on a medial brace under the subtop (fig. 9), and the inscription "Jos B. Barry & Son" is written on the bottom of the plinth in Wright's hand (fig. 10). Commissioned by Louis Clapier, who fled Santo Domingo in 1793 and arrived in Philadelphia in 1796, the pier table indicates that Barry's shop was capable of working in the latest English and French styles. Clapier married Philadelphia native Mary Heyl in 1801, and several pieces of furniture commissioned by the couple for their house at Sixth and Lombard streets and their country house in Nicetown survive. A sofa carved with dogs and fleur-de-lis and a matching pair of chairs that descended in the same line as the pier table may also have been made in Barry's shop.[7]

Like many of Philadelphia's French immigrants, Clapier settled in an area of the city that was home to several important cabinet shops (fig. 2). Local furniture makers were influenced by the work of French tradesmen as well as furnishings imported by French merchants. Wealthy patrons like Clapier and merchant and financier Stephen Girard typically imported some furnishings from France and commissioned others from Philadelphia craftsmen.[8]

The Clapier pier table is a superb example of Philadelphia furniture in the French antique taste, or *le goût antique*. Beginning in 1802 Parisian architect and designer Pierre de La Mésangère began publishing *Collection de Meubles et Objets de Goût,* a serial publication responsible for the dissemination of

Figure 11 Design for a pier table illustrated on pl. 10, no. 2 in Pierre de La Mésangère. *Collection de Meubles et Objets de Goût* (1802). (Courtesy, Metropolitan Museum of Art, Harris Brisbane Dick Fund, 1930 [30.80.1]. Image © Metropolitan Museum of Art.)

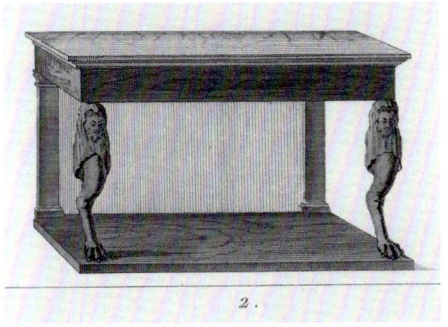

Figure 12 Detail of the carving on the pier table illustrated in fig. 8. (Photo, Gavin Ashworth.)

Figure 13 Design for a frieze or tablet illustrated on pl. 36 in Thomas Sheraton's *The Cabinet-Maker and Upholsterer's Drawing Book* (1791). (Courtesy, Philadelphia Museum of Art.)

French neoclassical style to other fashion centers in the Western world. A pier table illustrated in that work is similar in form to the Clapier example (fig. 11), although the latter has columns with spiral garlands rather than the verdigris caryatids advocated by Mésangère. Barry had probably seen ormolu garlands on European furniture while traveling abroad, but they may have been prohibitively expensive or difficult for his shop to obtain. Wright's alternative was to have the garlands executed in mahogany. The carved lyre alludes to the seventh-century Greek poet Arion, who was celebrated in classical mythology for his skill on that instrument. Like other American and European furniture adorned with such imagery, the Clapier table was most likely made for a room where music and dancing occurred.[9]

The seated griffins and arabesques on the frieze of the Clapier table are derived from plate 36 in Thomas Sheraton's *Drawing Book* (1791) (figs. 12, 13). The inclusion of these details is somewhat unusual, since they reflect an earlier phase of neoclassicism somewhat at odds with the table's avant-garde

French form. New York cabinetmaker Charles Honoré Lannuier began making pier tables in *le goût antique* as early as 1805, but that style did not attain widespread popularity in America until the 1820s. A narrow and early date range can be assigned to the Clapier table based on the pencil inscription on its label (fig. 14) and Wright's departure from Barry's shop in 1813. The words "& Son" refer to Joseph Barry Jr. (active 1810–1840) who became a partner in 1810.[10]

Figure 14 Detail of the label on the pier table illustrated in fig. 8. Barry's shop was located at 132 South Second Street in 1804 and 1805. (William Macpherson Hornor Jr., *Blue Book Philadelphia Furniture* [Philadelphia: By the author, 1935], pl. 432.)

Furniture Documented to George Wright's Shop

A pair of "mechanical" card tables initialed and dated by Wright are benchmarks for attributing other work to his shop (figs. 15, 16). New York cabinetmaker John Hewitt mentioned that form in his account book in 1809, but the earliest reference to mechanical tables in Philadelphia is in *The Journeyman Cabinet and Chair Makers' Pennsylvania Book of Prices* published two years later. This design may have arrived through the venture cargo trade or been transmitted by New York journeymen who moved to Philadelphia (fig. 17). Given the fact that Joseph Barry advertised in a New York newspaper for four experienced journeymen cabinetmakers in 1810, it is possible that Wright learned to make mechanical tables while working as a journeyman in his former master's shop. Based on the number of surviving examples, mechanical tables appear to have been less popular in Philadelphia than in New York. Price may have been a factor. According to the *Pennsylvania Book of Prices*, workmen received $16.36 for making a mechanical table. That was more than seven times the amount received for a standard square card table with swing leg ($2.31) and more than three times the amount received for a standard kidney-shaped table with a commode front ($4.68). Wright's mechanical tables (figs. 15, 16) would probably have been more expensive than any mechanical table listed in the Pennsylvania price book, owing to the lavish use of satinwood.[11]

Figure 15 George G. Wright, card table, Philadelphia, Pennsylvania, 1813. Satinwood and satinwood, birch, and burl veneers with mahogany and white pine. H. 30", W. 38¼", D. 20⅛". (Private collection; photo, Gavin Ashworth.) On a mechanical card table the two rear legs are hinged to swing back simultaneously as the leaf supports rotate out, thereby supporting the table as its center of gravity shifts owing to the top opening. An iron rod running through the pillar is attached to a series of pivoting iron bars housed in a box underneath the top of the table and to iron straps on the underside of the legs. This structure is found on both rear pillars of this table.

Figure 16 Detail of George Wright's initials and the date 1813 cut into the underside of the card table illustrated in fig. 15. (Photo, Gavin Ashworth.)

Figure 17 Michael Allison, card table, New York City, ca. 1810. Mahogany with unidentified secondary woods. (From the Collections of the Henry Ford Museum.) This table is one of a pair representing the only documented New York examples of the "mechanical" form known.

Unlike most New York mechanical tables, which have a single columnar support, Wright's examples have three thin pillars that rest on a trefoil-shaped plinth. This unusual design required him to bore out two columns (rear) to accommodate the iron rods of the swivel mechanism rather than one. The curved shoulders of his legs are modifications of the "sweep" pattern common on New York tables as well as in French Directoire and English

121 CABINETMAKER GEORGE G. WRIGHT

Figure 18 Detail of the plinth of the card table illustrated in fig. 15. (Photo, Gavin Ashworth.)

Figure 19 Detail of the apron construction of the card table illustrated in fig. 15. (Photo, Gavin Ashworth.)

Figure 20 Detail of the rear rail and mechanical system of the card table illustrated in fig. 15. The mechanism box is made of mahogany and beveled on three sides. The paired struts forming the short sides are half-dovetailed into the front rails. (Photo, Gavin Ashworth.)

Regency designs. Wright used contrasting panels to decorate the plinth and the tops and sides of the legs. Later examples made by Wright and his competitors often have legs with paneled sides and acanthus carving on the top.

Probably made of horizontally laminated boards, the plinths of the satinwood tables are capped with thin, thumbnail-molded boards that overhang slightly (fig. 18). This feature occurs on other tables documented and attributed to Wright's shop. On the convex sections of the plinth, the veneer that covers the vertical surfaces is tucked into grooves in the pine core. Wright knew this would prevent the veneer from popping off if the glue joint weakened.

The aprons of the satinwood tables consist of solid boards at the front and sides glued to horizontally laminated, curved sections with butt joints staggered for strength (fig. 19). Typical of Wright's work, the laminated sections are nailed from the underside at each end. The concave sections of the façade are made from a separate vertical board so the veneer on the outside never

goes over end grain. Wright eventually abandoned this feature, probably because of the extra work it required. The fly rails are attached to a birch block and their joints are held together with a metal pin. Like many cabinetmakers, Wright made the fingers circular for greater clearance and gave them a shoulder to stop the fly rails from rotating past ninety degrees (fig. 20).

The *Pennsylvania Book of Prices* described card tables similar to the documented examples as having "Serpentine Corners with Straight Front and

End Rails." In all of his later card tables, Wright used a slightly elliptical, or "round," front—a standard Philadelphia design for which journeymen received an additional twenty-eight cents. The tops of the satinwood tables are constructed in the method specified in contemporary price books, with two pine boards held in place with "square clamps," or battens, and a narrow "slip" of mahogany glued across the exposed rear edges of the tops. Wright made his clamps out of mahogany, for strength and stability, and attached them to the pine center boards with a tongue-and-groove joint. Afterward, he applied the veneer and crossbanding (fig. 21). On later tables, he set the clamps at an angle to provide additional strength and more glue surface for the crossbanding.[12]

A breakfast table (fig. 22) made en suite with the card tables has another feature typical of Wright's work. The crossbanding below the drawers is set

Figure 21 Detail of the top of the card table illustrated in fig. 15. When veneering tops in this pattern, Wright always used an odd number of rays to ensure symmetry and to have one segment centered at the front. The underside of the fly leaves and the tops of the stationary leaves of these tables are veneered with single flitches of what appears to be birch. The edges of the tops are crossbanded with the same wavy satinwood used in the rays. (Photo, Gavin Ashworth.)

Figure 22 George G. Wright, breakfast table, Philadelphia, Pennsylvania, 1813. Satinwood and satinwood, mahogany, birch, and burl veneers with mahogany, white pine and yellow pine. H. 30", W. 36¼", D. 18". (Private collection; photo, Gavin Ashworth.)

into a separate mahogany strip that is glued and nailed to the underside of the apron (fig. 23). This made the crossbanding less susceptible to damage and loss.

Furniture Attributed to George Wright's Shop

Several tables can be attributed to Wright's shop based on details shared with his documented work. The mechanical table illustrated in figure 24 is made of mahogany with no contrasting inlay. Except for having a single pillar, which dictated a slightly different mechanism, and a glued and nailed bead on the lower edge of the apron, the construction of this table matches that of the satinwood examples (figs. 15, 16). The top has pine clamps attached to the core board with tongue-and-groove joints, and its primary veneered surface features nine rays emanating from a semicircle. The sweep legs follow conventional Philadelphia style in having acanthus carving and reeding on top. Wright probably made this table before 1815, when mechanical examples became increasingly obsolete.[13]

Figure 23 Detail of the crossbanding under the drawers of the breakfast table illustrated in fig. 22. The underside of the apron is tooth-planed beneath the strips housing the crossbanding. (Photo, Gavin Ashworth.)

Figure 24 Card table attributed to George G. Wright, Philadelphia, Pennsylvania, 1813–1815. Mahogany and mahogany veneer with white pine and oak. H. 29⅝", W. 36", D. 18". (Private collection; photo, Gavin Ashworth.)

During the early to mid-1810s, Wright began making swivel-top card tables. The examples illustrated in figures 25 and 26 are attributed to his shop based on parallels with the marked satinwood tables: the tops have nine rays of highly figured veneer; the plinths are capped with a thin, thumbnail-molded board; and the tables have similarly constructed aprons. The pillars on the table illustrated in figure 25 also have turnings similar to those on furniture in the satinwood suite (see figs. 15, 22). On the other swivel-top

Figure 25 Card table attributed to George G. Wright, Philadelphia, Pennsylvania, 1813–1817. Mahogany and mahogany veneer with unidentified secondary woods. H. 28½", W. 37", depth not recorded. (Courtesy, Photo Archives, National Gallery of Art.) The table descended in the Biddle, Priestley, and Lyon families of Philadelphia.

Figure 26 Card table attributed to George G. Wright, Philadelphia, Pennsylvania, 1815–1817. Mahogany and mahogany veneer with white pine and white cedar. H. 30", W. 35¾", D. 19¼". (Courtesy, Winterthur Museum.) The secondary surfaces of this table are covered with a red wash, or "pinking." Several similar tables attributed to Wright are known. A pair made for Robert and Elizabeth Barnhill of Philadelphia (Sewell C. Biggs Museum of American Art) have playing surfaces covered in broadcloth and edged with mahogany veneer. *The Journeyman Cabinet and Chair Makers' Pennsylvania Book of Prices* (1811) referred to that edge treatment as "lipping the top for cloth." Another card table differs primarily in the execution of its carving (Northeast Auctions, *The Charles V. Swain Collection of Pewter*, Portsmouth, New Hampshire, February 24, 2007, lot 849).

example (fig. 26), the pillars are superimposed balusters with reeding at the top and leaf carving below. The leaves mirror those on the legs and harmonize with the floral carving on the curved sections of the plinth. This concave plinth design is found on all swivel-top tables attributed to Wright. On the table illustrated in figure 26, he added decorative veneer to the playing surface (fig. 27), an option that would have increased the cost.[14]

Figure 27 Detail of the playing surface of the card table illustrated in fig. 26. (Photo, Gavin Ashworth.)

Figure 28 Detail of the lower edge of the apron of the card table illustrated in fig. 26. (Photo, Gavin Ashworth.)

Figure 29 Detail of the plinth construction of the card table illustrated in fig. 26. (Photo, Gavin Ashworth.)

Although the construction of Wright's swivel-top tables is relatively consistent, minor variations can be observed. On the card table illustrated in figure 26, he glued and nailed wide strips of lightwood (possibly satinwood) to the tooth-planed lower edges of the apron (fig. 28) just as he did on the satinwood breakfast table (figs. 22, 23). These strips were intended to simulate stringing and protect the veneer on the lower edge. The plinth construction represents a more significant departure. To form the core, Wright used six pieces of mahogany, two boards arranged in an X-shape and four blocks to fill in the interstices (fig. 29). The circa 1815 addendum to the *New-York Revised Prices for Manufacturing and Cabinet and Chair Work* (1810) described this structure as "lapp'd and the corners filled in." The *Philadelphia Cabinet and Chair Makers' Union Book of Prices for Manufacturing Cabinet Work* (1828) referred to "lapping and filling in blocks."[15]

A similar pair of card tables (fig. 30) has slightly different carving, suggesting that Wright may have employed more than one carver or purchased

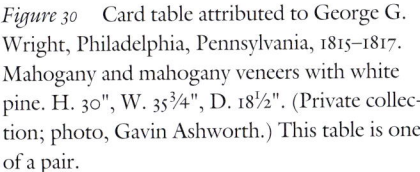

Figure 30 Card table attributed to George G. Wright, Philadelphia, Pennsylvania, 1815–1817. Mahogany and mahogany veneers with white pine. H. 30", W. 35¾", D. 18½". (Private collection; photo, Gavin Ashworth.) This table is one of a pair.

piecework (plaques, legs, pillars) from specialists who employed different carvers. Although these tables originally had thin strips of wood glued and nailed to the lower edges of their aprons like the objects illustrated in figures 22 and 26, Wright made the front and side rails out of solid mahogany, rather than his customary laminated white pine, and joined them at the front corners with large mahogany "keys" (fig. 31). He also used a solid block of mahogany for the core of the plinth.

Figure 31 Detail of the apron construction of the card table illustrated in fig. 30. (Photo, Gavin Ashworth.) The underside is tooth-planed, indicating that it originally had strips of contrasting wood.

Although Wright was a native-born artisan, his stylistic vocabulary emerged in a cosmopolitan setting. During the 1790s craftsmen from England and France came to Philadelphia in search of opportunities created by that city's burgeoning economy. Wealthy patrons like William and Mary Waln, Louis Clapier, and Stephen Girard were eager to furnish their homes in the latest European neoclassical styles, and immigrants like Wright's master John Aitken were more than capable of meeting their demands. To maintain a competitive edge, some Philadelphia tradesmen ventured abroad. When his shop produced the sideboard illustrated in figure 1, Joseph Barry was traveling through England and France, ostensibly to keep abreast of current designs and acquire European-made furnishings that he

Figure 32 Robert McGuffin, card table, Philadelphia, Pennsylvania, 1807. Satinwood and satinwood, mahogany, and rosewood veneers with white pine and oak. H. 29½", W. 35⅝", D. 18". (Collection of Mrs. George M. Kaufman; photo, Gavin Ashworth.) McGuffin was a journeyman in Henry Connelly's shop when he made this table. It is one of a pair.

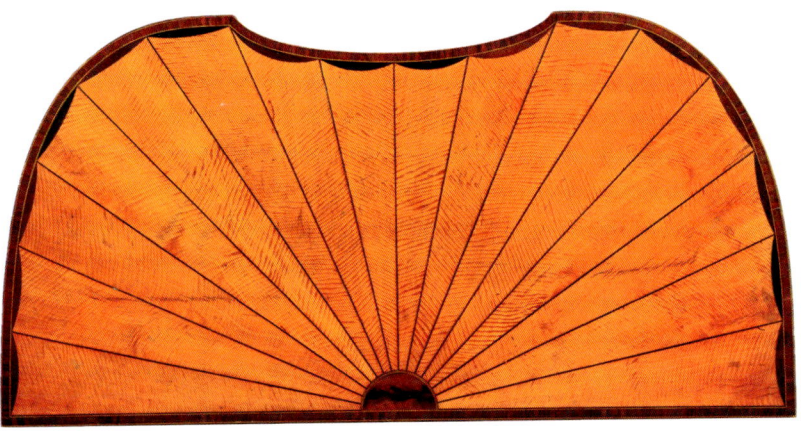

Figure 33 Detail of the top of the card table illustrated in fig. 32. (Photo, Gavin Ashworth.)

could sell at home. As an apprentice in Aitken's shop and then as a journeyman working for Barry, Wright experienced a broader range of stylistic influences than many of his peers.

Wright also appears to have been familiar with the work of Philadelphia cabinetmakers Robert McGuffin (b. 1778) and Henry Connelly. McGuffin worked as a journeyman for Connelly from before 1806 to at least 1809, producing elaborate satinwood tables with veneered tops similar to those made by Wright (figs. 32, 33). This suggests that Wright may have worked with McGuffin in Connelly's shop before joining Barry's workforce.[16]

Wright's furniture attests to his training in an immigrant tradition, his experience as foreman in a major cabinetmaking shop, and his ability to make the transition from journeyman to master. His innovative construction, eye for wood selection, and mastery of veneer decoration set him apart from many of his contemporaries. The tables documented and attributed to Wright further suggest that he was an astute businessman. Faced with the nuances of the Philadelphia marketplace, he developed a range of forms and options to satisfy the different tastes and budgets of his customers. Undoubtedly case furniture and possibly seating by Wright will come to light and provide a clearer picture of this talented cabinetmaker's total output.

ACKNOWLEDGMENTS

For assistance with this article, the authors thank Irfan Ali, Louisa Bartlett, Nicholas R. Bell, Lynda Cain, Katherine Chabla, Tara Chicirda, Jeff Cohen, David H. Conradsen, Wendy A. Cooper, Kathryn Coyle, David deMuzio, J. Michael Flanigan, Samuel M. Freeman II, John Stuart Gordon, Ryan Grover, Michael Harkless, Brock W. Jobe, Linda Kaufman, Peter M. Kenny, Kelly Lyles, Robert Lyles, Lisa Minardi, Robert D. Mussey Jr., Sumpter Priddy III, Karl J. C. Saberg, Christopher Swan, Christine Thomson, Matthew A. Thurlow, Nicholas Vincent, and Gregory Weidman.

1. George Wright's full middle name remains unknown, but he regularly identified himself using his middle initial. For the marked card table, its mate, and a breakfast table from the same suite, see Sotheby's, *Fine Americana*, New York, October 24, 1993, lots 366, 367. Wright's initials and date are on the underside of the card table illustrated in figure 15.

2. The Pennsylvania census of the early nineteenth century did not record the town where Wright was born. *Vital Records of Cambridge, Massachusetts to the Year 1850* (Boston: New England

Historic Genealogical Society, 1914), 1: 785. Archives of the City and County of Philadelphia (hereafter cited as ACCP), record no. 60.14, Apprenticeship and Redemptioner's Index (hereafter cited as ARI), p. 49. The only reference to Wright in Philadelphia newspapers is a notice for the Fire Hose Association signed by "Geo. G. Wright, Sec'ty" in the *United States Gazette* on September 27, 1806.

3. Deborah Ducoff-Barone, "Checklist of Cabinetmakers and Chairmakers of Philadelphia, 1800–1815," *Antiques* 139, no. 5 (May 1991): 986–95. Wright was in partnership with Joseph Roseman, who was a fancy-chair maker, ornamentor, and gilder in Pittsburgh in 1818. They advertised in the Pittsburgh newspapers in January, July, August, and September of that year, with their shop at Fourth Street, above Wood Street. J. M. Riddle and M. M. Murray, *The Pittsburg Directory for 1819* (Pittsburg, Pa.: Butler & Lambdin, 1819), p. 100. Information on Wright's Pittsburgh career can be found in Pittsburgh Furniture Project, American Decorative Arts Department, Carnegie Museum of Art, Pittsburgh, Pennsylvania. In 1819 Wright partnered with "M'Kown," and the city directory listed their place of business as Fourth Street between Wood and Smithfield streets. In 1826 the city directory listed Wright alone at that address (*City Directories of the United States, circa 1655–1881* [Woodbridge, Conn.: Research Publications, 1983], microfiche, pp. 100, 150). The authors thank Jeffrey Cohen, Professor of Architecture at Bryn Mawr College for suggesting the Paxton map. Will and Estate Inventory of George Wright, Court of Common Pleas, Brown County, Ohio, John B. Higgins Will Book (1853), pp. 99–101 (will recorded Aug. 22, 1853; inventory recorded Nov. 4, 1853).

4. ACCP, record number 60.14, ARI, p. 49. Aitken signed a certificate vouching for the value of a "draught board" made by a Mr. Dunavan on September 21, 1789 (Joseph Downs Collection of Manuscripts, no. 55.520, Winterthur Library). Unlike Henry Connelly, Aitken took few apprentices. *Federal Gazette* (Philadelphia), June 9, 1790. Alexandra Alevizatos Kirtley, "The Painted Furniture of Philadelphia: A Reappraisal," *Antiques* 169, no. 5 (May 2006): 137. Cocks (Cox) is listed in the 1790 census at the same address mentioned in his 1796 advertisement (www.familyhistory.com). He trained renowned cabinetmaker William Camp, who moved to Baltimore after completing his apprenticeship in 1801. Charles Montgomery, *American Furniture: The Federal Period* (New York: Viking Press, 1966), p. 147, fig. 96. Washington's Philadelphia Household Account Book, March 2, 1793–March 25, 1797, Historical Society of Pennsylvania, Philadelphia. Washington purchased the chairs and sideboards on February 21, 1797, and the cylinder desk-and-bookcase on March 13, 1797.

5. *Philadelphia: Three Centuries of American Art* (Philadelphia: Philadelphia Museum of Art, 1976), p. 219. *Federal Gazette and Baltimore Daily Advertiser,* February 9, 1803. Tax Assessment Records, New Market Ward, ACCP, as cited in *Philadelphia: Three Centuries of American Art*, p. 220.

6. Latrobe and Bridport were both particular about quality of workmanship. For example, Latrobe ordered painted furniture from the renowned Finlay brothers of Baltimore for James and Dolley Madison in 1809. It is only logical that he and Bridport would have hired one of the leading cabinet shops in Philadelphia to make the Waln painted suite. The Waln sideboard (fig. 1) establishes the fact that Barry's shop was capable of producing elaborate and sophisticated painted furniture. Kirtley, "Painted Furniture of Philadelphia," pp. 138–41. Alexandra Alevizatos Kirtley, "Collector's Notes," *Antiques* 169, no. 5 (May 2006): 76–80. In each city where he worked, Latrobe appears to have patronized a small group of artisans. Mr. and Mrs. Oliver Hopkinson sold the sideboard to the Philadelphia Museum of Art in 1913. It had descended in the male line of her family from her grandfather Dr. William Swaim, who purchased the Waln house in 1826.

7. For other objects documented to Barry's shop, see *Antiques* 65, no. 2 (February 1954): 135–36 (breakfront bookcase); *Antiques* 171, no. 4 (April 2007): 92–93 (tall clock case, Philadelphia Museum of Art); *Antiques* 135, no. 5 (May 1989): 1218–19 (sideboard dated 1813); *Antiques* 135, no. 5 (May 1989): 1223 (tall-post bed billed to Eleuthère Irénée du Pont, 1807–1810, Hagley Museum and Library); Page Talbot, *Classical Savannah* (Savannah, Ga.: Telfair Museum of Art, 1995), pp. 148–49 (set of upholstered-back open armchairs owned by Isaac Minis of Savannah, 1829–1833); and Alexandra Alevizatos Kirtley, "Philadelphia Furniture in the Empire Style," *Antiques* 171, no. 4 (April 2007): 94–95 (sideboard table stenciled "Joseph Barry and Lewis Krickbaum"). The authors thank Peter Kenny and Matthew Thurlow for making the Clapier table accessible.

8. Andrew Brunk, "To Fix the Taste of Our Country Properly: The French Style in Philadelphia Interiors, 1788–1800" (master's thesis, University of Delaware, 2000), p. 6. Robert D. Schwarz, *The Stephen Girard Collection: A Selective Catalog* (Philadelphia: Girard College, 1980), n.p.

9. It is possible that Barry owned a copy of Mésangère's publication. In the January 12, 1812, issue of the *Aurora General Advertiser* (Philadelphia), Barry reported that he had "lately returned from . . . London and Paris [where] he made some selections of the Most Fashionable and Elegant Articles . . . which [are] well worth the attention of the respectable citizens of Philadelphia." Some of these objects may have been in *le goût antique*. For more on that style in America, see Peter M. Kenny, Frances F. Bretter, and Ulrich Leben, *Honoré Lannuier: Cabinetmaker from Paris* (New York: Metropolitan Museum of Art, 1998), passim. The authors thank Nicholas Vincent for pointing out European pier tables with spiral ormolu garlands. See Enrico Collee, *Italian Empire Furniture: Furnishings and Interior Design from 1800 to 1843* (New York: Rizzoli, 2001), fig. 30; Christopher Wilk, *Western Furniture: 1350 to the Present Day in the Victoria and Albert Museum, London* (New York: Cross River Press, 1996), pp. 132–33, 138–39; and James Hall, *Dictionary of Subjects and Symbols in Art* (New York: Harper & Row, 1979), p. 31.

10. Barry had at least three printed labels: Old Print Shop advertisement, *Antiques* 34, no. 1 (July 1938): 36; the label on the pier table illustrated in figure 8; and the label on a breakfront desk-and-bookcase originally owned by Savannah, Georgia, merchant Robert Mackay, who shared commercial space with Barry (Mrs. Charlton M. Theus, "Furniture and Cabinetmakers of Coastal Georgia," *Antiques* 65, no. 2 [February 1954]: 135–37). The latter two labels have changes made to James Akin's original plate. The words "From London" were eliminated and the address changed to "N 132 South Second Street." Two female figures and an eagle (on the brass rail of the sideboard) were added. To the label on the pier table illustrated in figure 8, the words "& Son" were added in pencil to Barry's name. On the Mackay breakfront label, the words "& Son" were added to the engraved plate. The images on Barry's labels were taken directly from Thomas Sheraton's *Appendix to the Cabinet-Maker and Upholsterer's Drawing-Book* (1802). Thomas Sheraton, *The Cabinet-Maker and Upholsterer's Drawing-Book* (New York: Dover Publications, 1972), pp. 145–204. Baltimore cabinetmaker William Camp also commissioned Akin to engrave his label, using different plates from Sheraton's *Cabinetmaker and Upholsterer's Drawing Book*. Camp's label is owned by the Baltimore Museum of Art and illustrated in Robert Bishop, *Centuries and Styles of the American Chair, 1640–1970* (New York: E. P. Dutton, 1972), p. 222, fig. 314.

11. For the term "mechanical table," see *The New-York Revised Prices for Manufacturing Cabinet and Chair Work* (1810), p. 25. Mechanical tables are also mentioned in the 1817 edition. For more on Hewitt, see David L. Barquist, *American Tables and Looking Glasses in the Mabel Brady Garvan and Other Collections at Yale University* (New Haven, Conn.: Yale University Art Gallery, 1992), p. 217; and Marilyn A. Johnson, "John Hewitt, Cabinetmaker," *Winterthur Portfolio* 4 (1968): 185–205. *The Journeyman Cabinet and Chair Makers' Pennsylvania Book of Prices* (1811) uses the term "Pillar and Claw Card Table" instead of "mechanical table." *Mercantile Advertiser* (New York), December 3, 1810.

12. *Journeyman Cabinet and Chair Makers' Pennsylvania Book of Prices*, p. 33. The *New-York Revised Prices for Manufacturing Cabinet and Chair Work* (1810), specified "3 joints in each top, and clamp'd, slip'd on the back edges, and veneered on 3 sides, or the inside lipped for cloth, the edges banded" (Philip D. Zimmerman, "New York Card Tables, 1800–1825," *American Furniture*, edited by Luke Beckerdite [Hanover, N.H.: University Press of New England for the Chipstone Foundation, 2005], pp. 122–26). The top construction of Philadelphia and New card tables follows the same patterns (Zimmerman, "New York Card Tables," p. 125).

13. Zimmerman, "New York Card Tables," p. 130. The first known use of the swivel-top in America is the card table from the Waln suite designed by Latrobe in 1808 (fig. 7).

14. The former table is illustrated as "better" in Albert Sack, *The New Fine Points of Furniture, Early American* (New York: Crown Publishers, 1993), p. 294; Sotheby's, *American Heritage Auction of Americana*, New York, November 17–19, 1977, lot 733.

15. The strips (fig. 28), which bear fine circular saw marks, may have been purchased from a veneer specialist.

16. For more on McGuffin and Connelly, see Merri Lou Scribner Schaumann, "Henry Connelly, Cabinetmaker and Chairmaker," *Cumberland County History* 13, no. 2 (Winter 1996): 95–96. A sideboard at the Philadelphia Museum of Art has a Henry Connelly label, McGuffin's signature, and the date 1806. The Philadelphia tax assessment for 1808–1809 lists McGuffin and Connelly together (Archives of the City and County of Philadelphia, County Tax Assessment Ledger for the South Ward, 1785–1844, vol. 2 [1808–1809], in "Philadelphia Early Tax Records," comp. Allen Weinberg, Department of Records, Philadelphia, 1960). The authors recently discovered that the card table illustrated in figure 32 is marked "McGuffiin 1807." We thank Wendy Cooper, Tara Chicirda, and Christopher Snow for inspection and infrared photography of that object.

Figure 1 Armchair attributed to Robert Rhea (d. 1719), Monmouth County, New Jersey, 1695. White oak and yellow pine. H. 42 3/4", W. 25 3/4", D. 27 3/4". (Courtesy, Monmouth County Historical Association; gift of Mrs. J. Amory Haskell.)

Philip D. Zimmerman

Early American Furniture Makers' Marks

▼ THE MAKERS OF most surviving examples of early American furniture are unknown, but to the great joy of today's collectors and students, a few early artisans inscribed, branded, labeled, or stenciled their work. These distinguishing marks wrest pieces of furniture from historical anonymity and transform them into representatives and artifactual evidence of specific places and/or times of manufacture and the products of particular people. Marked objects can also serve as Rosetta stones for the identification and evaluation of anonymous examples. No regulations governed where, when, or why any of the various kinds of marks were used on any given furniture form, although the type of mark and its purpose influenced placement. Furniture historian Margaretta Lovell argues that labels—notably those of Newport cabinetmaker John Townsend—promoted the essentials of an artisan's business. Morrison Heckscher recently countered that Townsend's labels primarily served to establish his legacy in a very self-conscious manner. In fact, no single explanation describes the many functions labels and other marks served. They range from the personal and private to public roles. Important to furniture appreciation and history, makers' marks also affect current market values, which in turn inspires the production of fakes. That practice and the methods to detect false marks lie beyond the scope of this study. Occasionally, early furniture owners—as opposed to makers—marked their objects, but that practice also is not addressed here. Instead, this study focuses on the types of marks that makers used, speculates on the reasons for their use, and suggests some interpretative implications.[1]

Seventeenth-century American furniture makers may have marked their products, but no authentic inscriptions have come to light. Some scholars might argue that Shrewsbury, New Jersey, joiner Robert Rhea was the first to mark his work, since a joined armchair has his initials and the date 1695 carved into the back (fig. 1). However, the initials represented him and his wife. They were part of the chair's ornament and conformed to broader practices of identifying owners of furniture, silver, and other valuable household furnishings with prominently displayed initials rather than trade practices of identifying the artisan. The earliest-known American maker's mark, "EDWARD EVANS 1707," is on the Philadelphia scrutoire illustrated in figures 2 and 3. This mark looks as if it was created by striking one character at a time, rather than by striking a single multicharacter marking iron. Assuming that 1707 is the year when Evans began using this mark, that date is only four years later than the earliest English furniture maker's mark.

Figure 2 Edward Evans, scrutoire, Philadelphia, Pennsylvania, 1707. Walnut with white cedar and white pine. H. 66½", W. 44½", D. 20". (Courtesy, Colonial Williamsburg Foundation.)

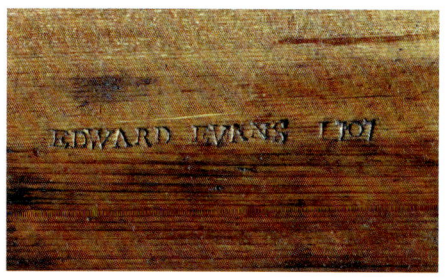

Figure 3 Detail of the "EDWARD EVANS 1707" mark stamped into the bottom of a drawer in the writing compartment of the scrutoire illustrated in fig. 2.

Unfortunately, little is known about Evans, and other men with the same name lived in Philadelphia during the late seventeenth and early eighteenth centuries. Despite the fact that a marking iron or set of dies can be used multiple times, no other furniture with Evans's stamped name is known.[2]

Philadelphia joiner William Beake signed and dated a four-drawer chest in 1711 (figs. 4, 5).[3] Although details of his life are sketchy, Beake's inscription may have been related to his release from an apprenticeship. Furniture historian Cathryn McElroy cites a 1709 bequest of money to "Wm Beakes Junr who is now an Apprentice wth Wm Till of Phil. Aforesd Joyner." Inasmuch as no other William Beake or Beakes appears in contemporary Philadelphia records, this joiner-in-training was likely the maker of the chest. His master Till died in 1711, assuring that Beake was no longer in his employ. The 1711 chest, therefore, may mark and celebrate his entry into the trade as a free artisan. Another youthful signature is that of Joel Baily

Figure 4 William Beake, chest of drawers, Philadelphia, Pennsylvania, 1711. Walnut with white cedar and pine. H. 36¾", W. 40⅛", D. 22⅛". (Collection of Joseph A. McFalls Jr.; photo, Decorative Arts Photographic Collection, Winterthur Museum.)

Figure 5 Detail showing the chalk inscription "William / Beake 1711" on the inside right case side of the chest illustrated in fig. 4.

(1732–1797) of West Chester, Pennsylvania, who signed a desk-and-bookcase in 1747 at age fifteen. Regrettably, no further evidence enlightens the seemingly audacious act of a youngster setting his mark for the world to see. Too often, marks lack contemporary explanation or context, although other apprentice signatures are known and discussed below.[4]

One of the more enigmatic American marks was used in the Boston area in the first decades of the eighteenth century. Made of punch marks arranged as an "I" with a dash through the center (also interpreted by some furniture scholars as back-to-back *E*s), this monogram occurs on several baroque turned chairs (figs. 6, 7). Several furniture historians and dealers assigned the mark to Edmund Edes, a joiner reported to have been in

Figure 6 Caned side chair. Boston, Massachusetts, 1715–1730. Maple. H. 45⅞", seat W. 17" (seat), D. 14½". (Courtesy, Winterthur Museum.)

Figure 7 Punched "I" mark on the back of the stay rail of the chair illustrated in fig. 6.

Boston by 1709. Furniture historian Benno Forman studied the evidence more thoroughly and found great variety among the nearly thirty marked chairs that he recorded. These differences effectively eliminate the possibility of the mark being that of an owner. Similarly, structural and ornamental variations indicate that several different chair makers were responsible for this seating. One "I"-monogrammed chair is made of beech, suggesting a British origin. The common denominator among all the "I"-marked chairs is that they are caned. Forman's theory that the mark likely belonged to a Boston-area caner is compelling, although a suitable candidate has not been identified.[5]

Labels printed on paper are the most widely recognized form of furniture makers' marks. English usage is documented from before 1712, the latest working date for John Guilbaud at the "Crowne and Looking Glasse in Long Acre" in London. How much earlier Guilbaud may have used this label is unknown. Similarly, the first use in America cannot be dated precisely. Philadelphia makers William Savery (1721/22–1787) and John Elliott (1713–1791) are among the earliest candidates. None of the six different paper labels Savery used is dated, nor does any furniture on which they survive establish specific dates. In the absence of any chronology, similarities and differences in wording among the various labels suggest a probable sequence. The earliest label is likely the one that stated Savery made "all sorts of rush bottom chairs," reflecting his apprenticeship under turned–chair maker Solomon Fussell (figs. 8, 9). Three of four labels advertised "chairs and joiner's work made and sold by William Savery" and directed readers to his place of business "at the sign of the Chair." The remaining label in this group

Figure 8 William Savery, side chair, Philadelphia, Pennsylvania, after 1750. Maple with rush seat. H. 41", W. 21 3/8", D. 20 3/4". (Private collection; photo, Decorative Arts Photographic Collection, Winterthur Museum.)

of four referred potential customers to the "Sign of the Chest of Drawers, Coffin, and Chair," suggesting that he diversified his shop production further. This label is probably later than the three "sign of the Chair" labels. The sixth label records only Savery's name above "[No. — —]," with space left for inscriptions in ink. It is probably the latest because it occurs on a serpentine-front chest of drawers, a furniture form that is not documented as having been made in Philadelphia (or elsewhere in America) before 1771.[6]

Establishing precise dates or date ranges for individual labels used by Savery is more problematic. The earliest reference to him as an independent artisan is in the November 1, 1750, issue of the *Pennsylvania Journal*, where Savery described himself as a "Chair-maker in Second Street." In the

Figure 9 Printed label of William Savery (advertising rush-seat chairs) on the rear of the stay rail of the chair illustrated in fig. 8.

absence of other biographical evidence, it seems reasonable to speculate that Savery would have described himself as a chair maker and joiner if he had been using a label mentioning both types of work at that time (fig. 9). Moreover, it is unlikely that Savery used labels when his career began, circa 1742. At that date, his personal circumstances were modest, and the use of printed labels was not an established practice among Philadelphia furniture makers. Savery may have begun using labels in the 1750s, concurrent with a few other American furniture makers.

John Elliott used three different labels on the looking glasses that he imported from England and sold from his "Looking-glass Store." His earliest, "Chestnut Street" label dates before 1762 (fig. 10), when he moved to the Walnut Street address noted on his other two labels. Although his first

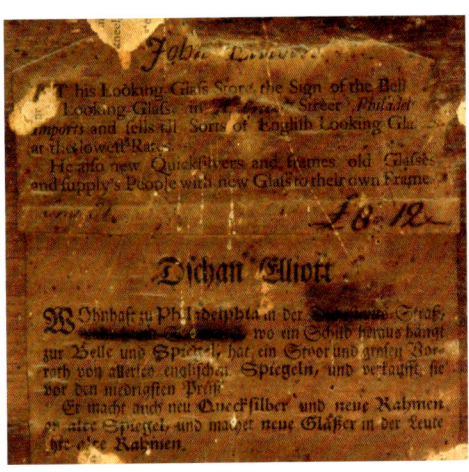

Figure 10 Printed two-part label of John Elliott with "Walnut" written over obliterated "Chestnut" Street address, ca. 1762. (Courtesy, Winterthur Museum.) This label is on a looking glass.

American label cannot have been produced earlier than 1753, when he arrived in Philadelphia from Leicester, England, several years may have passed before he had it printed. While working in England, Elliott labeled a dressing table with a paper label identifying himself as a cabinetmaker, chair maker, joiner, and turner who also repaired looking glasses. Written records show that he first worked as a cabinetmaker on Chestnut Street, where he made and repaired furniture for Philadelphians Edward Shippen and Charles Norris. Not until 1757 did Elliott alter his advertisement to note that instead of working as a cabinetmaker, he now sold imported goods. Presumably, this date approximates the introduction of his first American label, printed in both English and German, which announced that he "imports and sells all sorts of English looking-glasses" and repairs them.[7]

Elsewhere in the American colonies, upholsterer Joseph Cox of New York City labeled a sofa between 1757 and 1760, a date range determined by his tenure at the address listed below his name (fig. 11). Based on a strict

Figure 11 Printed label of Joseph Cox (active 1756–1773) originally pasted to the under upholstery of a New York sofa. (Courtesy, Metropolitan Museum of Art, gift of Mrs. John. J. Riker, 1932 [32.51.2]. Image © Metropolitan Museum of Art.)

Figure 12 Printed label of Benjamin Frothingham. (Courtesy, Currier Museum of Art, Manchester, New Hampshire, gift of Mrs. Norwin S. Bean, 1967.2.) The label bears the initials of engraver Nathaniel Hurd. It is on the small interior drawer of a desk.

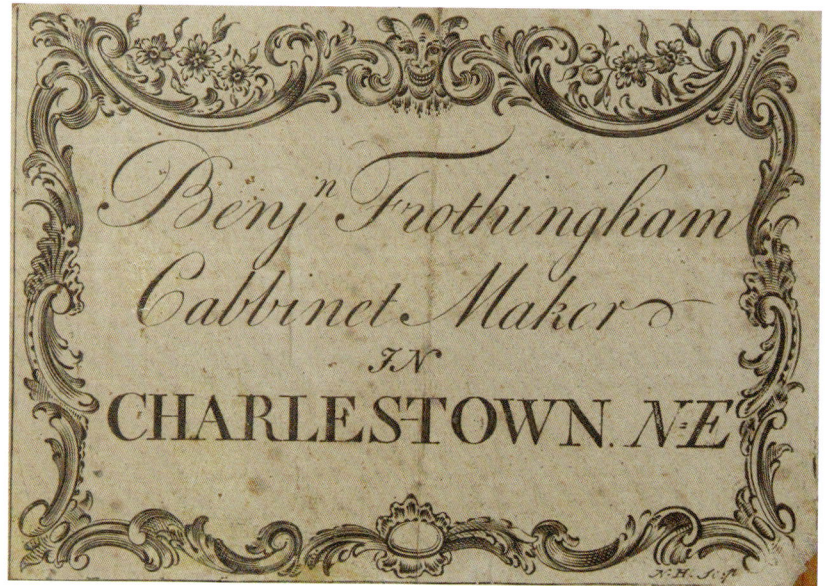

reading of the evidence, this printed label could be the earliest one used by an American furniture maker. Benjamin Frothingham of Charlestown, Massachusetts, began using printed paper labels many years after 1753, when he signed a bombé desk at the youthful age of twenty-one. Because Froth-

138 PHILIP D. ZIMMERMAN

Figure 13 Paper label inscribed in ink "Made by / John Townsend / Rhode Island / 1765" and applied to the inside of the top drawer of a four-drawer chest. (Courtesy, Metropolitan Museum of Art, Rogers Fund, 1927 [27.57.1]. Image © Metropolitan Museum of Art.)

ingham's labels bear the initials of Boston silversmith and engraver Nathaniel Hurd, they must predate the latter's death in 1777 (fig. 12). Even so, these labels continued to be used well into the 1790s and perhaps until Frothingham's death in 1809. Newport furniture makers Job, Edmund, and John Townsend used paper labels with their names handwritten in ink. John inscribed and dated furniture by 1756, but his earliest handwritten label is dated nineteen years later (fig. 13). In 1786 he penned the date on the first of many printed labels. All of the manuscript and printed labels used by the Townsends also include their place of business.[8]

When placed in locations that would be visible while the piece of furniture was being used, labels with addresses served as advertisements for their makers. Toward that end, some makers also described the products they sold or the services they provided. In addition to listing his wares, John Elliott's Philadelphia labels incorporated German text, clearly intended to attract business from people who might otherwise not think of him as a convenient or suitable supplier. Elliott's first English-German label, marked "Chestnut Street," was printed on two pieces of paper pasted together to appear as one (see fig. 10). New York looking-glass maker Charles Del Vecchio, who arrived from Italy in 1800, used a label in the 1830s that was printed entirely in Spanish (fig. 14). In it Del Vecchio noted his fluency in Spanish, French, English, and Italian. This label may have been produced for furniture intended primarily for export from New York to the Caribbean and South America.[9]

Labels, like newspaper advertisements, directed patrons to a maker's place of business. Moves to new addresses, such as Elliott's relocation from Chestnut to Walnut Street, occasioned new labels. Over the course of his

Figure 14 Printed label of Charles Del Vecchio, New York, 1830. (Courtesy, Bernard & S. Dean Levy.) This label is on a looking glass.

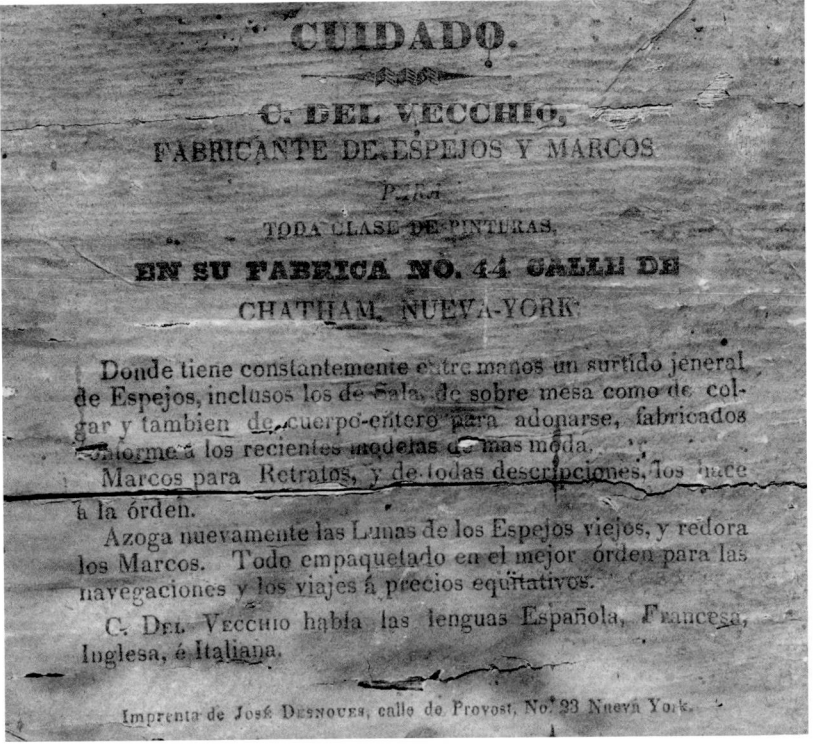

long career, New York furniture maker Michael Allison (1773–1855) used more than a dozen different labels and painted stencils, which cited three different business addresses between 42 and 48 Vesey Street. Six of his labels were printed with dates between January 1817 and November 1825, so for Allison, having new labels made was a regular affair. In contrast, George Shipley, also of New York, cautiously left the street number blank on one of his two known labels, which featured a neoclassical secretary-and-bookcase within an oval border of bell flowers (fig. 15). He inked in "161" when

Figure 15 George Shipley label with engraved street address attached to the seat of an upholstered side chair. (Courtesy, Decorative Arts Photographic Collection, Winterthur Museum.)

Figure 16 George Shipley label attached to a card table of probable Rhode Island origin. (Courtesy, Yale University Art Gallery, gift of Benjamin Hewitt in memory of Sarah and Attmore Tucker.)

he used it sometime between 1791 and 1795, the dates he occupied those quarters on Water Street. Shipley's other label, simpler than the first but ornate by most standards, was engraved with the full address (fig. 16). Historical evidence does not confirm whether it was printed before or after the inked example. Similarly, Jacob Forster (1764–1838) of Charlestown, Massachusetts, had labels printed with "179" with space for adding the year in ink. He used these labels at least through 1814.[10]

By the 1790s several labels incorporated attractive illustrations of furniture into their compositions, suggesting the makers' familiarity with fashionable designs as well as their implied competence to make them. New York City artisans in particular used this strategy, perhaps building on a tradition established by Samuel Prince, whose 1770s label featured a chest-on-chest and an armchair. Surviving labels of Andrew Anderson (1794–1805), Elbert Anderson (5 Maiden Lane label, 1786–1796), Thomas Burling (36 Beekman Street label, 1787–1793), Joseph Vail (ca. 1790–ca. 1806), and William Whitehead (75 Pearl St. label, 1794–1799) include two or more different furniture forms in each, as did the partnership of Samuel Kneeland and Lemuel Adams of Hartford, Connecticut. In addition to George Shipley's label, William Rollinson (1762–1842) engraved a membership certificate for the Society of Journey-men Cabinet-makers in New York that was issued in the mid-1790s. It featured an inlaid fall-front desk and a shield-back side chair with five carved ribs (fig. 17). Abraham Godwin (1763–1835), another New York engraver, executed other labels for local furniture makers, notably Burling's. In Philadelphia, James Akin engraved very ambitious and nearly identical labels for William Camp (1773–1822) of Baltimore and

Figure 17 Certificate of John Hewett for membership in the Society of Journey-men Cabinet-makers in New York, 1796. (Gift of Cooper Union Library, 1953-10-80, Cooper-Hewitt, National Design Museum, Smithsonian Institution; photo, Matt Flynn.)

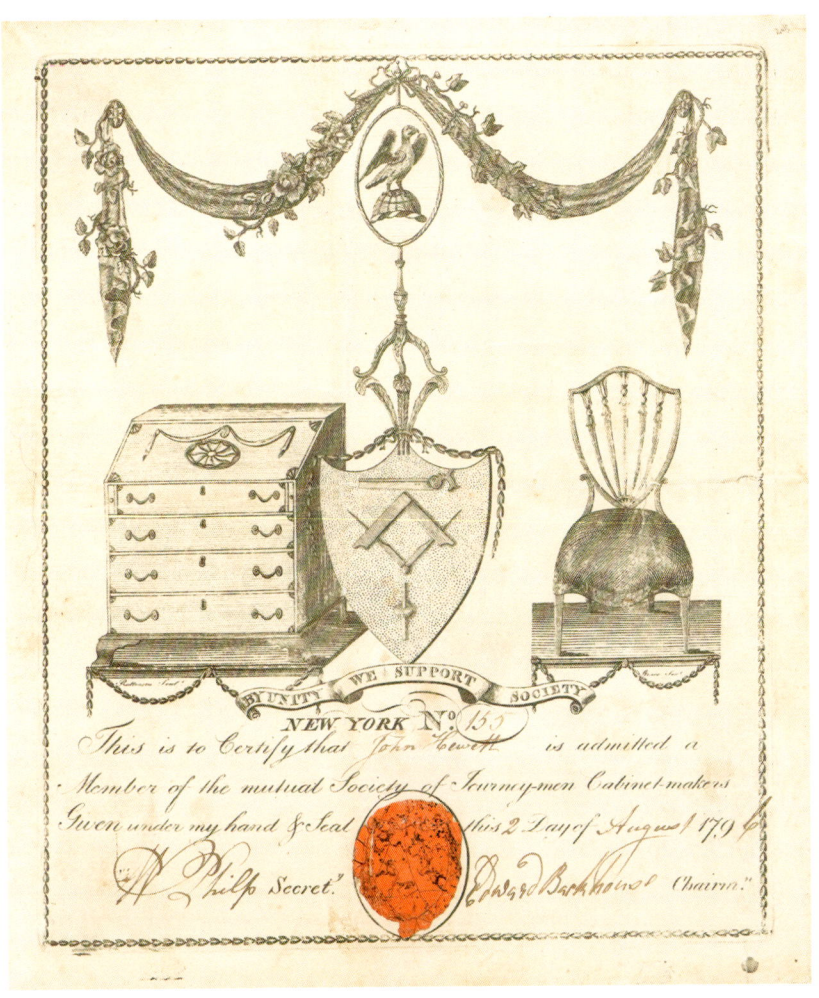

Figure 18 Label or trade card of William Camp. (Courtesy, Baltimore Museum of Art; photo, Decorative Arts Photographic Collection, Winterthur Museum.)

Joseph B. Barry (1757–1838) (figs. 18, 19). In addition to the maker's name and address, each label depicts six pieces of furniture borrowed directly or slightly modified from Thomas Sheraton's *Cabinet-Maker and Upholsterer's Drawing-Book and Appendix* (London, 1793), and Barry's also features two draped figures. The labels are not dated, but Barry added "& Son" in ink to his printed example. His son joined him circa 1810. Akin returned to Philadelphia in 1808 after a four-year absence, which suggests a narrow date range for his work. In a second version of the Barry label, the line naming him and his son is completely engraved and centered properly (fig. 20). The Camp label, which is not attached to a piece of furniture, probably dates from the period 1808–1810 as well.[11]

Label placement on furniture was typically—but not always—in unobtrusive but readily accessible places, such as drawer bottoms, inside rear rails of chairs, or tops of tilt-top table pillars. Certain chalk or ink inscriptions written in visible places may have been intended to serve as advertising, but most were not. When "CB" scrawled his initials in red chalk across the bottom board of a chest-on-chest on April 16, 1779, he marked the work as his own but not in a way that communicated that fact to the world at large

Figure 19 Label of Joseph B. Barry with "& Son" added. (Photo, Decorative Arts Photographic Collection, Winterthur Museum.)

Figure 20 Label of Joseph B. Barry & Son. (Mrs. Charlton M. Theus, *Savannah Furniture, 1735–1825* [Savannah, Ga.: privately printed, 1967], p. 85.) This label is later than the example illustrated in fig. 18.

Figure 21 Chest-on-chest probably made by Caleb Byrnes, probably Stanton, Delaware, 1779. Walnut with tulip poplar, white cedar, and yellow pine. H. 80½", W. 43¼", D. 23¾". (Courtesy, Sewell C. Biggs Museum of American Art.)

Figure 22 Inscription "C.B. April 16th / 1779" written in chalk on the inside bottom board of the lower case of the chest-on-chest illustrated in fig. 21.

(figs. 21, 22). Modern identification of the maker as probably Caleb Byrnes of Stanton, Delaware, rests on accurate identification of regional characteristics and the absence of any other maker in the region with suitable initials. The fact that CB may have been well known in the community he served reduces the utility of his signature as advertising. Outside that community, he was anonymous, a circumstance aggravated by the lack of an accompanying place-name.[12]

The private role of most signatures lies outside the mechanics of the marketplace. Motivation for signing a piece of furniture arose from different causes. Rather than advertisements, these signatures were personal proofs of accomplishment or statements of authorship, typically for an audience that never materialized in a way that benefited the maker. Sometimes a personal message or caricature accompanied the signature, as on the underside of a Philadelphia center table: "Made by Elias Reed in the year 1831 this table cause me to give a Black Eye to a frenchman." Recognition of the private function of these signatures makes comprehensible the practice of signing furniture in hidden places. Beake's 1711 inscription (figs. 5) cannot be read or even recognized without removing the drawers of the chest. Many makers' signatures have recently been discovered only when the signed piece of furniture was partially disassembled. In the early 1980s the Winterthur Museum took a chest of drawers off display because questions had arisen about the age of the object and the originality of its top. Removal of the top revealed a chalk signature on the subtop, which elevated the chest into the best-documented example of a sizable group of Connecticut furniture. Many other obscure signatures have been found.[13]

Signatures that commemorate transitions from apprenticeship to independent artisan are among the most common makers' marks. A chest-on-frame probably made near Kennett Square, Pennsylvania, bears the bold chalk signature "John W. Thomas / Cabinet Maker" and the date "December 27th 1805" across the inside bottom of the second-largest drawer (figs. 23, 24).

Figure 23 John W. Thomas, chest-on-frame, probably Kennett Square, Pennsylvania, 1805. Walnut with tulip poplar. H. 70", W. 41", D. 23¾". (Private collection.)

Figure 24 Chalk inscription "John W. Thomas / Cabinet Maker / December 27th 1805" on the inside bottom of the second-largest drawer of the chest-on-frame illustrated in fig. 23.

A second chalk inscription at the upper right corner of the backboards and in a different hand reads "George Gregg" (fig. 25). Few details of Thomas's life are known, although he is listed in Philadelphia directories from 1809 through 1814 as working at two addresses on South Fifth Street. From 1796

Figure 25 Chalk inscription "George Gregg" at the upper right corner of the backboards of the case of the chest-on-frame illustrated in fig. 23.

through 1819, George Gregg (1763–1833) was listed regularly as either a joiner or a cabinetmaker in tax assessments of Kennett Square, a small rural community southwest of Philadelphia. A receipt for making a coffin indicates that he was working on his own in Kennett Square by 1791. Gregg's inventory taken on March 18, 1833, includes the usual variety of joiner's tools and a turning lathe and chisels. Combining inscriptions and evidence again suggests the likelihood that the chest-on-frame represented Thomas's coming-of-age as a cabinetmaker, after serving an apprenticeship with Gregg. His talents then propelled him into Philadelphia, where he became sufficiently established by 1809 to appear in city directories. Several years later, Thomas signed another piece of furniture. This chalk inscription, on the outside back of the large bottom drawer of a federal worktable, carries the date October 16, 1813. Although the significance of the date is simply lost, the presence of the date provides precise documentation for when the table was made.[14]

William Houston (1755–1830) signed a high chest of drawers made in a style associated with John (1746–1792) and Samuel Dunlap (1752–1830) of Goffstown (also inscribed on the high chest) and Bedford, New Hampshire, although very few pieces of this distinctive furniture form are specifically documented to either Dunlap. Had not the Dunlaps' name already been established before Houston's was discovered on this high chest, furniture historians would likely have elevated Houston's name as the progenitor of a shop or school. In fact, Houston was an apprentice or part-time employee of John Dunlap when he probably made the high chest. A parallel exists in the Joel Joselyn (b. 1776) signature on another high chest of drawers. Joselyn was apprenticed to Samuel Dunlap, who charged work by Joselyn to third parties from 1793 to 1797. Soon after Joselyn completed his apprenticeship and married, he moved from Henniker, where Samuel Dunlap was then working, to Lebanon, some thirty-five miles away, where Joselyn continued to make furniture. Provenance of the high chest, reinforced by another inscription that appears to be the first owner's name, places it in Henniker.[15]

Multiple signatures on a single piece of furniture typically signify a cooperative venture. Moses Bayley (1716–1778) and Joshua Morss (1714–1756) of Newbury (now Newburyport), Massachusetts, memorialized their partnership in 1749 when each signed the high chest illustrated in figures 26–29. The

Figure 26 Moses Bayley and Joshua Morss, high chest, Newburyport, Massachusetts, 1749. Maple with white pine. H. 71", W. 36½", D. 19½". (Photo, Decorative Arts Photographic Collection, Winterthur Museum.)

Figure 27 Inscription "Made by Moses Bayley Newbury / February AD 1748/9" in the upper case of the high chest illustrated in fig. 26. Bayley signed the upper case twice.

Figure 28 Inscription "Made by / Josha Morss / Jany 1748/9" on the back of a lower case drawer of the high chest illustrated in fig. 26. Morss signed the lower case twice.

Figure 29 Painted inscription "For / Elizabeth / Noyes / E N" crossing the back of both cases of the high chest illustrated in fig. 26.

Figure 30 Printed label for Josiah Caldwell with a small piece of paper bearing the handwritten name "Mark Pitman." (Courtesy, Winterthur Museum.) This label is on a mahogany serving table or "enclosed pier table."

duration of that venture is not known, although the two artisans married sisters. Multiple labels pasted to the same object occasionally mask more complex business relationships. Looking-glass retailer Joseph White of Wilmington, Delaware, applied his label directly on top of John Elliott Jr.'s label. On the backboard of another looking glass, White inscribed "Sold at Joseph White's / Apocathery Shop / Wilmington" below an Elliott label. After White's death in 1798, his executors paid Elliott almost six hundred dollars to settle debts, which presumably included many purchases of looking glasses. In a similar vein, Salem maker Mark Pitman's name, written in ink on a small piece of paper, is pasted over the printed name of Josiah Caldwell, for whom the label must have originally been made (fig. 30). Caldwell is known to have worked on Essex Street, also Pitman's address, but except for a few pieces of furniture with similarly altered labels, his work is not identified. Historical details have not come to light, but evidence suggests that Pitman bought out Caldwell's labels, and perhaps his business.[16]

Figure 31 Desk-and-bookcase, probably northeastern Massachusetts, 1799. Maple with white pine. H. 100½", W. 45", D. 24¾". (Courtesy, Currier Museum of Art, Manchester, New Hampshire; Museum Purchase, 1958.6.)

Figure 32 Chalk inscription "Upper Edge" on the lower case backboards of the desk-and-bookcase illustrated in fig. 31. This same inscription is on a northeastern Massachusetts secretary-and-bookcase also marked "Gilmanton" (New Hampshire) and dated June 5, 1799.

The location of inscriptions on furniture helps distinguish owners from makers and destinations from places of origin. Since the late 1940s, a striped maple desk-and-bookcase was thought to have been signed "Walter Edge" (figs. 31, 32). Closer examination of the inscription decades later indicated that the inscription was a shipping mark reading "Upper Edge." Similarly, the "1794 / T. Back" inscription was once considered a maker's mark, but the letters more likely designate "top back." Several large case pieces have "bottom" written in chalk on the bottom boards and/or "top" on the top boards. During the eighteenth and nineteenth centuries, large pieces of furniture were often crated for protection, but backs and bottoms were apparently left partially exposed and used as a surface for shipping instructions. Most inscriptions simply stated which end was up.[17]

Place-names are more problematic. In some examples, a named locale seems more logically a destination rather than a place of origin. Marking furniture according to destination has a long history, although not many objects have been so identified. In 1705, for example, Boston upholsterer Thomas Fitch billed Mrs. Judith Pease in New York "for Six Rushia leather Chairs, and . . . for six more of the same sort all marked P with chalk on the ba[ck]." Anyone transporting the Newburyport high chest by Bayley and Morss could not overlook "For/ Elizabeth/ Noyes/ E N" written in large letters across the backs of both cases in black paint (see fig. 29). Eighteen-year-old Elizabeth Noyes Smith (1731–1816) received the high chest as a wedding present from her parents. A Massachusetts chest-on-chest has "To Bo[x]ford" inscribed in chalk across the back. Boxford is a small rural town northwest of Salem. A southeastern New Hampshire bowfront chest of drawers has a crude map to its destination drawn on the inside of the backboards. Ambiguity surrounds the Gilmanton name on the 1799 desk-and-bookcase (fig. 32). Independent of the misinterpretation of "upper edge," furniture scholars have assumed that Gilmanton marks its place of origin. Accordingly, they postulated a small but vital furniture-making community there, although evidence of any specific activity remains to be discovered. Absent the place-name, furniture scholars would readily identify the desk-and-bookcase as a product of Salem or some other prominent northeastern Massachusetts furniture-making center. At present, Gilmanton seems more likely a destination than an origin.[18]

There is little ambiguity about the inscription on the top board of the lower section of another desk-and-bookcase: "Nath Gould not his work" (fig. 33). When the desk and bookcase are assembled, the inscription is invis-

Figure 33 Incised inscription "Nath Gould not his work" on the top board of the lower section of a mahogany desk-and-bookcase made in Salem. (Courtesy, Metropolitan Museum of Art, gift of Mrs. Russell Sage, 1909 [10.125.81]. Image © Metropolitan Museum of Art.)

ible. This is a furniture maker's message to other artisans, who would likely have seen the object when it was disassembled and temporarily stored, perhaps in a shop. The reason for the inscription is less apparent. Morrison Heckscher speculates that it was written by a "disaffected workman" who created the object that Gould—the richest cabinetmaker in Salem, Massa-

Figure 34 William Fisk and Thomas Wightman, swivel-top Grecian card table, Boston, Massachusetts, 1817–1825. Mahogany with white pine. H. 29½", W. 36½", D. 18". (Courtesy, Historic New England, museum purchase with funds provided by an anonymous gift, 2005.26; photo, David Carmack.)

Figure 35 Ink inscription "Thomas Whightman / Carver back of [illegible] Horton's [?]" on the card table illustrated in fig. 34.

chusetts—merely sold. A recently discovered inscription by Boston carver Thomas Wightman (1759–1827) illuminates occasional needs for worker-to-worker communication. He wrote, "Thomas Whightman / Carver back of [illegible] Horton's [?]" in ink on the top of the pillar base of a card table (figs. 34, 35). The inscription can be seen only when the table frame is removed from the base, a task easily accomplished by unfastening the long iron bolt that joins the two parts. As with the Gould desk-and-bookcase, this card table was probably disassembled during storage and shipping. In contrast to Wightman's hidden inscription, Boston cabinetmaker William Fisk's (1770–1844) oval mark was stenciled onto the inside bottom of the

Figure 36 Stencil mark of William Fisk of Boston inside the well under the folding top of the card table illustrated in fig. 34.

well of the same card table, where it is clearly visible whenever the top is swiveled open (fig. 36). Historical circumstances suggest that Wightman was shifting much of his work and affiliations from Thomas Seymour to Fisk at about the time this card table was made. It was important to Wightman during this time of transition that fellow workers know where he could be contacted.[19]

Certain kinds of initials, sometimes accompanied by a full last name, readily identified the maker of the object in question to contemporary business associates familiar with the furniture-making community but not necessarily to the general public and potential consumers. Because furniture shipping, ventures, piecework arrangements, and other cooperative furniture-making and merchandizing practices created an ongoing and repetitive need for this kind of identification, most of these kinds of marks were made by striking the wood with an iron mark to impress the lettering (fig. 37). Such marking

Figure 37 Branding or marking irons of owners Peter Elmendorf II and Solomon Van Vechten Van Rensselaer, Albany area, New York, late eighteenth century. Iron with cast copper letters. L. 19". (Courtesy, Historic Cherry Hill.)

or branding irons—called a "marking hamor" in a 1676 Philadelphia account book entry—made marking furniture quick and cost-free except for the initial purchase price of the tool.[20]

English chair makers probably began using branding or marking irons in the late seventeenth century. Although no specific dates accompany the earliest marked chairs, the numbers of stamps recorded and the variety of carved and caned seating suggests that the practice was well established. Although research is incomplete, English two-initial stamps are widely believed to represent journeymen. Presumably, journeymen in the employ of masters marked the chairs and other furniture forms they made with these small, unobtrusive stamps to document their productivity and receive proper compensation. The closest parallel in America is the Boston-based "I" monogram, which likewise identified specific work executed for a segment of the furniture-making community. Typically, these marks were two serif letters denoting first and last names of a furniture maker. They formed a rectangle and were sometimes separated by a raised pellet or followed by periods (figs. 38, 39). Perhaps because brands or strike marks were small and cost-free to apply, they were occasionally stamped more than once onto the same piece of furniture. The tools used to impress these marks were made of iron or sometimes copper or brass. Copper marks "far exceed Iron ones, for Neatness and Continuance of Heat; . . . they neither burn nor scale away," as Philadelphia brass founder Daniel King claimed in a 1763 advertisement.

Figure 38   Side chair, England, 1725–1750. Walnut. H. 39⅜", W. 22½", D. 21¾". (Private collection; photo, Philip Zimmerman.)

Figure 39   Stamped mark "WH" on the bottom of the rear rail of the chair illustrated in fig. 38.

On the basis of this and other references, furniture historian Nancy Goyne Evans theorizes that marking irons were probably heated before use but not enough to char the wood. In any event, charred marks are very rare. Some furniture historians distinguish brands denoting burnt marks from struck marks made with cold dies, but given the apparent flexibility in period terminology and the subtle or invisible differences between marks made with heated versus cold marking irons, this distinction seems artificial.[21]

American Windsor chair makers began stamping their work with first initials and full last names by the 1760s. Windsor chair makers produced seating in bulk and probably found marks useful for tracking ownership and maintaining accountability. Port records document thousands of Windsor chairs in the export trade, giving credence to New York maker Thomas Hays's claim that "Masters of Vessels or Merchants, can be supplied with from 1 to 1000 chairs in one hour." As was the case with journeymen marks, Windsor makers' stamps were intended as identifiers for the furniture-making community rather than for the populace at large. Relatively few of the hundreds of recorded marks cite the cities where the maker worked. Even those bearing place names were often vague. The stamp "W[alter] · MACBRIDE / N–YORK" would have been sufficient for a distant customer to locate the maker, but that was not the case with the stamp "E[zekian] · HEWES / SALEM" (fig. 40). In the case of Hewes, a potential customer might incorrectly assume that he worked in Salem, Massachusetts, rather than his hometown of Salem, New Jersey. The mark "S · ROBERTS / Newmill (New Mills is now Pemberton, New Jersey) presented an even greater challenge because of the small size and relative obscurity of that community. True advertisements, such as those in numerous newspapers, provided adequate directions for contacting the maker, even if it meant contacting a factor at another, more prominent place of business.

Figure 40 Stamp "E[zekian] · HEWES / SALEM" on the bottom of a fanback Windsor side chair. (Private collection; photo, Decorative Arts Photographic Collection, Winterthur Museum.)

For most Windsor chair makers, business was either local or based on volume. Local makers could rely on word of mouth in most communities, perhaps augmented by occasional newspaper notices. Those who sought distant markets used merchants or middlemen, whose own selling efforts eliminated the need for furniture labels as advertisements. Only a few Windsor makers marked their chairs with the more expensive paper labels, and some of them, such as Joseph Birdsey Jr. of Huntington, Connecticut, and William Chappel of Danbury, Connecticut, called themselves cabinetmakers (figs. 41, 42).[22]

Figure 41 Joseph Birdsey Jr., sack-back Windsor armchair, Huntington, Connecticut, 1790–1800. Maple, basswood, oak, and hickory. H. 36", W. 24¾", D. 20½". (Private collection; photo, Philip Zimmerman.)

Figure 42 Paper label of Joseph Birdsey Jr. (1769–1805) of Huntington, Connecticut, pasted to the seat bottom of the armchair illustrated in fig. 41.

155   EARLY MAKERS' MARKS

Although the use of struck marks increased with expansion of the furniture export trade, the identities of some makers remain difficult to establish. Philadelphia furniture maker Edward James removed uncertainty about the multiple "E·J" marks in a clock case he made by pasting in his descriptive printed label (fig. 43). Similarly, Peregrine Janvier (1781–1865) signed and branded a chest of drawers in 1801. Identifying an "IE" mark on a clock case with movement by Jonas Alrichs of Wilmington, Delaware, as that of John Erwin or his son James is more problematic. It requires searching for all name possibilities in historical records in the presumed area of manufacture. Candidates remain viable unless and until new possibilities are discovered.[23]

Figure 43 Paper label and initial die stamps of Edward James (d. 1798) on the inside backboard of a mahogany tall clock case. (Courtesy, Philadelphia Museum of Art, purchased with the Germantown Tribute Fund, 1931.)

Identifying "S.F" marks as those of Samuel Fisk (1769–1797) reminds one of the caution that must be exercised when only circumstantial evidence is available to corroborate identity. The marks in question accompany an "S·BADLAM" stamp on a side chair and a lolling chair, each of a type made in eastern Massachusetts circa 1800. The name is that of Stephen Badlam

(1751–1815), a cabinetmaker who is best known for making an extraordinary chest-on-chest for Elias Haskett Derby in 1791. Badlam worked in Dorchester Lower Mills, south of Boston and Roxbury at the southern end of Washington Street. He also had a son of the same name, but custom dictated that the younger Badlam distinguish himself by adding "junior," which he did in his printed label. Samuel Fisk was the most prominent artisan with the requisite initials working in the Boston area at that time, but he was not the only one. Simon Francis signed a bowfront chest of drawers, which bears the second inscription "I + Rouse / Boston" that establishes a place of origin for the piece of furniture. Francis was listed in directories from 1797 until 1803, but he worked on Middle Street, a different neighborhood. Although no formal working arrangements between Fisk and Badlam are documented, additional evidence makes the case for Samuel more compelling. Fisk worked along Washington Street at the Roxbury-Boston line. For at least a few years before his early death in 1797, Samuel was in partnership with his brother William. A side chair and a card table each bear the "S.F" struck mark along with a "WF" mark. Another side chair has an "S & WF" die stamp, which more directly reflects a partnership (figs. 44, 45). Other furniture survives with just the "WF" mark, and one is

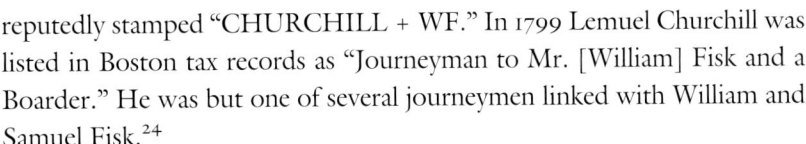

Figure 44 Side chair, attributed to the partnership of Samuel Fisk and William Fisk, Boston, Massachusetts, 1791–1797. Dimensions not recorded. (Courtesy, David Dunton; photo, Decorative Arts Photographic Collection, Winterthur Museum.)

Figure 45 Stamp "S & WF" on the rear rail of the chair illustrated in fig. 44.

reputedly stamped "CHURCHILL + WF." In 1799 Lemuel Churchill was listed in Boston tax records as "Journeyman to Mr. [William] Fisk and a Boarder." He was but one of several journeymen linked with William and Samuel Fisk.[24]

The lively network of relationships documented by struck marks should not obscure the fact that the Boston area is especially notable for the number of makers' struck marks that survive, also evident in late-eighteenth- and early-nineteenth-century furniture of the Hudson River Valley and the North Shore of Massachusetts. Salem furniture makers in particular were not only active markers of their products, a practice that paralleled a thriving export trade, but also some of them left voluminous and revealing records. An 1802 shipping invoice for cabinetmaker Jacob Sanderson (1757–1810) lists crates identified by number and "I+S," implying that each crate was so marked. In 1803 Jacob's brother Elijah (1752–1825) wrote his export agent, "you will find that my furniture is all marked with a brand E S on the back of each piece besides the mark of the case." Yet another Salem cabinetmaker, Samuel Barnard (1776–1858), also documented this practice when he noted on an 1805 invoice for furniture bound for the West Indies that his property was to be marked "SB." Jacob's marks were probably painted, whereas Elijah's were clearly branded on the piece of furniture in addition to the crate.[25]

Two "ES" die-struck pieces of furniture, a night cabinet (or commode) and a side chair, have long been identified as the work of Elijah Sanderson, who made the tambour desk illustrated in figures 46 and 47. Elijah worked in partnership with Jacob until the latter's death. Furniture survives bearing the printed label "E. & J. Sanderson, CABINET AND CHAIR-MAKERS In FEDERAL-STREET, SALEM, MASSACHUSETTS" (fig. 48). But partnerships did not necessarily preclude individual ventures, and makers employed multiple types of marks. Both Elijah and Jacob exported furni-

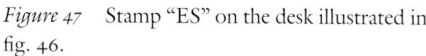

Figure 46 Tambour desk attributed to Elijah Sanderson, Salem, Massachusetts, 1800–1810. Mahogany with white pine. H. 47½", W. 37", D. 20½". (Private collection; photo, Decorative Arts Photographic Collection, Winterthur Museum.)

Figure 47 Stamp "ES" on the desk illustrated in fig. 46.

Figure 48 One of four paper labels of Elijah and Jacob Sanderson pasted to the underside of the top (one) and the skirt rails (three) of a Marlborough-leg breakfast table. (Courtesy, Winterthur Museum.)

ture on their own accounts. In 1804, for example, Jacob consigned twenty-two cases of furniture to Savannah, and two years later he shipped another thirty-eight cases of mahogany furniture, including "secretaries, sideboards, &c." to Madeira, the Canary Islands, and Surinam. Surviving manuscripts document numerous other Sanderson ventures to ports all over the world. In addition to Elijah's printed label and probable "ES" die stamp, a Salem-area card table bears the painted mark "E·S" on the fixed rear rail (fig. 49).

Figure 49 Painted initials on the stationary rear rail of a Salem-area card table, possibly by Elijah Sanderson. (Private collection; photo, Museum of Early Southern Decorative Arts, Old Salem Museums and Gardens.)

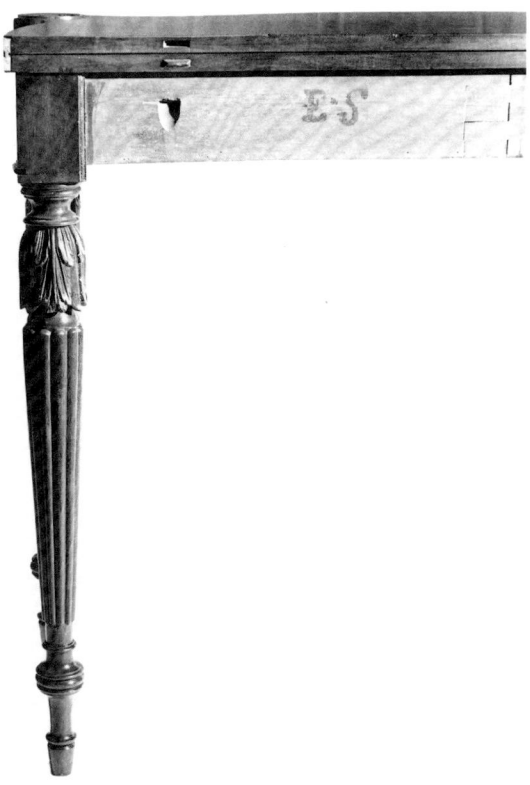

Jacob also used multiple marks. In addition to the printed label, he signed his name to a mahogany desk-and-bookcase. A pair of federal card tables, each painted "I + S" on the underside of the top, may also be by him. Another mahogany desk-and-bookcase bears a "JS" brand on the outside center of the outer lower-case backboards (figs. 50, 51).[26]

Figure 50 Desk-and-bookcase, Salem, Massachusetts, 1795–1805. Mahogany with white pine. H. 101½", W. 46", D. 26½". (Private collection; photo, Ali Elai, Camerarts.) This object is marked "JS," probably for Jacob Sanderson (1757–1810).

Figure 51 Impressed mark "JS" on the center of the outer lower case of the desk-and-bookcase illustrated in fig. 50. (Private collection; photo, Philip Zimmerman.)

Unlike the "ES" mark, which depicts relatively rare initials, the "JS" mark (and painted "I + S" mark) refers to more common initials and consequently introduces uncertainty about the maker's identity. If a Salem origin for the card tables and desk is correct, then Jacob is the leading and virtually only candidate. Joseph Short (1771–1819) worked in Newburyport, although his several documented pieces of furniture are less ambitious. Several Boston makers have JS as initials. They include John Smith of the short-lived partnership of Smith & Hitchings (ca. 1803–1804), John Simpkins and Joseph Simpson, each of whom is listed as a cabinetmaker in a 1789 directory, and John Seymour. Not surprisingly, several early-nineteenth-century pieces of furniture from eastern Massachusetts bear unidentified painted or struck "JS" or "IS" marks (by ca. 1790, *J*s had largely—but not entirely—displaced J-sounding *I*s). Assigning identities to these possibilities requires independent evidence that either confirms or contradicts manufacture by a specific maker. Regarding the "JS" marks, for example, the card tables and desk-and-bookcase each have pluses and minuses. Nothing of the urbane design or construction of the "I + S" pair of card tables distinguishes them as an exclusive Salem product. They may be from somewhere in the complex Boston furniture-making community. Similarly, an indistinct chalk signature on the underside of one tabletop begins with a "J," but the name is not Jacob. It may be that of a first owner, as could the "I + S" initials. Yet the card tables are marked in the same manner as specified on the 1802 Jacob Sanderson invoice. Likewise, the desk-and-bookcase is probably, but not definitely, of Salem origin. Also, the "JS" die has not been recorded on other furniture. In support of the Sanderson attribution, the location of the mark is appropriate for exported furniture.[27]

Although no shipping cases have yet come to light, Elijah's 1803 letter noted that his "ES" mark was to be struck on each piece of furniture "besides the mark of the case," suggesting that the mark was visible from outside the crate along with a crate number or other identifier. Similarly, chalk inscriptions on furniture carcasses indicating "back," "top," or "bottom" were intended to be read after the object had been crated and was being handled by shippers. Stephen Badlam was very specific regarding his shipping instructions for the monumental and ornately carved Derby chest-on-chest. Handwritten labels pasted to the tops of both the upper and lower cases state: "Keep this side up & preserve it from the Sun from wet & from bruises. It is of Consequence enough to merit great attention." Depending on specific needs, shipping crates probably did not always fully enclose the furniture but were constructed primarily to protect corners, fronts, and sides. In contrast, the pine boards that formed furniture backs, bottoms, and some tops were not very susceptible to damage and were convenient message boards.[28]

By the 1810s some furniture makers began using stencils to create maker's marks. New York furniture maker Michael Allison was among the first. In addition, over the course of his long career, he used more than a dozen different paper labels, some of which include printed dates. One of his stencils located Allison at 42 and 44 Vesey Street, an address that he occupied

Figure 52 Stencil mark of Michael Allison. (Courtesy, New York State Museum.) This mark is on a mahogany chest of drawers.

Figure 53 Printed paper label of Michael Allison from a chest of drawers. (Courtesy, Newark Museum; photo, Decorative Arts Photographic Collection, Winterthur Museum.)

between 1808 and 1815. As with all stencil marks, its appearance was modeled on printed labels, although the stenciling process produced a much coarser image. Allison's name, street address, and reference to being near "Bear Market," which must have been a familiar landmark, fit within an oval border. One of his printed labels displaying the identical address (a second version with that address also survives) has an oval surround and may have been a direct design source (figs. 52, 53). Several other Allison labels record number 42 only and may be earlier. His later labels, including one dated 1817 that pictures his "Cabinet and Upholstery Furniture Warehouse" at numbers 46 and 48 Vesey Street, are wordier and graphically more complex (fig. 54). Several Boston-area furniture makers used stencils, as did some makers in Philadelphia and various other locales.

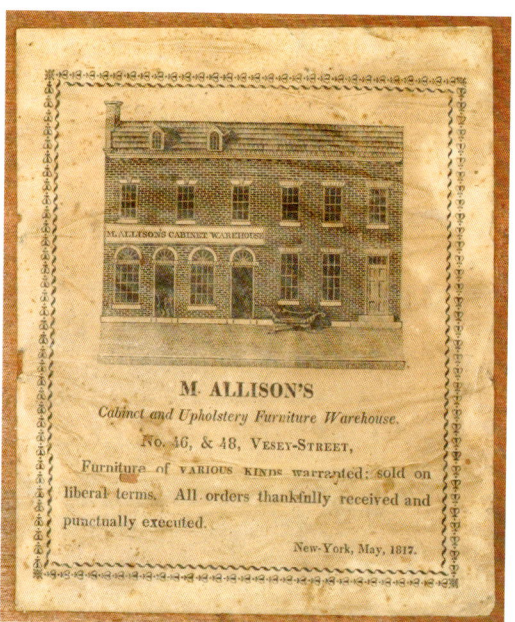

Figure 54 Printed paper label of Michael Allison dated May 1817. (Courtesy, New York State Museum.) This label is on a mahogany sideboard.

Figure 55 Printed paper trade card of Benjamin Randolph. (Courtesy, Library Company of Philadelphia.)

Although stencils were used on many types of decorative arts, they never replaced paper labels on furniture. Mid-eighteenth-century British trade cards set graphic standards that far exceeded the constraints of stencils. These distinctive forms of advertising were larger than labels and communicated more complex messages through ornate illustrations. Although not necessarily applied to pieces of furniture, they influenced label design. A rare American trade card, made for Benjamin Randolph circa 1770, used the same wording as conventional labels (fig. 55). The power of all these graphics—regardless of size—lay in their use of imagery and design to confer on the named furniture maker such values as exceptional skills, position within the trade, and good taste. The Barry and Camp labels (figs. 18–20) used furniture designs that were more than fifteen years old, indicating that the suggestive qualities of the images were more important than specific style information. Similarly, an illustration of a large furniture warehouse, such as Michael Allison's, implied investment, permanence, and success, all of which suggested that a furniture order from that source would probably be more than satisfactory.

Early American furniture has acquired new layers of meaning since it was first made and used. The presence of makers' labels and marks on a few pieces of that furniture has contributed value and interest—both historical and monetary—because of the information they contain. In either case, greater attention to the particulars of these markings results in more nuanced and accurate interpretations.

ACKNOWLEDGMENTS

For assistance with this article the author thanks Jay Robert Stiefel and Anne A. Verplanck.

1. Margaretta M. Lovell, "'Such Furniture as Will Be Most Profitable': The Business of Cabinetmaking in Eighteenth-Century Newport," *Winterthur Portfolio* 26, no. 1 (Spring 1991): 44–48. Morrison H. Heckscher, *John Townsend, Newport Cabinetmaker* (New York: Metropolitan Museum of Art, 2005), pp. 56, 61. For further comment, see Jay Robert Stiefel, review of *John Townsend, Newport Cabinetmaker* in *Journal of the Early Republic* (Winter 2006): 672–74.

2. The Nicholas Disbrowe inscription cited as seventeenth-century in early-twentieth-century publications is not authentic. See Penrose R. Hoopes, "Notes on Some Colonial Cabinetmakers of Hartford," *Antiques* 23, no. 5 (May 1933): 171; Patricia E. Kane, "The Seventeenth-Century Furniture of the Connecticut Valley: The Hadley Chest Reappraised," in *Arts of the Anglo-American Community in the Seventeenth Century,* edited by Ian M. G. Quimby (Charlottesville, Va.: University Press of Virginia for the Winterthur Museum, 1975), p. 79. David B. Warren, Michael K. Brown, Elizabeth Ann Coleman, and Emily Ballew Neff, *American Decorative Arts and Paintings in the Bayou Bend Collection* (Houston, Tex.: Museum of Fine Arts in association with Princeton University Press, 1998), no. F31. Christopher Gilbert states, "no [English] furniture marked by a maker is known that can be dated before 1700, although some may date slightly before," in *Pictorial Dictionary of Marked London Furniture, 1700–1840* (Leeds, Eng.: Furniture History Society and W. S. Maney and Son, 1996), p. 2. According to Gilbert, John Gumley carved his name and the date May 1703 into a large mirror at Chatsworth (*Pictorial Dictionary,* p. 4). *Philadelphia: Three Centuries of American Art* (Philadelphia: Philadelphia Museum of Art, 1976), pp. 13–14; Cathryn J. McElroy, "Furniture in Philadelphia: The First Fifty Years," in *American Furniture and Its Makers,* edited by Ian M. G. Quimby, special issue, *Winterthur Portfolio* 13 (1979): 76–77; Jack L. Lindsey, *Worldly Goods: The Arts of Early Pennsylvania, 1680–1758* (Philadelphia: Philadelphia Museum of Art, 1999), pp. 133–34. According to Lindsey's problematic biographical sketch, Evans, born in 1679, completed his apprenticeship in 1704 at age twenty-five yet sold William Penn a chest of drawers in 1701 and worked as a ship's joiner from 1703 to 1709. These biographical references may describe more than one individual of that name.

3. A second chest of drawers with Beake's inscribed name has no accompanying date (Decorative Arts Photographic Collection, file no. 78.877, Winterthur Museum, Winterthur, Delaware) [hereafter cited as DAPC].

4. Quoted in McElroy, "Furniture in Philadelphia," pp. 73, 79. Benno M. Forman challenges the Beakes-Till relationship but does not cite McElroy's article in "The Chest of Drawers in America, 1635–1730: The Origins of the Joined Chest of Drawers," *Winterthur Portfolio* 20, no. 1 (Spring 1985): 28. Margaret Berwind Schiffer, *Furniture and Its Makers of Chester County, Pennsylvania* (1966; reprint, Exton, Pa.: Schiffer Publishing, 1978), pp. 22–23, figs. 2, 3.

5. William C. Ketchum Jr., with the Museum of American Folk Art, *American Cabinetmakers: Marked American Furniture, 1640–1940* (New York: Crown Publishers, 1995), pp. 107–8. Benno M. Forman, *American Seating Furniture, 1630–1730: An Interpretive Catalogue* (New York: W. W. Norton, 1988), pp. 260–66. Forman notes another mark struck into the back of the crest rail of a Philadelphia leather-upholstered side chair of 1695 to 1710. This unidentified symbol is "too deliberate to be an accident, although its meaning is at the moment obscure" (p. 296).

6. Adam Bowett, *English Furniture from Charles II to Queen Anne, 1660–1714* (Woodbridge, Suffolk, Eng.: Antique Collectors' Club, 2002), pp. 204–5. See also Gilbert, *Pictorial Dictionary,* pp. 3–4. R. W. Symonds, "Old English Furniture and Its Makers: The Problem of Identification," in Ambrose Beal, *The London Furniture Makers from the Restoration to the Victorian Era, 1660–1840* (London: B. T. Batsford, 1953), p. 216. The labels are reproduced as pls. 88–93 in

William Macpherson Hornor Jr., *Blue Book, Philadelphia Furniture: William Penn to George Washington* (Philadelphia: privately printed, 1935). Savery's life and work are summarized in Philip D. Zimmerman, "William Savery," in *American National Biography* (New York: Oxford University Press, 1999), 19: 320–21. The walnut chest and label are illustrated in "Another Savery Label," *Antiques* 9, no. 2 (February 1926): 77. The 1771 reference is in Thomas Affleck's January 2 bill to John Cadwalader that lists "2 Commode Card Tables" and "2 Mahogany Commode Sophias for the Recesses" among many other items. For discussion of the terminology, see Philip D. Zimmerman, "A Methodological Study in the Identification of Some Important Philadelphia Chippendale Furniture," in Quimby, ed., *American Furniture and Its Makers*, pp. 193–208; see also pp. 200, 204.

7. Judith Coolidge Hughes, "The Labels of John Elliott Jr.," *Antiques* 91, no. 4 (April 1967): 514–17. "Collectors' Notes: John Elliott Sr.," *Antiques* 107, no. 5 (May 1975): 1068. The first American label appears in Alfred Coxe Prime, "John Elliott: Cabinet and Looking-Glass Maker of Philadelphia," *Pennsylvania Museum Bulletin* 19, no. 85 (April 1924): 135. Mary Ellen Hayward, "The Elliotts of Philadelphia: Emphasis on the Looking Glass Trade, 1755–1810" (master's thesis, University of Delaware, 1971), pp. 25–34.

8. Morrison H. Heckscher, *American Furniture in The Metropolitan Museum of Art, Late Colonial Period: The Queen Anne and Chippendale Styles* (New York: Metropolitan Museum of Art and Random House, 1985), no. 81. Clement E. Conger and Alexandra W. Rollins, *Treasures of State: Fine and Decorative Arts in the Diplomatic Reception Rooms of the U.S. Department of State* (New York: Harry N. Abrams, 1991), pp. 94–95, no. 13. For many labeled Frothingham pieces of furniture, see Richard H. Randall Jr., "Benjamin Frothingham," in *Boston Furniture of the Eighteenth Century*, edited by Walter Muir Whitehill (Boston: Colonial Society of Massachusetts, 1974), pp. 223–49. Only one label each for Job and Edmund Townsend is known. For a flat-top desk-and-bookcase labeled by Job Townsend, see Christopher P. Monkhouse and Thomas S. Michie, *American Furniture in Pendleton House* (Providence: Museum of Art, Rhode Island School of Design, 1986), pp. 94–96, no. 38. For a bureau table bearing the label of Edmund Townsend, see Edwin J. Hipkiss, *Eighteenth-Century American Arts: The M. and M. Karolik Collection* (Cambridge, Mass.: Harvard University Press for the Museum of Fine Arts, Boston, 1941), no. 68. Heckscher, *John Townsend, Newport Cabinetmaker*, pp. 61–64.

9. Bernard & S. Dean Levy advertisement, *Antiques* 94, no. 3 (September 1978): 356; Betty Ring, "Check List of Looking-Glass and Frame Makers and Merchants Known by Their Labels," *Antiques* 119, no. 5 (May 1981): 1182.

10. Meyric R. Rogers, "George Shipley: His Furniture and His Label, A Set of Side Chairs," *Antiques* 79, no. 4 (April 1961): 374; Martha Gandy Fales, "A Classical Sideboard," *Antiques* 79, no. 4 (April 1961): 375. Benjamin A. Hewitt, Patricia E. Kane, and Gerald W. R. Ward, *The Work of Many Hands: Card Tables in Federal America, 1790–1820* (New Haven, Conn.: Yale University Art Gallery, 1982), no. 32. Illustrated in Ketchum, *American Cabinetmakers*, p. 123.

11. Illustrated in Joseph Downs and Ruth Ralston, *A Loan Exhibition of New York State Furniture* (New York: Metropolitan Museum of Art, 1934), n.p. Illustrated in Hornor, *Blue Book*, pl. 432; Robert Bishop, *Centuries and Styles of the American Chair, 1640–1970* (New York: E. P. Dutton & Co., 1972), fig. 314. Maureen O'Brien Quimby, "The Political Art of James Akin," *Winterthur Portfolio* 7 (1972): 59–112. Illustrated in Robert T. Trump, "Joseph B. Barry, Philadelphia Cabinetmaker," *Antiques* 107, no. 1 (January 1975): 161, fig. 5.

12. Philip D. Zimmerman et al., *Sewell C. Biggs Museum of American Art: A Catalogue*, 2 vols. (Dover, Del.: Biggs Museum, 2002), 1: no. 81.

13. The motivation behind leaving a signature seems similar to that of western explorer William Clark, who scratched his name and date in the rock face of Pompeys Piller, Montana, in 1806. Cited in Kathleen Matilda Catalano, "Cabinetmaking in Philadelphia, 1820–1840" (master's thesis, University of Delaware, 1972), p. 111. Nancy E. Richards and Nancy Goyne Evans, *New England Furniture at Winterthur* (Winterthur, Del.: Winterthur Museum, 1997), no. 182. A signature on a sideboard eluded separate examinations by a dealer and an independent consultant as well as former owners and interested parties. Viewing the signature requires peering around the lower center cupboard doors to see the back surface of the fixed front panels. Philip D. Zimmerman, "A Rare Eight-Legged Federal Sideboard, Connecticut, 1795–1805" (unpublished report for Bernard & S. Dean Levy, 1997); Thomas Kugelman, Alice Kugelman, and Robert Lionetti, *Connecticut Valley Furniture: Eliphalet Chapin and His Contemporaries, 1750–1800* (Hartford: Connecticut Historical Society, 2005), pp. 368–70, no. 169. Another sideboard bears its maker's signature on a framing member underneath the top and is visible only when the top is removed. Zimmerman, *Sewell C. Biggs Museum*, 1: no. 49.

14. Furniture historians Thomas and Alice Kugelman and Robert Lionetti cite several examples of this practice in their study of Hartford-area case furniture; Kugelman, Kugelman, and Lionetti, *Connecticut Valley Furniture*, pp. 114, 148–50, 162–64, 196, 366. Deborah Ducoff-Barone, "Philadelphia Furniture Makers, 1800–1815," *Antiques* 145, no. 5 (May 1991): 994. Schiffer, *Furniture and Its Makers of Chester County*, pp. 100, 101, 316. The 1800 and 1810 United States Census also records Gregg in Kennett Square. Chester County inventories #8938, as cited in Schiffer, *Furniture and Its Makers of Chester County*, pp. 100–101. Ducoff-Barone, "Philadelphia Furniture Makers, 1800–1815," 983, pl. 3.

15. Donna-Belle Garvin, "Two High Chests of the Dunlap School," *Historical New Hampshire* 35, no. 2 (Summer 1980): 165ff.; Richards and Evans, *New England Furniture at Winterthur*, no. 175. Garvin, "Two High Chests of the Dunlap School," pp. 180–83.

16. Israel Sack advertisement, *Antiques* 115, no. 5 (May 1979): inside front cover. Peter Benes, *Old-Town and the Waterside: Two Hundred Years of Tradition and Change in Newbury, Newburyport, and West Newbury, 1635–1835* (Newburyport, Mass.: Historical Society of Old Newbury, 1986), pp. 50–51, no. 23. Elizabeth Noyes (1731–1816) married James Smith III (1725–1787) of Newbury. She received furniture from her parents. Deborah D. Waters, *Delaware Collections in the Museum of the Historical Society of Delaware* (Wilmington, Del.: Historical Society of Delaware, 1984), pp. 30–31, no. 12. Collections of the Biggs Museum of American Art, Dover, Delaware. Inconsistent nail-hole patterns indicate that the backboards are not original to the looking-glass frame. This looking glass seems to be the same one described with a different inscription in Charles G. Dorman, *Delaware Cabinetmakers and Allied Artisans, 1655–1855* (Wilmington, Del.: Historical Society of Delaware, 1960), p. 88. Margaret Burke Clunie, "Salem Federal Furniture" (master's thesis, University of Delaware, 1976), pp. 158, 210.

17. Israel Sack advertisement, *Antiques* 56, no. 6 (December 1949): 399; M. Ada Young, "Five Secretaries and the Cogswells," *Antiques* 88, no. 4 (October 1965): 479–81. Morrison H. Heckscher interprets the inscription as "I [?] Back" in *American Furniture in The Metropolitan Museum of Art*, no. 179. Gerald W. R. Ward, *American Case Furniture in the Mabel Brady Garvan and Other Collections at Yale University* (New Haven, Conn.: Yale University Art Gallery, 1988), nos. 62, 67, 160, 168, 177.

18. Fitch to Pease, May 8, 1705, Fitch Letterbook, American Antiquarian Society, as quoted in Forman, *American Seating Furniture*, p. 264. Benes, *Old-Town and the Waterside*, p. 51. Ward, *American Case Furniture*, pp. 169–70, no. 80. Brock Jobe, *Portsmouth Furniture: Masterworks from the New Hampshire Seacoast* (Boston: Society for the Preservation of New England Antiquities, 1993), pp. 109–10, no. 9.

19. Heckscher, *American Furniture in The Metropolitan Museum of Art*, no. 181. Philip D. Zimmerman with David Jorgensen, "A Grecian Card Table by William Fisk and Thomas Wightman of Boston," *Antiques* 169, no. 5 (May 2006): 146–51.

20. Account Book of maritime joiner Gregory Marlow, as quoted in *Philadelphia: Three Centuries of American Art*, p. 15.

21. Victor Chinnery argues that initial and name brands on seventeenth-century-style furniture and earlier are ownership rather than makers' marks (Victor Chinnery, *Oak Furniture: The British Tradition* [Woodbridge, Suffolk, Eng.: Antique Collectors' Club, 1979], pp. 57–59). Bernard D. Cotton treats struck makers' marks as routine in his study of late-eighteenth- and nineteenth-century chair making, *The English Regional Chair* (Woodbridge, Suffolk, Eng.: Antique Collectors' Club, 1990). Bowett, *English Furniture from Charles II to Queen Anne*, pp. 89–90. Gilbert, *Pictorial Dictionary*, p. 3. *Philadelphia Gazette*, September 22, 1763, as quoted in Nancy Goyne Evans, *Windsor-Chair Making in America: From Craft Shop to Consumer* (Hanover, N.H.: University Press of New England, 2006), p. 80; see also p. 81.

22. For a detailed study of similarly marked owners' names, see Myrna Kaye, "Marked Portsmouth Furniture," *Antiques* 113, no. 5 (May 1978): 1098–104. Nancy Goyne Evans, "American Painted Seating Furniture: Marketing the Product, 1750–1840," in *Perspectives on American Furniture*, edited by Gerald W. R. Ward (New York: W. W. Norton & Co, 1988), pp. 160–64. Thomas Hays advertisement, *Daily Advertiser* (New York), April 8, 1801, quoted in Rita Susswein Gottesman, *The Arts and Crafts in New York, 1800–1804: Advertisements and News Items from New York City Newspapers* (New York: New-York Historical Society, 1965), p. 144. Nancy Goyne Evans, *American Windsor Chairs* (New York: Hudson Hills Press in association with the Winterthur Museum, 1996), pp. 180–83, 205; see also pp. 337–38.

23. *Philadelphia: Three Centuries of American Art*, pp. 93–94. Deborah D. Waters, *Plain and Ornamental: Delaware Furniture, 1740–1890* (Wilmington: Historical Society of Delaware,

1984), p. 26, no. 14. Philip D. Zimmerman, *Delaware Clocks* (Dover, Del.: Biggs Museum, 2006), pp. 48–49.

24. Charles F. Montgomery, *American Furniture: The Federal Period* (New York: Viking Press, 1966), nos. 30, 110, p. 479. Montgomery speculated that the "SF" mark was possibly that of an owner but more likely that "of a journeyman who made the chairs for Badlam." Ward, *American Case Furniture*, pp. 171–77, no. 82. Montgomery, *American Furniture: The Federal Period*, no. 253. DAPC, 75.292. Ethel Hall Bjerkoe, *The Cabinetmakers of America* (1957; reprint, New York: Bonanza Books, n.d.), p. 95. Chair marks illustrated in Ketchum, *American Cabinetmakers*, p. 120. Hewitt, Kane, and Ward, *The Work of Many Hands*, no. 15. The card table is incorrectly identified as made in Salem rather than Boston-Roxbury. DAPC, 97.829-.830. Richard H. Randall Jr., *American Furniture in the Museum of Fine Arts, Boston* (Boston: Museum of Fine Arts, 1965), no. 158; Paul J. Foley, *Willard's Patent Time Pieces: A History of the Weight-Driven Banjo Clock, 1800–1900* (Norwell, Mass.: Roxbury Village Publishing, 2002), p. 251. The author does not illustrate the mark or describe further the furniture form. Anne Rogers Haley, "Boston Cabinetmakers and Allied Craftsmen, 1780–1799: A New Source," *Antiques* 149, no. 5 (May 1996): 763.

25. Quoted in Mabel M. Swan, "Elijah and Jacob Sanderson, Early Salem Cabinetmakers," *Essex Institute Historical Collections* 70, no. 4 (October 1934): 331. Hewitt, Kane, and Ward, *The Work of Many Hands*, no. 19.

26. Dean A. Fales Jr., "Essex County Furniture—Documented Treasures from Local Collections, 1660–1860," *Essex Institute Historical Collections* 101, no. 3 (July 1965): nos. 36, 37; Randall, *American Furniture in the Museum of Fine Arts, Boston*, no. 158. For a tambour desk with the same brand, see Sotheby's, *The Collection of Mr. and Mrs. Lammot du Pont Copeland*, New York, January 19, 2002, lot 316. Montgomery, *American Furniture: The Federal Period*, no. 322. [Henry Wyckoff Belknap], "Furniture Exported by Cabinetmakers of Salem," from notes left by Henry Wyckoff Belknap, *Essex Institute Historical Collections* 85, no. 4 (October 1949): 350–55. DAPC, 73.341. Israel Sack advertisement, *Antiques* 72, no. 6 (December 1957): inside front cover. Wendy Cooper and Kemble Widmer II, "Seeing Double: Winterthur's Sanderson Card Table Finds Its Mate," *Catalogue of Antiques and Fine Art* 4, no. 6 (2004): 274–79.

27. Martha G. Fales, "The Shorts, Newburyport Cabinetmakers," *Essex Institute Historical Collections* 102, no. 3 (July 1966): 233–34, figs. 3–5. David L. Barquist, *American Tables and Looking Glasses in the Mabel Brady Garvan and Other Collections at Yale University* (New Haven, Conn.: Yale University Art Gallery, 1992), no. 94; Bjerkoe, *Cabinetmakers of America*, p. 201.

28. Ward, *American Case Furniture*, p. 172, no. 82.

Ethan W. Lasser

Reading Japanned Furniture

▼ RECENTLY SCHOLARS HAVE interpreted works of literature by focusing on the way in which authors describe and characterize material objects, including pieces of furniture. This essay attempts a similar, but slightly reformulated, version of that project: it endeavors to reveal period-specific meanings of furniture by considering several different genres of literature. Its focus is a group of japanned cabinets-on-stands and high chests of drawers made in late-seventeenth- and early-eighteenth-century London and Boston (see figs. 1, 2, 14, 18). The adjective "japanned" refers to the exotic surface ornament of the objects. This ornament, which includes gold-colored human figures, bouquets of flowers, flocks of birds, and rows of pagoda-roofed houses, resembles the imagery on the Asian lacquerware screens and boxes that were imported into Boston and London from China and Japan in the late seventeenth and early eighteenth centuries. Despite the furniture's Asian connotations, Western craftsmen, known as japanners, decorated surfaces of the japanned cabinets and high chests. These craftsmen, whose names are largely unknown today, practiced a labor-intensive and expensive craft. Wealthy merchant families purchased many of the japanned objects that were produced during the style's height of fashion, from roughly 1680 to 1740. Wills and inventories suggest that these families often owned a range of japanned objects, from high chests and cabinets to dressing tables, chairs, and mirrors.[1]

Dozens of japanned high chests and cabinets survive from late seventeenth- and early eighteenth-century London and Boston. Although concerned with this entire class of objects, this essay concentrates on a single exemplary piece: a high chest made in Boston between 1730 and 1740 (fig. 2). This object is one of the best-preserved examples of japanned furniture, in that the decoration that covers most of its surface is original. There are identical images of buildings and trees on its sides; abstract, curvilinear patterns on its legs and moldings; cherub heads on its pediment; and, most spectacularly of all, clusters of images on each of its ten drawer fronts.[2]

The first owner of the chest was probably Benjamin Pickman, a wealthy merchant from Salem, Massachusetts. Like many of the owners of japanned furniture, Pickman made a fortune shipping and exchanging various types of commodities between Boston, London, Portugal, and ports to the south, including the West Indies. The high chest is thought to have stood in Pickman's home on Union Street in Salem. There it would have served as both a showpiece and a container for household goods such as bed linens and clothing.[3]

Figure 1 Cabinet-on-stand, London, ca. 1700. Cabinet, oak and pine; stand, pine and basswood. H. 35⅞", W. 38", D. 19¾". (Courtesy, V&A Images, Victoria & Albert Museum.)

Figure 2 High chest of drawers, Boston, Massachusetts, 1730–1740. Maple, white pine, and birch with white pine. H. 86½", W. 38¼", D. 20⅞". (Courtesy, Metropolitan Museum of Art, purchase, Joseph Pulitzer Bequest, 1940 [40.37.1]; photo, Gavin Ashworth.)

Generations of English and American furniture historians have studied Pickman's high chest and other surviving japanned furniture from the period. Their analyses primarily address connoisseurial questions. Focusing closely on artifactual evidence and consulting primary sources such as wills, inventories, and treatises, scholars have studied the process of japanning, have carefully authenticated the japanned objects in museums and private collections, and have attributed a small percentage of these objects to the hands of individual period craftsmen. (Pickman's high chest has been loosely attributed to Thomas Johnston, a Boston craftsman. Johnston worked primarily as an engraver, but he also advertised his services as a japanner in the 1730s.) Beyond these connoisseurial studies, scholars have drawn two general conclusions about japanned furniture. First, they argue that it, like many household goods from the early eighteenth century, was used to broadcast its owners' wealth and status. Second, they tie japanned furniture to the eighteenth-century taste for chinoiserie, or Asian-style, domestic objects.[4]

This essay does not dispute these conclusions, nor does it question the connoisseurial studies—indeed, it relies on their findings and employs their method of close analysis. However, in addition to the standard sources of the furniture historian—wills, inventories, and treatises—I also turn to other forms of literature, including professional manuals, novels, and poems. These works help reveal a long-overlooked aspect of objects like Pickman's high chest: their literary function. I first argue that japanned high chests and cabinets are narrative objects whose ornament tells a story. I then address questions of audience and reception. Although scholars have long associated the chinoiserie style with women, I argue that these narrative objects cater equally to a masculine, and specifically mercantile, sensibility.

Furniture as Literature
The best point of entry into the narrative character of the high chests and cabinets is John Stalker and George Parker's *Treatise of Japanning and Varnishing* (1688), which outlines the process of japanning. Intended, in its authors' words, for both "practitioners" and the "ingenious gentry" who owned japanned furniture, the treatise carefully describes the steps necessary to transform a piece of pine into a spectacular surface of gesso and gilt. In certain passages, however, Stalker and Parker digress from their discussions of method to describe the appearance and character of japanned furniture. These descriptions are important because they provide insight into the ways in which period viewers thought about objects such as Pickman's chest. The descriptions focus principally on japanning's visual splendor. Stalker and Parker use phrases such as "delightful and ornamental beyond expression" and words such as "beautiful," "rich," and "Majestick" to characterize the style. Yet in other passages, the authors describe japanned furniture in very different terms. At the conclusion of the preface, for example, they write that japanned furniture "calls to mind the fictions of the poets." Pages later, they note that some of this furniture risks being "registered in doggrel ballad." At other points, they refer to japanning's "errata," "passages," and

171 READING JAPANNED FURNITURE

"conclusions," and they speak of the object's "author" and his "pen." By aligning japanned objects with narrative forms and narrative structures, these characterizations indicate that Stalker and Parker and, by extension, their readers thought that there was something storylike about japanned furniture.[5]

Today, one is tempted to dismiss Stalker and Parker's descriptions as poetic license. Japanned furniture, after all, presents pictures, not words, which are generally considered the primary ingredient of "fictions," "poems," and "ballads." Narratives, though, as scholar Mieke Bal has explained in her extensive writings on the subject, can be presented in a variety of media, including images. In eighteenth-century London and Boston, where literacy rates were low, stories told through images were common. In Boston, they surfaced in children's books such as the *New England Primer,* whose pictures told stories to help children learn to read. In London, they appeared in public spaces such as churches, where stained-glass windows presented stories from the Bible. In both cities, significantly, they

Figure 3 Needlework picture depicting David and Bathsheba, England, late seventeenth century. 14 5/8" x 19". (Courtesy, Ashmolean Museum, Oxford.)

could be seen on a variety of domestic objects. The homes of early-eighteenth-century Boston and London elites contained many narrative objects. These included imported porcelain vases decorated with images that told the story of the hunt by showing its different stages (the successive spotting, tracking, and killing of the deer), porcelain plates that told the story of a voyage from Canton to London by showing the same ship at various points between the two coasts, and panels embroidered with colorful images that presented familiar stories from the Bible. One such panel from 1680s London tells the story of King David's seduction of the beautiful Bathsheba (fig. 3). At the upper left corner of this object is an image of Bathsheba's initial seduction; below that, an image of David deliberating with her husband; at the upper right corner, an image of Bathsheba's husband being murdered; and, finally, in the lower right corner, an image of the concluding moment in the story, when the prophet Nathan admonishes David for his behavior. It is crucial to understand that the images in all of these examples are not just illustrations. By presenting the same characters (the deer, the hunters, the ship, David) at different times in different places, they tell stories—and constitute narratives—themselves.[6]

Japanned furniture can be counted among these narrative objects. The exotic images on Pickman's chest do not, of course, tell a story from the Bible. Rather, they tell a version of the stories of exotic cultures that were presented in one of the most popular literary genres of the late seventeenth and early eighteenth centuries, sea narratives. This genre consisted of works such as William Symson's *New Voyage to the East Indies* (1715) and William Betagh's *Voyage Round the World* (1728). As these titles suggest, English explorers who had circumnavigated the globe or sailed to its "unknown" coasts, places such as Asia and the Indies, were the authors of the sea narratives. These explorers were famous for the painstaking observations they made in their attempts to record every aspect of the coastlines they encountered, from their geography to their human inhabitants to their commercial opportunities. The result was a series of best sellers: the sea narratives were read by a wide variety of social groups in Boston and London, including the cities' craftsmen. Art historians Carl Dauterman and Leslie Grigsby have shown that both English silver chasers and ceramists decorated their vessels with images based on illustrations from this kind of travel book.[7]

The japanners of London and Boston went a step further. They created objects that actually told sea narratives rather than objects that simply

Figure 4 Detail of the lower drawer of the upper case of the high chest illustrated in fig. 2. (Photo, Gavin Ashworth.)

Figure 5 View of "ANHING" from Johan Nieuhof, *Embassy from the East India Company, of the United Provinces, to the Grand Tartar Cham, Emperor of China, ...* (London, 1673). (Courtesy, Beinecke Rare Book and Manuscript Library, Yale University.)

Figure 6 Detail of the drawer directly above the one illustrated in fig. 4. (Photo, Gavin Ashworth.)

Figure 7 "CHINESE MEN" from Johan Nieuhof, *Embassy from the East-India Company, of the United Provinces, to the Grand Tartar Cham, Emperor of China, ...* (London, 1673). (Courtesy, Beinecke Rare Book and Manuscript Library, Yale University.)

resembled the narratives' illustrations. We can begin to understand how japanned furniture tells a story by considering the way the images on the Pickman high chest echo two of the sea narrative's essential characteristics. First, they evoke a location that almost all of the sea narratives illustrate and describe, the Asian coast. Comparing the japanned surface to the images of the coastline that appear in one of the most lavishly illustrated sea narratives, Johan Nieuhof's *Embassy from the East-India Company . . .* (1673), makes this connection clear. The houses on the lower drawer of the upper case of the Pickman chest (fig. 4) bear a strong resemblance to the small town pictured in Nieuhof's engraving of the Anhing section of the Chinese coast (fig. 5). Like the houses in this image, the buildings on the high chest are horizontally proportioned and positioned low to the ground and close to one another in a single line. Similarly, the figures on the drawer above (fig. 6) are depicted in the manner of the coastal inhabitants illustrated in Nieuhof's book (fig. 7). Like Nieuhof's engraving of "Chinese Men," the high chest presents small groups of men and children walking across the landscape wearing loose, flowing clothing.[8]

In addition to these details, other images on the japanned surfaces correspond to aspects of the Asian coastline that the authors of the sea narratives discuss in their texts (fig. 8). Many of the images, for example, relate to the descriptions of the coast of St. John's, an island off China, in William Dampier's *A New Voyage Round the World*, a best-selling sea narrative published in its fifth edition in 1729. The two long-necked birds stationed behind the keyhole on the uppermost large drawer and the small birds hovering on the

Figure 8 Detail of the upper section of the high chest illustrated in fig. 2.

Figure 9 Detail of the decoration on the right side of the large drawer at the top of the upper section of the high chest illustrated in fig. 2. (Photo, Gavin Ashworth.)

bottom drawer resemble the "tame fowls . . . ducks and cocks and hens and small birds" that Dampier described flying around the coast, the triangular bridges on the upper large drawer call to mind the bridges he encountered, and the figures spread across each drawer of the high chest resemble the inhabitants the captain observed as he sailed toward the island. As he notes,

> The natives of this island are Chinese . . . the Chinese in general are tall, straight-bodied, raw-boned men. . . . The Chinese have no turbans, but when they walk abroad, they carry a small umbrello in their hands, wherewith they fence their heads from the sun or the rain, by holding it over their heads. . . . The common apparel of the men is a loose frock and breeches.[9]

The figures on the high chest match Dampier's description: they wear loose frocks and breeches, lack turbans, and—in the case of the figure on the far right side of the detail shown in figure 9—hold umbrellas. Dampier later describes the way that the inhabitants of the coast "gazed on us as we past by." The figures on the high chest also match this aspect of the coastal inhabitants. All of them appear to look out at some presence beyond their immediate landscape.[10]

Figure 10 Detail showing how the decoration continues from the right edges of the drawers on the right side of the upper section of the chest illustrated in fig. 2 to the left side of the drawers below. (Photo, Gavin Ashworth.) (*A*) On the right edge of the small drawer at the top of the upper case, a tree limb arcing up behind a small house intersects the drawer edge and disappears. But its missing portion, which matches the other half of the tree perfectly, reappears on the left-hand side of the large drawer below. (*B*) The bridge that appears on the right edge of the upper large drawer is repeated on the left side of the drawer below. (*C*) The flowers on the right side of the second large drawer from the top continue as foliage behind the house on the left-hand side of the drawer below. (*D*) The fences and trees on the right side of the third drawer down reappear behind the houses on the left side of the bottom drawer.

The connections between the japanned surface and the coastlines discussed in the sea narratives, however, are more than a matter of these details. Looking closely reveals that the entire japanned surface represents the kind of place that the sea narratives describe. That is to say, the japanner organized the images into a coherent whole. Although the images on each drawer of the high chest appear to be separated into discrete, horizontal units, they are, in fact, closely linked. The image on the far right side of each drawer corresponds directly to the image on the far left side of the drawer below (fig. 10). This pattern, which extends to the drawers below the waist mold-

Figure 11 Looking glass, Boston, Massachusetts, 1730–1740. White pine. H. 57 1/2", W. 19 1/8", D. 1 1/4". (Courtesy, Metropolitan Museum of Art, purchase, Joseph Pulitzer Bequest, 1940 [40.37.4]; photo, Gavin Ashworth.)

Figure 12 Detail of the crest of the looking glass illustrated in fig. 11. (Photo, Gavin Ashworth.)

ing, presents the images on the high chest's drawers as one continuous, linear image that is similar to those featured on the Asian screens and scrolls that inspired many of the motifs used in japanning. Indeed, if one were to line up the drawers side by side, one could view a panorama of the kind of coastline that the authors of sea narratives such as *Embassy from the East-India Company* and *A New Voyage Round the World* explored.[11]

The similarities between the high chest and the sea narratives run even deeper. In addition to their setting, they share the same point of view. Captains such as Dampier and Nieuhof typically viewed and described the coast from the perspective of their ships. For example, Dampier views the shore from his "canoa" and takes note of the gaze of the coasts' inhabitants as he "pas[ses] by." Similarly, the large body of water in the foreground of Nieuhof's image of Anhing (fig. 5) indicates that he portrayed this coast as he viewed it from the deck of a ship still at sea. The japanner of the Pickman chest rendered the coastline on the high chest from this same "ship's-eye" perspective. The horizontal lines that appear in front of the houses on the pediment drawers, in front of the fences below the waist molding, and in front of the figure on a japanned mirror that scholars believe Pickman bought at the same time as the high chest all make this clear (figs. 11, 12). These lines match those that engravers used to depict waves in period views of Boston, such as William Burgis's 1743 view of the city from the southeast

Figure 13 William Burgis, *South East View of the Great Town of Boston*, Boston, Massachusetts, 1743. 9⅞" x 20⅞". (Courtesy, American Antiquarian Society.)

(fig. 13). The position of these lines in the foreground of the high chest's landscapes indicates that there is water in front of the coast, and thus that it is viewed from the sea. The images on other pieces of japanned furniture sometimes signal this perspective more explicitly. One high chest from the 1730s, for example, shows a boat sailing in front of a rocky coastline, indicating unambiguously that the view is from the water (figs. 14, 15). Similar boats cruise past the landscapes depicted on several other contemporaneous English chests.[12]

Pickman's high chest thus represents the same region of the world that the sea narratives describe, and it does so from a similar ship's-eye point of view. Despite these similarities, the Pickman chest and the sea narratives differ in one important way. Because the sea narratives are characterized by a strong authorial presence in their prose and illustrations, the reader of works such as *A New Voyage Round the World* is always at a remove from the discovered coast. Dampier consistently writes in the first person: "I shall now add this account," "I will share my observations," and the illustrations often show the author in the act of encountering the things he writes about, as opposed to just showing what he encountered. In many of the images of the Asian coast in Nieuhof's *Embassy from the East-India Company*, for example, the author's ship, shown as such by its Western design and Dutch flag,

Figure 14 High chest of drawers, Boston, Massachusetts, 1730–1740. White pine and maple with white pine. H. 95¾", W. 42", D. 24½". (Courtesy, Winterthur Museum.)

Figure 15 Detail of the decoration on a drawer from the upper case of the high chest illustrated in fig. 14.

Figure 16 View of "HEYTAMON" from Johan Nieuhof, *Embassy from the East-India Company, of the United Provinces, to the Grand Tartar Cham, Emperor of China,* . . . . (London, 1673). (Courtesy, Beinecke Rare Book and Manuscript Library, Yale University.)

presides in the foreground (fig. 16). These marks of the author make the reader very aware that he is reading about the explorer's adventures and learning about the exotic coast through the explorer's mediating eyes. Daniel Defoe makes this clear in his unfinished 1731 work *The Compleat English Gentleman,* in which he writes that *A New Voyage Round the World* invites the reader "to go round the globe *with* Dampier" (my emphasis). To read a sea narrative, then, is to experience exotic places but to do so only secondhand, with the author as a filter and a guide.[13]

On the japanned surface, in contrast, there are no obvious signs of authorial presence. The images on the high chest match the coasts that the sea narratives describe and they match the point of view that the authors had of those coasts, but they do so without depicting the Western ship that marks the presence of the author-explorer. As a result, the viewer has the illusion of an unmediated, "first-person" experience of exploration and discovery. With the right amount of imaginative engagement, a viewer can assume the captain's place in the "canoa" and experience the coast firsthand. Ultimately, she or he can observe and come to know the coastline on the chest's surface just as Dampier came to know the coast of China.

This is the sense in which the images on the surface of the high chest tell a story. This story chronicles the reader's own exploration and discovery of the exotic coastline. The japanner actually arranged the images to imply the progress of an explorer: the ship's-eye view is that of a gradually approaching vessel. At the top of the high chest, the "ship" is only close enough to allow the viewer to see buildings; as it "sails in closer" in the middle drawers, figures become visible; and, finally, on the drawer above the molding, it retreats to a point from which once again only buildings are visible. To paraphrase Defoe, then, the viewer of the high chest does not go round the world *with* Dampier, he goes *as* Dampier himself.

Two pieces of evidence solidify this interpretation. The first is the *Treatise on Japanning and Varnishing*. Authors Parker and Stalker conclude their discussion of japanning by describing the opportunity for a firsthand experience of exploration as one of the primary attractions of their style: "I had rather see an embassy thus in miniature than go to China that I might really behold one." The authors refer to the experience of exploration in other passages as well. They advise the viewer of the japanned surface to expect a "Terra incognita and undiscovered provinces," and they salt their volume with nautical metaphors. The process of placing ornament on the surface is like that of "a ship that ploughs and divides the sea, makes a channel in an instant, but as it sails off, the waters return"; the process of following the plates they lay out for japanners to copy is like "sailing between this scylla and charybdis, passing the rock on one hand, the gulph on the other." These references are important both because they shed light on the meaning of the Pickman chest and because they suggest that other pieces of japanned furniture likewise present sea narratives.[14]

The second piece of evidence that buttresses this interpretation specifically concerns Pickman's high chest. The japanner arranged its images in a manner that calls to mind the site in which the sea narratives were originally presented, the printed page. The left-to-right and top-to-bottom linear sequence (created by the repetition of the form at each drawer's right edge on the left edge of the drawer below, as described above) makes each drawer function like a line of text that is interrupted at the right margin but that resumes on the left-hand side of the line below. The cherub heads placed around the pediment also resemble a type of decoration common in early-eighteenth-century books. Engravers, including Thomas Johnston, the Boston craftsman thought to have japanned the Pickman chest, placed similar heads at the tops of title pages and at the beginnings of chapters (fig. 17). The heads on the high chest occupy a similar position: stationed at the top

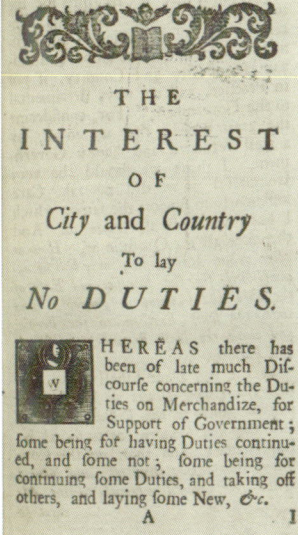

Figure 17   Detail of the opening page of chapter one of The Interest of City and Country to Lay No Duties (New York, 1726). (Courtesy, New York Public Library.)

of the high chest, they call attention to the beginning of a "text" composed of pictures and thus emphasize the way that the surface tells a story.[15]

It is no wonder, then, that Stalker and Parker used words such as "ballad" and "fiction" to describe japanned furniture. For what the viewer, or "reader," of a japanned high chest encountered was not just a visually striking, exotic object but a piece of furniture that told a captivating tale of discovery, one in which the viewer-reader played a starring role.

Audience

Scholars have long associated chinoiserie goods, including japanned furniture, with women. The arguments in one recent book are typical: "In Restoration London," writes historian David Mitchell, "it was in the chambers, dressing rooms and closets of the wives of City merchants . . . that porcelain, japanned furniture and Oriental textiles were most commonly found." Significant historical evidence supports this assertion. Inventories suggest that japanned furniture stood in the women's spaces of the home; treatises directed at amateur japanners have titles—*The Art of Japanning Published at the Request of Several Ladies* and *Ladies Amusement, the Whole Art of Japanning Made Easy*—that propose these practitioners were often female; and, most significantly, period literature connects japanned furniture with women. Alexander Pope, for example, associated japanned decoration with the subject of his 1710 poem "Chloe": "She while her lover pants upon her breast / Can mark the figures on an Indian chest." (Britons and Anglo-Americans used the word "Indian" to refer to all Asian peoples.) Also in 1710, in his "Advice to an Author," the Earl of Shaftesbury sarcastically commented, "Effeminacy pleases me. The Indian figures, the Japan work, the enamel strikes my eye." The feminine connotations of japanned furniture were operative well into the mid-eighteenth century; in 1762 Swedish painter Olof Fridsberg pictured a woman in an interior that featured a japanned chest.[16]

This evidence would seem to suggest that the Pickman chest and others like it were intended for a female audience, and indeed, the literary character of japanned furniture probably added to its appeal for women. Women of the classes that could afford japanned furniture spent significant time reading in the early eighteenth century, and they often acquired and produced domestic goods, such as ceramics and needlepoint, that told stories with pictures. Yet other evidence points to an audience broader than that of the typical chinoiserie object. Close examination of the japanned cabinets and chests indicates that this furniture caters to a decidedly masculine and particularly mercantile sensibility.

The first indicator that the story on the Pickman chest caters specifically to men is the fact that it positions the viewer in a role with which (male) merchants were especially familiar. Though any member of an English or American household could probably imagine him- or herself as an explorer viewing a coast from the deck of a ship, the merchant could assume this position quite literally, for many such men had firsthand familiarity with the explorer's perspective. Early in their careers, they had often sailed on ships as captains or as travelers and had seen the coast from a similar point of view. Merchants who did not have this experience also were adept at assuming the deck-of-the-ship perspective. As owners of and investors in trading ships, they spent time planning the courses of sea voyages. Many of the maps they were likely to have consulted in this process portrayed coastlines from the sea and thus habituated the merchant to the captain's position.[18]

The deck-of-the-ship perspective that the japanners adopted also asks the viewer to assume a role that male merchants particularly, even feverishly, desired: that of explorer. Many of the merchants portrayed in the era's new realistic novels and plays fantasize about exploring distant shores. Robinson Crusoe, son of a merchant in Defoe's 1719 story, is distracted by his wish "to see the world"; Lemuel Gulliver from Jonathan Swift's story of 1726 has an "insatiable desire to see foreign lands"; and George Barnwell, the aspiring merchant in George Lillo's 1731 play *The London Merchant*, speaks of "quit[ting] his ease and trust[ing] to rocks and sands and stormy seas; in hopes [of] some unknown golden coast to find." Exploration appealed to these merchants not only because of the prospect of encountering exotic places but also for the opportunity to discover new markets in which to buy and sell goods, and, ultimately, from which to grow rich. Thus, the merchants in Lillo's play describe "the populous east, luxuriant" that "abounds with glittering gems, bright pearls," while Gulliver, who eventually submits to his desires and sails to a coastline populated by miniature figures like those on the japanned surface, likewise emphasizes the "commerce" and the "marketplace" in the places he discovers.[19]

The japanned story invites its reader to fulfill these fantasies of what one might call commercial discovery. For it not only offers the reader an experience of exotic peoples and animals, but it also gives him the chance to encounter a range of commercial opportunities. Though Pickman's chest makes no direct allusions to commerce, other japanned high chests show figures selling goods, signaling that the coast is ready to trade. On one high chest built in Boston in the 1720s, for example, japanned figures stand around a table that displays the kind of porcelain wares—teapots, bowls, and pitchers—that the English actually brought back from China (figs. 18, 19). On a more basic level, the gold colors of the japanned surface emphasize that the coastline is a place so wealthy, as the nameless author of *The Pleasant and Profitable Companion* wrote of China in 1733, that "all the bridges, doors, Gates, tops of the windows . . . and all the roofs of the houses were cover'd with Plates of gold."[20]

The implied masculine audience for the high chests is not only a matter of the way these objects appealed to merchants' daydreams of exploration and wealth. These objects also affirmed and effectively taught their viewers what merchants, in their professional role as traders, viewed as the proper way to approach material objects. The many treatises written while japanning was at the height of fashion to educate aspiring and practicing merchants counseled their readers to observe and build a comprehensive knowledge of the objects they exchanged. In 1734 English author Edward Hatton opened his treatise *The Merchant's Magazine* by noting that the merchant had to have "clear notions" of "the quality of the most material and best commodities." Lewes Roberts treated this subject more extensively in his book *The Merchant's Map of Commerce,* published in its fourth edition in 1700. This work, intended for the edification of "all merchants . . . in any part of the habitable world," devotes an entire chapter to the importance of the merchant's knowledge of "commodities in general." Roberts writes, "a principal part of [being a merchant] is to know and learn" commodities. He must have "unlimited knowledge" of them and "have a generall inspection in every part and member of them," from their "colours" to their "goodnesses, substance, vertue, taste, seeing, or feeling." This knowledge, Roberts notes, "is best gotten by often viewing the same, and heedfully marking the qualitie and properties thereof."[21]

Figure 18 High chest of drawers, Boston, Massachusetts, 1710–1720. White pine and maple with white pine. H. 61", W. 40¼", D. 22". (Chipstone Foundation; photo, Gavin Ashworth.)

The story on the japanned surface invites its reader to approach a material object in precisely this manner. For insofar as it asks a viewer to consider a piece of furniture from the point of view of an explorer, it puts him in a position from which he is expected to closely observe and "heedfully mark" all of the properties of the object. Certain period writings actually allude to the benefits of viewing commodities with a captain's careful eye. For example, Swift's 1730 poem "The Lady's Dressing Room" details Strephon's exploration of his lover's dressing room and his "strict survey" of the objects in this space, which included a chest. This "survey," a kind of looking characteristic of sea narrative explorers, reveals that the chest is not quite what it seems. As Strephon "ventur'd" to consider the chest, he realized that though it looked like an expensive cabinet with drawers that opened from

Figure 19   Detail of the decoration on the upper case of the high chest illustrated in fig. 18. (Photo, Gavin Ashworth.)

the front, it was in fact a less expensive chest whose top opened up: "In vain, the Workman shew'd his wit / With Rings and Hinges counterfeit / To make it seem in this Disguise, / A Cabinet to vulgar Eyes." By inviting the viewer to "survey" and "venture" through a real object, the japanned story thematizes the close looking that Swift describes.[22]

The japanned narrative instructs its reader in the proper way to look at an object in another respect, too. Roberts writes that the close observation and knowledge of the commodity had a single objective:

> Neither yet must his knowledge rest it selfe here upon the consideration of the meere goodnesse of commodities, but must also extend it selfe to the consideration of the true worth and value thereof . . . their maine scope and aime should be to make this knowledge and skill profitable and beneficiall unto them.

To move from "knowledge" to "value" and thus to profit, a merchant needed to make a deduction: he had to translate the "goodness" of the commodity into a monetary price. The japanned story calls for its reader to execute just this kind of conversion. Insofar as it caters to the merchant's fantasies of commercial discovery, it invites him to extrapolate his observations about the coast into an assessment of its value.[23]

Despite the imaginative engagement it invites, the japanned story ultimately imparts a very practical lesson. With every "sail" past the japanned coast, the viewer is subtly reminded of the proper way to engage with a commodity. An object such as a high chest or cabinet was a particularly appropriate means by which to convey such a reminder. As a permanent fixture in the home, it constantly broadcast its lessons. Moreover, furniture was itself a traded commodity in the early eighteenth century. Chairs and sometimes chests were actively exchanged between Boston and London and other colonial ports. The kind of looking that japanning encouraged was thus especially relevant to the type of object it ornamented.[24]

One is thus led to question or at least to qualify the nature of the audience typically associated with japanned furniture. Though women no doubt "read" these literary objects, most japanned high chests and cabinets catered to a masculine, mercantile sensibility. These objects brought the imaginative life and perceptive modes of the countinghouses into the home.

ACKNOWLEDGMENTS

For their valuable insights and assistance, the author thanks Dennis Carr, Edward S. Cooke Jr., Karina Corrigan, Carma Gorman, Jennifer Raab, Jessica Roth, and the American Art Reading Group at Yale University. Particular thanks are also owed to David Raizman for his enthusiasm and encouragement. A version of this essay was first published in David Raizman and Carma Gorman, eds., *Objects, Audiences and Literatures: Alternative Narratives in the History of Design* (Cambridge: Cambridge Scholars Press, 2007). The author thanks Cambridge Scholars Press for granting permission to reprint the article.

1. For interpretations of literature, see Bill Brown, *A Sense of Things: The Object Matter of American Literature* (Chicago: University of Chicago Press, 2003) and *Things,* edited by Bill Brown (Chicago: University of Chicago Press, 2004). The high chest of drawers was principally a Boston form. The cabinet-on-stand was principally a London form. However, examples of each object existed in both Boston and London. See Benno Forman, "The Chest of Drawers in America, 1635–1730: The Origins of the Joined Chest of Drawers," *Winterthur Portfolio* 20 (spring 1985): 1–30. For images of the two types of objects, see John Kirk, *American Furniture and the British Tradition to 1830* (New York: Knopf, 1982). Often the cabinets-on-stands had doors. My arguments, however, concern the decorated surfaces behind these doors. For lacquerware examples, see Hans Huth, *Lacquer of the West: The History of a Craft and an Industry, 1550–1950* (Chicago: University of Chicago Press, 1971); and Adam Bowett, *English Furniture, 1660–1714: From Charles II to Queen Anne* (London: Antique Collectors' Club, 2002). Most japanned objects with known provenances are associated with wealthy merchant families in Boston and London. For London, see David Mitchell, "A Passion for the Exotic," in *City Merchants and the Arts, 1670–1720,* edited by Mirelle Galinou (London: Oblong, 2004), pp. 72–82. For Boston, see Phyllis Hunter, *Purchasing Identity in the Atlantic World: Massachusetts Merchants, 1670–1780* (Ithaca, N.Y.: Cornell University Press, 2001), pp. 117–18; and Dean Fales, "Boston Japanned Furniture," in *Boston Furniture of the Eighteenth Century,*

edited by Walter Whitehill (Boston: Colonial Society of Massachusetts, 1972), pp. 49–71. Fales lists many of the merchant families that owned japanned objects in Boston, including the Governor James Bowdoin family, the Captain Joshua Loring family, and the Benjamin Pickman family. On the period of japanning's fashion, see Huth, *Lacquer of the West*, pp. 36–51.

2. Many of these objects are discussed in Fales, "Boston Japanned Furniture," pp. 49–71; Huth, *Lacquer of the West*, pp. 36–41; and Bowett, *English Furniture*, pp. 144 69. The Boston high chest is discussed in Morrison Heckscher, *American Furniture in the Metropolitan Museum of Art, Late Colonial Period: The Queen Anne and Chippendale Styles* (New York: Random House, 1985), pp. 241–43; the condition of the object is discussed in Morrison H. Heckscher and Frances G. Safford, "Boston Japanned Furniture in the Metropolitan Museum of Art," *Antiques* 129, no. 5 (May 1986): 1049. Heckscher dates the high chest to 1730–1750. I have narrowed his date to a shorter, decadelong period for three reasons. First, several similar high chests from Boston have been dated to this decade; second, the likely japanner of the high chest, Thomas Johnston, was particularly active in this decade (for more on Johnston, see Heckscher, *American Furniture in the Metropolitan Museum of Art*, p. 240; and Elizabeth Rhoades and Brock Jobe, "Recent Discoveries in Boston Japanned Furniture," *Antiques* 105, no. 5 [May 1974]: 1082–91); and third, Benjamin Pickman, the original owner, was married in 1731, and high chests were often presented as wedding gifts. The case for this object as exemplary is made throughout this essay; I consistently show how my arguments about Pickman's high chest apply to japanned furniture more broadly. Japanned furniture is well suited to this kind of case-study approach because its ornament is so consistent. Though individual objects were made by different hands, the surfaces of the objects, as Bowett writes, "varied little over the period" when they were in fashion (Bowett, *English Furniture*, p. 162).

3. This provenance follows from a family history. See Heckscher, *American Furniture in the Metropolitan Museum of Art*, p. 240. Pickman traded in barrels, wood, codfish, vinegar, and rum. See James Phillips, *Salem in the Eighteenth Century* (Boston: Houghton Mifflin Company, 1937), pp. 244–56; and *The Diary and Letters of Benjamin Pickman (1740–1819) of Salem, Massachusetts with a Biographical and Genealogical Sketch of the Pickman Family*, edited by George Francis Dow (Newport, R.I., 1928).

4. For process, see John Hill, "The History and Technique of Japanning and the Restoration of the Pimm Highboy," *American Art Journal* 8 (November 1976): 59–84; R. W. Symonds, "The Craft of Japanning," *Antique Collector*, September–October 1947, 149–54; R. W. Symonds, "The Craft of Japanning, Part II," *Antique Collector*, November–December 1947, 183–89. For museums and private collections, see Bowett, *English Furniture*; Fales, "Boston Japanned Furniture"; J. Michael Flanigan, *American Furniture from the Kaufman Collection* (Washington, D.C.: National Gallery of Art, 1986), pp. 50–53; Heckscher and Safford, "Boston Japanned Furniture"; Huth, *Lacquer of the West*; Danielle Kisluk-Grosheide, "A Japanned Cabinet in the Metropolitan Museum of Art," *Metropolitan Museum Journal* 19–20 (1984–1985): 85–95; Rhoades and Jobe, "Recent Discoveries"; Nancy Richards and Nancy Goyne Evans, *New England Furniture at Winterthur: Queen Anne and Chippendale Periods* (Winterthur, Del.: Winterthur Museum, 1997), 304–9; and David Warren, *American Decorative Arts and Paintings in the Bayou Bend Collection* (Houston: Museum of Fine Arts, Houston, 1998), pp. 44–46. For attributions, see Rhoades and Jobe, "Recent Discoveries"; Richard Randall, "William Randall, Boston Japanner," *Antiques* 105, no. 5 (May 1974): 1127–31; and Skinner, *American Furniture and Decorative Arts*, Boston, Massachusetts, November 7, 2004, lot 230. A design book created by Boston japanner Jean Berger is reproduced in Robert Leath, "Jean Berger's Design Book: Huguenot Tradesmen and the Dissemination of the French Baroque Style," in *American Furniture*, edited by Luke Beckerdite (Hanover, N.H.: University Press of New England for the Chipstone Foundation, 1994), pp. 137–62. For Johnston, see Heckscher, *American Furniture in the Metropolitan Museum of Art*, p. 240. For a discussion of Johnston and other Boston japanners, see Rhoades and Jobe, "Recent Discoveries." For japanning and social status, see Hunter, *Purchasing Identity*, pp. 117–18. For japanning and the taste for chinoiserie, see Hugh Honour, *Chinoiserie: The Vision of Cathay* (New York: Harper & Row, 1961), pp. 64–67; and Oliver Impey, *Chinoiserie: The Impact of Oriental Styles on Western Art and Decoration* (New York: Charles Scribner's Sons, 1977), pp. 111–29.

5. John Stalker and George Parker, *A Treatise of Japanning and Varnishing* (Oxford: printed for the authors, 1688), Epistle 25. For a discussion of the continued use of this publication in the eighteenth century, see Hill, "The History and Technique of Japanning and Restoration of the Pimm Highboy," p. 61. Stalker and Parker, *Treatise*, preface, pp. 9, 29.

6. Mieke Bal, *Narratology* (Toronto: University of Toronto Press, 2002). For vases, see Ronald Fuchs, *Made in China: Export Porcelain from the Leo and Doris Hodroff Collection at Winterthur* (Hanover, N.H.: University of New England Press, 2005), p. 169. For plates, see Kee Il Choi, "Hong Bowls and the Landscape of the China Trade," *Antiques* 156, no. 4 (October 1999): 500–509. For panels, see Mary Brooks, *English Embroideries of the Sixteenth and Seventeenth Centuries in the Collection of the Ashmolean Museum* (Oxford: Ashmolean Museum, 2004), p. 12.

7. Philip Edwards, *The Story of the Voyage: Sea Narratives in Eighteenth-Century England* (Cambridge: Cambridge University Press, 1994), pp. 2–3. English writer the Earl of Shaftesbury identified these "wonders of the terra incognita" as the "chief material to furnish out a library." See his *Soliloquy or Advice to an Author* (London, 1710), p. 178. William Dampier, author of *A New Voyage Round the World*, one of the most widely read sea narratives, even conceded that he chose "to be more particular than may have been needful." William Dampier, *A New Voyage Round the World* (1697; reprint, London: Argonaut Press, 1927), p. 3. Leslie Grigsby, "Johan Nieuhof's *Embassy*: Inspiration for Relief Decoration on English Stoneware and Earthenware," *Antiques* 143, no. 6 (January 1993): 173–83. Carl Dauterman, "Dream Pictures of Cathay: Chinoiserie on Restoration Silver," *Metropolitan Museum of Art Bulletin* 23, no. 1 (summer 1964): 11–25. Both Grigsby and Dauterman focus on the connections between English objects and one specific book: Nieuhof's *Embassy from the East-India Company*. This volume is discussed in greater detail below. Dauterman also speculates about connections between early chinoiserie and the theater.

8. Johan Nieuhof, *An Embassy from the East-India Company, of the United Provinces, to the Grand Tartar Cham, Emperor of China . . .*, translated by John Ogilby, 2nd ed. (London, 1673). This volume was originally published in Dutch in 1665.

9. Dampier, *New Voyage*, p. 275. For the reception of Dampier in London, see Diane Preston and Michael Preston, *A Pirate of Exquisite Mind: The Life of William Dampier* (New York: Walker and Company, 2004), p. 242; in Boston, see "From the Magazine," *Boston Gazette*, September 11–18, 1738.

10. Dampier, *New Voyage*, p. 275.

11. Ibid., p. 309. This is also true of the two figures below the waist molding that are not shown in this illustration.

12. One also wonders if the japanner was familiar with Asian handscrolls, since the continuous structure and proportions of the bands of imagery on the high chest evoke these objects.

13. Dampier, *New Voyage*, p. 275. Heckscher discusses the mirror illustrated in figure 11 in *American Furniture in the Metropolitan Museum of Art*, p. 328. For a similar coastline, see the boat placed centrally on the London cabinet-on-stand illustrated in Huth, *Lacquer of the West*, pl. 55.

14. Dampier, *New Voyage*, p. 3. Daniel Defoe, *The Compleat English Gentleman* (London: D. Nutt, 1890), p. 225.

15. Parker and Stalker, *Treatise*, pp. 50, 40–42. For other japanned pieces that appear to present sea narratives, see the objects illustrated in David Dewey, *The Geffrey Museum: A Brief Guide* (London: Geffrey Museum Trust, 1998), p. 16; Fales, "Boston Japanned Furniture," pp. 55, 58; Flanigan, *American Furniture from the Kaufman Collection*, p. 50; Heckscher, *American Furniture in the Metropolitan Museum*, p. 238; Honour, *Chinoiserie*, pls. 30 and 31; Huth, *Lacquer of the West*, pls. 55, 59, 60, 90, 92; Brock Jobe and Myrna Kaye, *New England Furniture: The Colonial Era* (Boston: Houghton Mifflin, 1984), p. 197; and Richards and Evans, *New England Furniture at Winterthur*, pp. 305–7. As these illustrations suggest, and as mentioned in note 2, in the case of cabinets, the narrative images appear on the cabinet's interior drawers, behind the doors.

16. Cherub heads also have a precedent in furniture design in that similar heads occasionally appear in the carved stands of English lacquered cabinets. See Bowett, *English Furniture*, p. 156. The connections between the Pickman chest and the printed page support the chest's attribution to Thomas Johnston. Johnston had an established connection to the Boston book industry. He engraved trade cards for Boston bookseller Thomas Hancock and Boston bookbinder Andrew Barclay that feature cherub heads above lines of text. The trade cards are illustrated in Sinclair Hitchings, "Thomas Johnston," in *Boston Prints and Printmakers*, edited by Walter Whitehill (Boston: Colonial Society of Massachusetts, 1973), pp. 86, 118–19. There are also established connections between the bookmaking and japanning industries in London. John Baskerville, the important Birmingham type founder, trained as a japanner early in his career, in the 1720s. John Dreyfus, "The Baskerville Punches, 1750–1950," in Dreyfus, *Into*

Print: Selected Writings on Printing History, Typography and Book Production (London: British Library, 1994), p. 13. The author thanks David Raizman for this reference. In addition to its front, the sides of the high chest also emphasize the surface's storytelling function. They loosely resemble bookbindings and therefore evoke a part of another material object that presents stories. As noted earlier, the two sides of the high chest feature identical images of a house and tree placed within painted rectangular frames. While this composition has parallels in Asian lacquerware, it also resembles high-style eighteenth-century bindings, which often include similar ornamental "centerpieces," set, as their name suggests, in the center of rectangular frames. For a specific binding that the sides of the high chest resemble, see David Pearson, *English Bookbinding Styles, 1450–1800* (New Castle, Del.: Oak Knoll, 2005), p. 74, fig. 3.75. Insofar as the front of the high chest resembles a printed page and the two sides loosely resemble bindings, the entire object could be said to represent a book, with its two covers opened to reveal a page of text.

17. Mitchell, "A Passion for the Exotic," p. 82. For another recent work that connects chinoiserie with women, see David Porter, "Monstrous Beauty: Eighteenth-Century Fashion and the Aesthetics of the Chinese Taste," *Eighteenth Century Studies* 35 (2002): 395–411. Pope and Shaftesbury, as quoted in Honour, *Chinoiserie*, p. 81. The Fridsberg painting is illustrated in Peter Thornton, *Authentic Décor: The Domestic Interior, 1620–1920* (London: Seven Dials, 2000), p. 128.

18. On women and reading, see John Brewer, *The Pleasures of the Imagination: English Culture in the Eighteenth Century* (New York: Harper Collins, 1997), p. 193. On women as the creators of narrative objects, see Brooks, *English Embroideries in the Ashmolean Museum*, p. 12.

19. David Hancock, *Citizens of the World: London Merchants and the Integration of the British Atlantic Community* (Cambridge: Cambridge University Press, 1995), p. 41. Pickman came from a family of ship captains and he himself traveled to Canada during the period when he owned the high chest (Phillips, *History of Salem*, p. 210). For the merchants' use of coastline maps, see Hancock, *Citizens of the World*, p. 34. Historian Catherine Delano-Smith has also discussed the way that cartographers made maps for merchant companies such as the East India Company; see Catherine Delano-Smith, *English Maps: A History* (London: British Library, 1999), p. 156.

20. Daniel Defoe, *Robinson Crusoe* (1731; reprint, New York: Tor, 1989), p. 5. Jonathan Swift, *Gulliver's Travels* (1726; reprint, New York: Putnam, 1999), p. 74. George Lillo, *The London Merchant* (1731; reprint, Lincoln: University of Nebraska Press), pp. 24, 34. Swift, *Gulliver's Travels*, p. 87. The connections between Lilliput and the japanned coast are more than a matter of scale. The Lilliputians also look like the japanned figures: their dress is "plain and simple, and the fashion of it between the *Asiatic and the European; but he had on his head a light helmet of gold adorned with jewels,* and a plume on the crest. . . . The ladies and courtiers were all most magnificently clad, so that the spot they stood upon seemed to resemble a petticoat spread on the ground, embroidered with *figures of gold and silver,*" pp. 19–20 (my emphasis). This connection is not coincidental: Swift owned a japanned cabinet. The fact that he wrote a story about discovery that concerns figures like the ones on this cabinet buttresses my readings of the japanned narrative and generally opens up new possibilities for thinking about the role of furniture in *Gulliver's Travels*. For Swift's cabinet, see Victoria Glendinning, *Jonathan Swift* (London: Hutchinson, 1998), p. 138.

21. *The Pleasant and Profitable Companion: Being a Collection of Ingenious and Diverting Historys; With Suitable Applications or Morals for Instructing the Mind, and Encouraging Virtue* (Boston, 1733), p. 137.

22. Edward Hatton, *The Merchant's Magazine, or, Trades-man's Treasury*, 9th impression, corrected and improved (London, 1734), preface. Lewes Roberts, *The Merchant's Map of Commerce* (London, 1700), pp. 40–45. Jonathan Swift, "The Lady's Dressing Room" (1730), in *Norton Anthology of Poetry*, edited by Alexander Allison and Blake Herbert, 3rd ed. (New York: W. W. Norton, 1983), p. 396.

23. Roberts, *Merchant's Map*, p. 43. Historian Joyce Appleby discusses the need for this kind of conversion in *Economic Thought and Ideology in Seventeenth Century England* (Princeton: Princeton University Press, 1977), p. 201.

24. In the longer discussion of japanned furniture that I present in my dissertation, I argue that the way that japanning made furniture into something to explore or know had more than just an instructional purpose. It also radically changed the position that furniture maintained relative to its owner. In the seventeenth century and earlier, Anglo-Americans conceived of furniture as an almost sentient entity that, though material, possessed certain subject capacities

over and above its materiality, including the capacity to know and understand like a person. Japanning, by making furniture something to *be* known, reversed this traditional position, making furniture an object rather than a subject. This shift is symptomatic of the new Cartesian conception of the object that emerged in the early eighteenth century. See Ethan Lasser, "Figures in the Grain: The Enlightenment of Anglo-American Furniture, 1660–1800" (Ph.D. diss., Yale University, 2007). For furniture exports from London, see Bowett, *English Furniture,* p. 31. For furniture exports from London to Boston specifically, see Jobe and Kaye, *New England Furniture,* p. 19. For furniture exported from Boston, see Leigh Keno, "'The Very Pink of the Mode': Boston Georgian Chairs, Their Export and Their Influence," in *American Furniture,* edited by Luke Beckerdite (Hanover, N.H.: University Press of New England for the Chipstone Foundation, 1996), pp. 266–306.

Nancy Goyne Evans

The Written Evidence of Furniture Repairs and Alterations: How Original Is "All Original"?

▼ NEW FURNITURE CONSTITUTED only part of the output of the typical furniture craftsman in the late colonial and federal periods. Another mainstay of business and the focus of this article and its sequel was the repair of furniture already in use. Forming the basis of this analytical study is a sizable body of material describing period repair work, as gleaned from a database of more than 250 original documents, varying from craftsmen's accounts to clients' business records. The geographic range of the documents is broad, extending from Maine to Georgia, with major emphasis centering on Massachusetts, Connecticut, New York, and Pennsylvania. Eighty-three percent of the documentation dates between the Revolution and the mid-nineteenth century. Based on document date and origin, the material falls into three arbitrary groups, reflecting varying economies. Primary urban locations represent 46 percent of the sample; rural and semirural areas account for another 35 percent; and secondary urban locations make up the remaining 19 percent of the total. Craftsmen working in secondary urban locations often were subject to the cross-economic influences of the rural region surrounding them and the trading economy at their elbows.

As many historians have learned, the study and interpretation of period documents is rarely straightforward. Entries in craftsmen's accounts typically are brief and bereft of descriptive embellishment. More information is left unrecorded than noted, and ambiguities are common. Multiple terms often apply to the same task or object. In this study, for instance, the words "mend," "repair," and "fix" appear to have had the same meaning, and craftsmen often used them interchangeably, even in a single document. If nuances of meaning actually existed, they are subtle.

For clarity and ease of discussion, the large body of information documenting furniture repairs and alterations consulted for this study has been divided into seven main categories and further subdivided, as appropriate. Seating furniture makes up the largest group, followed by tables and case furniture. More modest in number are references to bedsteads, children's furniture, and looking glasses, in that order. Somewhat of a surprise is the notable body of material dealing with dozens of miscellaneous household and personal items that includes objects as diverse as teapot handles and musical instruments.

To better manage the length and complexity of this study, the text will be presented in two parts. Complementing the relatively simple frames of the seating furniture, bedsteads, and tables that form part 1 will be the complex cases of the desks, chests, and cupboards forming part 2 (forthcoming 2008), augmented by looking glasses and the wealth of miscellaneous items associated with everyday life two hundred and more years ago.

Chairs

Craftsmen's records of repairs made to chairs and other furniture forms are primarily general in nature, often identifying neither the specific details of the work undertaken nor the particular style of the furniture. Insights may be gleaned, however, from the small number of account entries that contain more than basic descriptive information and by making cost comparisons. The majority of recorded chair repairs focuses on vernacular seating. In describing this activity, craftsmen employed the term "mend" three times as often as "repair." Other terms include "fix" and "work on" or "work at" a specific object or furniture group. In dealing with damaged vernacular chairs, craftsmen appear to have replaced parts more commonly than they repaired them.

The front runner in chair repairs was seat "bottoming," a process also known as "matting" and "seating." Until the introduction of the plank-seat Windsor chair in the mid-eighteenth century, most chairs had seats of woven plant material. The common choice was "rush," also called "flag," a plant (genus *Juncus*) with pith-filled stems that grows in marshes or near water. Craftsmen made frequent note in their accounts of the acquisition of "bunches" or "bundles" of flags.

Amos Denison Allen of South Windham, Connecticut, bottomed "6 fidlebackd Chairs" for a customer in 1798 at a charge of 1s. 6d. apiece. In the new decimal-based currency of the nation, this was equivalent to 25¢ per chair. Craftsmen working in prosperous regions of the country in the 1790s could expect to earn at least 6s. ($1.00) a day at their trade, suggesting that one-quarter of a day was required to replace each chair seat in Allen's order. John and Samuel Durand Jr., father and son, also made and repaired fiddle-back chairs along the Connecticut coast at Milford in the late eighteenth century (fig. 1).[1]

With few exceptions, bottoming a chair with rush required no further explanation in craftsmen's accounts. When Daniel and Samuel Proud of Providence, Rhode Island, wove a seat bottom for 34¢ in 1818, they also repaired the chair with a new "side list." A list is a seat framing member, one of four, concealed by the rush (see fig. 1). On another occasion the Proud brothers were engaged to provide rushwork of a quality above standard weaving. The tightly twisted "fine" seat they wove cost the customer 50¢. Some years earlier Thomas Moody supplied Captain Edmund Kimball of Newburyport, Massachusetts, with fine rush bottoms for two chairs, along with a "Coars" bottom for another seat. "Superior work" was another term for a fine seat. John Proud of Providence charged a substantial 66¢ for this work in 1824, although the seat may have been of large size.[2]

When Elizur Barnes, a cabinetmaker of Middletown, Connecticut, undertook to refurbish eight vernacular chairs for Arthur Magill in 1822, the painted and decorated fancy chair had achieved prominence. Its rush bot-

Figure 1 Side chair possibly by John Durand (1735–1780), Samuel Durand I (1738–1829), or Samuel Durand Jr. (1762–1838), probably Milford, Connecticut, 1760–1790. Maple and hickory; rush. H. 41 3/4", W. 19 1/8", D. 14 1/4". (Courtesy, Winterthur Museum.)

tom was no less vulnerable to wear and tear, however, than those of its fiddle-back, slat-back, and banister-back predecessors. To address this problem, householders could elect to have their woven chair seats coated with varnish or paint, which, as described by Thomas Sheraton in his *Cabinet Dictionary* (1803), "preserves the rushes, and hardens them." Magill chose yellow paint for his chair seats and further engaged Barnes to paint and varnish the chairs' wooden surfaces.[3]

Aside from rush, consumers could choose from several other seating materials, although none was substantially more popular than any other. At

Providence, William Barker described a cheaper substitute for rush when he billed a customer 1s. 4d. for a "Straw matt," the price being 2d. less than his rush bottoms. Splint was another option. Harvested from the inner bark of trees, frequently the hickory tree, the material also was used in basketwork. Stephen Whipple, who worked in the Boston area in 1805, recorded a job of "bottoming 3 chairs, 2 of them with bark & the other with flags." Chairmaker Simon Perkins of Weare, New Hampshire, was more specific when he noted that he had bottomed chairs with "elm bark." The basketweave pattern of splint was described by Solomon Fussell, a chairmaker active at Philadelphia in the 1740s, when he recorded matting three chairs with "Checkt bottoms." One drawback of splint seats was their tendency to damage the clothing of the sitter. A rarity in craftsmen's accounts is the activity recorded by Thomas Boynton at Windsor, Vermont, in 1816: "Board bottoming 5 chairs" at 9d. apiece, or 63¢ for the lot. These were not the planks used in Windsor chair seats, although on occasion householders who furnished with Windsors might encounter a problem, as suggested by an entry in the accounts of Silas Cheney of Litchfield, Connecticut. In October 1820 Cheney noted that before he could repaint eight chairs he was, of necessity, employed in "giting out nails out of 8 Chairs Chair Seat."[4]

Rockers were the second most common repair or addition to vernacular seating. Even a small sampling of craftsmen's records reveals hundreds of references. Rocking chairs, sometimes called "easy chairs," were in limited use from the second to the fourth quarters of the eighteenth century. After craftsmen introduced rockers to the Windsor in the 1790s, interest began to grow. By the late 1820s the rocking chair had become a household fixture.[5]

Although many chairs entered the market as rockers, many more were converted to that form from any of a variety of vernacular chairs common to most households. In this respect two direct references to replacement rockers on rocking chairs are unusual. Allen Holcomb of New Lisbon, New York, noted that he put "a new Rocker on a rocking chair" in July 1825, followed three years later by Chapman Lee of Charlton, Massachusetts, who recorded a job of "putting Rockers on [a] Rocking Chair." Still other craftsmen recorded altering or repairing rockers already in place. Chairs chosen by householders for conversion to rockers were at times in need of repair. A replacement foot and stretchers refurbished a chair in 1819 to which George Landon of Erie, Pennsylvania, added rockers. Arms also were vulnerable to damage from sitters using them to support too much weight as they sat or rose from chairs. When Daniel Ford of Plainfield, Massachusetts, had new arms made for a chair in 1807, he also directed Samuel Davison to add rockers and paint the chair. Some insights into the types of chairs converted from stationary to rocking form appear in the accounts of True Currier of Deerfield, New Hampshire. In 1824 he recorded that he had made "rockers and *slats* for chairs." A year later the same customer requested the craftsman to make "a bow & rockers" for a Windsor chair.[6]

On occasion, craftsmen modified chair feet for purposes other than installing rockers. Titus Preston of Wallingford, Connecticut, completed a job for a customer in 1805 by "puting 2 rounds to a chair & sawing it lower."

At Albany, New York, in the same year James Chestney accommodated Peter E. Elmendorf by "cutting off and bottoming 2 Cottage chairs." Chestney then painted the chairs and ornamented the surfaces with fine lines, or "penciling."[7]

As stated previously, furniture makers appear to have replaced damaged parts in vernacular chairs more often than they repaired them. Records identify replacement work in a range of chair styles: fiddle backs; banister backs; Windsors, also known as dining chairs; kitchen, or slat-backs; and fancy chairs, some in the Grecian style. The terms "old" and "old fashioned" occur with regularity. Rounds, or stretchers, suffered the greatest number of mishaps because these low braces were a convenient place for the sitter to park his feet. Vulnerable to a lesser degree were arms, or "elbows," legs, also called "feet," crest pieces, and even entire backs. Craftsmen had less call for individual slats, banisters, and "sticks," or spindles. Entries for repairs to great chairs, or armchairs, occur with some regularity, and the Proud family of Providence mended their share. A typical account notation, made in 1782, reads: "To 1 Grate Chair Bottoming, To 1 Top and 4 Banester."[8]

With the introduction of the fancy chair at the close of the eighteenth century, seat casings, or moldings, introduced new concerns for conscientious householders (fig. 2). These thin strips of shaped wood nailed to four sides

Figure 2 Side chair, Baltimore, Maryland, 1820–1830. Maple and yellow poplar; rush. H. 32¾", W. 17½", D. 15½". (Private collection; photo, Winterthur Museum.)

of a rush seat frame were vulnerable to cracking, chipping, and falling off. When a rush seat was replaced, casings were removed then reattached to the new seat, providing another opportunity for these delicate parts to be damaged. David Alling bought chair moldings in quantity from suppliers in and around Newark, New Jersey, where he had an extensive chair business for more than fifty years, beginning circa 1800. When chairs came into the shop for repair, appropriate replacement parts likely were at hand. A typical repair, made in 1836, called for matting and molding a rocking chair and painting the new seat "2 coats," all at a cost of 62¢. Several years later Alling recorded a somewhat extreme repair: "To mending 1 badly broke grecian chair."[9]

Painting ranked with bottoming as a service most requested by householders. As a surface coating, paint was suitable for any type of vernacular chair in the market in the late colonial and federal periods. Samuel J. Tuck, proprietor of a Windsor and fancy chair manufactory at Boston, knew the public mind when he advertised in 1802: "Chairs repaired and painted, to look as good as new."[10]

Little detail accompanies craftsmen's records of repainting chairs. Colors are only occasionally identified. Green and black appear to have been the common choices; other named selections include blue and white. Titus Preston of Wallingford, Connecticut, combined green and black in 1801 when painting a large set of fourteen chairs, probably Windsors, introducing a striking contrast between the seat and the other surfaces. The mahogany-color chairs John Sager painted for a customer in 1808 at Bordentown, New Jersey, likely were of solid color, as grain painting was not introduced to seating furniture until almost a decade later. By the time that David Alling of Newark, New Jersey, repainted a sewing chair in 1836 to resemble curled maple, "imitation" finishes had swept the market.[11]

Craftsmen rarely noted how many new coats of paint they applied to chair surfaces. One coat appears to have been the norm unless special circumstances or the customer dictated otherwise. Silas Cheney recorded instances of painting chairs with two coats and four coats. His work at "Painting 6 chairs twise" for Bettey Shepard at Litchfield, Connecticut, in 1817 cost his customer $2.00, the equivalent of two days' pay for many workmen. Cheney also made note on occasion of scraping, or "Smoothing Out," chair seats before repainting. When work had been completed at a shop, it was customary for a customer to call for his furniture. In a few rare instances craftsmen noted otherwise. Silas Cheney, for example, both "fetched" and carried to a customer eight chairs he painted and ornamented in 1815, charging 33¢ for the service. When James Gere of Groton, Connecticut, mended, painted, and ornamented six Windsor chairs for a customer in 1831, he noted a charge for "Carting home the same" to Preston, a distance of more than fifteen miles.[12]

By the early nineteenth century chairs that received a fresh coat of paint in a woodworker's shop often were ornamented. Descriptions usually end there, however, and the nature of most ornamental work is unknown. A typical record is that of Elizur Barnes, who mended, painted, and ornamented a large rocking chair for 38¢ in 1823 at his shop in Middletown, Connecticut, but who gave no further details. More specific are references to striping, penciling, and tipping. Striping identifies decoration of fine to broad lines used to accent and define chair parts. Penciling and tipping refer specifically to fine lines executed with a small camel's-hair brush known as a "pencil" (fig. 2). Painting and decorating both new and old chairs were often undertaken at David Alling's Newark, New Jersey, manufactory. In 1839 a customer deposited "8 ballback Bamboo," or fancy, chairs, which Alling mended, matted, molded, painted, and striped. The following year another customer paid to have six Windsor chairs painted and tipped. Still other types of ornament are recorded in Alling's accounts. An entry made in 1840 for seating and painting a sewing chair describes the decoration as "gilding & bronzing" (fig. 2). "Bronzing" refers to stenciling, the term derived from the pulverized metallic powders used in the process. Whether painted surfaces were decorated or left plain, a final coat of varnish to protect the finish was common.[13]

A process known in woodworking circles as "coloring" was relatively common as a method of coating chair surfaces, although it did not have the popularity of painting. In coloring wooden surfaces, one or more thin coats of size, made from animal glue diluted with water, were applied to the wood to fill the pores and smooth the surface. Finely ground pigment added to a size coat produced the desired color. Elisha Hawley of Ridgefield, Connecticut, identified the color green in his accounts for 1800. A colored surface could be renewed when necessary by applying another coat of pigmented size. Alternatively, some householders requested a protective coat of varnish to seal the colored surface and protect the finish. Colored size appears to have been most common on the cheapest utilitarian seating, including kitchen chairs, four-slat and five-slat chairs, "old" chairs, low chairs, and rocking chairs, as recorded in period documents.[14]

Within the large body of general, often ambiguous, material relating to seating furniture in craftsmen's accounts is a small core of records relating to structural repairs made to formal seating. Terms such as "hair bottom," "leather," "Joiner," "compass seat" (fig. 3), and "carved" identify some of the chairs. Primary construction woods and circumstantial evidence relative to the cost and nature of the repairs serve to identify other examples. Mahogany, walnut, maple, and cherry are the woods noted, mahogany being named the most frequently. The records also contain references to repairs made to specialized seating: close-stool chairs, easy and lolling chairs, and roundabout chairs.

Deborah Morris, a wealthy Philadelphia Quaker, engaged Richard Johns in 1765 to make and repair household furniture, including "mending ye arms & Legs of a Arm Chair." Johns was a relative newcomer to the woodworking trade, having in 1760 ordered from London through William Wilson, a local merchant, a joiner's chest and an extensive selection of tools. Wilson had instructed his London factor, William Neate, that "all things be of the best and the Chest neatly fitted." A few years later James Brice, Esq., of Annapolis, Maryland, engaged the firm of John Shaw and Archibald

Figure 3 Armchairs, Philadelphia, Pennsylvania, 1730–1750. Walnut. H. 41¼", W. 32¾", D. 21" (chair facing forward). (Courtesy, Winterthur Museum.)

Chisholm for work that included "putting a new top rail on a Mahogany Chair." Repairs made by Silas Cheney in 1807 at Litchfield, Connecticut, for Tapping Reeve included mending and "putting in blocks" in eight chairs. Reeve had arrived in the community in 1772 following graduation from Princeton (then the College of New Jersey) and founded the Litchfield Law School. In Newport, Rhode Island, in the lively household of Dr. Isaac Senter, who with his wife raised five children, furniture repairs were an ongoing need. Senter called on Walter Nichols in 1797 to provide "2 new front posts and [a] front rail to a mahogany chair" at a charge of 9s. Two years earlier Nichols had accommodated the family with a new arm for a mahogany chair.[15]

Anonymous repairs made to chairs identified by their primary wood include work done by notable craftsmen for clients or families of prominence. At Philadelphia in 1769 young Quaker merchant Stephen Collins called on Daniel Drinker to mend two walnut chairs. These may well have been chairs from one or both groups of walnut seating Collins bought from Drinker three years earlier at a cost of 26s. and 33s. 4d. apiece. For both new furniture and repairs Captain Lawrence Taliaferro patronized an unidentified craftsman working in the vicinity of Fredericksburg, Virginia. He is recorded as having paid the cabinetmaker 15s. for "Repairing 6 Chirrie Wood Chairs & Restuffing the Bottoms." Other records focus on unnamed repairs to mahogany chairs. In the mid-1780s both Chancellor Robert R. Livingston of New York and eminent Philadelphia merchant Stephen Girard patronized local craftsmen for repairs to their seating furniture. Thomas Burling mended "9 Mahogany Chairs much Broke" for Livingston. Daniel Trotter repaired a single chair for Girard, although his charge of 17s. 6d. suggests the seating piece was in much the same condition as the chancellor's furniture. Another eminent merchant, Elias Hasket Derby of Salem, Massachusetts, called on the Sanderson brothers, Elijah and Jacob, in 1793 to carry out repairs on six of his mahogany chairs in a period when a contemporary regional craftsman, Stephen Badlam of Dorchester near Boston, accommodated General Henry Knox by mending four carved chairs. Several decades later David Alling of Newark, New Jersey, who is known mainly as a vernacular chairmaker, undertook work for Frederick T. Frelinghuysen Jr., Esq., described as "repairing, varnishing & upholstering" two "old fashioned" mahogany chairs. Alling also fitted one of the chairs with a set of casters.[16]

The accounts of Job Danforth of Providence further detail the installation of chair casters in work undertaken for two clients. In 1803 Stephen Jackson brought a chair to the shop to be cut down and fitted with casters. The same year Elisha Dyer paid for a set of chair casters with screws to be installed. Richard Alexander's work for the Francis family of Philadelphia, although lacking detail, lists one item that is sufficiently unusual in craft records to warrant note. In an account covering numerous repairs to formal furniture, one entry dated May 28, 1820, reads, "To Repairing 7 chairs with Iren Plates."[17]

Surface coating sometimes followed formal furniture repairs. In Connecticut Silas Cheney varnished Tapping Reeve's chairs at his shop in Litchfield after repairing them with new blocks, as noted. Eight mahogany chairs varnished in Elizur Barnes's shop at Middletown were repaired and cleaned before coating. The term "clean" as used here is open to speculation. Did Barnes merely remove surface soil or did he smooth surfaces to eliminate any irregularities in the previous coat? Most surface coating of furniture took place in the woodworker's shop, whether or not repairs were made. References to varnishing furniture at a customer's house are rare, although Philemon Robbins of Hartford, along with Silas Cheney and Elizur Barnes, made note of this activity. The cost of the job likely included travel time, and Cheney also made a special charge for the varnish. Transporting furniture to and from a woodworker's shop for any type of work was the responsibility of the customer. This may be why Duncan Phyfe noted in a lengthy bill to James L. Brinckerhoof, a dry-goods merchant of New York, "Removeing & varnishing 12 chairs" and a "Sofa." The refurbishing may have been prompted by Brinckerhoof's purchase on the same date, September 29, 1815, of a "Set Dining Tables" for the substantial sum of $180.00. In lieu of varnishing furniture, householders could choose merely to have the surfaces polished. Job E. Townsend of Newport, Rhode Island, recorded in the 1790s refurbishing in this manner both black walnut and mahogany chairs.[18]

Information about upholstering seats in formal chairs, also referred to as "covering" or "stuffing" and occasionally as "bottoming," is elusive, although it is somewhat more comprehensive than that for surface coating. Of a general nature are David Alling's record of upholstering two old-fashioned mahogany chairs and a Virginia craftsman's work in restuffing six cherry chairs. Benjamin Lander's work for Joshua Ward in 1787 provided the Salem, Massachusetts, merchant with a new bottom for a "joiner comp[ass] s[ea]t" chair (fig. 3), possibly an inherited piece, given the older seat shape. New York land and real estate speculator Isaac Bronson employed a workman at Fairfield, Connecticut, to "take the covering from & clean the seats of 3 chairs" at what may have been a summer residence on Long Island.[19]

Removable stuffed seats in joined chairs are the subject of several references. Richard Magrath, a cabinetmaker and chair maker of Charleston, South Carolina, described chair bottoms of this type as "seats to take in and out." When undertaking upholstery work for Stephen Girard at Philadelphia, probably in the 1790s, Samuel Benge referred to this type of seat as "Loose." Some years later Silas Cheney was occupied part of a day at his shop in Connecticut with making a frame for a seat of this type and stuffing it, likely in a linen undercover only, as the customer charge was a mere 50¢. Another Connecticut householder sought the services of Solomon Cole at Glastonbury for "fiting Chair bottoms" at the same price.[20]

A few documents identify materials used as finish covers in restuffing chair seats. Leather was a utilitarian selection and the choice in 1813 of David S. Greenough, Esq., of Roxbury, now part of Boston. The charge for covering six chairs was $6.00. Four years earlier Captain John Derby of Salem paid Benjamin Beckford Jr. $27.00 for "new covering 12 Chairs with hair seating." Henry Connelly of Philadelphia carried out similar work at a comparable charge in 1808 for Stephen Girard. By this date haircloth had been popular with consumers for many decades. As early as 1775 William Savery mended a "hair bottom arm chair" at Philadelphia for James Pemberton. Haircloth was available in a selection of colors and in plain, striped, or patterned grounds; however, few details appear in woodworker's records. Another selection was moreen, a durable worsted, or woolen, cloth dyed in a variety of colors. The fabric might be glazed or embossed with a pattern, although the common finish was a process called "watering," which created a waved surface. Daniel Trotter of Philadelphia accommodated the merchant Samuel Coates in 1792 by "Covering 8 Chair Seats in Moreen" at a cost of £1.6.3, or $4.38 in decimal currency. The most comprehensive information on materials used in a set of replaced seat covers is detailed in Samuel Benge's work for Stephen Girard: "12 Mah'y Loose Chairs Seats restuffed; new webb, new Canvas & curld Hair with Stripe Satin Seats at 11/3" per chair. The total charge was $15.00.[21]

Figure 4 Armchair, Philadelphia, Pennsylvania, 1745–1755. Maple with pine. H. 41 3/8", W. 29 7/8", D. 23 3/8". (Courtesy, Winterthur Museum.)

Woodworkers rarely noted repairs to easy chairs and lolling chairs in their accounts. Householders likely placed a substantial part of this business in the hands of the upholsterer. Records provide considerably more information on another specialized form—the "close stool," or "close-stool chair" (fig. 4). That was the preferred term for this form, although the name "night chair" also had currency among craftsmen and consumers. Variations of the term were "night cabinet" and "night pot." Mahogany is the only wood named in records describing close-stool repairs. Richard Booker, a cabinetmaker of Williamsburg, Virginia, repaired a mahogany "night Chaire" in 1791 for St. George Tucker, Esq. Other information sheds light on the nature of close-stool repairs.[22]

The principal request of close-stool owners seeking repairs was for a new seat, or bottom, in their specialized furniture. Notes of repairs carried out by David Evans in 1780 for Benjamin Saixes of Philadelphia at a cost of 10s. enlarge on this work: "to making a Seat for [a] Close stool Chair & Putting [in] a Scollop'd rail." The fancy rail, probably of some vertical depth, concealed the pot that was part of the chair's equipment (fig. 4). Some closestool chairs received a coat of varnish at the time repairs were made. A "night chair" belonging to Samuel Larned, Esq., of Providence received both a coat of varnish and a set of casters while in the shop of H. Dancaster. Two close stools of early date and likely of box form, one repaired at Salem, Massachusetts, in September 1733 by Miles Ward and another mended in New York in 1743 at the shop of Joshua Delaplaine, had handles fixed to the wood, one set described as brass, while in the respective shops.[23]

Job E. Townsend, a cabinetmaker of Newport, Rhode Island, was among the group of craftsmen who mended close-stool chairs. One repair for John Taylor in 1808 replaced a damaged "bottom" with a new one. Townsend's work with this specialized seating also took on another aspect. Three customers approached him to "Alter . . . a Chair for a Clostool," one in 1787 and the others in 1800 and 1808. The first alteration cost 50¢, the other two 75¢ apiece, although there is no indication of what type of chairs were altered. Elizabeth Lovett of Beverly, Massachusetts, also sought this service in 1804 at the shop of Ebenezer Smith Jr. The alteration cost 75¢, and Miss Lovett paid an additional 42¢ for painting and 88¢ for a "Pan," or pot.[24]

Stools

Stools as a seating form were not abundant in society until well into the nineteenth century. The records on repair work are sparse and varied, many merely citing anonymous work, or "mending." This section will cover briefly a body of general material followed by specific references to low stools and high stools.

General references provide some insight on stools by type, function, and nature of repairs. The lingering presence of the seventeenth-century joint stool in some households is attested in the accounts of two cabinetmakers. Both Richard Johns of Philadelphia and Nathaniel Kinsman of Gloucester, Massachusetts, charged customers for "making a New Leg To Joynt stool." Several accounts describe a specialized stool, variously termed a "music," "piano," or "spinet" stool. The music stools received a coat of paint. Duncan Phyfe covered a piano stool for James L. Brinckerhoof of New York and in the same month, May 1816, repaired his piano. At Newport, Rhode Island, Christopher Champlin engaged Townsend Goddard in 1787 to put "Rails" in a spinet stool. Circumstances surrounding all the music-stool references suggest the owners were affluent members of society, and their ownership of an expensive musical instrument appears to confirm this.[25]

Craftsmen mended several stools by replacing damaged parts. In 1814 Alexander Shaw of Philadelphia provided a new top for a stool. A few years later at Middletown, Connecticut, Elizur Barnes made and installed four stool legs. A more extensive entry, made by David Alling of Newark, New Jersey, in an account dated 1838, describes work for his business customers Shugarth and Macknet: "To mending seat and putting new legs & rounds to one shop stool." The charge was 50¢. Other craftsmen "bottomed" stools, which usually describes weaving a rush seat. Alling also repaired a "broken cane seat stool" for a private customer the same year as the above work, the date suggesting the piece was a contemporary fancy stool rather than a relic of the seventeenth century.[26]

The cricket is a small stool of low height, usually in the six-to-ten-inch range. "Footstool" and "low stool" were alternative terms in the period of this study, although "cricket" was by far the common name for this form from an early date. John Gaines II of Ipswich, Massachusetts, made a new cricket as early as 1718 for the mother of one of his customers. The form came into its own, however, only after the Revolutionary War as the number of middle-class consumers in the marketplace rose substantially, and leisure time, especially among women, became more widespread. Crickets of both framed and stick construction were current in this period.[27]

Craftsmen's accounts identify the replacement of a leg or legs as the principal repair to the cricket. The cost of replacing a single leg varied from about 8 to 18¢. True Currier of Deerfield, New Hampshire, undertook more extensive work in 1834, probably to a pair of crickets, when he charged a customer 34¢ for "putting legs to crickets & painting them." The exposed surfaces of the cricket were vulnerable to wear, and a new coat of paint was a reasonable call. A good time to have the work done was when the household chairs needed refurbishing. A Mrs. Silsbee of Windsor, Vermont, engaged Thomas Boynton in 1811 to paint two armchairs and a cricket, suggesting the furniture was linked in use.[28]

Varnish was another surface coating requested by consumers. When Elizur Barnes of Middletown, Connecticut, varnished two crickets for Jacob Williams in 1822, he also recovered the tops, noting that he used "50 Nails." The charge of 50¢ for the entire job suggests the customer supplied the material for the covers. Several clients residing in larger urban centers approached cabinetmakers for more sophisticated work. In 1810 Stephen Girard of Philadelphia sent a footstool with other furniture to the shop of Henry Connelly, who charged $1.75 to recover the top. Several years earlier, Fenwick Lyell, who worked in the shadow of New York City at Middletown, New Jersey, had stuffed a pair of footstools for a customer at the substantial charge of £1.6 ($4.33).[29]

High stools were particularly useful in places of business, whether a shop or countinghouse. The high stool Thomas Boynton repaired at a charge of 25¢ in July 1816 for Stephen Conant likely stood in Conant's Windsor, Vermont, shop, a facility Boynton identified six months earlier when he sold Conant a "Candle S[t]ick for Shop." The lighting device probably was made of wood and may have been of standing form. David Alling had many business customers at his manufactory in the bustling commercial center of Newark, New Jersey, a community located a short distance by water from New York City. His record of "mending & pting a green high stool" for a customer in 1839 could well identify a seat of Windsor construction, "green" being an alternative term. Alling usually stocked a supply of "3 ft plain stool legs," which may describe the height of the green stool.[30]

Long Seats

One of the early long seats in the American household was the one-person bed, or recliner, called a couch, which was constructed with a large chair back at one end (fig. 5). The initial expense of this furniture form and its principal daytime use limited its possession primarily to affluent householders. Introduction of a caned couch from England in the late seventeenth century gave rise to a small trade in American imitations in the early eighteenth century. One example belonged to Joshua Humphries, a shipbuilder of Philadelphia, who in 1774 engaged Samuel Walton to put "Canns on a Sarfe" (canes on a sofa). Repairs made to two other couches at an early date describe examples with either cane or canvas bottoms. On February 7, 1739, John Gaines II of Ipswich, Massachusetts, entered in his accounts a job of "Carving a Top to Maj'r Apletons Couch," at a charge of 7s. 6d. for the new crest piece. Two years later at Philadelphia Solomon Fussell mended a couch for Jeremiah Elfreth Sr., a silversmith.[31]

Several references further identify the types of repairs made to couches. Job E. Townsend of Newport, Rhode Island, accommodated Captain John Oldfield in 1783 by "mending a Twisted Baul [ball] for a Couch," apparently describing a finial surmounting one of the chair-back framing posts. Repairs to "Couch bed poasts" were undertaken by Samuel Matthews in 1766 for Charles Norris, a wealthy Philadelphia merchant. Other work for Norris provides rare insight into couch accessories, as detailed in 1764 by Plunket

Figure 5 Couch, Massachusetts or Rhode Island, 1730–1760. Walnut and maple. H. 38", W. 23¾", L. 68". (Courtesy, Winterthur Museum.)

Fleeson, an upholsterer: "To making a Case for a Couche bed and 4 pillows." Samuel Coates, another Philadelphia mercantile figure, owned a couch as late as 1792, when he employed Daniel Trotter to make repairs. Trotter, coincidentally, was the nephew of Jeremiah Elfreth Sr., the silversmith noted above.[32]

Contrary to expectations, woodworking craftsmen were considerably more active in repairing and refurbishing stuffed sofas than in mending their single-sitter counterparts, the easy chair and lolling chair. Although many account entries lack description, and the term "sofa" at times identified a vernacular-style long seat, internal evidence in some documents provides insight into stuffed-sofa repairs and the cost of the work. Four documents further describe the geographic range of shops that repaired the form. William Bentley, who worked in Butternuts (Gilbertville) in rural Otsego County, New York, completed $7.00 worth of sofa repairs for a customer in 1814, a cost that is too high for vernacular work. More modest repairs undertaken for Stephen Girard in the 1820s were completed by Michael Bouvier, a French émigré craftsman in Philadelphia. John Collins, a cabinetmaker of Portsmouth, Virginia, twice repaired a sofa for the local merchant Richard Blow, charging $9.00 in 1802, when he stuffed and covered a frame, and $3.00 two years later for miscellaneous work. It is tempting to speculate that this was the sofa shipped to Virginia in 1785 by George Seddon and Son of London and described as a "6 ft 6 Sofa, back & heads [ends] to take off, in Sattin hair cloth & brass nailed" with socket casters on the feet. In a transaction of 1786, which was likely more common than is indicated in records, David Evans, a cabinetmaker of Philadelphia, repaired a sofa at the request of an upholsterer, Thomas Hurley, rather than a private customer.[33]

Structural repairs to sofas, when identified, focus on the legs and vary from making a repair, as recorded in 1806 by John Sager of Bordentown, New Jersey, to replacing a leg, as noted by Fenwick Lyell of Middletown. Several craftsmen supplied and installed casters. Samuel and Joseph Rawson of Providence undertook this work in 1842 for Samuel W. Greene, Esq. During earlier sofa repairs Greene acquired two pillows. Sometimes a coat of varnish supplemented repairs. Albert C. Greene, Esq., had this work done in 1834 by John G. Hopkins of Providence. In 1791, not long after removing from New York City to the new seat of national government at Philadelphia, General Henry Knox, secretary of war, called on Pennell Beale for a variety of cabinetwork, including mending and restuffing a sofa.[34]

Repairs to the settee form, as documented in records, describe vernacular seating. The types of work called for are best summarized in the accounts of David Alling of Newark, New Jersey, and Silas Cheney, of Litchfield, Connecticut, active woodworkers in the early nineteenth century. Both men produced and mended cane-seat and rush-seat fancy settees and wood-bottom Windsor settees. Alling made particular note in 1837 of altering, repairing, and putting new arms on four Windsor settees. When the repairs were complete, he painted the settees "plain yellow," a perfect complement to seating whose turned work simulated bamboo. Another time Alling repaired a settee painted green, a Windsor color that had its genesis in early-eighteenth-century England, when Windsors initially were used out of doors in the grounds of country estates. Work in both shops also included ornamenting painted surfaces. Striping and gilding are mentioned. On one occasion in 1815, when Cheney painted and gilded a settee, he noted the work was equal to that of five chairs and charged accordingly. When necessary, a craftsman undertook the task of "cleaning off seats" before repainting. Varnish, a common surface-coating material, often was used after repainting or "tuching up." It also was the common finish on unpainted wood. After repairing a partial suite of curled maple seating, consisting of two chairs, two long seats, and two short settees, Alling varnished the wood and then rubbed the surface to enhance the sheen.[35]

The bench, a utilitarian object, was useful both inside and outside the home. When Paul Jenkins of Kennebunk, Maine, repaired a bench in 1839, he noted specifically that it was for the house. Few other notices provide more than a general note of repair work. Jacob Brouwer mended a small bench in 1798 for Nicholas Low, a New York City merchant and upstate landholder. This was also the year that Peter Ranck, a German-American woodworker from Lebanon County, Pennsylvania, mended and painted a bench for a customer, along with supplying a new bench. Not all benches were for sitting, as demonstrated in a job recorded in 1823 by Elizur Barnes of Middletown, Connecticut: "painting Bench green for Flower pots."[36]

Children's Furniture
Chairs and cradles are the furniture forms for children that suffered most from daily use and required regular attention by the local woodworker. Children's low chairs (as opposed to high chairs) are identified by several names in craftsmen's records. Most common is "little chair," followed by "child's chair," then "small chair." Some confusion surrounds the term "small chair" because at times it appears to identify a small adult's chair or a youth's chair. Confirmation of the term's use to identify children's seating on occasion occurs in a bill of 1837 directed by W. and R. Tucker of Albany, New York, to Peter Gansevoort, Esq.: "1 Small chair for child."[37]

The majority of children's chairs requiring repair work were of the vernacular type (fig. 6). The records consulted are almost devoid of references to examples made of fine cabinet woods. Given the economies practiced in many American households in the eighteenth and early nineteenth centuries, this is understandable. Similar to the material referencing adult seating, specific repairs to children's chairs are identified only infrequently: chair bottoming with rush was common, rockers were a moderately popular enhancement, and a few special references are worthy of note.

Two accounts describe early activity in "mending and bottoming" a "Childs" chair and a "Littel" chair. Jacob Hinsdale of Harwinton in western Connecticut charged 1s. circa 1728 for this work. Four years later at Newbury in coastal Massachusetts, Joseph Brown Jr. charged only slightly more. Similar records continue well into the nineteenth century. Another seating job, probably using a wood bottom, was that described by Job

Figure 6 Child's armchair, New England, 1750–1800. Red oak and maple. H. 26", W. 15¼", D. 10¾". (Courtesy, Winterthur Museum.)

E. Townsend of Newport, Rhode Island: "To Putting a New Bottom to a Small Chair with a hole in the Same." Other records contain particular information about structural repairs. In 1758 Isaiah Tiffany, a furniture craftsman and general storekeeper of Norwich, Connecticut, put both a new arm and a new bottom in a little chair. A new arm in a child's chair was still a call years later in 1836 at the Wytheville, Virginia, shop of Thomas J. Moyers and Fleming K. Rich. By the start of the nineteenth century, chair rockers, which were becoming popular for adult seating, were also an option for children's chairs. When George Landon undertook this work for a customer in 1818 at his shop in Erie, Pennsylvania, he found it necessary first to replace the "feet," or legs. Other rocker installations were initiated because of the need to replace a chair bottom, or woven seat, as recorded at Framingham, Massachusetts, in 1810 by Abner Haven.[38]

Repairs and/or new bottoms often went hand in hand with repainting. When Elizur Barnes mended, painted, and ornamented a little chair for a customer in 1823 at Middletown, Connecticut, he identified it as part of a suite containing eight adult chairs refurbished at the same time. A year earlier Barnes had painted the woven seat of a little chair, thereby enhancing both its durability and appearance. Making or mending children's seating was fairly routine by the early nineteenth century at the Newark, New Jersey, chair manufactory of David Alling. The facility also undertook specialized ornamental work when refurbishing these chairs, described as "tipping" and "striping," which introduced fine or broad lines to the painted surfaces. Coloring wood with pigment in size was another technique borrowed from adult seating to enrich children's chairs. Evidence of its use in Rhode Island, for example, ranges from the bottoming and coloring undertaken by Daniel Dunham for the Senter family at Newport in 1788 to similar work recorded in 1825 in the accounts of Daniel and Samuel Proud at Providence. Varnish was an uncommon surface coating for refurbished children's chairs; however, William Savery of Philadelphia undertook this work in 1772 for General John Cadwalader.[39]

Two early references to high-chair mending by William Savery for Joseph Pemberton, a Quaker merchant of Philadelphia, appear to refer to the same piece of furniture. Unspecified repairs made to a "childs high Chair" in February 1774 cost 1s. Less than a year later, in January 1775, the cost of repairing a high chair identified as walnut was the same. Thomas Boynton had only just begun his woodworking career when he painted a "childs dining chair" in 1811. At this date he was in Boston, although he soon removed to the neighborhood of Windsor, Vermont. "Dining" was a favored term among Windsor chair-makers for the child's tall chair. At Bennington, Henry F. Dewey identified still another style of dining chair in 1841, when he matted a high chair and painted the wooden surfaces. Until well into the nineteenth century, most children's high chairs were devoid of footrests and feeding trays. The purpose of the tall chair was to accommodate the child at the family dining table. Thus, David Alling's reference to making a "table for [a] childs chr" at Newark, New Jersey, in 1839 is unusual and may have heralded the start of an innovation that changed dining patterns for young children.[40]

Few references to mending, or repairing, children's cradles provide details (fig. 7). The exception is the repair or replacement of rockers. In view of the cradle's constant use in the early American home, the extent of this work comes as no surprise. The cost ranged from 16.7 cents (1s.) to one dollar, with the majority of charges falling between 25 and 62½¢, an indication that replacement rather than repair was the usual approach. Rockers made of a fine cabinet wood—mahogany and cherry are named—cost 50¢ or more. The accounts of John Durand, a turner and woodworker of coastal Milford, Connecticut, contain unusual terminology when identifying rocker replacement work. In June 1767 Durand debited the account of a

Doctor Carrington by about 42¢ for "Cradle feet and putting on." Entries in the accounts of two other craftsmen, Fenwick Lyell of Middletown, New Jersey, and Job E. Townsend of Newport, Rhode Island, describe another repair: "Puting a new top to a Cradle." If in use at all, the term "hood" for a cradle top likely was rare.[41]

A body of material highlighting cradle repairs at Philadelphia provides further insight into and may reflect activity in other urban centers from the mid-1750s to the early 1780s. Named in the records are cabinetmakers of moderate to prominent stature: Thomas Affleck, George Claypoole, Daniel Drinker, Samuel Matthews, William Savery, Francis Trumble, Thomas Tufft, and Samuel Williams. Equally impressive is the list of patrons, all influential members of the merchant community in the city: Stephen Collins, Michael Gratz, Levi Hollingsworth, Samuel Meredith, Charles Norris and his widow Mary Norris, Joseph Pemberton, and Thomas Wharton. Collins, Hollingsworth, and perhaps others also owned interests in sailing vessels, and Wharton included maritime brokerage in his business. Part of the work William Savery carried out for Joseph Pemberton in 1774 was "Making Rockers to a Mahogany Cradle," as indicated in an account entry dated May 13. Savery appears to have mended the same mahogany cradle less than a year later on January 21, 1775. Samuel Matthews made several cradle repairs for Charles Norris during the 1760s. He first installed a new bottom and followed that shortly with mending and polishing a cradle, an activity that suggests the cradle was made of a fine cabinet wood. Several years later Matthews altered a cradle for the family, although the nature of the alteration is not indicated.[42]

Polish is just one of several surface coatings for cradles mentioned in furniture records. More common was a new coat of varnish, which sometimes followed repair work, as indicated in 1829 by Elisha Harlow Holmes of

Figure 7 Cradle, Pennsylvania or New Jersey, 1740–1800. Walnut and yellow poplar. H. 28½", W. 24⅜", L. 42". (Courtesy, Winterthur Museum.)

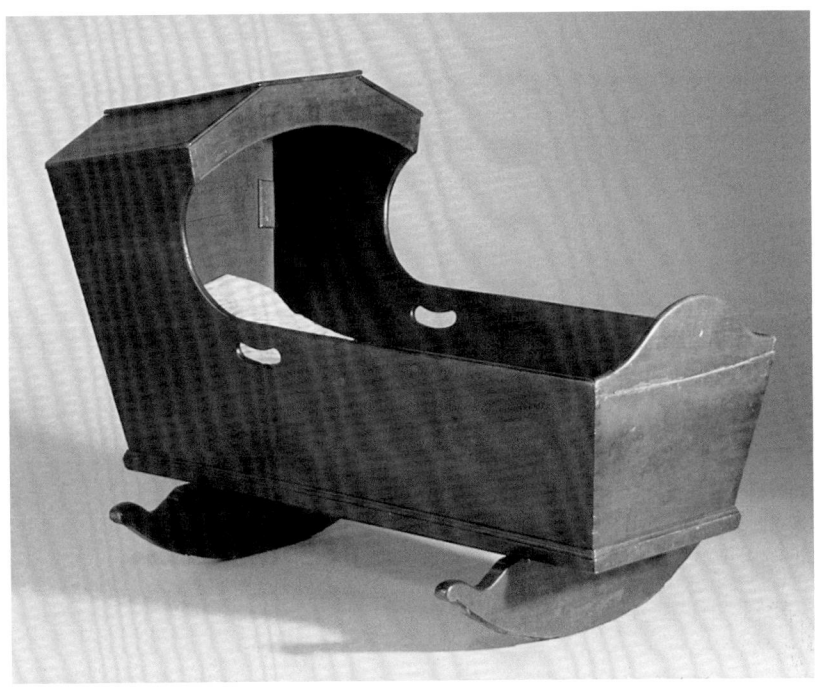

Essex, Connecticut. Several craftsmen made note of painting a cradle. Joseph Griswold of Buckland, Massachusetts, was quite specific in 1817, when he recorded "painting Cradle once." The charge was 25¢. Job Danforth of Providence followed a job of mending a cradle in 1805 by staining the surfaces.[43]

Rarely mentioned in craftsmen's accounts are cradles constructed primarily of woven plant material. Richard Alexander, a cabinetmaker of Philadelphia, in undertaking extensive work for Mrs. John Francis, recorded on April 24, 1820, that he had put "a pair of Rockers in a Willow Cradle." The willow (genus *Salix*), a shrub or small tree with pliant branches and shoots, was suitable for basketwork. This may be the same material identified by Elizur Barnes in 1822, when he noted in his accounts a job of "putting Rockers on Basket Cradle" for Reuben Chaffee of Middletown, Connecticut.[44]

References to mending children's cribs date, for the most part, to the post-Revolutionary period. An exception is William Savery's job of painting a crib in 1774 for Joseph Pemberton of Philadelphia. At New York in 1813, Jacob Brouwer described this furniture form as a "cribe bedsted" when he carried out extensive repair work on the household furniture of Nicholas Low. The mahogany crib Brouwer repaired for the merchant a decade earlier may have been the same child's bedstead. Like the cradle, the crib was subject to considerable wear, as noted in a bill to St. George Tucker of Williamsburg, Virginia, from Rookesby Roberts, who in 1794 installed "fore legs" and a bottom in a child's crib and charged $1.25. Alterations to cribs occurred from time to time. Elizur Barnes of Middletown, Connecticut, noted one in 1823, when he lengthened a crib and bored holes in the horizontal frame to receive a cord lacing.[45]

Furniture craftsmen undertook repairs to several other specialized forms for children. Twice, Joseph Pemberton of Philadelphia called on William Savery to mend a "hobby horse," once in 1774 and again in 1775. Meanwhile, Charles Norris, another member of the merchant community, had engaged Samuel Matthews on several occasions during the 1760s to mend a "go-cart." This term describes a small cage, or pen, sometimes fitted with wheels used to teach a child to walk and to control its movements once that skill had been mastered. Other craftsmen associated with go-cart repairs include John Durand of Milford, Connecticut, and Job E. Townsend of Newport, Rhode Island. In identifying go-cart repairs Townsend sometimes used the alternative term "standing stool" and indicated that he both mended and painted this form during the 1790s. In the following decade the term appears in the accounts of Job Danforth of Providence, who charged 1s. to repair a standing stool. Solomon Cole's fee for this work at Glastonbury, Connecticut, in 1799 was about the same.[46]

Bedsteads

The number of unidentified bedstead repairs in woodworkers' accounts is substantial; however, the presence of a modest body of more detailed material provides cogent insights. Many repairs included both mending and supplying new parts for the bedstead, the wooden frame that supports the bed (mattress) and bedding. Repaired and replaced bedstead parts identified in the records consulted can be ranked from most to least frequently mentioned: bedposts, headboards and footboards, post-top structures, bed screws and accessories, bedrails, casters, and trundles (wheels). In the course of recording bedstead repairs, craftsmen occasionally identified the principal structural woods, although by no means is this short list inclusive of the options: mahogany, black walnut, red cedar, and birch.

Many craftsmen fashioned one or more new posts for clients' bedsteads. Descriptive information in several late-eighteenth-century accounts is revealing. Two craftsmen, David Evans of Philadelphia and an unidentified woodworker of Middletown, New Jersey, fabricated footposts for client's bedsteads at the modest figures of 1s. 6d. and 1s. per post, respectively, suggesting they were of low height and common wood. Cost comparison indicates that Joseph Griswold's 83¢ (5s.) replacement post for a customer at Buckland, Massachusetts, probably was of tall form. This supposition seems confirmed in the records of Job E. Townsend of Newport, Rhode Island, who made a pair of high posts for a customer's bedstead, charging 5s. 3d. apiece. Townsend had already repaired another bedstead for a customer and made "Two Black Walnuts Posts fluted" for 18s. Adjusting for the unnamed repairs, each walnut post could have cost 7 or 8s. apiece, suggesting that the cheaper high posts were made of a cabinet wood of lesser stature, such as maple (fig. 8).[47]

A few documents identify turning as the method of fabricating some replacement posts. The cost was low. Joseph Short of Newburyport, Massachusetts, undertook more detailed work for Abigail Woodbury in 1818, when he turned just the "lower ends of 2 long bedposts" and varnished the new supports along with the headposts, which were plain because they would be concealed by the bed curtains. Several craftsmen working in the first decade of the nineteenth century undertook a job for clients described in records as "splicing Bedstead posts." Sometimes all four posts were treated in this manner. The expense was minimal, and the work does not appear to have been initiated due to broken posts. The purpose of the activity is unclear. Was this a way to convert a low-post frame to a high-post bedstead or to update old or plain posts in style or embellishment, using the original feet or bases? Indeed, Nehemiah Adams of Salem, Massachusetts, spliced and varnished "old posts" in 1808 for Captain Benjamin Webb. Perhaps Ebenezer Smith Jr's. work at "Piecing bed Posts" in neighboring Beverly for Robert Rantoul, and Cook and Greene's job at Providence in "raising up bed post[s]" for Richard W. Greene describe the same work. Two embellishments for post tips, recorded by Paul Jenkins of Kennebunk, Maine, and Vose and Coates of Boston, respectively, were balls and urns. Work at the lower ends of the posts, described by John Hockaday in Williamsburg, Virginia, as "plinthing . . . four mehogoney Bedstead posts," appears to have introduced a low block to the base of each foot or cased the bases to resemble blocks (fig. 8). The purpose of similar work undertaken at Newport, Rhode Island, for Mary Ann Marble was spelled out in specific terms by Job E. Townsend: "To Making four Blocks for To Raise her Bedstid."[48]

Figure 8 Bedstead, North Shore, Massachusetts, or Portsmouth, New Hampshire, 1770–1810. Maple and white pine. H. 88¾", W. 58", L. 80¾". (Courtesy, Winterthur Museum.)

Next to bedposts, headboards are mentioned most frequently in craftsmen's records. A few were mended; however, most appear to have been replacements or entirely new additions to the frame. Most repairs were modest. Thomas Boynton's charge of 13¢ for a headboard repair at Windsor, Vermont, in 1817 was comparable to that made by Elizur Barnes five years later at Middletown, Connecticut. The cost of a new board was at times not much more. Fifty cents or less covered most purchases. The form was simple, given that fabrication and installation required less than half a day of the craftsman's time, as indicated by the cost. Boards of this type were made in the late eighteenth century at Philadelphia by William Wayne for his customer merchant Stephen Collins and at Providence by Job Danforth for prominent pewterer Gershom Jones. At 3s. 6d. (58½¢) General Henry Knox paid slightly more for a headboard bought from William Roberts in 1795 for his house at the seat of government in Philadelphia.[49]

Some craftsmen furnished both a headboard and a footboard to fill a customer's order. Elisha Crane, a cabinetmaker of Albany, New York, carried out work of this description in 1824 for Peter Gansevoort, Esq. When a craftsman supplied a board, he might undertake other bedstead work. Josiah P. Wilder, a chairmaker of New Ipswich, New Hampshire, made a footboard for a customer in 1839 and then completed the job by painting the entire bedstead. Two customer orders dating to the 1820s stand above the others in cost and sophistication. In a three-party transaction at Middletown, Connecticut, Elizur Barnes supplied John B. Southmayd, a craftsman, with "8 feet Shaded Veneers for Headboard for Mrs Lewis Bedsted." In New York Henrietta Low, daughter of merchant Nicholas Low, employed Abraham S. Egerton in February 1824 to panel "the ends" of her bedstead, that is, the headboard and footboard, at a cost of $10.00. Less than a month later, Nicholas Low himself paid Egerton the same sum for similar work to his bedstead.[50]

Basic to the post-top structure of a tall bedstead is a slender wood framework that joins the posts and is secured to the tops by means of vertical pins known as "pintles." Craftsmen identified this skeletal frame by various terms, including "Strips for teaster," "vallance rails," "side pieces to a Bedsted top," and "curtain rails." The framework supported a short cloth valance, or tester, tacked to the top surface and suspended. Paul Jenkins repaired a tester in 1838 for a customer at Kennebunk, Maine. When introducing a newly fabricated valance, the installation required careful "fitting," as indicated by George Merrifield of Albany, New York. The word "cornice" appears at times to have been an alternative term for this feature. Other cornices were more massive structures made of wood. A "Sett bed cornices" made by Nehemiah Adams at Salem, Massachusetts, in 1808 for Captain Benjamin Webb was "gilt" and cost a substantial $8.00. Several decades earlier Joseph Pemberton of Philadelphia had ordered a "Scollop'd" bed cornice complete with pulleys for drawing the curtains from William Savery at a cost of £1.5 (approximately $4.17). Sometimes a ceiling cloth filled the void inside the framework of the top, a fixture described by Alexander Low of Freehold, New Jersey, as a "roof." The top frame also served to secure rods to accommodate full-length bed curtains, which could be made to open and close or draw up in festoons. For this purpose Daniel Trotter spent part of a day in 1793 "fixing pullies" in a bedstead for prominent Philadelphia merchant Stephen Girard. The "canopy top" mentioned in several craftsmen's records appears to have been a complete unit of cloth, consisting of a roof, valances, and, at times, perhaps, the curtains.[51]

Periodically, the rails that form the basic framing of the bedstead required attention. Joseph Pemberton of Philadelphia called on William Savery in 1775 for this type of work. Two bedsteads owned by William Lord and identified as birch by Paul Jenkins in 1837, when brought to his shop in Kennebunk, Maine, required moderate work, consisting between them of two new rails and alterations to a headboard. In the shop at the same time was Lord's mahogany bedstead, which was refurbished with "2 new side rales & headboard & balls to posts." Some years earlier Fenwick Lyell had put a mahogany rail in a bedstead for a customer at Middletown, New Jersey. Lyell's bedstead work also included other tasks that were a frequent call at American woodworking shops. On one occasion when he repaired a field bedstead with "new Sides" and a post, he also supplied "5 Screws," the metal bolts used to secure the mortise-and-tenon joints at the four corners of many bedstead frames. Another time Lyell installed "Caps" on a bedstead, the small pivoting metal disks used to conceal the screw heads (fig. 8). Daniel Trotter described the material of these caps as brass in 1790, when he repaired a mahogany bedstead at Philadelphia for Stephen Girard. Two prominent New England cabinetmakers carried out similar work for their patrons. William Hook of Salem, Massachusetts, supplied a "Set of New Caps" for a field bedstead belonging to Benjamin Hathorne (Hawthorne), and Townsend Goddard of Newport, Rhode Island, fixed the screws in a bedstead owned by Christopher Champlin. Relative to installing bed screws, *The Workwoman's Guide,* first published in 1838, advised using a "bed key to turn each screw till firmly fixed in the hole."[52]

The installation of casters on bedstead feet, whether at purchase or as a later addition, introduced a measure of mobility to an otherwise unwieldy form. St. George Tucker of Williamsburg, Virginia, found a good opportunity in 1806 to have two casters replaced when he sent his bed frame to the cabinet shop of John Hockaday for repairs. The complete "Set of Castors for Bedstead" that William Ranken provided two decades later for Philadelphia merchant Samuel Coates at a cost of $1.00 appears to have replaced a damaged set, as no new installation charge was made. A more complete record is work done for Richard W. Greene of Providence by the Cleveland Brothers, when in 1844 the firm billed him $1.75 for "Brass Castors for Bedstead & putting in." Craftsmen provided wheels of a different type for the trundle bedstead. Samuel Douglas of Connecticut described the fabrication method in 1816, when charging a customer 34¢ for "turning 8 rounds for trundle bead." Other craftsmen referred to these cylinders of wood as "trundles," a term that also identifies the low bedstead fitted with wheels, permitting it to be rolled away beneath a larger frame. Two early references to supplying "Trundles for a Bedsted" in the accounts of Peter Emerson of Reading, Massachusetts, and Robert Crage of Leicester date to 1756 and 1759, respectively. Years later, in 1811, Titus Preston of Wallingford, Connecticut, precisely identified the purpose of similar work, when he recorded "puting trundles to a trundle bedsted."[53]

The application of some type of coating to refurbish worn bedstead frames or to cover a repair or addition was a fairly common task in the woodworking shop. Varnish, paint, stain, color, oil, and blacking all are mentioned in craftsmen's accounts, although the latter three are uncommon. Woodworkers usually applied varnish on its own; occasionally it covered a fresh coat of stain. Painting was the most common way to refurbish a worn surface, however. Sometimes a customer deposited more than one bedstead for repainting at the shop of the local woodworker, and on occasion a repair was involved. When Joseph Griswold of Buckland, Massachusetts, repainted two bedsteads for Jesse Pratt in 1822, he also put a new post in one frame. Some bedstead parts were painted independent of the main frame. Both John Sager of Bordentown, New Jersey, and George Landon of Erie, Pennsylvania, recorded their work in painting bed cornices. Of the color options available for painted bedsteads, green alone is mentioned in a few references; most records are without description. David Evans painted a bedstead green in 1791 at Philadelphia. Similar work carried out by Silas

Cheney at Litchfield, Connecticut, some years later also included replacing a side rail in his customer's bedstead.[54]

Parallels exist in the type of work undertaken by woodworkers when customers chose stain instead of paint. Sometimes a craftsman refurbished and stained more than one bed frame for a householder. At other times he merely added finish to a new feature. Job E. Townsend of Newport, Rhode Island, made a "roof" for a bedstead in 1802 and finished it with stain. When choosing stain, the customer had several options. A patron of Josiah P. Wilder's shop at New Ipswich, New Hampshire, chose to have his stained frame varnished to protect the colored surface. Jacob Rodriguez Rivera, a Newport, Rhode Island, merchant who was a customer of Benjamin Baker, selected a cheaper finish by having his newly stained bedstead polished. Silas Cheney described another option when he oiled a stained bed frame at Litchfield, Connecticut, for Oliver Wolcott. Some bedsteads were oiled without further surface treatment.[55]

Short of having an entire bedstead revarnished, some customers elected to have their woodworker coat only the repaired or replaced parts, including cornices, testers, headboards, rails, and posts. At Williamsburg, Virginia, St. George Tucker engaged John Hockaday in 1812 for "plinthing, Working Over, and Varnish[ing] four mehogoney Bedstead posts." Some work required that bedstead surfaces be "smoothed," probably scraped, before varnishing. Occasionally, a customer requested special work, as when Miles Benjamin of Cooperstown, New York, recorded, "Varnishing bedstead twice." The accounts of Solomon Fussell of Philadelphia, which date principally to the 1740s, name two other surface finishes that could be sealed with a coat of varnish. In August 1741 Fussell charged Thomas Sugar 1s. 6d. for "blacking and varnishing the Cornish [cornice] of a bead tester." Two years later he "colored" and varnished a bed cornice for Benjamin Franklin at the same charge. Coloring utilized a size coating mixed with powdered pigment to the desired shade. This finish remained a limited option for bedsteads into the early nineteenth century, when in 1809 Oliver Avery of North Stonington, Connecticut, colored a bedstead at the request of Aaron Newton.[56]

The sacking bottom was the most common support for the bed (mattress) and bedding that furnished a bedstead. The sacking filled the entire area within the open frame formed by the bed rails (fig. 8). Craftsmen placed sacking bottoms in all types of bed frames—high post, low post, field, press, and trundle. The material of this sturdy support is identified in a bill of 1772 from upholsterer Thomas Lawrence of Philadelphia to Stephen Collins: "To Sail Duck & mending Sacking Bottom." Duck is a strong linen fabric, lighter than canvas, with a glazed surface that sheds water; thus the name. A stout grade was serviceable for heavy use. Craftsmen's records also provide insights on the various methods of installing the sacking bottom. Most common was lacing the sacking directly to the inside frame of the bedstead, using cord interlaced through grommets spaced along the outside edges of the rectangular sacking cloth. When Henrietta Low of New York employed Abraham S. Egerton to panel the ends of her bedstead in 1824, she also ordered a "new sacking bottom & cord." To secure the lacing to the bed frame, a rabbet along the interior face of the rails was fitted with small spaced pegs, probably of mushroom shape to prevent the cord from slipping off. John Paine, a woodworker of Southold, Long Island, described the fabrication method of these small knobs in a 1797 account entry: "To turn 15 pags [pegs] for bedsted." The terminology varied. Earlier, in 1765, John Durand of Milford, Connecticut, recorded turning "butens" for a bedstead. These were not the most common names, however. In the period between 1767 and 1814 at least four craft shops—those of John and William Richmond and John Danforth at Providence, Charles C. Robinson at Philadelphia, and Aaron Leaming at Cape May, New Jersey—used the word "pin" to describe these small knobs. The bedstead illustrated in figure 8 has an unusual system of pins. The small cylinders are secured within a channel cut into the upper inside face of the rails.[57]

Job Townsend Jr. of Newport described another method of installing a sacking bottom in a bed frame in 1762, when working at the house of William Wanton, a governor of Rhode Island: "to Nailing on a Bed Sacking . . . To Leathar for Ditto." In this process Townsend nailed a narrow strip of material, probably the leather, to either the rail tops or an interior rabbet. This border was then laced to the main sacking panel. Paralleling Townsend's work was another job undertaken in the community less than two decades later for Jacob Rodriguez Rivera by Benjamin Baker, who billed the merchant for "glewing sacking in Bedsted." The support system appears to have been similar to that of Wanton's frame—a border, lacing, and sacking panel. Had the sacking been one large unit glued to the bed frame, it would have been impossible to disassemble the bedstead for repairs or moving without compromising the sacking. No matter what the method of installing the sacking, the author of *The Workwoman's Guide* advised that the lacing be of strong cord and "be pulled together and knotted by a man, as a woman is scarcely strong enough to do it effectually."[58]

In 1767, when Jesse Hand discharged a debt with woodworker Aaron Leaming at Cape May, New Jersey, he provided payment in the form of two bedstead frames. One, as noted above, was fitted "with pins for a Sackin bottom." The other was "a Beadsted with holes for a cord." This type of support system appears to have been considerably less common than the sacking bottom. The "new cord" for bedsteads acquired at New York a year apart in the mid-1810s by Nicholas Low and James L. Brinckerhoof from Jacob Brouwer and Duncan Phyfe, respectively, may have been for frames with this type of support for the bed and bedding, as neither account makes mention of a sacking.[59]

A single reference to the use of rope in "putting up the old Bed" describes the uncommon occurrence of that support system versus the sacking bottom, or even the corded bottom, in the American bedstead. A few references document still another uncommon type of mattress support in this study, best described in a bill of 1809 from John T. Ball of New York to Nicholas Low: "repairing & putting slatt bottom to bedsted." Other individuals who ordered slats for a bedstead include Richard W. Greene of Providence and Mrs. St. George Tucker of Williamsburg, Virginia.[60]

A regular, recurring activity in the lives of householders and woodworkers and one easily overlooked in furniture studies was the routine assembly and disassembly of the bedstead and its accessories. Some households seem always to have been in a flurry of "putting up" and "taking down" their bed frames or parts thereof. The reasons for this activity, which brought the woodworker to the house of the client, are varied. Most obvious is the erection of a newly purchased frame or the disassembly of another one for repair, surface refurbishing, alteration, or the addition of an accessory, such as a set of casters. Seasonal cleaning sometimes necessitated the disassembly of the bedstead, as vermin were always a problem in a society with few window screens or effective insecticides. Even relocating a bed frame from one room to another required that it be dismantled to negotiate doorways, hallways, and staircases. If the main frame did not require assembly or disassembly, a householder might focus on particular accessories. Samuel Morris, a member of the Philadelphia merchant community, called on David Evans in 1775 to put up both a cornice and a set of tester rails. Elizabeth Bleecker McDonald was a newlywed in New York in 1800, when she noted in her diary on November 21, "A snow stormy morning—the first snow that has fallen this season . . . my Bed Curtains were put up." Once the cold weather had passed, the bed curtains were taken down to provide adequate ventilation during the warm months.[61]

Still another reason for disassembling the bedstead loomed large in the lives of some householders. It is best described in a bill dated June 24, 1828, at Philadelphia by William Ranken and directed to his client Samuel Coates: "[to] taken down & puting up Bedsteads at moving." Nowhere was this activity more prominent than at New York. During a visit to America in the 1790s, Moreau de St. Méry observed: "A strange habit of New Yorkers is their mania for moving on May 1, if they do not own a house. This moving must be seen to be believed." Several years later Frances M. Trollope, inveterate British traveler and commentator, offered a more detailed picture of this "changing house once a year": "On the 1st of May the city of New York has the appearance of sending off a population flying from the plague, or of a town which had surrendered on condition of carrying away all their goods and chattels. Rich furniture and ragged furniture, carts, waggons, and drays, ropes, canvas, and straw, packers, porters, and draymen . . . occupy the streets from east to west, from north to south."[62]

The more affluent the American household, the more substantial the year-round disposition of bedsteads was likely to be. John Eyre's work for the first Samuel Powel at Philadelphia in 1736 included "taking down" and "Seting up" no fewer than six bedsteads in the month of September alone. Three of those frames were furnished with a cornice. A running account of William Savery's work for the Joseph Pemberton family several decades later details a varied and significant amount of bedstead work. Between June 30, 1774, and January 16, 1775, Savery took down five bedsteads and set up six. In addition he made a scalloped bed cornice, a bedstead made of stained poplar, and a plain, but large, mahogany bedstead, all requiring assembly. Savery's charge for the disassembly and reassembly of a bedstead was 1s. 6d., or 25¢ in the decimal currency introduced in the 1790s. In calculating a master craftsman's average pay at 6s. ($1.00) a day, the complete work of taking down and putting up one bed frame required one-quarter of a working day, one that at best was no fewer than ten hours. These figures are corroborated in an account recorded by Hiram Taylor of neighboring Chester County, Pennsylvania: "To half day at putting up bedsteads" (two) at 50¢. Much the same activity described for the household of Joseph Pemberton occurred in that of Stephen Girard in the mid-1780s and again in the mid-1790s, as recorded by his cabinetmaker of choice, Daniel Trotter.[63]

Equally substantial was work carried out in New York for Nicholas Low by Jacob Brouwer from June through September 1796, when the cabinetmaker took down nine bed frames and set up eleven. Brouwer was still Low's cabinetmaker in 1813–1814, when the figures for similar work were almost the same. One account entry stands out, however: "A bedsted on loan takeing down & putting up" at 16s. Even a household well equipped with sleeping accommodations might on occasion require a temporary supplement. By the early nineteenth century urban craftsmen, in particular, frequently had a small store of used furniture taken in trade for new, which was available for loan or resale.[64]

As a body of furniture, bedsteads were subject to a significant number of alterations. Frames were made wider, or narrower, or shorter, and sometimes both shorter and narrower. In the course of this work and in carrying out general repairs, craftsmen occasionally identified the style of bedstead either directly or by inference. In converting a high-post bedstead to a low-post frame for the Norris family of Philadelphia, Thomas Tufft described what the work entailed: "To pulling down and puting up a bedsted Cuting posts and mending." At times the procedure was reversed, as in 1826 when Allen Holcomb of New Lisbon in central New York State altered a field bedstead to a high-post frame and finished the work with a coat of varnish. A more radical conversion occurred when David Evans of Philadelphia made a high-post bedstead out of a low-post frame. When the alteration was complete, Evans stained the tall frame, resecured the post-and-rail joints with four new screws, and fitted the frame with a new cornice. Converting the bedstead led to other work for the client's bedchamber. Evans next made a trundle bedstead and stained it to coordinate with the tall frame. The cabinetmaker completed the job by making "4 window rails with boards." The total bill came to £6.10 ($21.67).[65]

The field bedstead, with its medium-high posts and flat, peaked, or low-arched roof, began as a frame suitable for military use; therefore, it originally was hinged to fold completely into a case for travel. The folding feature was retained in some nonmilitary use, as demonstrated in 1772 in the work of an unidentified Middletown, New Jersey, cabinetmaker for George Taylor, "tavern keeper": "to making of lath for a feild bed & finding of hinges." The folding feature of this new canopy frame for the bedstead would have been of particular relevance in a public inn, where furnishings were moved about frequently. Other craftsmen provided replacement side rails or corner posts for field bedsteads owned by their patrons.[66]

The "press," or "turn-up," bedstead was reasonably popular in the late eighteenth and early nineteenth centuries, judging by the number of standard bedsteads converted to this form (fig. 9). Raised and concealed by day behind the curtains of a short tester frame, within a slipcover, or inside a cupboardlike box, the folding bedstead could be lowered, ready for service,

Figure 9 Bedstead, New England, 1780–1830. Maple and ash. H. 85¾", W. 52½", L. 73⅝". (Courtesy, Winterthur Museum.)

at nightfall. Nehemiah Adams altered a bedstead "to Turn up" for a mariner client in 1808 at Salem, Massachusetts. True Currier, who worked across the border in Exeter, New Hampshire, referred to this frame as a "Rule joint Bedstead." With the side rails jointed near the headposts, the entire frame folded up close to the wall, the pivoting front legs dropping when raised to lie flat against the frame. Account entries of several craftsmen attest to the use on occasion of a wooden box, called a "press," to conceal the bed frame. When Elizur Barnes of Middletown, Connecticut, altered a bedstead in 1822 to turn up, he also charged his client for "Making Case to Enclose Bedsted." At a later date George Merrifield of Albany, New York, entered a charge in his accounts for repairing a door to a bedstead press. Hartwell Holmes had already spent an entire day at Woodstock, Connecticut, painting a "Bed press" for a customer, as indicated by his $1.00 charge.[67]

The "cot bedstead" mended by several craftsmen appears to have been a frame for stationary use rather than the hanging bed of the same name used by mariners and suspended from ships' beams. George Merrifield of Albany referred to the form as a "Camp Cot" when making repairs in 1838, suggesting that some cots could be folded for easy transport. Ephraim Haines, a prominent Philadelphia cabinetmaker, replaced "a Bottom on [a] Cott Bedstead" for Stephen Girard in 1802 on the same day he sold a painted lowpost bedstead to the merchant. Putting new legs on a cot bedstead nine years later was one task of many undertaken by Langley Boardman at Portsmouth, New Hampshire, for the household of Captain Reuben S. Randall. Providing insight on the appearance of the cot form in the early nineteenth century is a small image in a printed plate of bedstead forms in *The Workwoman's Guide,* a volume first published in London in 1838. The image depicts a rectangular lath-type wooden frame stretched with a laced canvas and supported on X-shaped legs at the head and foot. The illustrated low rectangular headboard was slotted into the frame for easy removal; otherwise, the crossed legs of the bed frame would not have folded for storage or transport.[68]

Tables

Most repair work noted in craftsmen's records references tables of anonymous type, although the nature, range, and extent of activity provide a comprehensive overview of repair work to the form as a whole. The work falls into four categories: general repairs; installation of new parts; surface smoothing, identified by the terms "planing," "dressing," "smoothing," "scraping," and "cleaning"; and surface coating. In addition, a few notations relate to table alterations.

The language of table repairs is much like that for chairs. "Mend" was the word of choice over "repair" by more than two to one, and the terms "fix" and "work on" appear in records only occasionally. The introduction of a new table part often is preceded by the words "put on" or "put in." Only on rare occasions is the material of the table identified. Named are cherry, mahogany, maple, pine, poplar, and walnut. Mahogany is recorded more than all the other woods combined, likely because of its market stature rather than its household prevalence. John Sager of Bordentown, New Jersey, and Hiram Taylor of Chester County, Pennsylvania, identified work on pairs of tables, and in both instances the wood was mahogany. Table shapes identified in repair work are round, oval, and square, in that order of frequency, although all such references are uncommon. Of more frequent occurrence are notations of size—large and small, and a number of craftsmen made special note when making repairs to "old" tables.[69]

The body of material identifying repairs to tables by special task, although small, appears representative of the types of jobs undertaken by craftsmen for their clients. A minor job noted by Jacob Brouwer in 1810 was the repair of a "table Ketch" (possibly a tea table) for the New York household of Nicholas Low, a task that required at least half a day, judging by the charge of 4s. (67¢). Oliver Moore repaired a drawer lock several years later for a customer at East Granby, Connecticut. Structural repairs were more usual. Isaiah Tiffany recorded a single task of "mending a Table frame" at Norwich in 1757, although this work often accompanied repairs to a tabletop or leaf. In 1790 Walter Nichols focused on mending the end rails and legs of a mahogany table for the Senter family of Newport, Rhode Island. Other craftsmen mended table drawers. Benona Segar of western Connecticut paid 8¢ in 1812 for drawer repairs, the same price as his new rolling pin.[70]

Table-leg repairs often were part of a larger job at the cabinet shop. When listed alone, the cost appears to have been moderate. Repairs to a single leg in a federal-period table in the early nineteenth century are recorded at 17 to 20¢. Even "Mending the Claw of a Table" at the Annapolis, Maryland, shop of Shaw and Chisholm in 1772 cost a customer only 1s. (16.7¢). Damage of a substantial nature likely resulted in a replaced leg. Tabletops also were the object of repair and adjustment. Mending a "Top of a Table" could vary in cost from the 1s. repair (16.7¢) made by Job E. Townsend at Newport, Rhode Island, to the $1.00 charged in 1829 by E. G. and A. Partridge of Worcester, Massachusetts. More particular in description is Job Townsend Jr's. note of "fasting Down a Top of Table" at Newport and James Linacre's record of "reparing a tabel and Cuting the Corners" at Albany, New York.[71]

Work on table leaves was extensive and involved mending, rehanging, and new fabrication plus installation. Some records are straightforward, as when in the post-Revolutionary years John Paine of Southold, Long Island, mended a table leaf for 25¢ and a "Littel tabel lefe" for 8¢. A table leaf mended by Titus Preston of Wallingford, Connecticut, had to be rehung as well, although the total cost was just 33¢. When new screws were required, Preston charged 4¢ for a set of six, the requisite number for one hinge. A complete new hinge and installation cost 16¢. Problems lie in interpreting the extent of work completed on other table leaves.[72]

Jonathan Herrick's work at "makeing leaf to table" in 1815 for Robert Rantoul, a druggist-merchant of Beverly, Massachusetts, describes a new leaf that replaced a damaged one. With no other charges recorded, it can be assumed that the cost of the work at $1.40 covered a proper finish on the leaf and hanging. By contrast, a charge made two decades earlier by Hartwell Holmes of Woodstock, Connecticut, for supplying a new table leaf was just 50¢. The cost of a replacement leaf was a direct reflection of its size, material, structural detail, and finish. Terminology equally clear in describing replacement work is John Durand's account at Milford, Connecticut, of "putting a new Leaf on a table." Problems arise when interpreting other phraseology, however, such as "puting leaf to Table," "puting fall to Table," and "hanging a table." Were these new leaves or old ones rehung? Here, cost must be taken into account. Probably very little new work was priced under 25¢. The average cost of fabricating and installing a new leaf, based on almost sixty references, was about $1.00.[73]

One dollar was Moses Parkhurst's charge in 1834 for spending a day making and putting a new leaf on a table for Deacon David Davis at Paxton, Massachusetts. Titus Preston provided more detail about a one-day job he undertook in 1822 at Wallingford, Connecticut. The materials, consisting of "about 3 feet of cherry bord 2s., 1 pr: butts [hinges] 8d., 14 screws 4d.," cost a total of 3s. (50¢). Preston's charge for "the labor at the table" was 6s. ($1.00).

Cherry is mentioned again along with other woods in the leaf-replacement work undertaken by several craft shops. John Paine of Southold, Long Island, made a "table lefe cheretree" in 1786 for 6s. ($1.00). The maple table leaf fabricated by Edward Slead at Dartmouth, Massachusetts, more than a decade later cost his customer somewhat less money at 75¢. A job of making a pine table leaf for 58¢ recorded by Reuben Loomis in the early nineteenth century was bespoke by Rev. Joseph Mix of Suffield, Connecticut.[74]

Several early-nineteenth-century craftsmen recorded the installation of leaves in tables identified by their length. At Charlton, Massachusetts, Chapman Lee provided a "New Leaf" for a three-foot table and finished the job by varnishing the entire structure. Two New Hampshire craftsmen, James Chase of Gilmanton and True Currier of Deerfield, made new leaves for four-foot tables. The broad price range for the replacement work in the three tables, 75¢ to $3.25 for the varnished example, describes considerable variety in wood choice. The number of table leaves replaced by furniture makers for customers may have equaled that of all replaced tops, legs (and their metal accessories), and drawers combined.[75]

In replacing a tabletop, craftsmen sometimes found that other tasks were necessary: replacing a drawer or adding a drawer lock; mending a frame or installing new rails; painting a new top or coating an entire table. Tops are identified for large and small tables on occasion; wood selection noted includes mahogany, pine, and maple. In one account entry dated in 1793, Job E. Townsend, of Newport, Rhode Island, recorded a special arrangement with a customer: "To a Mapol Table and he found an old Top."[76]

With specifics such as size and material often unknown, the cost of making and installing a new tabletop is difficult to access. Nathaniel Kinsman of Gloucester, Massachusetts, and Samuel Wayne of Philadelphia made and attached new tabletops for as little as 42¢ to 44¢. Job E. Townsend of Newport priced a "Top to a Small Table" at 50¢. A mahogany tabletop could vary in cost from £1 ($3.34) to as much as £6 ($20.00). Even the utilitarian pine top was subject to a substantial range in price. Samuel Walton made a pine tabletop in 1773 for Joshua Humphries, a Philadelphia shipbuilder, charging 10s. ($1.67). At New York several decades later Nicholas Low paid Jacob Brouwer £2.8 ($8.00) for "a large pine table top."[77]

Craftsmen replaced single legs in common tables for as little as 25¢, the charge made in 1837 by Paul Jenkins at Kennebunk, Maine, for "reparing tabel 1 new Leg." Replacing two legs at one time could be cheaper per unit under certain circumstances because basic table disassembly was the same whether repairing one or more legs. Silas Cheney of Litchfield, Connecticut, charged a customer thirty-eight cents in 1805 for "puting 2 lags to table." Robert Crage provided some insight into leg form at Leicester, Massachusetts, in 1757–1758, when he identified "turning" as a fabrication method. His charge was about 50¢ per leg, which presumably included framing. A customer of Job E. Townsend's at Newport, Rhode Island, paid twice that price in 1785 for "mending a Table With a New Leg mohogony." Walter Nichols undertook more radical work for the local Senter family five years later, when he repaired two legs and replaced several others in a pair of mahogany tables.[78]

At times craftsmen substituted the word "foot" for "leg." An early instance of its use occurs in the accounts of Samuel McCall Sr. of Philadelphia, who paid the joiner Daniel Swan £1 ($3.34) in 1745 for "making a foot to ye Table." The replacement cost suggests a carved walnut example. The same term was still current years later in 1796, when St. George Tucker of Williamsburg, Virginia, employed Charles Hyland to put a new foot on a table of more modest construction, judging by the 4s. (67¢) cost of the repair. Casters appeared on table legs in some numbers by the start of the nineteenth century. Some were part of the original construction, others were added later for convenience, as recorded at New Haven, Connecticut, in 1844 by Howard Smith, who placed casters on a client's table at a charge of $1.37. Occasionally, minor repairs were in order, as when Walsh and Egerton of New York supplied Nicholas Low with "A new wheel for Castor of table."[79]

More often than not, the replacement of a drawer was the occasion for more extensive work on a table. In the pre-Revolutionary years Joseph Symonds of Salem, Massachusetts, and Job Townsend Jr. of Newport, Rhode Island, both recorded a job of replacing a drawer and a tabletop. At the turn of the century coloring a customer's table accompanied drawer-making in the shops of Ezekiel Smith at Taunton, Massachusetts, and Oliver Avery at North Stonington, Connecticut. One of the most extensive jobs recorded is that undertaken in 1826 by James Gere of Groton, Connecticut, for a client in Preston, some fifteen miles distant: "To making Leaf, Draw &c painting & Varnishing Table @ 9 / $1.50." Transporting the table to and from Gere's shop was the customer's responsibility.[80]

Original surfaces on tables often were renewed or refurbished during the lifetime of the first owner. Frequently, a new surface coating was preceded by surface preparation, identified in craftsmen's accounts as "planing," "dressing," "smoothing," "scraping," or "cleaning." The first three words—planing, dressing, and smoothing—describe the same process, that of making a wood surface level, or smooth. Most shops, regardless of geographic location, favored the term "planing," although whatever the word selection, its use usually was consistent within a shop. A rare exception occurs in the records of Job E. Townsend of Newport, Rhode Island. In a ledger entry dated January 26, 1798, under the account of John Taylor, Townsend used his standard term: "To Plaining an old Table." The initial record of this charge in his daybook reads differently: "To Smoothing an old Table." The charge was 3s. (50¢).[81]

Frequently, the process of planing a tabletop, a leaf, or dual surfaces was followed by coating the smoothed areas, if not the entire table, in some manner. Craftsmen often applied stain, sometimes alone, sometimes followed by varnish. Abner Taylor planed and stained a table in 1810 at Lee, Massachusetts, for 34¢. When Jeduthern Avery planed, stained, and varnished a table a few years later at Bolton-Coventry, Connecticut, his charge was slightly higher at 50¢. Other craftsmen described more particular jobs. At New Lisbon, New York, Allen Holcomb recorded work for a customer in 1824 that included "Dressing over Staining & varnishing A Curlmaple table." A large job, undertaken at East Granby, Connecticut, in 1817 by Oliver Moore, involved three tables from one household, which the cabinetmaker planed, stained, and varnished. The work was preceded by "mending one table, Glewing leaf, fixing lock and &c." Some references describe planing and varnishing a table without staining the surfaces. After planing a large table in 1817 at Litchfield, Silas Cheney completed the work by "varnishing [the table] twise." The entire job cost $1.25.[82]

In lieu of varnishing, some householders elected to have their tables polished after the surface was planed, although the materials used for this finish are not specified. At New York in 1738 Joshua Delaplaine recorded "planing over & polishing a Small table." The craftsman's charge of 6s. at this early date suggests the work may have taken longer than a day to complete. Late in the century Pennell Beale of Philadelphia planed and polished "a Large Table" for General Henry Knox, who served as secretary of war in the new federal government, then located in the city. Furniture craftsmen in New England also renewed their share of tables for customers. For example, in the absence of William Greene from Newport, Rhode Island, in 1787, his fellow merchant, Christopher Champlin, looked after the needs of Greene's family. On one occasion Champlin engaged the shop of Stephen and Thomas Goddard to smooth and polish two large tables for Mrs. Greene.[83]

Planing and oiling appears to have been an infrequent option among householders. Silas Cheney planed and oiled a table for 50¢ in 1819 at Litchfield, Connecticut. Some years earlier he oiled another table after scraping the surface. Other options for scraped tables include staining, as recorded by Job E. Townsend at Newport, and painting, noted by True Currier in his accounts at Deerfield, New Hampshire. The most popular coating among householders who chose to have their tables scraped was varnish. Two Connecticut craftsmen named mahogany as the wood of tables refinished in this manner in the 1820s and 1830s. Philemon Robbins scraped and varnished a mahogany table at Hartford. Near the coast at Essex, Elisha Harlow Holmes charged a customer $2.50 to scrape and varnish two mahogany tables, 50¢ more than the client paid for a new trundle bedstead from the shop.[84]

The term "cleaning" or "cleaning off," in reference to restoring a surface, may have several meanings. It could refer simply to cleansing a surface of soil, or it may identify more vigorous activity, such as scraping a surface or smoothing it with a light abrasive. Two shops, those of Fenwick Lyell at Middletown, New Jersey, and Moyers and Rich at Wytheville, Virginia, specifically identified cleaning off and polishing tabletops in the early nineteenth century. Cabinetmaker Jacob Brouwer was asked to clean and polish a table in the household of New York merchant Nicholas Low on several occasions at the turn of the century. The cost varied from 4 to 6s. (67¢ to $1.00), the higher figure similar to Brouwer's charge for putting up three bedsteads in the same household.[85]

In this survey about 69 percent of the tables that received some type of new surface coating were refinished without having the surface first smoothed with hand tools, as described. Six basic surface materials are recorded, whether used alone or in combination with one or more of the other materials. These are ranked from most to least requested: polish, 26.4 percent; varnish, 25.8 percent; stain, 16.6 percent; paint, 16 percent; color, 13.5 percent, and oil, 1.8 percent. "Oiling" and "polishing" a table may describe the same process. As a surface coating on tables, only color, a combination of size and pigment, has yet to be described.

Coloring household furniture in the eighteenth century was an option from an early date. On December 20, 1726, Joseph Brown Jr. of Newbury, Massachusetts, charged Benjamin Morse for "culering & varnishing a table." An average price for coloring a table without further work was 3 to 4s., and, when identified, the form is described as small, little, oval, or round. Lemuel Tobey of Dartmouth–New Bedford named another option when he spent about half a day in 1798 "Cullering and Pollishing [a] Table" for a customer. Other craftsmen carried out somewhat more extensive work when coloring a table, recording the replacement of a table leaf or a drawer.[86]

Craftsmen occasionally noted alterations that changed the structure and/or physical appearance of a table. An early alteration was one undertaken at Philadelphia by Francis Trumble for merchant Nathaniel Allen: "By mending & altring 2 Wallnut tables 10/, hinges & Screws 13/," making a total of £1.3. The substantial cost of the new hardware for the tables, more than that for the repairs and alteration, invites speculation. It appears that all four leaves were rehung, using twelve new hinges and seventy-two screws. This supposition, in turn, suggests that the "mending" occurred at the points where the old hardware was attached to the leaves and tabletops. The damage at the hinge sites appears to have severely compromised the inside edge of one or more leaves, prompting Trumble to suggest shortening, or altering, the leaves by cutting away the damaged wood at the hinge sites and rehanging. To shorten the table leaves in this manner, the original shape had to have been rectangular. Trumble's work for Allen extended over a period of several years and helped to offset some of the annual cost of renting his house from the merchant.[87]

Another alteration, one priced at 9s. and carried out at the end of the century for the household of St. George Tucker at Williamsburg, Virginia, by Charles Hyland, required a day and a half or more of the craftsman's time. The work, described as "altering a four foot mehogany table, cutting of it shorter and cleaning of it of[f] and a new joint," suggests a long rectangular frame with a fixed top and no leaves, given the cost of the job. Removing and shortening the top was minor compared to shortening the side framing pieces by disassembling one end and working two new mortise-and-tenon joints to reattach the legs to the shortened frame. Elisha Harlow Holmes of Essex, Connecticut, had an easier job when he billed Elias Redfield in 1826 for "Rounding table ends at his house." Two other craftsmen working in the early nineteenth century were requested by clients to produce two tables from one large one. At Middletown, New Jersey, Fenwick Lyell described the work as "altering a Table into two" and charged £1.2 ($3.67). Elizur Barnes, working at Middletown, Connecticut, recorded "making 2 tables out of one" for $1.25.[88]

Tea Tables

As a collective body, the repaired tables identified in craftsmen's records by particular function are far fewer in number than the mass of general tables listed without further description. This anonymity often carries over to the nature of repairs, even in named tables. For example, in reviewing references to tea tables, more than half lack details of the actual repair work. Fortunately, the snippets of information in the remaining material appear to represent a reasonable sampling of the range and scope of work carried out on this specialized form (fig. 10). The average cost of unidentified tea-table repairs was 47¢ per job, although two-thirds of the work actually cost householders 34¢ or less and required one-third or less of a craftsman's workday to complete.

Figure 10 Nathaniel Dominy V (1770–1852), tea table, East Hampton, Long Island, New York, 1796. Mahogany. H. 27⅜", Diam. (top) 26⅝". (Courtesy, Winterthur Museum.)

Mahogany is the only wood of the tea table identified in repair work, and the references are few. The work could cost as little as 1s. 6d. (25¢), the fee Samuel Williams charged prominent Philadelphia merchant Michael Gratz for "Glewing 2 Joints & mending a Mohogony teatable," or as much as

$1.00, which likely represented a full day's work on the part of the furniture craftsman. Repairs to or replacement of a tabletop are named more than other tasks in tea-table work. Lemuel Tobey of Dartmouth, Massachusetts, supplied a "Tea Table Top" at 4s. (67¢) in 1785 to "Mr Dillingham, Blacksmith." Thirteen years later the craftsman made a "Tea Table Top and Draw[er]" for another customer and charged him 9s. ($1.50). The term "tee table Leafe" used in 1757 by Peter Emerson of Reading, Massachusetts, may also identify a tabletop.[89]

An early reference of 1742/43 to "making a new molding to a tea table" at the New York shop of Joseph Delaplaine may describe a rectangular rather than a circular table, one with four legs rather than a single pillar on a tripod base. Late in the century Job Danforth of Providence recorded "putting frame on China Table," a reference that also appears to identify a rectangular tea table, one with a gallery around the edges of the top. There is less ambiguity about Titus Preston's work at Wallingford, Connecticut, in 1801, when he put "a dead head to a tea table." This long, slender block of wood with deeply chamfered ends mounted on the underside of a tabletop secured the top to a central pillar. Preston recorded another type of repair a dozen years later, described as "fastning a leg to a tea table." Job E. Townsend of Newport, Rhode Island, went one step further in "Putting a New Leg to a Tea Table." With or without structural repairs to the body, tea-table surfaces periodically required attention. Undoubtedly, some tables were painted. Others were stained, planed and stained, or, in the case of a table refurbished at Middletown, Connecticut, by Elizur Barnes, planed, stained, and varnished.[90]

Tea-table hardware was the concern of patrons of other woodworking shops from New England to the South. New "ketches" were supplied by Samuel Cheever at Salem, Massachusetts, to Colonel John Hawthorne and by Shaw and Chisholm at Annapolis, Maryland, to James Brice, Esq. Thomas Affleck's reference to a "Tea Table lock" at Philadelphia may describe the same hardware. Patrons of other cabinetmaking establishments requested casters to provide ease in moving tea tables. Charles Norris of Philadelphia acquired "A Set of new Castors" in 1764 when having his table "mended" by Samuel Matthews. A single replacement caster was all that St. George Tucker required of John Hockaday at Williamsburg, Virginia, after the turn of the century.[91]

Dining Tables
Craftsmen enjoyed a relatively brisk business in dining-table repairs. As expected, the average cost of the many anonymous repair jobs listed is significantly higher at 73¢ than the average unidentified tea-table repair. A rare descriptive entry for general mending in the accounts of David Evans provides some insight on work versus cost at this Philadelphia shop in 1776: "To making a Joint to a Dining Table 1/6, To a hinge for D[itt]o 1/0," the total being 2s. 6d. (42¢). What exactly did the customer, John Biddle, get for his 42¢? Evans's labor charge at 1s. 6d. was equal to about a quarter of a day's pay, and the additional shilling bought one hinge. The time devoted to the

job indicates that Evans did more than replace a broken hinge with a new one. Because of damage at the original hinge site, the craftsman made a new joint by paring away wood on the undersurface of the stationary top and the leaf, ensuring that the newly installed hinge would lie flush with the wood.[92]

Several accounts identify the wood of a table under repair. In 1822 in rural Cooperstown, New York, Miles Benjamin mended a cherry dining table. Walnut tables appear to have been favored at Philadelphia in the mid- to late eighteenth century, as three are named in accounts. One was almost new when repaired. On February 23, 1754, John Elliott Sr. completed a "Square Walnut Dineing table" for merchant Edward Shippen Jr., whom he charged £2.15. The table was back in Elliott's shop less than a week later, on March 1, for "Mending and working over a new Square Dineing table" at an additional charge of 12s. 6d. What had happened? Because carrying or carting furniture to and from a woodworker's shop was the responsibility of the customer, it appears that some mishap occurred between Elliott's shop and Shippen's house. Mahogany is named in a New York account of 1783, when Jonathan Cowdrey repaired a dining table described as "large" for Chancellor Robert R. Livingston. Considerably less pretentious was the table repaired and painted "Mehogany" color two decades later at Bordentown, New Jersey, by John Sager.[93]

Constant use of the dining table in the home and the size and weight of the fall leaves necessitated that some leaves would require replacement from time to time. When Jacob Sass undertook this work at Charleston, South Carolina, in 1805, he charged $6.00 for a single leaf. The table may well have been made of mahogany, although of modest size. Two years later at Middletown, New Jersey, Fenwick Lyell charged a customer the enormous sum of $18.00 for "Puting leaves to a Large Dining Table," which almost certainly was made of mahogany. Periodically a table leg required attention. Elisha Harlow Holmes repaired a "Dining table new leg two butts" (hinges) in 1829 at Essex, Connecticut. An unusual occurrence was William Turner's job of "Repairing a pillar & Claw Dining Table" in 1817 for New York merchant Nicholas Low. The table appears to have been part of a purchase Low made in 1808 from Robert McConachy described as "a Sett Pillar & Claw Dining tables." The purchase price of $190.00 suggests the tables were richly carved and perhaps gilded.[94]

More than the introduction of replacement parts, dining tables required renewed and refurbished surfaces. Planing, smoothing, dressing, or scraping was followed by stain, varnish, and polish, sometimes alone, sometimes in combination. In June 1814 Thomas Boynton of Windsor, Vermont, took on a job for William Leverett that included scraping and varnishing two dining tables, one described as circular. Boynton also made several new pieces of furniture for Leverett at that time, and at the end of the account entry he penned a rather uncommon note: "all mahogany varnished 4 times." Rarely did furniture receive more than two coats of varnish, and one coat was still more common. At Newport, Rhode Island, Job E. Townsend undertook special work of a different type in 1801 for Samuel Vaughn. After mending, staining, and polishing a dining table, he built "Two Sircler End

Figure 11   End section of dining table, probably Baltimore, Maryland, 1790–1800. Mahogany, mahogany veneer, and cedrella with white oak. H. 28¾", W. 51⅜", L. 43⅝". (Courtesy, Winterthur Museum.)

Tables" to complement the main dining frame (fig. 11), all at a cost of £3 ($10.00). Vaughn's was not the only request for this dining enhancement. In the same year Dr. John Rodgers of New York acquired "a pair of ends for a table" for his house in Cortlandt Street. General Moses Porter of Boston may already have owned the two end tables he had repaired by Nathaniel Bryant two decades later.[95]

Breakfast, or Pembroke, Tables
Small tables for the purpose of individual or private dining were in use prior to the eighteenth century in Europe, although it was almost the mid-eighteenth century before the small table became a reasonably common household form and one associated particularly with the breakfast meal (fig. 12). Thomas Chippendale illustrated only two designs for "Breakfast Tables" in

Figure 12   Elijah (1752–1825) and Jacob (1758–1810) Sanderson, breakfast, or Pembroke, table, Salem, Massachusetts, 1779–1800. Mahogany with white pine. H. 27½", W. 34", L. (open) 34⅞". (Courtesy, Winterthur Museum.)

the three editions of his *Director,* published between 1754 and 1762. A purchase for the English royal household in 1765 describes the structural features that became associated with the form: "a good mahogany 2 Flap Breakfast Table with a Drawer on Brass Casters." Toward the end of the century the form became known as a "Pembroke table," a term used by Thomas Sheraton in his *Drawing-Book* (1793) and by George Hepplewhite in his *Guide* (1794). Concerning the shape of the tabletop, Sheraton noted that "the long square and the oval are the most fashionable." Sheraton linked the name "Pembroke" with a lady who was an early owner of one of the small tables.[96]

References to repair work on the small dining frame known both as a breakfast and a Pembroke table in America first appear in this study under dates in the late eighteenth century. The earliest is 1791, when General Henry Knox engaged Pennell Beale of Philadelphia to plane and polish "4 Breakfast Tables @ 3/9 pr Table." The latest reference is 1830, with the bulk of material falling between 1791 and 1816. Although the breakfast/Pembroke-table sample in this study is relatively small, it may be of sufficient size to identify some regional preferences in the use of these terms. Craftsmen in Connecticut, New York City, New Jersey, and Philadelphia were consistent in their choice of "breakfast table," just as woodworkers in Salem, Massachusetts, Newport, Rhode Island, and Williamsburg, Virginia, preferred "Pembroke table."[97]

Structural repairs to the breakfast/Pembroke table focus on two elements, legs and tops. William Reger of Germantown, near Philadelphia, put a new leg in a table in 1816 for Charles Wistar. At New York Jacob Brouwer went a step further in 1802, when "Repairing a breakfast table with new legs & stretchers." It was the tabletop, however, that required the most attention. The work could vary from simply "screwing on the top of a pembroke Table," as recorded in 1795 by Rookesby Roberts at Williamsburg, Virginia, to making a new top. On this subject the records of Job E. Townsend of Newport, Rhode Island, are particularly comprehensive because they also shed light on materials. Two account entries dating to 1804 are noteworthy. Townsend charged Benedict Smith 13s. 6d. for "Making a New Birch top and staining the frame of a Pembroke Table." When Henry Freeborn paid 18s. for his work, the charge reflected the greater status of his choice of wood: "To a New Top To a Cherry Pembroke Table."[98]

Townsend's records for 1799 to 1801 also contain insights on new work that provide a basis for cost comparison. A plain cherry Pembroke table from the shop cost £2.2 (42s.). If the small frame was embellished with stringing, the charge was £2.8 (48s.). The 6s. difference between the two tables describes an additional day's labor to lay in the narrow threads of contrasting wood. The price of a mahogany table with stringing was £3 (60s.). By contrast, a householder could purchase a plain maple Pembroke table from Townsend for as little as 15s. Reuben Loomis identified "a breakfast table with a drawr" in 1824, when filling an order at Suffield, Connecticut.[99]

Surface refurbishing recorded for the breakfast/Pembroke table is not unlike that described for the dining table. Planing, oiling, and varnishing were options, either alone or in combination. Captain John Derby of Salem, Massachusetts, engaged Robert Cowan in 1803 to varnish and polish "a pembroke Table (made by Sanderson)," identifying either Elijah or Jacob, the entrepreneurial brothers who made and brokered quantities of furniture for exportation (fig. 12). Painting was another option. This was the choice in 1805 of a customer at John Sager's shop in Bordentown, New Jersey.[100]

Dressing Tables

The furniture form for the chamber, or bedroom, that functioned as a center for personal grooming from the late seventeenth century until well into the nineteenth century is termed in this study either a "dressing table" or a "toilet table" (also "toyelite," "twilite"). Whether craftsmen and customers made a distinction in using these terms is unclear. The word "dressing" is almost 2½ times as common as "toilet" in the present sample, and it occurs in records at an earlier date. Joshua Delaplaine of New York City billed Jane Gilbert 10s. in 1737 for "raising a dressing table with a new draw[er] & furniture" (hardware). The term "raise," as used here, may describe straightforward replacement work or a new feature designed to enhance the usefulness of the furniture. First mention of the toilet table in this study is January 21, 1775, when William Savery of Philadelphia completed a "Top to a toilet table" for Joseph Pemberton. Information on repair costs is fragmentary, although it appears that charges for mending a dressing table usually were higher than those for a toilet table.[101]

Most dressing tables have one or two tiers of drawers in the frame (fig. 13). A few tables have interiors fitted with compartments and, on occasion, an easel-style dressing glass in a drawer. Most of the dressing tables in

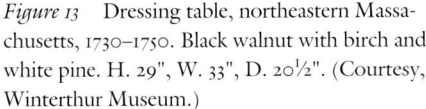

Figure 13 Dressing table, northeastern Massachusetts, 1730–1750. Black walnut with birch and white pine. H. 29", W. 33", D. 20½". (Courtesy, Winterthur Museum.)

this sample appear to have been of simple structure, with a few exceptions. One exception may be the "Dressing Table with Glass" repaired by Robert C. Scadin of Cooperstown, New York, in 1830 at a charge of $6.00 to the owner. Repairs carried out by Elizur Barnes at Middletown, Connecticut, several years earlier were modest by comparison. He charged one patron 25¢ for "Easing Draws to 2 Dressing tables at house." Because house calls were unusual in the cabinet trade, Barnes may have completed the work when in the vicinity on other business. On another occasion a customer paid Barnes $1.25 for "mending Dressing table Legg & painting D[itt]o." An early and unusual repair noted by Solomon Fussell of Philadelphia in 1741 was turning a "Ball for a Dressing Table." The 4¢ "ornament" for an earlier-style table likely replaced a lost or damaged pendent drop in the case frame or a finial at the center crossing of a pair of curvilinear stretchers.[102]

On occasion craftsmen noted replacing the entire top of either a dressing table or a toilet table. The cost usually was low, even when Job E. Townsend of Newport, Rhode Island, recorded "Making a New top and Splicing the legs Toy light" (for a toilet table). The 50¢ charge indicates the top was made of common wood and probably painted. Paint also was current for the dressing table. Allen Holcomb's charge of 50¢ in 1827 at New Lisbon, New York, describes embellishment he added to painted furniture: "Striping a wash stand and Dress[ing] table." Stain, color, and varnish were other surface options. Perhaps the table Townsend "cover[ed] . . . with oil Cloth" to protect the surface was for use in the toilet in the household of David Stephens, the client.[103]

If a chamber table was not supplied with a fitted drawer, a householder could purchase a dressing box to place on the top. Many boxes were framed with an accompanying looking glass. At times these accessories also required maintenance. When in Philadelphia during the 1790s, General Henry Knox sought the services of Pennell Beale and Isaac Ashton for this work on several occasions. One request to Ashton was for a "Kea for the Dressing Box & mending the Glass fraim." At Newport Job E. Townsend mended a "Shaving Glass," identifying another function filled by dressing furniture. Surfaces periodically needed attention. Mrs. John Francis of Philadelphia paid Richard Alexander the tidy sum of $2.50 in 1817 for "Pollishing in Varnish a Dressing box."[104]

Card Tables

The earliest repaired card tables recorded in this study were located in urban settings and date to the 1770s, identifying them as cabriole-style furniture (fig. 14). David Evans of Philadelphia made repairs to John Biddle's table, which required new hinges. At Salem, Massachusetts, the estate of Nathaniel Gould charged merchant Elias Hasket Derby 6s. for unspecified card-table repairs that, based on the cost, likely had required a day to complete. Between 1780 and 1794 craftsmen repaired eight other pre-federal tables, one described as mahogany, whose owners resided in urban or semi-urban centers, including Newburyport, Massachusetts, New York City, Philadelphia, Freehold, New Jersey, and Williamsburg, Virginia.[105]

Figure 14 Card table, Philadelphia, Pennsylvania, 1750–1775. Walnut with yellow pine. H. 28⅜", W. 31⅞", D. (open) 31⅜". (Courtesy, Winterthur Museum.)

Repair work on card tables often reflects work carried out on other table forms. For example, a customer at Freehold, New Jersey, asked Alexander Low to hinge a card table. David Evans of Philadelphia and Fenwick Lyell of Middletown, New Jersey, each framed a new leg in a card table. Eliakim Prindle of Salem, Massachusetts, requested Benjamin Ellery Jr. to put a new top on his table. Other structural repairs include the "new lath" (braces for the frame) that Jacob Brouwer of New York fitted into each of a pair of tables owned by Nicholas Low. The merchant also engaged Brouwer to install "new baze" on the top of a card table. Baize, a felted woolen cloth, was dyed green or brown. An unusual request made in 1829 by a customer of Robert C. Scadin at Cooperstown, New York, was for "pillers & Claws to Card Tables," with sets of casters for the feet. The total bill was $17.50. Without further information, it would appear that the customer updated older tops with new bases. Scadin's price for a new stand or a new tea table in the pillar-and-claw style was $25.00. Cabinetmakers also responded to customers' requests for surface refinishing by planing or scraping their card tables followed by stain, varnish, or polish. A customer of George Short at Newburyport, Massachusetts, was credited $1.50 for painting two card tables.[106]

Table games, aside from those employing cards, had some currency in the American household. Several records cite repairs to backgammon tables. Earliest is a record in the accounts of Benjamin Randolph of Philadelphia, who in 1767 billed Colonel George Croghan, Indian trader, agent, and land speculator, for "Mending 2 Backgammon Tables" at a cost of £1. Job Townsend Jr. and his son Job E. Townsend had similar calls for repair work between 1768 and 1785 at Newport, Rhode Island. Although the game of backgammon was available in board form, tables appear to have been preferred in some quarters. Young Elizabeth Bleecker McDonald of New York noted in her diary on January 11, 1802, that Peter Stuyvesant, one of a circle of friends she and her husband entertained, had made her a present of "a handsome Back gammon table." Four days later she noted: "Peter Stuyvesant was here—he and I sat playing Back Gammon till near twelve o'clock."[107]

Kitchen Tables

Whereas Philemon Robbins of Hartford, Connecticut, sold a new kitchen table for $1.75 in 1834, a general survey of table repairs indicates that some tables when new sold for considerably more. Some kitchen tables appear to have had stationary tops; others had one or more fall leaves. The cost of general repairs varied from 25¢ to almost $1.00. Repairs made with new parts are more revealing. Amos Denison Allen of Windham, Connecticut, the only craftsman to name a table material, supplied a patron with "1 citchen table leaf pine" and charged him $1.84 for the work. Some leaves supplied by other craftsmen were almost as expensive; others were about half the price, indicating that table size and material varied appreciably. Joseph Griswold of Buckland, Massachusetts, and David Haven of Framingham supplied customers with both a new leaf and a drawer for their kitchen tables, again at varied pricing. In "putting a Top & Draw to a Citchen Table" for $2.25 in 1803, Job Danforth of Providence appears to have replaced a stationary top. Another fixed top required "Smoothing & puting on Part kitche[n] table top" ten years later at the Litchfield, Connecticut, shop of Silas Cheney.[108]

Householders selected a suitable table finish from several options. At Glastonbury, Connecticut, in 1801, George Talcott paid Solomon Cole $1.67 for a "Citchen table leaf & staining frame." Stain followed by varnish was the choice of other householders. Following repair work on his kitchen table, David Crage of Charlton, Massachusetts, directed Chapman Lee to coat the surface with paint. Paint again was deemed a suitable finish for utilitarian furniture when Christian M. Nestell of Providence repaired and painted a "large wash Table" for Richard W. Greene, Esq.[109]

Tables of Special Note

Several tables of opulent feature from affluent households invite special notice because notes on their repair are uncommon in craftsmen's or clients' accounts. On March 10, 1795, Mathurin Tardy of New York received £10 ($33.40) from Chancellor Robert R. Livingston "for Mending and Polishing two Marble Tables." Equally handsome furniture stood in the home of Stephen Girard at Philadelphia in 1824, when the merchant paid William Sherman $20.00 to regild and varnish a "Carved Table." Girard again required Sherman's services three years later to mend a "Gilt Table."[110]

Stands and Stand Tables

Craftsmen's records identify a large group of small tables of varied feature as stands or stand tables. Some stands filled general household needs, while others served specialized functions. A large body of material relating to this form addresses repair work of a general nature without identifying function or feature. In summarizing data of a more specific type, legs and tops appear to have required the most attention, whether for repair or replacement. New leaves or screws for leaves are noted, and craftsmen installed new or replacement locks on box-style stands. Mahogany is named occasionally as the construction wood; cherry is mentioned once. Surface preparation and finish run the gamut. Surfaces were planed, smoothed, scraped, and cleaned. Finishes include stain, varnish, paint, oil, polish, and wax.

Candlestands and Light Stands

A candlestand in the form of a small table (fig. 15) was relatively uncommon in America before the 1740s, and the form may have remained a rarity in rural areas for several decades longer. When Abraham David of Southold on eastern Long Island ordered half a dozen out-of-fashion cane-back chairs in 1761, he also directed John Paine "to mack a stand to set a candle on." The wording suggests some unfamiliarity with the form. Only two years later, William Barker, a furniture maker of Providence, where society was considerably more cosmopolitan, was already "mending [a] candle stand" for a client. Toward the end of the century another term for this furniture form

Figure 15 Joseph Short (1771–1819), candlestand, Newburyport, Massachusetts, 1795–1805. Mahogany. H. 26⅝", W. (top) 13⅝", L. (top) 18½". (Courtesy, Winterthur Museum.)

came into relatively common use. The earliest "light stand" repair recorded in this study dates to 1788, when Job E. Townsend of Providence produced "a Crose [cross] stick for a Lite Stand," presumably a cleat for the underside of the top. There appears to be little, if any, difference in meaning between the terms "light stand" and "candlestand," although records indicate the word "candlestand" was in more general use.[111]

Most stand repairs cost 50¢ or less. Higher charges reflect work of an extensive nature or the use of costly materials. A review of accounts from the shops of a group of New England craftsmen identifies prices for new stands, ranging from $1.34, possibly for a painted example, to $5.00 for a "mahogany turn up" stand. The review also indicates that 80 percent of the stands purchased by householders cost $2.00 or less. A "second hand light-stand" from the shop of True Currier at Deerfield, New Hampshire, could be acquired for 58¢. In reviewing repairs, two woods are named in the general sample, mahogany and cherry, and each just once. The reference to the cherry stand actually identifies another, somewhat unusual, circumstance. In 1813 Oliver Moore of East Granby, Connecticut, accommodated Phineas Newton Jr. by "turning a Candle stand post" for 25¢ and then providing "Cherry pieces for leggs" at 6¢. Obviously, Newton planned to build his own candlestand, highlighting a craftsman-customer arrangement repeated from time to time in other shops.[112]

A replacement candlestand or light-stand top to be finished in varnish, other than one of mahogany, cost about 50¢ at either a rural or urban shop. Luke Houghton of Barre, Massachusetts, and Isaac Vose of Boston noted these charges in their accounts. Silas Cheney's "Bord for top of Candle Stand" cost 20¢ and likely received a coat of paint at his shop in Litchfield, Connecticut. The "leaf" for a candlestand listed in craftsmen's accounts appears to have been an alternative term for a top. Use of the term was widespread—from the accounts of George Landon in Erie, Pennsylvania, to those of Allen Holcomb in New Lisbon, New York, and William Mather in Whately, Massachusetts.[113]

Because of its design, the candlestand, or light stand, was vulnerable to tipping over, sometimes resulting in damage to the pillar. Philip Deland recorded mending a pillar in 1819 at his shop in West Brookfield, Massachusetts. True Currier's description of this construction element at Deerfield, New Hampshire, was "light stand body." Frequently, damage to the pillar was sufficient that replacement was necessary, leading craftsmen, including Samuel Douglas of near Canton, Connecticut, to note, "repairing Candle Stand made new pillar." Douglas's charge of 67¢ was half the price of a new stand. James Gere of Groton identified turning as the usual method of fabricating the pillar. Most vulnerable of all were the legs. Fortunately, several accounts contain more than the basic information common to most records. Daniel Trotter of Philadelphia described "putting a new Claw foot to a Stand" at a charge of 5s. (84¢) in 1788, three years following Townsend Goddard's record of "makeing a Leg to Stand, paw foot" at Newport, Rhode Island, for merchant Christopher Champlin. Silas Cheney carried out more extensive work at Litchfield, Connecticut, in the early nineteenth century, when Tapping Reeve, Esq., bespoke a job of "putting 3 Lags to mehogeny Candlestand and varnishing the same for O Woolcot" (probably Oliver Wolcott). The charge was 8s. ($1.34).[114]

Plain varnish was the common finish of the candlestand. Occasionally a craftsman planed and stained the wood first. Other options included applying a coat of paint or color. Hartwell Holmes of Woodstock, Connecticut, probably spent no more than one-twelfth of a day (less than one hour) painting a candlestand in 1806, since his charge was just 8¢. Edward Slead's fee for "colouring and pollishing one candle stand" in 1798 at Dartmouth, Massachusetts, was only slightly more at 12½ cents.[115]

Worktables and Work Stands

The lady's worktable, first produced in Paris circa 1750, was current in England within a few years. Thomas Sheraton illustrated two designs for worktables in the 1793, or first, edition of his *Drawing-Book,* and production of this form in America may have begun before the close of the century (fig. 16). As early as 1804 a client brought a worktable to the shop of Fenwick Lyell at Middletown, New Jersey, a community lying within the sphere of New York influence, to be varnished and fitted with casters. The charge of 18s. ($3.00) for the work was substantial, perhaps reflecting the quality of the table, which could have been of English or American construction. The next reference, which dates to 1811, leaves little doubt that American furniture was the subject. On August 7 Captain Reuben S. Randall brought two work tables for repair to the shop of Langley Boardman in Portsmouth, New Hampshire. These tables appear to have been the "two work tables" Randall bought from Boardman earlier in the year on January 26 for the sum of $18.00.[116]

Whereas "work table" appears to have been the general term in England for the box-style frame with a drawer or drawers used by ladies to store needlework and sewing equipment, American craftsmen and consumers identified the form by either of two names, "work table" or "work stand." Both terms were concurrent and appear to have followed no clear pattern of regional use, although "table" may have been preferred in New York City and Philadelphia. A relatively common call at cabinet shops was for "new triming work Stand & finding knobs," as recorded by Paul Jenkins in 1839 at Kennebunk, Maine. The work cost 50¢ or less. More expensive was "a Set of Casters on a Worktable" for which Richard Alexander of Philadelphia charged $1.25. Alterations occurred from time to time. Thirty-four cents was Elizur Barnes's fee in 1824 for "Lowering workstand & mending Casters" for a customer at Middletown, Connecticut. Some worktables had a cloth bag, or pouch, for storing current needlework or sewing. Whether this accessory was an item in a bill of 1827 from Michael Bouvier of Philadelphia to Stephen Girard is unclear: "To Repairing & furnishing cloth & silk for Tables $20." When renewing the finish of a worktable, furniture craftsmen routinely cleaned, stained, varnished, and/or polished the surface. George Button of Groton, Connecticut, engaged James Gere in 1828 to stain and varnish one of two work stands he brought to the shop; the craftsman painted and ornamented the second stand.[117]

Figure 16 Worktable or -stand, New York, 1800–1810. Curled maple and curled maple veneer with yellow poplar. H. 32", W. 19⅛", D. 15". (Courtesy, Winterthur Museum.)

Washstands and Basin Stands

A piece of furniture designed especially for the purpose of washing the hands and body was current in England only about the mid-eighteenth century. Chippendale introduced designs for basin stands with the third edition (1762) of the *Director*. Early stands have tripod bases with slender, tiered, open skeletal bodies. Designs for stands illustrated by Hepplewhite and Sheraton toward the end of the century include cupboards, drawers, backsplashes, and other conveniences. Most frames are rectangular or triangular. These features and shapes are more in keeping with the stands represented in the repair work described in this study (fig. 17).[118]

Terminology is again a consideration in reviewing repairs made to this specialized stand because craftsmen in America used two names to identify the form — "basin stand" and "wash stand." Basin stand is the less common of the two, although it may have been in use earlier. In 1784 Thomas Affleck, a prominent Philadelphia cabinetmaker who had emigrated from Scotland,

Figure 17 Jacob Forster (1764–1838), corner wash, or basin, stand, Charlestown, Massachusetts, 1790–1800. Mahogany with white pine. H. 34", W. 29¼", D. 16¼". (Courtesy, Winterthur Museum.)

repaired a "Bason Stand" for General John Cadwalader, owner of a handsome house in Second Street furnished in an opulent style. Twelve years earlier the first printed furniture price book was published in the city and included among the entries two listings for a "Bason Stand." Materials for the present study indicate this term was also in use in Charleston, South Carolina, New York City, and adjacent Middletown, New Jersey. Otherwise "wash stand" appears to have been the preferred term from New England to the South.[119]

The triangular washstand with rounded front illustrated in figure 17 is identified as a "Corner Basin Stand" in design books. Of this form, Hepplewhite stated, "This is a very useful shape, as it stands in a corner out of the way." Sheraton commented further on the design of the front legs, noting in his *Cabinet Dictionary* that they were made to "spring forward" to protect the stand from "tumbling over." Another feature here is the two hinged top boards to be raised "to prevent water from spraying the wall." When folded over completely, the boards form a cover for the top well. A convenient shelf for linens supports a central drawer flanked by two sham drawers, and a bottom stretcher provides structural reinforcement for the delicate legs.[120]

Craftsmen's records identify a variety of structural repairs to wash- and basin stands. Fenwick Lyell put "a Top on a Basin Stand" in 1809 at Middletown, New Jersey. A new drawer for a washstand cost a customer 50¢ at the shop of Miles Benjamin in Cooperstown, New York. Benjamin's records indicate that he sold new washstands in a range of prices from $2.25 to $12.00. Retrimming a stand was a regular call at many shops. After making repairs to a washstand, Alexander H. Gilbert of Chester, Connecticut, charged a customer 50¢ for a mahogany knob. The "New Stretcher" installed in a basin stand at Charleston, South Carolina, by Nicholas Silberg in 1799 may have been of triangular form to support turned-out legs of the type in figure 17. Occasionally a craftsman made a quick repair using glue, as indicated in the records of Silas Cheney at Litchfield, Connecticut.[121]

Finishes for wash- and basin stands are divided between varnish and paint. Daniel Dewey of Hartford, Connecticut, scraped three washstands for Daniel Wadsworth in 1829 before applying varnish. Painting records are somewhat more descriptive. Philemon Robbins, another Hartford craftsman, charged a customer 50¢ to paint a washstand yellow; a coat of varnish followed. Fifty cents also was William Beesley's fee at Salem, New Jersey, in 1831 for "painting a wash stand maple." Beesley's charge raises the question of whether the new paint was merely maple color or a grained surface simulating the figure of the wood. At New Lisbon, New York, Allen Holcomb decorated a washstand by introducing "Striping." Sometimes the work was more extensive than indicated in that simple descriptor.[122]

Summary
Although substantive information highlighting furniture repairs and alterations in the late-colonial and federal periods forms only a small part of the related general body of material in craftsmen's records, careful analysis, cost

comparison, and even reading between the lines provide further illumination of this important branch of the furniture trade. These avenues of investigation will be continued in part 2, which, as noted, will explore the recorded activity of craftsmen who undertook to repair, refurbish, and, on occasion, alter their patrons' case furniture, looking glasses, and small household and personal items.

1. Amos Denison Allen Memorandum Book, Windham, Connecticut, 1796–1803, account with John Jenings, August 27, 1798, Connecticut Historical Society, Hartford (hereafter cited as CHS).

2. Daniel and Samuel Proud Account Book, Providence, Rhode Island, 1810–1834, accounts with George Sprag[u]e, February 13, 1818, and Samuel B. Mumford, May 23, 1815, Rhode Island Historical Society, Providence (hereafter cited as RIHS). Thomas Moody Bill to Captain Edmund Kimball, Newburyport, Massachusetts, May 30, 1801, Kimball Family Papers, Peabody Essex Museum, Salem, Massachusetts (hereafter cited as PEM). John Proud Bill to Albert C. Greene, Providence, Rhode Island, June 1824, A. C. and R. W. Greene Collection, RIHS.

3. Elizur Barnes Account Book, Middletown, Connecticut, 1821–1825, account with Arthur W. Magill, April 9, 1822, Middletown Historical Society, Middletown, Connecticut. Thomas Sheraton, *The Cabinet Dictionary*, 2 vols. (1803; reprint, New York: Praeger, 1970), 2: 423.

4. William Barker Account Book, Providence, Rhode Island, 1784–1787, account with Welcome Arnold, May 4, 1785, RIHS. Stephen Whipple Account Book, Boston and northeastern Massachusetts, 1803–1811, account with Joseph Kendall, June 1805, Ipswich Historical Society, Ipswich, Massachusetts. Simon Perkins information from Charles S. Parsons, "New Hampshire Notes," Visual Resources Collection, Winterthur Museum, Winterthur, Delaware (hereafter cited as WM). Solomon Fussell Account Book, Philadelphia, Pennsylvania, 1738–1748, account with John Richardson, 11:12:1739/40, Stephen Collins Papers, Library of Congress, Washington, D.C. (hereafter cited as LC). Thomas Boynton Ledger, Boston, Massachusetts, and Windsor, Vermont, 1810–1817, account with William Leverett, April 22, 1816, Special Collections, Dartmouth College, Hanover, New Hampshire. Silas Ellis Cheney Daybook, Litchfield, Connecticut, 1813–1821, account with Jonathan Buel, October 17, 1820, Litchfield Historical Society, Litchfield, Connecticut (hereafter cited as LHS).

5. For more insight on rocking chairs, see Nancy Goyne Evans, "The Genesis of the Boston Rocking Chair," *Antiques* 122, no. 1 (January 1983): 246–53; and Nancy Goyne Evans, *American Windsor Furniture: Specialized Forms* (New York: Hudson Hills Press, 1997), "The Rocking Chair," pp. 52–85.

6. Allen Holcomb Account Book, New Lisbon, New York, 1809–ca. 1828, account with Ira Skidmore, July 1825, Metropolitan Museum of Art, New York. Chapman Lee Ledger, Charlton, Massachusetts, 1799–1850, account with James Irons, December 10, 1828, Old Sturbridge Village, Sturbridge, Massachusetts (hereafter cited as OSV). George Landon Account Book, Erie, Pennsylvania, 1813–1832, account with Robert Murray, April 28, 1819, Joseph Downs Collection of Manuscripts and Printed Ephemera (hereafter cited as DCM), WM. Samuel Davison Ledger, Plainfield, Massachusetts, 1795–1824, account with Daniel Ford, July 1807, Pocumtuck Valley Memorial Association, Deerfield, Massachusetts. True Currier Account Book, Deerfield, New Hampshire, 1815–1838, account with Stephen Cram, May 1824 and April 1825, DCM.

7. Titus Preston Ledger, Wallingford, Connecticut, 1795–1817, account with Jared Alling, February 27, 1805, Sterling Library, Yale University, New Haven, Connecticut (hereafter cited as YU). James Chestnut Bill to Peter E. Elmendorf, Albany, New York, November 19, 1805, Sanders Papers, New-York Historical Society, New York (hereafter cited as N-YHS).

8. William, Daniel, and Samuel Proud Ledger, Providence, Rhode Island, 1770–1825, account with Amos Atwell, March 4, 1782, RIHS.

9. David Alling Daybook, Newark, New Jersey, 1836–1854, accounts with Colonel Graham, September 19, 1836, and L. E. Barnes, October 31, 1837, New Jersey Historical Society, Newark, New Jersey (hereafter cited as NJHS).

10. Advertisement of Samuel J. Tuck, *Columbian Centinel* (Boston), May 5, 1802.

11. Preston Ledger, account with Samuel Cook, May 2, 1801. John Sager Daybook, Bordentown, New Jersey, 1805–1817, account with Frederick Brooks, September 21, 1808, Historical Society of Pennsylvania, Philadelphia (hereafter cited as HSP). Alling Daybook, account with Mrs. Cummings, August 13, 1836.

12. Silas Ellis Cheney Ledger, Litchfield, Connecticut, 1799–1817, account with Bettey Shepard, 1817, and Daybook, 1802–1807, account with C. Goodwin, May 28, 1805, LHS (scraping). Cheney Daybook, 1813–1821, accounts with Mary Lord, September 16, 1815 (chair delivery), Jonathan Buel, October 17, 1820 (smoothing), and Orin Judd, May 18, 1821 (four coats). James Gere Ledger, Groton, Connecticut, 1822–1852, account with George Harvey, September 30, 1831, Connecticut State Library, Hartford (hereafter cited as CSL).

13. Barnes Account Book, account with John C. Pratt, July 17, 1823. Alling Daybook, accounts with A. S. Prisson, June 18, 1839 (ball-back chairs), and Mrs. J. Beam, April 2, 1840. David Alling Ledger, Newark, New Jersey, 1803–1853, account with Fitch Smith, April 1, 1840, NJHS.

14. Elisha Hawley Account Book, Ridgefield, Connecticut, 1781–1805, account with Col. David Olmstead, May 20, 1800, CHS (green chairs, kitchen chairs). Isaiah Tiffany Account Book, Norwich, Connecticut, 1746–1767, account with Elijah Bliss, August 25, 1756, CHS (four-slat chairs). Fussell Account Book, account with Richard Swan, 3:6:1747 (five-slat chairs). John Durand Account Book, Milford, Connecticut, 1760–1783, account with Mr. Lownsbury, April 18, 1764, Milford Historical Society, Milford, Connecticut (old chairs). William Barker Account Book, Providence, Rhode Island, 1750–1772, account with Ephraim Bowen, February 1774 (rocking chair), and Account Book, 1753–1766, account with Simon Lowring, April 1772 (low chair), RIHS.

15. Richard Johns Bill to Deborah Morris, Philadelphia, September 18, 1765, Gratz Collection, HSP. William Wilson Order to William Neate, Philadelphia to London, August 23, 1760, Letter Book of William Wilson, Mercantile Papers, New York Public Library, New York (hereafter cited as NYPL). John Shaw and Archibald Chisholm Bill to James Brice, Annapolis, Maryland, July 30, 1772, Brice-Jennings Papers, Maryland Historical Society, Baltimore. Cheney Daybook (1802–1807), account with Tapping Reeve, May 17, 1807. John F. Page, *Litchfield County Furniture* (Litchfield, Conn.: Litchfield Historical Society, 1969), p. 51. Dr. Isaac Senter in Joseph K. Ott, "Recent Discoveries among Rhode Island Cabinetmakers and Their Work," *Rhode Island History* 28, no. 1 (February 1969): 9.

16. Daniel Drinker Bill to Stephen Collins, Philadelphia, June 24, 1766–July 17, 1769, Collins Papers. Anonymous Cabinetmaker's Account Book, probably Fredericksburg, Virginia, 1767–1777, account with Capt. Lawrence Taliaferro, May 25, 1775, DCM. Thomas Burling Bill to Chancellor Robert R. Livingston, New York, May 6, 1786, Robert R. Livingston Papers, N-YHS. Daniel Trotter Bill to Stephen Girard, Philadelphia, April 2, 1787, Girard Papers, Girard College, Philadelphia. E. and J. Sanderson Bill to Elias Hasket Derby, Salem, Massachusetts, June 14, 1793, Derby Family Papers, PEM. Stephen Badlam Bill to Gen. Henry Knox, Dorchester, Massachusetts, November 3, 1784, Henry Knox Papers, Massachusetts Historical Society, Boston (hereafter cited as MHS). Alling Daybook, 1836–1854, account with Frederick T. Frelinghuysen Jr., May 25, 1840.

17. Job Danforth Sr., Ledger, Providence, Rhode Island, 1788–1818, accounts with Stephen Jackson, May 23, 1803, and Elisha Dyer, April 13, 1803, RIHS. Richard Alexander Bill to Mrs. John Francis, Philadelphia, November 6, 1817–November 13, 1822, Cadwalader Papers, Gen. Thomas Cadwalader, HSP.

18. Cheney Daybook, 1802–1807, account with Tapping Reeve, May 7, 1807. Barnes Account Book, account with John L. Lewis, June 1822. Philemon Robbins Account Book, Hartford, Connecticut, 1833–1836, account with E. B. Stedman, March 1834, CHS. Cheney Daybook, 1813–1821, account with Betsey Collins, May 12, 1813. Barnes Account Book, account with Eleazer Doud, July 12, 1823. Duncan Phyfe Bill to James L. Brinckerhoof, New York, September 29, 1815, Papers of Robert Troup, NYPL. Job E. Townsend Account Book and Ledger, Newport, Rhode Island, 1778–1794, accounts with Constant Taber, November 29, 1790, and Capt. Caleb Gardner, July 23, 1791, Newport Historical Society, Newport, Rhode Island (hereafter cited as NHS).

19. Alling Daybook, 1836–1854, account with Frederick T. Frelinghuysen Jr., May 25, 1840. Anonymous Cabinetmaker's Account Book, probably Fredericksburg, Virginia, account with Capt. Lawrence Taliaferro, May 25, 1775. Benjamin Lander Bill to Joshua Ward, Salem, Massachusetts, October 10, 1787, Ward Family Manuscripts, PEM. Samuel Perry Bill to Isaac Bronson, Fairfield, Connecticut, May 1827, Bronson Papers, Papers of Isaac Bronson, NYPL.

20. Advertisement of Richard Magrath, *South Carolina Gazette* (Charleston), July 9, 1772. Samuel Benge Bill to Stephen Girard, Philadelphia, n.d., Girard Papers. Silas Ellis Cheney Daybook, Litchfield, Connecticut, 1807–1813, account with Joseph L. Smith, December 13,

1808, LHS. Solomon Cole Account Book, Glastonbury, Connecticut, 1794–1809, account with Isaac Plumer, 1800, CHS.

21. John Clap Bill to David S. Greenough, Roxbury, Massachusetts, April 26, 1813, Greenough Papers, MHS. Benjamin Beckford Jr. Bill to Capt. John Derby, Salem, Massachusetts, September 1809, Derby Family Papers. Henry Connelly Bill to Stephen Girard, Philadelphia, September 15, 1808, Girard Papers. William Savery Bill to James Pemberton, Philadelphia, June 28, 1775, in W. M. Hornor Jr., "William Savery: 'Chairmaker and Joiner,'" *Antiquarian* 15 (July 1930): 32. Florence M. Montgomery, *Textiles in America, 1650–1870* (New York: W. W. Norton, 1983), pp. 254–55, 300, 302–3. Daniel Trotter Bill to Samuel Coates, Philadelphia, June 16, 1792, Reynell and Coates Collection, Baker Library, Harvard University, Cambridge, Massachusetts (hereafter cited as BL).

22. Richard Booker Bill to St. George Tucker, Williamsburg, Virginia, February 14–October 6, 1791, Tucker-Coleman Collection, Swem Library, College of William and Mary, Williamsburg, Virginia (hereafter cited as W&M).

23. David Evans Daybook, Philadelphia, 1774–1781, account with Benjamin Saixes, October 20, 1780, HSP. H. Dancaster Bill to Samuel Larned, Providence, Rhode Island, September 5, 1829, Greene Collection. Miles Ward Ledger, Salem, Massachusetts, 1725–1738, account with Capt. Ichabod Plasted, September 1733, PEM. Joshua Delaplaine Account Book, New York, 1720s–1770s, account with Jane Gilbert, January 31, 1743, N-YHS.

24. Job E. Townsend Daybook, Newport, Rhode Island, 1803–1828, account with John Taylor, January 29, 1808, NHS. J. E. Townsend Account Book and Ledger, account with Phillip Morse, June 12, 1787. Job E. Townsend Daybook, Newport, Rhode Island, 1778–1803, account with Gardner Thurston, August 21, 1800, NHS. J. E. Townsend Daybook, 1803–1828, account with Benedict Smith, March 1, 1808. Ebenezer Smith Jr. Bill to Elizabeth Lovett, Beverly, Massachusetts, March 5, 1804, Papers of Captains John and Jonathan Lovett, PEM.

25. Richard Johns Bill to Deborah Morris, Philadelphia, July 28, 1765, Gratz Collection. Nathaniel Kinsman Bill to Jacob Parsons, Gloucester, Massachusetts, February 20, 1783, Nathaniel Kinsman Papers, PEM. Boynton Ledger, account with Samuel Barrett, October 16, 1816 (painted music stool). Duncan Phyfe Bill to James L. Brinckerhoof, New York, May 6 and 11, 1816, Troup Papers. Townsend Goddard Bill to Christopher Champlin, Newport, Rhode Island, March 21, 1787, Wetmore Papers, MHS.

26. Alexander Shaw Bill to Zacheus Collins, Philadelphia, October 1814, Daniel Parker Papers, HSP. Barnes Account Book, account with Charles Dyer, September 15, 1821. Alling Daybook, accounts with Shugarth and Macknet, August 12, 1838, and Milo Heath, April 9, 1838.

27. John Gaines II and Thomas Gaines Account Book, Ipswich, Massachusetts, 1712–1762, account with Phillip Fowler, July 29, 1718, DCM.

28. Currier Account Book, account with Peter Jenness, November 1834; Boynton Account Book, account with Mrs. Silsbee, June 25, 1811.

29. Barnes Account Book, account with Jacob Williams, May 30, 1822. Henry Connelly Bill to Stephen Girard, Philadelphia, July 13, 1810, Girard Papers. Fenwick Lyle Account Book, Middletown, New Jersey, 1800–1813, account with John H. Sickles, February 9, 1804, Monmouth County Historical Association, Freehold, New Jersey (hereafter cited as MCHA).

30. Boynton Account Book, account with Stephen Conant, July 26 and January 26, 1816. Alling Ledger, accounts with James Agens, June 8, 1839, and D. B. Brown and Co., November 5, 1836.

31. Samuel Walton Bill to Joshua Humphries, Philadelphia, May 28, 1774, Early Cabinetmakers of Philadelphia, Harrold Gillingham Collection, HSP. Gaines Account Book, account with Nathaniel Dutch, February 7, 1739. Fussell Account Book, account with Jeremiah Elfreth Sr., 6:15:1741.

32. J. E. Townsend Daybook, 1778–1803, account with Capt. John Oldfield, June 5, 1783. Samuel Matthews Bill to Charles Norris, Philadelphia, July 1766, Norris Family Accounts, HSP. Plunket Fleeson Bill to Charles Norris, Philadelphia, September 24, 1764, Norris of Fairhill Manuscripts, Family Accounts, vol. 1, HSP. Daniel Trotter Bill to Samuel Coates, Philadelphia, June 16, 1792, Reynell and Coates Collection.

33. William Bentley Ledger, Butternuts, New York, 1812–1815, account with Robert L. Bounds, June 29, 1814, DCM. Michael Bouvier Bill to Stephen Girard, Philadelphia, July 28, 1829, Girard Papers. John Collins Bills to Richard Blow, Portsmouth, Virginia, January 28, 1802, and June 30, 1804, and George Seddon and Son Account, London, August 15, 1785, Richard Blow Papers, W&M. Evans Daybook, account with Thomas Hurley, October 20, 1786.

34. Sager Daybook, account with Doctor Barnes, April 29, 1806. Lyell Account Book, account with John Post, November 7, 1808. Samuel and Joseph Rawson Bills to Richard W. Greene, Providence, Rhode Island, August 11, 1842, and July 24, 1839, and John G. Hopkins Bill to Albert C. Greene, Providence, September 29, 1834, Greene Collection. Pennell Beale Bill to Gen. Henry Knox, Philadelphia, November 25, 1791, Henry Knox Papers, Maine Historical Society, Portland (hereafter cited as MeHS).

35. Alling Ledger, accounts with D. D. Chandler, April 17, 1837 (yellow settees), Alexander N. Dougherty, April 14, 1836 (green settee), and Jonas Agens, April 1, 1840 (cleaning off). Cheney Daybook, 1813–1821, account with Oliver Wolcott, September 16, 1815. Alling Daybook, accounts with I. G. Goble, April 27, 1837 (touching up), and Caleb P. Crockett, September 14, 1839 (long and short settees).

36. Paul Jenkins Daybook, Kennebunk, Maine, 1836–1841, account with Barnabas Palmer, November 23, 1839, DCM. Jacob Brouwer Bill to Nicholas Low, New York, February 10, 1798, Nicholas Low Collection, LC. *The Accounts of Two Pennsylvania German Furniture Makers*, edited by Alan G. Keyser, Larry M. Neff, and Frederick K. Weiser, Sources and Documents of the Pennsylvania Germans, vol. 3 (Breinigsville, Pa.: Pennsylvania German Society, 1978), Peter Ranck Account Book, Jonestown, Pennsylvania, 1794–1817, account with George Merk, May 18, 1798, p. 85. Barnes Account Book, account with John L. Lewis, March 26, 1823.

37. W. and R. Tucker Bill to Peter Gansevoort, Albany, New York, January 17, 1837, Gansevoort-Lansing Collection, NYPL.

38. Jacob Hinsdale Ledger, Harwinton, Connecticut, 1723–1774, account with anonymous customer, probably 1828, YU. Joseph Brown Account Book, Newbury, Massachusetts, 1725–1783, account with Abel Huse Jr., March 1732/33, PEM. J. E. Townsend Daybook, 1803–1828, account with Christopher Ellery, December 20, 1823. Tiffany Account Book, account with Nathaniel Backus Jr., August 2, 1758. Thomas J. Moyers and Fleming K. Rich Account Book, Wytheville, Virginia, 1834–1840, account with Robert Kent, December 30, 1836, DCM. Landon Account Book, account with Thomas Wilkins, February 20, 1818. Abner Haven Account Book, Framingham, Massachusetts, 1809–1830, account with Aaron Pratt, March 1810, DCM.

39. Barnes Account Book, accounts with Aaron Treet, May 21, 1823, and William Scranton, April 16, 1822. Alling Ledger, accounts with Fitch Smith, April 1, 1840, and William Garthwaite, March 25, 1841. Daniel Dunham, account with Dr. Isaac Senter, Newport, Rhode Island, May 1788, in Ott, "Recent Discoveries," p. 8. W., D., and S. Proud Ledger, account with Stephen Potter, March 9, 1825. William Savery Bill to Gen. John Cadwalader, Philadelphia, August 29, 1772, Cadwalader Papers, Gen. John Cadwalader.

40. William Savery Bill to Joseph Pemberton, Philadelphia, February 2, 1774, and January 10, 1775, Pemberton Papers, HSP. Boynton Ledger, account with Jacob Carter, June 15, 1811. Henry F. Dewey Account Book, Bennington, Vermont, 1837–1864, account with Daniel Conklin, September 1841, Shelburne Museum, Shelburne, Vermont. Alling Ledger, account with William Fatout, January 16, 1839.

41. Durand Account Book, account with Dr. Carrington, June 8, 1767. Lyell Account Book, account with James Morrison, October 24, 1808. J. E. Townsend Daybook, 1778–1803, account with Robert Taylor, September 15, 1780.

42. Cradle repairs and replacement parts: Thomas Affleck Bill to Levi Hollingsworth, Philadelphia, 1780, Society Collection, Levi Hollingsworth Papers, Bills and Receipts, HSP (new rockers). George Claypoole Bill to Samuel Meredith, Philadelphia, September 24, 1781, Clymer-Meredith-Read Papers, Samuel Meredith Accounts, NYPL (repairs). Daniel Drinker Bill to Stephen Collins, Philadelphia, February 28, 1768, Collins Papers (new rockers). Francis Trumble Bill to Thomas Wharton, Philadelphia, November 10, 1756, Wharton Manuscripts, Thomas Wharton, HSP (new rockers). Thomas Tufft Bill to Mary (Mrs. Charles) Norris, Philadelphia, April 1775, Norris of Fairhill Manuscripts (repairs). Samuel Williams Bill to Michael Gratz, Philadelphia, December 18, 1770, Various Bills and Receipts, Library Company of Philadelphia, Philadelphia (hereafter cited as LCP) (new rockers and repairs). William Savery Bill to James Pemberton, Philadelphia, May 13, 1774, and January 21, 1775, Pemberton Papers. Samuel Matthews Bills to Charles Norris, Philadelphia, 1761 and April 1765, Charles Norris Cash Book, Norris Family Accounts.

43. Elisha Harlow Holmes Daybook, Essex, Connecticut, 1825–1830, account with Mrs. Post, July 11, 1829, CSL. Joseph Griswold Ledger, Buckland, Massachusetts, 1804–1836, account with Daniel Ward, April 15, 1817, private collection (microfilm, DCM). Danforth Ledger, account with Thomas Jackson, November 27, 1805.

44. Richard Alexander Bill to Mrs. John Francis, Philadelphia, April 24, 1820, Cadwalader Papers, Gen. John Cadwalader. Barnes Account Book, account with Reuben Chaffee, October 9, 1822.

45. William Savery Bill to Joseph Pemberton, Philadelphia, July 15, 1774, Pemberton Papers. Jacob Brouwer Bill to Nicholas Low, New York, April 16, 1813, Nicholas Low Papers, Rutgers University Library, New Brunswick, New Jersey. Jacob Brouwer Bill to Nicholas Low, New York, May 11, 1803, Low Collection. Rookesby Roberts Bill to St. George Tucker, Williamsburg, Virginia, December 3, 1794, Tucker-Coleman Collection. Barnes Account Book, account with William B. Ward, August 12, 1823.

46. William Savery Bills to Joseph Pemberton, Philadelphia, May 19, 1774, and October 23, 1775, Pemberton Papers. Samuel Matthews Bills to Charles Norris, Philadelphia, February 1764, June 1766, and September 1766, Norris Family Accounts. Durand Account Book, account with Dr. Elisha Whiting, June 23, 1763. J. E. Townsend Daybook, 1803–1828, account with Rachel Gardner, August 18, 1807. J. E. Townsend Daybook, 1778–1803, accounts with Will Boss Black, September 19, 1794, and Joshua Crandel, September 28, 1795. Danforth Ledger, account with Elisha Dyer, May 12, 1804. Cole Account Book, account with Dr. Joseph Hale, July 13, 1799.

47. Evans Daybook, account with Thomas Hurley, December 2, 1788. Anonymous Cabinetmaker's Account Book, Middletown, New Jersey, 1763–1768, account with Daniel Kowenhoven, October 1770, N-YHS. Griswold Ledger, account with Jesse Pratt, May 1822. J. E. Townsend Daybook, 1778–1803, account with Dr. Easton, December 19, 1800. J. E. Townsend Account Book and Ledger, account with Constant Taber, May 26, 1792.

48. George Short Account Book, Newburyport, Massachusetts, 1807–1821, account with Abigail Woodbury, August 8, 1818, PEM. Abner Taylor Account Book, Lee, Massachusetts, 1806–1832, account with Ephraim Williams, November 1809, DCM (splicing). J. E. Townsend Daybook, 1778–1803, account with John Taylor, September 8, 1801 (splicing). Pennell Beale Bill to Jonathan Meredith, Philadelphia, February 22, 1806, DCM (splicing). Nehemiah Adams Bill to Capt. Benjamin Webb, Salem, Massachusetts, November 1, 1808, Papers of Samuel and John Barton, PEM. Ebenezer Smith Jr. Bill to Robert Rantoul, Beverly, Massachusetts, July 14, 1809, Papers of Robert Rantoul, Beverly Historical Society, Beverly, Massachusetts. Cook and Greene Bill to Richard W. Greene, Providence, Rhode Island, November 1839, Greene Collection. Jenkins Daybook, account with William Lord, November 15, 1837. Vose and Coates Bill to Francis Dana Jr., Boston, December 16, 1805, Dana Papers, MHS. John Hockaday Bill to St. George Tucker, Williamsburg, Virginia, October 31, 1812, Tucker-Coleman Collection. J. E. Townsend Daybook, 1803–1828, account with Mary Ann Marble, September 8, 1823.

49. Boynton Ledger, account with Thomas Leverett and Son, January 6, 1817. Barnes Account Book, account with Samuel Cooper, February 23, 1822. William Wayne Bill to Stephen Collins, Philadelphia, May 25, 1775, Collins Papers. Danforth Ledger, account with Gershom Jones, June 2, 1797. William Roberts Bill to Gen. Henry Knox, Philadelphia, January 27, 1795, Knox Papers (MeHS).

50. Elisha Crane Bill to Peter Gansevoort, Albany, New York, February 6, 1824, Gansevoort-Lansing Collection. Josiah P. Wilder Daybook and Ledger, New Ipswich, New Hampshire, 1837–1861, account with G. B. Gardner, January 25, 1839, private collection (typescript, DCM). Barnes Account Book, account with John B. Southmayd, August 28, 1821. Abraham S. Egerton Bills to Henrietta Low, New York, February 14, 1824, and Nicholas Low, March 10, 1824, Low Collection.

51. Gere Ledger, account with Jabez Giddings, May 21, 1825 (pintles). Evans Daybook, account with John Pemberton, March 1776 (strips). Barnes Account Book, account with Horace Clark, December 30, 1823 (valance rails). Holcomb Account Book, account with Cornelius Jeney, November 1826 (side pieces). Daniel Trotter Bill to Stephen Girard, Philadelphia, May 27, 1793, Girard Papers (curtain rails, pulleys). Jenkins Daybook, account with Joseph Dane, April 18, 1838. George Merrifield Account Book, Albany, New York, 1831–1847, account with Mrs. Godley, May 30, 1832, DCM. Nehemiah Adams Bill to Capt. Benjamin Webb, Salem, Massachusetts, November 1, 1808, Barton Papers. William Savery Bill to Jospeh Pemberton, Philadelphia, December 15, 1774, Pemberton Papers. Alexander Low Account Book, Freehold, New Jersey, 1784–1826, account with Capt. Dennis Forman, MCHA. *Bed Hangings: A Treatise on Fabrics and Styles in the Curtaining of Beds, 1650–1850,* compiled by Abbott Lowell Cummings (Boston: Society for the Preservation of New England Antiquities, 1961), pp. 8–9.

52. William Savery Bill to Joseph Pemberton, Philadelphia, October 23, 1775, Pemberton Papers. Jenkins Daybook, account with William Lord, November 15, 1837. Lyell Account

Book, accounts with Thomas Post, June 13, 1804, John Lang, November 11, 1806, and William Popham, June 25, 1808. Daniel Trotter Bill to Stephen Girard, Philadelphia, August 25, 1790, Girard Papers. William Hook Bill to Benjamin Hathorne, Salem, Massachusetts, April 22, 1812, Ward Family Manuscripts. Townsend Goddard Bill to Christopher Champlin, Newport, Rhode Island, June 2, 1787, Wetmore Papers. By a lady, *The Workwoman's Guide,* 2d ed. (London: Simpkins, Marshall and Co., 1840), p. 191.

53. John Hockaday Bill to St. George Tucker, Williamsburg, Virginia, October 15, 1806, Tucker-Coleman Collection. William Ranken Bill to Samuel Coates, Philadelphia, June 24, 1828, Reynell and Coates Collection. Cleveland and Brothers Bill to Richard W. Greene, Providence, Rhode Island, May 11, 1844, Greene Collection. Samuel Douglas Account Book, area Canton, Connecticut, 1810–1858, account with Moses Douglass, October 3, 1816, CSL. Peter Emerson Daybook, Reading, Massachusetts, 1749–1759, account with Joseph Smith, March 2, 1756, Boston Public Library, Boston, Massachusetts. Robert Crage Ledger, Leicester, Massachusetts, 1757–1781, account with Nathaniel Tolman, May 9, 1759, OSV. Preston Ledger, account with William Johnson, April 2, 1811.

54. Griswold Ledger, account with Jesse Pratt, May 1, 1822. Sager Account Book, account with Doctor Burns, March 3, 1807. Landon Account Book, account with William Barton, June 26, 1820. Evans Daybook, account with Jonathan D. Sergeant, January 15, 1791. Cheney Daybook, 1813–1821, account with Ozias Seymore, May 3, 1815.

55. J. E. Townsend Daybook, 1778–1803, account with Gilbert Chase, February 11, 1802. Wilder Daybook, account with Leonard Morse, June 2, 1838. Benjamin Baker Account Book, Newport, Rhode Island, 1760–1792, account with Jacob Rodriguez Rivera, August 17, 1785, NHS. Cheney Daybook, 1802–1807, account with Oliver Wolcott, January 19, 1803. Evans Daybook, account with Benjamin Saixes, October 12, 1780 (oiling).

56. John Hockaday Bill to St. George Tucker, Williamsburg, Virginia, October 31, 1812, Tucker-Coleman Collection. Benjamin Ellery Bill to estate of Eliakim Prindell, Gloucester, Massachusetts, May 12, 1818, Papers of Daniel Rogers Jr., PEM (smoothing). Miles Benjamin Daybook and Ledger, Cooperstown, New York, 1821–1829, account with H. Luce and Co., October 28, 1826, DCM. Fussell Account Book, accounts with Thomas Sugar, 8:28:1741, and Benjamin Franklin, 6:20:1743. Oliver Avery Account Book, North Stonington, Connecticut, 1789–1813, account with Aaron Newton, July 30, 1809, DCM.

57. Thomas Lawrence Bill to Stephen Collins, Philadelphia, September 16, 1772, Collins Papers; Montgomery, *Textiles in America,* p. 228. Abraham S. Egerton Bill to Henrietta Low, New York, February 14, 1824, Low Collection. John Paine Account Book, Southold, Long Island, 1761–1815, account with John Franks, February 27, 1797, Institute for Colonial Studies, State University of New York at Stony Brook. Durand Account Book, account with Joseph Marshall, 1765. William and John Richmond Bill to Almy and Brown, Providence, Rhode Island, August 1799, in Joseph K. Ott, "Still More Notes on Rhode Island Cabinetmakers and Allied Craftsmen," *Rhode Island History* 28, no. 4 (November 1969): 119. Danforth Ledger, account with James Burrell, November 12, 1789. Charles C. Robinson Daybook, Philadelphia, 1809–1825, account with Francis Goncher, September 15, 1814, HSP. Aaron Leaming Ledger, Cape May, New Jersey, 1764–1785, payment in kind received from Jesse Hand, March 1767, DCM.

58. Job Townsend Jr. Daybook, Newport, Rhode Island, 1762–1778, account with William Wanton, December 15, 1762, NHS. Baker Account Book, account with Jacob Rodriguez Rivera, August 8, 1785; *Workwoman's Guide,* p. 191.

59. Leaming Ledger, payment in kind received from Jesse Hand, March 1767. Jacob Brouwer Bill to Nicholas Low, New York, June 6, 1814, Low Papers. Duncan Phyfe Bill to James L. Brinckerhoof, New York, October 15, 1815, Troup Papers.

60. John Mason Bill to Stephen Collins, Philadelphia, 1763, Collins Papers. John T. Ball Bill to Nicholas Low, New York, May 27, 1809, Low Collection. Caleb C. Cook Bill to Richard W. Greene, Providence, Rhode Island, October 19, 1827, Greene Collection. Charles Hyland Bill to Mrs. St. George Tucker, Williamsburg, Virginia, 1797–1798, Tucker-Coleman Collection.

61. Evans Daybook, account with Samuel Morris, 1775. Elizabeth deHart Bleecker (McDonald) Diary, New York, 1799–1806, entry for November 21, 1800, NYPL.

62. William Ranken Bill to Samuel Coates, Philadelphia, June 24, 1828, Reynell and Coates Collection. *Moreau de St. Méry's American Journey [1793–1798],* edited and translated by Kenneth Roberts and Anna M. Roberts (Garden City, N.Y.: Doubleday, 1947), p. 165. Frances M. Trollope, *Domestic Manners of the Americans,* 2 vols. (London: Whitaker, Treatcher and Co., 1832), 2: 209–10.

63. Samuel Powel Daybook, Philadelphia, 1735–1739, account of work by John Eyre, September 22–23, 1736, DCM. William Savery Bill to Joseph Pemberton, Philadelphia, June 30, 1774–January 16, 1775, Pemberton Papers. Hiram Taylor Account Book, Chester County, Pennsylvania, 1828–1855, account with David Rickabaugh, November 12, 1835, DCM. Daniel Trotter Bills to Stephen Girard, Philadelphia, October 23, 1787–February 23, 1788, and August 5–October 27, 1796, Girard Papers.

64. Jacob Brouwer Bills to Nicholas Low, New York, March 29, 1796, June 14–July 27, 1796, and September 24–27, 1796, Low Collection. Jacob Brouwer Bills to Nicholas Low, New York, April 16–28, 1813, June 3, 1814, and October 3–21, 1814, Low Papers.

65. Thomas Tufft Bill to Mrs. Mary Norris, Philadelphia, August 1775, Norris of Fairhill Manuscripts. Holcomb Account Book, account with Cornelius Jeney, August 21, 1826. Evans Daybook, account with Leonard Dorsey, June 14, 1781.

66. Anonymous New Jersey Cabinetmaker's Account Book, account with George Taylor, February 16, 1772. Lyell Account Book, account with John Lang, November 11, 1806 (side rails and post). Oliver Moore Account Book, East Granby, Connecticut, 1808–1821, account with Benijah Owen, March 5, 1817, CHS (posts).

67. Nehemiah Adams Bill to James Proctor, Salem, Massachusetts, July 28, 1808, Papers of John Prince Jr., PEM. Currier Account Book, account with True S. Thrasher, January 1827. Barnes Account Book, account with William B. Hall, December 29, 1822. Merrifield Account Book, account with Mr. Whitney, October 22, 1836. Hartwell Holmes Account Book, Woodstock, Connecticut, 1793–1827, account with Sanford Holmes, March 1810, CHS.

68. Phillip Filer Account Book, area Rome, New York, 1798–1839, account with Steven Weight, September 4, 1803, DCM (repairs). Avery Account Book, account with William Avery, July 10, 1799 (repairs). J. E. Townsend Daybook (1778–1803), account with Elizabeth Townsend, October 6, 1784 (repairs). Merrifield Account Book, account with Mr. Ferguson, March 7, 1838. Ephraim Haines Bill to Stephen Girard, Philadelphia, March 17, 1802, Girard Papers. Langley Boardman Bill to Capt. Reuben S. Randall, Portsmouth, New Hampshire, May 11, 1811, Wendell Papers, BL. *Workwoman's Guide*, pl. 22.

69. Sager Daybook, account with Mrs. Norris, May 8, 1806. H. Taylor Account Book, account with Jonathan Morris, December 30, 1834.

70. Jacob Brouwer Bill to Nicholas Low, New York, November 30, 1810, Low Collection. Moore Account Book, account with Benijah Owen, March 5, 1817. Tiffany Account Book, account with Jonathan Huntington, June 16, 1757. Walter Nichols Bill to Dr. Isaac Senter, Newport, Rhode Island, February 1790, in Ott, "Recent Discoveries," p. 8. Garret Account Book, account with Benona Segar, March 4, 1812, and January 12, 1814.

71. Perez Austin Account Book, Canterbury, Connecticut, 1811–1832, account with Rufus Adams, October 1, 1826, CHS. Josiah White Account Book, Ashburnham, Massachusetts, 1811–1821, account with Capt. Caleb Wilder, September 1814, DCM. Shaw and Chisholm Bill to James Brice, Annapolis, Maryland, October 6, 1772, Brice-Jennings Papers. J. E. Townsend Daybook (1778–1803), account with John Hadwen, November 12, 1781. E. G. and A. Partridge Bill to Henry Miller, Worcester, Massachusetts, October 13, 1829, accounts of Henry W. Miller, DCM. Job Townsend Jr. Ledger, Newport, Rhode Island, 1750–1778, account with Matthew Pates, February 9, 1753, NHS. James Lineacre Bill to Peter E. Elmendorf, Albany, New York, December 8, 1806, Sanders Papers.

72. Paine Account Book, accounts with Jonathan Conklin, March 11, 1791, and Widow Abigail Moore, June 1785. Preston Ledger, 1795–1817, accounts with Doctor Brandin, January 30, 1804, and Daniel Ives, November 1809. Titus Preston Ledger, Wallingford, Connecticut, 1811–1842, account with Capt. Phineas Pond, January 1817, YU.

73. Jonathan Herrick Bill to Robert Rantoul, Beverly, Massachusetts, June 20, 1815, Rantoul Papers. H. Holmes Account Book, account with Jonathan Corbin, July 4, 1795. Durand Account Book, account with Nathan Netelton, June 1768. Stephen C. Webster Account Book, Salisbury, New Hampshire, 1804–1843, account with Jonathan Garland, March 1827 (leaf to table), Parsons, "New Hampshire Notes." Cole Account Book, account with Zephaniah H. Smith, February 9, 1802 (fall to table). Currier Account Book, account with John Hilton and Simeon Duey, February 14, 1816 (hanging a table).

74. Moses Parkhurst Account Book, Paxton, Massachusetts, 1814–1839, account with Deacon David Davis, April 2, 1834, OSV. Preston Ledger, 1811–1842, account with Asa Doolittle, March 10, 1822. Paine Account Book, account with Sylvester Lester, January 1786. Edward Slead Account Book, Dartmouth, Massachusetts, 1797–1827, account with Zoeth Shearman,

October 27, 1798, DCM. Reuben Loomis Account Book, Windsor-Suffield, Connecticut, 1793–1836, account with Rev. Joseph Mix, October 1821, CHS.

75. Lee Ledger, account with David Crage, May 1816. James Chase Account Book, Gilmanton, New Hampshire, 1797–1807, account with Stephen Perley of Meredith, July 22, 1806, Parsons, "New Hampshire Notes." Currier Account Book, account with John Sandborn, May 1837.

76. J. Townsend Jr. Daybook, 1762–1778, account with Joseph Bass, May 14, 1771 (top and drawer). J. Townsend Jr. Ledger, 1750–1778, account with Thomas Robinson, March 29, 1756 (top and drawer lock). Powel Daybook, account of work by John Eyre, 2:20:1736 (top and mending frame). J. Townsend Jr. Ledger, 1750–1778, account with Peter Cozzens, June 14, 1765 (top and new rails). Robinson Daybook, account with John Powell, September 28, 1815 (top and painting top). Barnes Account Book, account with John L. Lewis, January 11, 1823 (top and painting table). J. E. Townsend Account Book and Ledger, account with John Springer, August 10, 1793.

77. Nathaniel Kinsman Bill to Josiah Brown, Gloucester, Massachusetts, July 1768, Kinsman Papers. Samuel Wayne Bill to Samuel Coates, Philadelphia, June 12, 1788, Reynell and Coates Collection. J. E. Townsend Daybook, 1778–1803, account with Phoebe Cahoone, August 4, 1785. Benjamin Randolph Bill to Isaac Zane, Philadelphia, May 17, 1770, Zane Papers, Coates-Reynell Collection, HSP (mahogany tabletop). J. Townsend Jr. Ledger (1750–1778), account with Thomas Robinson, March 29, 1756 (mahogany tabletop). Samuel Walton Bill to Joshua Humphries, Philadelphia, August 20, 1773, Gillingham Collection. Jacob Brouwer Bill to Nicholas Low, New York, June 2, 1807, Low Collection.

78. Jenkins Daybook, account with George Littlefield, December 21, 1837. Cheney Daybook, 1802–1807, account with Thomas Collier, January 22, 1805. Crage Ledger, accounts with Hezekiah Merium Jr., November 1757 and February 1758, and Widow Smith of Charlton, December 1758. J. E. Townsend Account Book and Ledger, account with Nathan Beebe, February 9, 1785. Walter Nichols Bill to Dr. Isaac Senter, Newport, Rhode Island, April 1790, in Ott, "Recent Discoveries," p. 8.

79. Samuel McCall Sr. Account Book, Philadelphia, 1743–1749, account of work by Daniel Swan, September 9, 1745, HSP. Charles Hyland Bill to St. George Tucker, Williamsburg, Virginia, November 1796, Tucker-Coleman Collection. Howard Smith Account Book, New Haven, Connecticut, 1844–1849, account with Sidney M. Stone, April 31, 1844, CHS. Walsh and Egerton Bill to Nicholas Low, New York, March 12, 1820, Low Papers.

80. Joseph Symonds Account Book, Salem, Massachusetts, 1738–1766, account with Thorndike Procter, 1763, PEM. J. Townsend Jr. Daybook, 1762–1778, account with Joseph Bass, May 4, 1771. Ezekiel Smith Account Book, Taunton, Massachusetts, 1773–1831, account with Ebenezer Peck, January 2, 1792, DCM. Avery Account Book, account with Jedidiah Randall, March 28, 1810. Gere Ledger, account with Jesse Wells, July 3, 1826.

81. Job E. Townsend Ledger, Newport, Rhode Island, 1794–1802, account with John Taylor, January 26, 1798, NHS. J. E. Townsend Daybook, 1778–1803, account with John Taylor January 26, 1798.

82. Taylor Account Book, account with Robert M. Ashley, August 27, 1810. Jeduthern Avery Account Book, Bolton-Coventry, Connecticut, 1811–1855, account with Nathaniel Kingsbury, May 1823, CHS. Holcomb Account Book, account with Jacob Tull, October 25, 1824. Moore Account Book, account with Benijah Owen, March 5, 1817. Cheney Daybook, 1813–1821, account with Phineas Miner, Esq., June 18, 1817.

83. Delaplaine Account Book, account with Jane Gilbert, 5:8:1738. Pennell Beale Bill to Gen. Henry Knox, Philadelphia, September 24, 1791, Knox Papers. William Greene in account with Christopher Champlin for bill of Stephen and Thomas Goddard, Newport, Rhode Island, February 2, 1787, Wetmore Papers.

84. Silas Ellis Cheney Ledger, Litchfield, Connecticut, 1816–1822, account with James Winship, March 30, 1819, LHS, and Cheney Daybook, 1807–1813, account with Ashbel Marsh, July 5, 1803. J. E. Townsend Daybook, 1778–1803, accounts with Esther Miller, July 4, 1780, and Matthew Layton, July 13, 1780. Currier Account Book, account with Joseph Harford, April 1829. Robbins Account Book, account with A. Saunders and Son, February 27, 1835. Elisha Harlow Holmes Ledger, Essex, Connecticut, 1825–1830, account with Samuel Ingham, April 25, 1828, CHS.

85. Lyell Account Book, account with Isaac Minard, June 24, 1806. Moyers and Rich Account Book, account with William Pearson, August 6, 1838. Jacob Brouwer Bills to Nicholas Low, New York, October 30, 1799, and October 25, 1800, Low Collection.

86. Brown Account Book, account with Benjamin Morse, December 20, 1726. Lemuel Tobey Daybook, New Bedford, Massachusetts, 1797–1806, account with Cornelius Jenne,

1798, OSV. Timothy Loomis Account Book, Windsor, Connecticut, 1768–1804, accounts with John Roberts, 1770, and Dr. Alexander Wolcott, 1785, CHS (leaves and color). E. Smith Account Book, accounts with Otis Peck, April 1800 (leaf and color), and Ebenezer Rich, January 2, 1792 (drawer and color). Avery Account Book, account with Jedidiah Randall, March 28, 1810 (drawers and color).

87. Nathaniel Allen Account Book, Philadelphia, 1732–1757, accounts of work by Francis Trumble, 10:28:1742 and 1741–1745, HSP.

88. Charles Hyland Bill to Mrs. St. George Tucker, Williamsburg, Virginia, November 1796, Tucker-Coleman Collection. E. H. Holmes Daybook, account with Elias Redfield, November 11, 1826. Lyell Account Book, account with Benjamin Stevens, February 22, 1808. Barnes Account Book, account with Gilbert Burrows, March 16, 1824.

89. Samuel Williams Bill to Michael Gratz, Philadelphia, December 20, 1771, Various Bills and Receipts, LCP. J. E. Townsend Daybook, 1778–1803, account with Samuel C. Carr, June 22, 1799 ($1.00 repair work). Lemuel Tobey Daybook, Dartmouth, Massachusetts, 1785–1786, account with Mr. Dillingham, March 11, 1785, OSV, and Tobey Daybook, 1797–1806, New Bedford, account with William Reynolds, April 1, 1798. Emerson Daybook, account with Thomas Emerson, May 5, 1757.

90. Delaplaine Account Book, account with Michael Thody, 1:1742/3. Danforth Ledger, account with Andrew Dexter, September 10, 1797. Preston Ledger, 1795–1817, accounts with Jerry Tuttle, June 9, 1801, and Abner Johnson, August 17, 1813. J. E. Townsend Daybook, 1803–1828, account with Mary Ann Marble, January 25, 1823. Barnes Account Book, account with Elihu Cox (Coe?), November 26, 1823.

91. Samuel Cheever Bill to Col. John Hawthorne, Salem, Massachusetts, April 15, 1809, Ha[w]thorne Family Manuscripts, PEM. Shaw and Chisholm Bill to James Brice, Annapolis, Maryland, February 17, 1775, Brice-Jennings Papers. Thomas Affleck Bill to Levi Hollingsworth, Philadelphia, March 2, 1789, Gillingham Collection. Samuel Matthews Bill to Charles Norris, Philadelphia, October 1764, Norris Family Accounts. John Hockaday Bill to St. George Tucker, Williamsburg, Virginia, May 30, 1807, Tucker-Coleman Collection.

92. Evans Daybook, account with John Biddle, June 1, 1776.

93. Benjamin Daybook and Ledger, account with Root and Foote, July 22, 1822. John Elliott Sr. Bill to Edward Shippen, Philadelphia, February 23, 1754, as reproduced in *Pennsylvania Museum Bulletin* 20, no. 91 (January 1925): 71. Jonathan Cowdrey Bill to Chancellor Robert L. Livingston, New York, December 16, 1783, Livingston Papers. Sager Account Book, account with James Toner, August 22, 1806.

94. Jacob Sass Bill to Peter Trezevant, Charleston, South Carolina, June 29, 1805, as quoted in Bradford Rauschenberg and John Bivins Jr., *The Furniture of Charleston, 1680–1820*, 3 vols. (Winston-Salem, N.C.: Old Salem / Museum of Early Southern Decorative Arts, 2003), 3: 1208. Lyell Account Book, account with Daniel Mumford, July 1807. E. H. Holmes Daybook, account with Mrs. Russell Post, December 4, 1829. William Turner Bill to Nicholas Low, New York, September 30, 1817, Low Collection.

95. Boynton Ledger, account with William Leverett, June 11, 1814. J. E. Townsend Ledger, 1794–1802, account with Samuel Vaughn, April 27, 1801. Dr. J. R. B. Rodgers Receipt Book, New York, 1790–1803, receipt of Joshua Tabele, August 20, 1801, N-YHS. Nathaniel Bryant Bill to Gen. Moses Porter, Boston, March 1, 1821, Gen. Moses Porter Papers, PEM.

96. Percy Macquoid and Ralph Edwards, *Dictionary of English Furniture*, 3 vols. (1924–27; reprint, 2nd rev. ed., Woodbridge, Eng.: Barra Books, 1983), 3: 190–92, 266–68, 271–72. Thomas Chippendale, *The Gentleman and Cabinet-Maker's Director*, 3 eds. (London, 1754, 1755, and 1762), pl. 53. Thomas Sheraton, *The Cabinet-Maker and Upholsterer's Drawing-Book* (1793; reprint, New York: Dover Publications, 1972), pl. 54; George Hepplewhite, *The Cabinet-Maker and Upholsterer's Guide* (1794; reprint, 3rd ed., New York: Dover Publications, 1969), p. 12, pl. 62. Sheraton, *Cabinet Dictionary*, 2: 284.

97. Pennell Beale Bill to Gen. Henry Knox, Philadelphia, September 24, 1791, Knox Papers, MeHS.

98. William Reger Bill to Charles Wistar, Germantown, Pennsylvania, October 24, 1816, Charles Wistar Papers, DCM. Jacob Brouwer Bill to Nicholas Low, New York, December 21, 1802, Low Collection. Rookesby Roberts Bill to St. George Tucker, Williamsburg, Virginia, 1795, Tucker-Coleman Collection. J. E. Townsend Daybook, 1803–1828, accounts with Benedict Smith, October 26, 1804, and Henry Freeborn, October 29, 1804.

99. J. E. Townsend Daybook, 1778–1803, accounts with Hugh Vickary, November 2, 1799 (plain cherry), Thomas Sheffield, September 20, 1799 (inlaid cherry), and William Cory, July 21, 1798

(inlaid mahogany). J. E. Townsend Ledger, 1794–1802, account with Samuel Vaughn, May 4, 1801 (plain maple). Loomis Account Book, account with David Hastings Jr., February 1824.

100. Robert Cowan Bill to Capt. John Derby, Salem, Massachusetts, January 9, 1803, Derby Family Papers. Sager Daybook, account with Thomas Rine, September 26, 1805.

101. Delaplaine Account Book, account with Jane Gilbert, 3:25:1737. William Savery Bill to Joseph Pemberton, Philadelphia, January 21, 1775, Pemberton Papers.

102. Robert C. Scadin Ledger, Cooperstown, New York, 1829–1831, account with E. B. Morehouse, August 3, 1830, New York State Historical Association, Cooperstown, New York (hereafter cited as NYSHA). Barnes Account Book, accounts with Samuel W. Dana, August 2, 1821, and Randolph Pease, August 15, 1822. Fussell Account Book, account with Edward Masters, 12:19:1741/2.

103. J. E. Townsend Daybook, 1803–1828, account with William E. Williams, April 9, 1823. Holcomb Account Book, account with Wildman How, April 11, 1827. J. E. Townsend Daybook, 1778 1803, account with David Stephens, July 21, 1800.

104. Pennell Beale Bill to Gen. Henry Knox, Philadelphia, September 24, 1791 (mending), and Isaac Ashton Bill to Gen. Henry Knox, Philadelphia, November 1, 1792, Knox Papers, MeHS. J. E. Townsend Daybook (1778–1803), account with William Stanhope, August 27, 1788. Richard Alexander Bill to Mrs. John Francis, Philadelphia, June 15, 1817, Cadwalader Papers, Gen. Thomas Cadwalader.

105. Evans Daybook, account with John Biddle, ca. September 1774. Estate of Nathaniel Gould Bill to Elias Hasket Derby, Salem, Massachusetts, January 1777, Derby Papers. Jonathan Kettell Account Book, Newburyport, Massachusetts, 1781–1794, account with Joshua Greenleaf, May 1791, PEM. Thomas Burling Bill to Chancellor Robert R. Livingston, New York, May 6, 1786, Livingston Papers. Thomas Affleck Bill to Levi Hollingsworth, Philadelphia, March 12, 1789, Gillingham Collection. Daniel Trotter Bill to Stephen Girard, Philadelphia, September 9, 1790, Girard Papers. Pennell Beale Bill to Gen. Henry Knox, Philadelphia, November 25, 1791, Knox Papers, MeHS. A. Low Account Book, account with Joseph Scudder, October 9, 1794 (Freehold, New Jersey). Richard Booker Bill to St. George Tucker, Williamsburg, Virginia, March 17, 1792, Tucker-Coleman Collection.

106. A. Low Account Book, account with Joseph Scudder, October 9, 1794. Evans Daybook, account with John Patton, October 21, 1780. Lyell Account Book, account with Thomas Buchanan, February 15, 1810. Benjamin Ellery Jr. Bill to estate of Eliakim Prindel, Salem, Massachusetts, July 1816, Rogers Papers. Jacob Brouwer Bills to Nicholas Low, New York, February 28 and June 2, 1807, Low Collection. Robert C. Scadin Daybook, Cooperstown, New York, 1829–1831, account with Mr. B. Sparrow, May 21, 1829, NYSHA. Scadin Ledger, inventory of property assigned to William H. Averill, December 30, 1830. Short Account Book, account of work by Daniel Somerby, July 1808.

107. Benjamin Randolph Bill to Col. George Croghan, Philadelphia, February 6, 1767, Cadwalader Collection, George Croghan Section. J. Townsend Jr. Daybook, 1762–1778, account with Joshua Isaiah, August 10, 1768. J. E. Townsend Daybook, 1778–1803, account with Mr. Hamilton, April 5, 1782. J. E. Townsend Account Book and Ledger, account with John L. Bass, March 5, 1785. Bleecker Diary, entries for January 11 and 15, 1802.

108. Robbins Account Book, account with Mr. Bates of Farmington, March 13, 1834. Allen Memorandum Book, account with Jabez Hazen, May 1797. Griswold Ledger, account with Samuel Bement of Ashford, April 1816. David Haven Account Book, Framingham, Massachusetts, 1785–1800, account with Samuel Park, Esq., November 1, 1787, DCM. Danforth Ledger, account with Jenkes Olney, November 16, 1803. Cheney Daybook, 1807–1813, account with Samuel Wick, June 11, 1813.

109. Cole Account Book, account with George Talcott, December 30, 1801. Lee Ledger, account with David Crage, May 1816. Christian M. Nestell Bill to Richard W. Greene, Providence, Rhode Island, April 3, 1827, Greene Collection.

110. Mathurin Tardy Bill to Robert R, Livingston, New York, March 10, 1795, Livingston Papers. William Sherman Bills to Stephen Girard, Philadelphia, November 20, 1824, and May 20, 1827, Girard Papers.

111. Paine Account Book, account with Abraham David, 1761. Barker Account Book, 1750–1772, account with Knight Dexter, October 26, 1763. J. E. Townsend Account Book and Ledger, account with Elizabeth Lamfiere (Lamphear?), November 17, 1788.

112. James Chase Account Book, Gilmanton, New Hampshire, 1807–1812, account with Josiah Ranlet, December 9, 1811, Parsons, "New Hampshire Notes" ($1.34 stand). Luke Houghton Ledger, Barre, Massachusetts, 1816–1827, account with Peter Hornor, January 1,

1824, Barre Historical Society, Barre, Massachusetts ($5.00 stand). Currier Account Book, account with Daniel Davis, February 1836. Moore Account Book, account with Phineas Newton Jr., February 26, 1813.

113. Houghton Ledger, account with Benjamin Wilson, September 1823. Isaac Vose Bill to Caleb Davis, Boston, May 10, 1791, Caleb Davis Papers, MHS. Cheney Daybook, 1813–1821, account with Jacob Thompson, June 10, 1815. Landon Account Book, account with Archibald McSparren, October 13, 1819. Holcomb Account Book, account with Phila Hitchcock, April 26, 1821. William Mather Account Book, Whately, Massachusetts, 1808–1825, account with Chester Belding, March 28, 1809, Historic Deerfield, Deerfield, Massachusetts.

114. Phillip Deland Account Book, West Brookfield, Massachusetts, 1812–1846, account with James Howland, December 9, 1819, OSV. Currier Account Book, account with Josiah Batchelder, February 1822. Samuel Douglas Account Book, near Canton, Connecticut, 1810–1858, account with Isaac Barnes, October 24, 1816, CSL. James Gere Ledger, Groton, Connecticut, 1809–1839, account with Peleg Rose, April 4, ca. 1814, CSL. Daniel Trotter Bill to Benjamin Thaw, Philadelphia, May 24, 1788, DCM. Townsend Goddard Bill to Christopher Champlin, Newport, Rhode Island, June 7, 1785, Wetmore Papers. Cheney Daybook, 1802–1807, account with Tapping Reeve, March 16, 1807.

115. H. Holmes Account Book, account with Plyna Woodward, March 29, 1806. Slead Account Book, account with Jonathan Tucker, November 28, 1798.

116. David L. Barquist, *American Tables and Looking Glasses in the Mabel Brady Garvan and Other Collections at Yale University* (New Haven, Conn.: Yale University Art Gallery, 1992), p. 274. Sheraton, *Drawing-Book*, Appendix, pl. 26. Lyell Account Book, account with Robert Golet, January 18, 1804. Langley Boardman Bills to Capt. Reuben S. Randall, Portsmouth, New Hampshire, August 7, 1811, and January 26, 1811, Wendell Papers.

117. Jenkins Daybook, account with Barnabas Palmer, May 13, 1839. Richard Alexander Bill to Mrs. John Francis, Philadelphia, November 6, 1817, Cadwalader Papers, Gen. Thomas Cadwalader. Barnes Account Book, account with Henry Chauncey, September 16, 1824. Michael Bouvier Bill to Stephen Girard, Philadelphia, October 7, 1827, Girard Papers. Gere Ledger, 1822–1852, account with George Button, August 1828.

118. Chippendale, *Director,* 3d ed. (1762), pls. 54, 55. Hepplewhite, *Guide,* pls. 83, 84; Sheraton, *Drawing-Book,* pl. 42.

119. Thomas Affleck Bill to Gen. John Cadwalader, Philadelphia, May 10, 1784, Cadwalader Collection, Gen. John Cadwalader. *The 1772 Philadelphia Furniture Price Book: A Facsimile*, compiled by Alexandra Alevizatos Kirtley (1772; Philadelphia: Philadelphia Museum of Art, 2005), p. 17.

120. Sheraton, *Drawing-Book,* p. 42. Hepplewhite, *Guide,* p. 15. Sheraton, *Cabinet Dictionary,* 1: 36.

121. Lyell Account Book, account with Ezra Sargeant, October 1809. Benjamin Daybook and Ledger, account with Horatio Averill, July 16, 1823. Alexander H. Gilbert Account Book, Chester, Connecticut, 1831–1852, account with Abraham W. Mitchell, July 1839, CHS. Nicholas Silberg Bill to William Wragg, Charleston, South Carolina, August 9–16, 1799, in Rauschenberg and Bivins, *Furniture of Charleston,* 3: 1217. Cheney Daybook, 1807–1813, account with Tapping Reeve, September 28, 1809.

122. Daniel Dewey Bill to Daniel Wadsworth, Hartford, Connecticut, August 26, 1829, Daniel Wadsworth Papers, CHS. Robbins Account Book, account with William James Humisly, May 15, 1834. William G, Beesley Daybook, Salem, New Jersey, 1828–1836, account with Thomas Daniels, October 28, 1831, Salem County Historical Society, Salem, New Jersey. Holcomb Account Book, account with Wildman How, April 11, 1827.

Book Reviews

Christopher Long. *Paul T. Frankl and Modern American Design*. New Haven and London: Yale University Press, 2007. xi + 225 pp.; 42 color and 120 bw illus., bibliography, index. $50.00.

Paul T. Frankl (1886–1958) was one of the most important and influential designers working in the United States during the first half of the twentieth century. His skyscraper bookcases, produced in New York City in the late 1920s, captured the optimism and bravura of modern urban life with their jaunty angles and expressive personalities. Not only were these objects popular enough in their day to inspire *New Yorker* cartoons, but they have become, in our time, the essential centerpiece in almost every major collection of twentieth-century American furniture. Frankl's ability to divine the attitude of an era did not end in the 1920s, however; his low-slung, upholstered Speed armchair of the early 1930s is a poetic, comfortable embodiment of streamlining, and his biomorphic cork-topped coffee table of 1951 aptly expresses the more casual lifestyles of the post–World War II era. In addition to his work as a designer and decorator, Frankl was an ardent, effective publicist for the modernist cause, and he published numerous articles and books over the course of his career; his *New Dimensions* (1928) and *Form and Re-Form* (1930) were among the earliest American modern design manifestoes.

With so many iconic designs and writings to his name, it is surprising that Frankl has not received more scholarly attention. When, in the 1980s, curators and academics began to study pre–World War II furniture, Frankl was always accorded a central place, yet the substance and complexity of his career were never fully examined.[1] A handful of master's theses and Ph.D. dissertations have been written on him, but before the arrival of Christopher Long's *Paul T. Frankl and Modern American Design*, Frankl was a bit of a mystery: easy to recognize, hard to know. Long's thoughtful, comprehensive monograph thus fills a major gap in the field. Long follows Frankl from his student days in Vienna and Berlin to New York, then to Southern California, where he lived and worked for the last two decades of his life. His narrative weaves together at least three different strands: it is a history of Frankl's furniture designs; a history of Frankl's interior decorating; and a history of the retailing of modern design in the United States. It is buttressed by an impressive wealth of research, both in archival collections and in period publications. Indeed, one of the most valuable parts of this book is its extensive bibliography, which includes a list of Frankl's own writings and of publications devoted to his work: in response to his modernist proselytizing in the 1920s and 1930s, he was the subject of countless articles in popular magazines, art journals, and newspapers across the country (such as the *Indianapolis News* and the *Allentown [Pa.] Call*), an impressive number of which are listed here.

Long's book reveals many new facts about Frankl and teaches us several important lessons about the rise of modern design in the United States. Long is a professor of architectural history and theory at the University of Texas at Austin, and his previous scholarship has focused on European modern architecture and design. He thus approaches Frankl's career with a sophisticated understanding of the cultural and artistic milieu in which Frankl trained, to which the designer looked for inspiration throughout his career. One of the great pleasures of this book is the ease with which Long perceives, and then dissects, the many European trends that informed Frankl's designs. His approach does not diminish the originality of Frankl's work but, rather, has the virtue of placing these iconic American objects in a thoroughly transatlantic dialogue. It is a model that the field of American furniture and design history would benefit from following.

Frankl was born into a wealthy Viennese family. The artistically inclined son reached a deal with his father: he would be allowed to pursue a degree in architecture with the understanding that he would design buildings for the family real-estate business. After mixed success at art schools in Vienna and Berlin, a few brief architectural apprenticeships, and the death of his father, he sailed for the United States in 1914. With the outbreak of World War I, Frankl decided to stay in the States. To make money, he opened a small retail store specializing in modern decorative accessories and hired himself out as an interior decorator. He returned home after the United States entered the war in 1917, but life in New York had clearly thrilled him, and he traveled back across the Atlantic, this time for good, in 1920.

As Long describes it (relying extensively on Frankl's own unpublished autobiography, written circa 1954), Frankl found New York City an exciting place with a surprisingly ambivalent attitude toward modernism: although modern technology had transformed daily life, the buying public was skeptical of modern design in the home. Frankl sensed an opportunity to make himself a prominent spokesman for the new cause, and he threw himself into a variety of projects, including his store, interior decorating, writing, and involvement in various art and design groups. He launched his first complete line of furniture in 1925, called Peasant Furniture. This rustic collection, which included trestle-style dining tables and benches to match, resonated in several arenas. As Long explains, Frankl was responding, in part, to American fascination with the colonial past, but the furniture's emphasis on handicraft also situates it in relationship to British and Continental arts and crafts sensibilities. Moreover, the severe simplicity of the forms has an ahistoric quality, as if Frankl were wresting modernism from the blunt realities of handcraftsmanship.

Frankl's unquestionable breakthrough came just a year or two later in the form of the skyscraper bookcases. These were tall case pieces that climbed to the ceiling in a series of irregular step backs, echoing the silhouette of the new building form rising throughout New York and other urban centers. The account of their origin is marvelously pragmatic: as Frankl recalled, he had piles of large magazines and books in his small cottage in Woodstock, New York, and he designed a bookcase to hold each pile efficiently; the inadvertent effect was a series of stepped-back shelves that his guests immediately associated with skyscraper architecture. By 1927 the skyscraper line had taken off, and Frankl was inundated with more orders than he could handle. This led to a problem that has concerned curators and collectors ever since. To keep up with demand, Frankl contracted with a variety of woodworkers in the city, and quality was thus uneven. In addition, several companies and many small-scale producers copied the idea, creating, in essence, a market of pirated skyscraper pieces. (To further confuse historians, some of these objects may have been made by Frankl's own suppliers, working after hours.) Although Frankl attempted to designate authentic designs with a paper (and later metal) label, this did little to prevent the sales of copies.

Frankl had been approached by an acquaintance in 1925 who offered to build a furniture factory for him in North Carolina. Had Frankl accepted, he would have had a centralized place to manufacture enough skyscraper objects to meet demand, and he would have obviated the subsequent piracy problem. The furniture made in this factory would also have been more affordable because of lower overhead and more efficient production. Ironically, Frankl rejected the offer because, from his base in New York, he would have been unable to oversee production and thus guarantee quality. The incident reveals much about Frankl's particular modernist vision: although he celebrated the power of the modern machine, and although he believed modern furniture should be available to the middle classes, his commitment to the object as an aesthetic expression usually led to individually crafted pieces that were far too expensive for most consumers. Long highlights incongruities such as this throughout Frankl's career without defending or casting aspersions on them. The result is that Frankl's modernism is carefully traced against competing models, with similarities and divergences highlighted. If the final assessment of Frankl is somewhat surprising, it gives us a more nuanced account of how modernism developed in this country, and what it represented to consumers, than heretofore.

With the rise of industrial design in the 1930s, Frankl's emphasis on the aesthetic, expressive object placed him further outside the mainstream of modernism. His style changed in this decade to encompass smooth curves, soft lines, and an even greater simplicity of overall form. Long describes a variety of furniture pieces designed in the early 1930s, situating them in an arc of stylistic change that should be helpful to scholars trying to date unprovenanced Frankl objects. Long attributes the shift toward curves and simplicity to the influence of streamlining as well as trends in European design, which Frankl learned about through magazines, trips, and fellow émigrés. But he goes on to highlight features of Frankl's work that were unique to him: an abiding interest in sensuous, tactile experience and in physical comfort. One word Long uses to describe this sensibility is "cozy"

(p. 109), and it proves to be an apt, if unexpected, adjective for Frankl's most successful design of these years, the Speed lounge chair. The Speed chair is undoubtedly streamlined, with its forward-thrusting arms and reclined back, but Frankl covered it in a variety of rich materials, ranging from deeply textured upholstery to pony skin. The deep seat envelops the sitter, creating the effect of being ensconced in a forward-surging cocoon.

After World War II (which he survived, financially, by selling plants at his Rodeo Drive store), Frankl finally found an opportunity to produce his designs affordably through collaboration with the Johnson Company, a Grand Rapids furniture firm. Between 1949 and 1953 he designed several lines of furniture, some quite conservative, with brass-colored drawer pulls or tambour fronts, and others more austerely modern, with bleached cork and mahogany. It is for this last group that the biomorphic coffee table was developed. Although the Johnson Company furniture was financially successful, on the whole it did not suffice to place Frankl at the forefront of postwar modern furniture design; Long himself notes that in comparison with the work of Ray and Charles Eames or Isamu Noguchi, Frankl's objects look "dowdy" (p. 164). It is at this point that Long's narrative seems lacking in the depth and nuance of previous chapters. While he illustrates a few advertisements and objects from the Johnson lines, several are not depicted at all; these are not as avant-garde as Frankl's earlier designs, but their presence in the book would have helped to articulate Frankl's aesthetic (and, one suspects, ideological) ambivalence at this late date in his career. In addition, a more sustained analysis of Frankl's relationship to popular modernism in the postwar years would have been helpful. What did Frankl think of the furniture being produced by manufacturers such as Herman Miller and Knoll? Is the biomorphic coffee table, the only piece in these years that resonates with the dominant aesthetic, simply his attempt to show he could stay on the bandwagon, or is it a glimpse of a nascent aesthetic idea, derived from changing patterns in domestic living, that he did not have the space to develop?

On a larger scale, *Paul T. Frankl* suffers from an insufficiently theorized and historicized account of American taste and design identity. At the outset, Long explains that his monograph "is also about the search for 'Americanness' in American design culture" (p. ix). Yet the quest to identify and isolate a characteristic that represents a specific national identity—whether in art, design, or literature—is problematic. As Long's own account reveals, with its rich layers of overlapping European and American ideas, irreducible "Americanness" in design is at best difficult to find, at worst a chimera. What is irrefutable, however, is the fact that many designers and artists working in the 1920s and 1930s in the United States were obsessed with the thought of establishing a uniquely American aesthetic. Frankl, despite (or, more likely, because of) his immigrant status, was eager to promote the idea of a distinct American taste, as countless quotes attest. Here he is describing, in his autobiography, one of his early skyscraper bookcases: "That large piece was made of redwood, which I used extensively to underscore the American origin of that furniture" (p. 67). Thus,

Long would be more successful if he historicized and contextualized this search for "Americanness," rather than referring to it, as he sometimes does, as a given quantity (see, for example, pp. 55 and 96).

This is, however, a minor complaint about a book that offers so much to the field. Not only has Long exhumed the complicated career of a pivotal figure in American furniture, but he has also provided an excellent example of how American design can be set in a global context. Long situates Frankl in dialogue with European design, but he does not force a comparison between the Continental work and the American work; the result is a much enriched understanding of some of the iconic pieces of American modern furniture. More broadly, the book offers a nuanced account of the rise of modernism in the United States—of its multiple sources, its varied interpreters, and its complex meanings.

Kristina Wilson
Clark University

1. See, for example, Karen Davies, *At Home in Manhattan: Modern Decorative Arts, 1925 to the Depression* (New Haven: Yale University Art Gallery, 1983); Alastair Duncan, *American Art Deco* (London: Thames and Hudson, 1986); and Richard Guy Wilson, Dianne H. Pilgrim, and Dickran Tashjian, *The Machine Age in America, 1918–1941* (New York: Brooklyn Museum of Art and Harry N. Abrams, 1986).

Boor, Allison, Jonathan A. Boor, Christopher Boor, Peter Boor, and John William Boor. *Philadelphia Empire Furniture*. West Chester, Pa.: Boor Management LLC, 2007. 596 pp.; 495 color and 126 bw illus., bibliography, index. Distributed by University Press of New England, Hanover and London. $139.00.

Once upon a time, not so very long ago, it was possible to buy pieces of American empire furniture, particularly very large pieces, for very little money. Back in the 1980s, when I was experiencing what might have looked like a decorative arts variant of midlife crisis, I became attracted to empire chests. I got into the habit of driving around to shops in eastern Pennsylvania, New York, and New England, looking for any empire chest in restorable condition that could be had for under $200. On a couple of occasions I paid $350 (and once or twice much more), but that was for pieces that were above average. Usually I gave less, and sometimes considerably so. At one point, I had about forty empire chests stored away in my garage, one piled on top of another. The scroll fronts were always easiest to find and therefore the cheapest. The first one I bought, in downstate New Hampshire, cost $150. The bigger and heavier Pennsylvania versions of the form were available for about the same price. Then as now, the market valued the earlier column-front chests more highly than the scroll fronts and priced them accordingly. Still, some very nice examples of this form could sometimes be had for around my limit of $200. I owned some dandy chests of drawers back then. Charles Montgomery was absolutely right. The best way to learn about a type of object is to buy one. Or two, or three, or four. . . .

Three aspects of this once undervalued furniture were particularly appealing. First, unless seriously damaged and missing a lot of veneer, these chests could be easily restored by an amateur (in this case, me), but mostly they didn't need it. Yes, the low-end New England examples were often pretty shoddily made, but the Pennsylvania pieces were as solid and sturdy as barns, built to last for years. A new drawer slide or two and a little glue here and there usually were enough to tighten everything up again for another century. I tried to stay away from pieces needing significant structural repairs, but most didn't. Some were in a wonderful state of preservation.

Then there was the wood. John Kirk may be generally right when he tells people to buy things ratty and leave them that way, but I think this practice is inappropriate when it comes to empire furniture. Muddy, old, opaque finish does not become objects in this style. And this was where the real delight of working with empire chests came in. A little bit of paint remover easily lifted unattractive old finish to reveal brilliantly figured mahogany veneer underneath. Even objects that had originally been relatively inexpensive were veneered with spectacular wood. I never got over the thrill of wiping away the old finish to reveal the lustrous and richly grained mahogany. Glorious transformation! My refinishing practices may not have conformed to prevailing professional standards, but I was tickled with the results. I often thought of myself as being in the resurrection business, bringing back to life old objects that had been all but dead. Sometimes the chests also still had their original pressed-glass pulls. Cleaned and reinstalled, these added brilliance and luster. In all, these objects yielded a lot of positive experience and sensory delight for not very much money.

Finally, there was and remains the simple matter of the powerful presence of empire case furniture. The New England chests, with some exceptions, were not particularly large, but some of the New York and Pennsylvania chests, both urban and rural, were big, heavy objects. Their substantiality was impressive. Agreeably formidable, they commanded attention and made their presence known in any room. You knew they were not about to blow away with the next wind. I briefly toyed with the idea of buying sideboards as well, for these were often even a better bargain, figuring dollars per cubic foot. But the greater size of these items posed a number of insuperable problems, and I reluctantly gave up on the idea.

There are plenty of chests of drawers, and sideboards too, in *Philadelphia Empire Furniture*. This handsome book, as weighty and substantial as some of the furniture it celebrates, is a spectacular pictorial testimony to the distinctive visual delights of this furniture. Somewhere in the vicinity of three hundred objects believed to be from Philadelphia appear in large-format photographs, almost always full color and often of outstanding quality. All of the major upmarket forms are represented, usually in multiple examples. The pieces illustrated come from a number of the usual expected sources, among them the Philadelphia Museum of Art, the Metropolitan Museum of Art, Winterthur, and Andalusia, and from the trade, Hirschl & Adler, Carswell Rush Berlin, Christie's, and a few others. A sizable percentage, however, are from private collections or institutional collections either little known or only recently publicized, such as the Biggs Museum in Dover, Delaware. So the images offer a mixture of familiar and less familiar goods.

Because even many of the major institutions have very limited holdings of Philadelphia empire furniture, it can be difficult to form an impression of the entire genre from the holdings of any one museum. The authors deserve considerable credit for bringing together in one place images of objects scattered around the country. Taken together and compared to one another, they help to create a composite picture of the genre. About the only caveat I would offer about the selection is that it is, indeed, biased in favor of the high end. There is very little here that could have been had for $200, not even twenty years ago. Midlevel Philadelphia empire, whatever that might be, is not very much in evidence here. Another project for another time, I suppose.

Philadelphia Empire Furniture is, frankly, a picture book, and it is best to treat it as such. Yes, it is distributed by a university press, but no, it is not a university product. Although there are no words to that effect anywhere in the text, my sense is that this was a labor of love of sorts for a family enamored of Philadelphia empire furniture. And why not? I fully understand the appeal. I enjoyed looking through this book, and I believe that others will, too. But the key to enjoyment is ignoring or skimming over the text. It is benignly disorganized and pleasantly muddled. By that I mean that it is partial, repetitive, sometimes relevant, sometimes not, inconsistent, unsystematic, underinformative, now and then inaccurate, occasionally outright wrong (even when quoting from museum publications), riddled with typos and grammatical and spelling errors, and on and on. The knowledgeable will be frustrated by the limitations of the text, and novices will be led astray or at best confused. There are matters to quibble with on nearly every page. A couple of short pieces by Don Fennimore and Alexandra Alevizatos Kirtley are mostly exempt from these criticisms, but unfortunately both have been subjected to the same generally inattentive editing that afflicts the entire volume. There is no point in belaboring this. Indeed, it is probably in poor taste to say as much as I already have. The folks responsible for this book wrote it because they love Philadelphia empire furniture. So be it. They are not alone.

So, how to use this volume? The value, I think, is in the gathering and grouping that the authors have done, in putting like with like that allows for a sense of a metropolitan or regional manner to become more apparent. There is value in attending to some of the authors' observations. Surely they are correct in noting that regional preferences were still visible in American furniture in the early nineteenth century when the empire style was in vogue. Some classes of Philadelphia goods are quite distinctive and not likely to be confused with those from New York or New England. Surely they are also correct in their observations about the wonderful quality of the mahogany used in much of this furniture, some of it applied as a surface veneer, some in the solid as running boards on sides and tops of case furniture, and some carved into lion's feet, wings, scrolls, baskets of fruit, leaves, or the other curious motifs of the era. There is no denying that those who find pleasure in contemplating—or meditating upon—the rich luster of mahogany will be well rewarded by *Philadelphia Empire Furniture*.

A perhaps more challenging claim that the authors make is that Philadelphia empire is worthy of the same attention and the same high regard as Philadelphia Chippendale furniture. Possibly so, but the aesthetic system and patterns of thought that gave form to Philadelphia empire differ so radically from those responsible for Philadelphia Chippendale that it is hard to justly compare the two. Both styles find some of their fullest expression in carving, yet how different the carving of the later manner is from the earlier. It is not just a matter of motif but also of touch, weight, scale, boldness, and force rather than delicacy, diminution, or nuance. And, at least at present, the empire style remains more of a cognitive challenge to modern viewers. Although not as old, it somehow seems more foreign, more alien, more culturally distant than the now canonical (but perhaps falsely familiar) forms of the eighteenth century.

In organizing their images, the authors have put like with like, usually by function, that is, chairs, chests of drawers, worktables, and so on. In one instance, they group what they call platform pedestal tables together, perhaps because this design or structural concept was used for tables of various sizes and functions. The descriptor is useful but the problem here is that several of the tables included in this section are not of the platform pedestal form. Nonetheless, it is clear from the images that this was a distinctive genre. The key features of Philadelphia versions of these tables are a central pedestal, typically carved and occasionally flanked by scrolls or other forms, resting on a veneered triangular platform with concave sides. This platform in turn is supported on either lion's feet adorned with the characteristic Philadelphia splash of foliage that curls away from the base or carved rounded feet. Some of these tables have marble tops, others wooden tops that tilt. A second type of table, unaccountably included in the section on platform pedestal types, retains the platform but in place of the pedestal has three or five scrolling legs with lion's feet.

The other sections, which group the furniture according to use, are a bit more coherent. In most of these, clusters of images document recurring types. One group of game or card tables is constructed along the lines of the platform pedestal types, but the pedestal is here replaced by some variation on the form of a lyre. A related group retains the lyre contour but replaces the musical instrument with a carved pair of sea monsters confronting each other. Both of these types of tables I would call federal in style, but the distinction between federal and empire is admittedly not always clear. Less ambiguous stylistically is a group of game tables of platform pedestal construction, the platform usually supported by the conventional Philadelphia lion's foot and foliage device and the pedestal richly carved with pendant leaves.

A small number of other very distinctive types bear mentioning. Apparently typical of Philadelphia are pier tables with shaped lower shelves, usually with a semicircular central device. A group of lady's worktables with lyre bases is clearly related to the game tables mentioned above and just as arguably federal in manner. On the other hand, another group of worktables follows the platform pedestal format and is definitely empire, characterized by rich mahogany, deep carving, and bold contrasts of large-scale features.

The section on chairs is a bit jumbled but does include a cluster of quite archaeologically informed klismos types characterized by a low, emphatically curved back, a broad, concave crest that extends beyond the stiles, very boxy seats, and strongly curved front and back legs, all sawed rather than turned. Some examples also sport brass inlay. Painted variations may have caned seats and back panels or turned rather than saw-shaped front legs. Otherwise, the chair section seems something of a mishmash, with too many clearly federal examples included. And is it true that there were no Philadelphia empire rocking chairs? None appears here.

The sofa section includes six examples of a very recognizable box or square sofa. This type of sofa has arm supports conceived as straight columns or posts aligned above a turned leg, rather than some combination of the more familiar scrolls, cornucopias, animal feet, and foliage, set in opposition to each other like reversed brackets. What is particularly noteworthy, considering the relative paucity of labeled Philadelphia empire furniture, is that four of these six very similar examples are marked in some way—and all by different firms. One has an inscription with the name of G. W. Pickering, who apparently worked in the shop of Joseph Barry. A second bears the dark but still legible stencil of Cook & Parkin. A third has a very clear and bright stencil for C. H. and J. F. White, while the fourth is labeled by David Fleetwood. The two remaining sofas are obviously part of this very tight grouping, which together documents how very similar objects bearing the labels of different shops might be. Although not pursued here, these sofas could provide the basis for a very instructive workshop on connoisseurship and close observation of objects. They also raise all the usual questions about shop practice, interchangeability of parts (or of workmen), subcontracting, retail sales, and all the rest of the murky and shifting inner workings of the trade.

Philadelphia empire chests of drawers come in a number of variants, with or without an overhanging top drawer, with the largest drawer at the top or at the bottom, with flat drawers or bowed, two drawers across the top or only one, and so on. A lovely example of what seems to be the most conventional form, in this instance in bird's-eye maple, appears as figure 305. This piece has two small bow-front drawers side by side over three flat-front drawers, the latter flanked by full-round columns with conventionalized Ionic scroll capitals topped with a bit of foliate fluting. As with all of the rest of the Philadelphia chests of drawers here and congruent with my own experience, the flat top is without a deck of smaller drawers or a backboard of any sort. This treatment is notably at odds with both New England and New York practice. Why this was the case in Philadelphia is one of those regional mysteries and clear evidence that local dialect still survived in American furniture in the early nineteenth century.

And then there are sideboards. Ah, yes. I would have liked to see more than the twenty-three shown here. I have often thought it would be glorious to produce an exhibition devotedly entirely to empire sideboards.

Think of the majesty of it all! The type of sideboard most fully represented here has a tripartite façade with a dropped central section, this last typically surfaced with a marble slab. The tripartite composition extends into the prominent backboard, where a raised central mirror is flanked by scrolls, cornucopias, or other empire decorative motifs. One of the examples illustrated in *Philadelphia Empire Furniture* bears the label of Anthony Gabriel Quervelle. All of the rest are obviously very much in the same manner, but, in light of the number of different shops represented in the small sampling of very similar box sofas mentioned above, it is not at all clear what that might mean.

These sideboards, like the sofas, raise questions that the authors are apparently disinclined to answer, let alone ask. What, we might wonder, was the relative cultural weight of various objects in the empire style for sale in Philadelphia in the early nineteenth century? Was one object just as meaningful (or meaningless) as another? Possibly not. Consider a few pieces of evidence offered in this volume. On the first page of his introductory commentary, Don Fennimore quotes two period Philadelphia advertisements. One is an auction notice posted by J. M. Evans in a Philadelphia newspaper for October 7, 1811. The first object for sale mentioned is an "elegant Mahogany sideboard." The other advertisement, for November 28, 1828, is from Anthony Gabriel Quervelle announcing that he has "so enlarged his manufactory, as to enable him to keep constantly on hand an extensive supply of CABINET WARE, such as Elegant Fashionable SIDEBOARDS" (p. 5). Note that sideboards are mentioned first in both texts. Then, if we turn to the pages in *Philadelphia Empire Furniture* reproducing a book of sketches said to be by Quervelle, we find one desk, one desk-and-bookcase, one worktable, one pier table, and one this, and one that, but also two bureaus, three sofas (including one box sofa), and seven sideboards! Yes, seven sideboards (five of them of the drop-center variety). How do we determine cultural weight or heightened significance? I am not sure that there is a simple formula that fits all cases, but here at least is a trail of clues about the significance of sideboards that we might want to follow and that might help us begin to unlock period comprehensions or appreciations or valuations of these objects.

Quervelle, of course, remains the reigning figure in Philadelphia empire furniture. This book does nothing to change that. It was that decorative arts polymath Robert C. Smith who brought Quervelle to the attention of the twentieth century, first with an article in *Antiques* in 1964 and, later, with a five-part series in that same journal in 1973–74. Taken together, these articles still constitute the most sustained scholarly study of Philadelphia empire furniture. Smith may have been optimistic in some of his attributions, but he located a substantial body of documented or otherwise probable Quervelle furniture that has provided useful touchstones for subsequent students. The spirit of Robert C. Smith hovers around this book, although there is little evidence of the extraordinary eye for a motif or a manner, the sweeping grasp of design history, or the felicitous way with words—in multiple languages, it should be said—that Smith brought to his work. Still,

Smith dearly loved the arts of Philadelphia, and I think that he would be pleased to see that others continue to study them.

Philadelphia Empire Furniture is an attractively packaged archive of a fascinating genre of American furniture. It is not truly comprehensive but it does present the major categories of the material in clear and easily read photographs. There will be other books about various aspects of this subject, but, for the present, this is a very useful compendium and reference. Yes, it would have been a better book if the authors had been more systematic and thorough in gathering and presenting data and if they had engaged a more demanding editor. But perhaps a revised and augmented edition at some point is not entirely out of the question.

Kenneth L. Ames
Bard Graduate Center

Martin Eidelberg, Thomas Hine, Pat Kirkham, David A. Hanks, and C. Ford Peatross. *The Eames Lounge Chair: An Icon of Modern Design.* London and New York: Merrell Publishers; Grand Rapids, Mich.: Grand Rapids Art Museum, 2006. 192 pp.; 200 bw and color illus., index. $45.00.

The careers of Charles (1907–1978) and Ray Kaiser Eames (1912–1988) and their contributions to design have been explored in publications and popular forums to such a degree that their names are nearly synonymous with mid-twentieth-century modernism, but it is nonetheless surprising to find a book dedicated to single work of theirs, notably a manufactured lounge chair that remains in production to the present day. Certainly, within the realm of design objects of the last century, few works have been accorded such an honor. As willing participants, design museums have embraced and furthered the lofty role chairs have been assigned in recent years, subjecting the form to an untold number of scholarly analyses. That the Grand Rapids Art Museum would undertake a touring exhibition and publication with this focus appears to affirm the iconic status to which the Eames lounge chair has ascended in the five decades since its creation. If because of their functional challenges and personal immediacy chairs have become the touchstone by which many aspirants as well as accomplished designers are often evaluated by and identified with, then the Eames lounge chair may stand, within the realms of those casting judgment upon design, as the consummate realization of casual luxury in a modernist work. The essays within *The Eames Lounge Chair: An Icon of Modern Design* not only frame the development of this object's design, production, and consumption but further the notion of select chairs serving as standard-bearers representative of their respective eras and, ultimately, fetishistic objects of status for the design-savvy consumer. This book seeks to fix this one design as the Eameses' supreme domestic achievement and a modern icon, but it also intriguingly raises questions, not necessarily answered, as to how and why a design may be considered iconic.

The first essay, written by Martin Eidelberg and suitably titled "Charting the Iconic Chair," establishes the rationale for the focus of the effort by noting the chair's representation of "engineering and manufacturing prowess" relative to modernism and, indicative of the issue of status and popular recognition, noting that "it celebrates important personalities" (p.10). The point of chairs being offered iconic status is presented as a more recent, mid-twentieth-century phenomenon with the ensuing discussion, framed through a survey of early twentieth-century chairs, perceptively pointing out the particular command architect-designed works have assumed in serving as a microcosm of style and culture and—through technology, materials, and form—proclaiming modernist ideals. The following sections, detailing innovations in furniture construction in tubular steel, plywood, and plastics, prove interesting as surveys of primary modernist materials and resultant chair forms dating from the 1920s through the 1960s. However, the inclusion of the first material—tubular steel—seems less applicable specifically to the Eameses given their predilection for working with the latter two materials. Bent plywood, which forms the primary shells of the lounge chair, is presented as descending directly from the early 1930s work of Finnish architect Alvar Aalto, reinforced by the comparison with the sled-footed chair from the Cranbrook Academy of Art Library of Eliel and Eero Saarinen (a colleague of and later collaborator of Eames) to Aalto's earlier design for the *Springleaf* armchair. Both provided cantilevered seats supported by two runners of laminated wood, and both the elder and younger Saarinen were quite familiar with Aalto's work. However, the argument that Eames was, at the time, equally "aping" (p. 21) this earlier work would be more convincing if additional evidence were introduced. Eidelberg finally promptly dismisses any significant technological achievements in the chair in questioning its iconic status, suggesting instead that its familiarity and "unabashed combination of modernity and traditionalism" served to "announce the shift in the direction that Modernism would take" (p. 26). This statement, challenging the notion of a purely progressive modernity, is central to the understanding of the chair and the plurality of modernism after World War II.

Thomas Hine's essay on the development of the image of the Eames lounge chair speaks both to its popularization as a fashionable marker of high-style domesticity and the duality of the design's image as both materially glamorous and comfortingly casual. As sales results indicate, the lounge chair was neither the most popular chair designed by the Eameses nor as ubiquitous within the American home as its appearance in later advertising and other media might suggest to contemporary audiences. It is especially interesting to note that the chair's highly theatrical premiere in 1956 on NBC's *Home* show, supported by the presence of Charles and Ray Eames, as well as its subsequent critical awards failed to propel sales of the $404 lounge chair above 500 units in its first year of production (p. 33). Given the apprehension of the Eameses about the chair's sales failing to meet tooling costs (as noted in Pat Kirkham's following essay [p. 59]) and the transcription of a 2004 interview with Max Depree (p. 154), who remarked, "From

Herman Miller's [the manufacturer] point of view, the Lounge Chair was not necessarily an expensive product," one cannot help but desire to know the firm's sales expectations (especially as the question of the chair's relative expense and market is raised repeatedly throughout the book). Only in the 1970s, following Herman Miller's reorientation away from the domestic and toward the office furnishing market, would the chair, "sold mainly as executive seating," reach its peak of units sold. Hine rightly, if ironically within the context of this book, asserts, "in our global consumer culture, the Eames Lounge Chair, like most other pieces of Modernist furniture, has played only a marginal role" (p. 33). However, his adjoining comparison of the chair's sales to the legacy of Ford's notoriously ill-conceived Edsel automobile seems forced, as does the unequivocal statement that the chair "looks like a classic." More telling is the mention of the mood of American consumers during the 1950s as being receptive to the promise of domestic security and higher standards of luxury that the chair seemed to evoke. The popular "sightings" of the lounge chair of the past half century—including in movies, television shows, and comic strips—is presented through anecdotes and images, reinforcing its status as a widespread signifier of modern taste and how the lounge chair, alongside the Eameses' other plywood chairs, has become synonymous with the Eames "brand." The misuse of a designer's or maker's name as a descriptive stylistic moniker for a host of unrelated contemporaneous objects is hardly unusual in the history of decorative arts, but Eames is one of the few names of the last half century that have become truly ubiquitous as a design reference. Although this particular chair retains a slightly rarified status within the context of their work, the name "Eames" does not, thanks both to their prolific careers and renewed interest in mid-twentieth-century design. The concluding focus on the specific and authentic is also particularly welcome. Concerning technical changes in the construction of the chair over the decades and providing points of connoisseurship for a manufactured work that has been subject to material improvements as well as competition from here-unmentioned imitators, ultimately Hine's popular culture approach implies the brand—and by relation the perception of the chair—is equally as significant as the veneers, leather, and metal that constitute the chair's physical framework.

"The Evolution of the Eames Lounge Chair and Ottoman" by Pat Kirkham provides a biographical sketch of the Eameses, affirming Ray's training in the fine arts and dance as a foundation for the later collaborative efforts of husband and wife. As recent scholarly efforts have attempted to increase the understanding and appreciation of Ray's collaborative role in their creations, Kirkham too weaves Ray into the picture as a figure integral to the Eames office and thus sharing in the development of the Plywood Group of furnishings and the lounge chair. Further emphasis is placed on Charles Eames's association with Eero Saarinen through Cranbrook Academy and their chair designs for the 1940 Museum of Modern Art "Organic Design in Home Furnishings" competition. This event marked the shift toward greater experimentation with plywood formed into compound curves and the importance of decidedly biomorphic shapes, which would dominate progressive furniture design in the decade to come. That in 1953–1954 the Eames may have been inspired by Saarinen's *Womb* chair design of 1948 to create their own version of a biomorphic lounge chair is asserted in terms of their ownership and subsequent replacement of an example of the former with the latter (p. 54). This can be accepted as Saarinen's design being one "point of reference" in the basic idea of a modern and protective lounge chair and ottoman, but the construction, upholstery, and lavish expression of veneer differentiate it from Saarinen's approach and provides the Eameses's design with a richness befitting its original intent as a gift to their close friend, acclaimed filmmaker Billy Wilder.

The author refutes her declaration "in the mid-twentieth century United States, there was a popular belief that modernist designers preferred to focus on minimal comfort" by asserting, "belief is one-dimensional" (p. 57). Even so, before the 1960s remarkably few modern works embraced the image of highly refined *casual* comfort as completely as does the lounge chair, prompting Charles Eames to reference 1930s club chairs as one inspiration (p. 150). The citation of another oft-proclaimed icon of twentieth-century furniture design, Mies van der Rohe's chair for the Barcelona Exhibition of 1929 as one of the sources "conscious or otherwise, for the Eames Lounge Chair" (p. 57), reinforces the difficulty of identifying references to European modernist works, largely eschewing anything that might intrude on their formalist qualities and suggest a bourgeois appearance. Even though it is button-tufted, the Barcelona chair retains its geometry through a taut grid of pleated leather in two slablike pads balanced on a chromed steel frame. The upholstery of the Eames chair not only provides actual cushioning but also exudes the appearance of comfort through the quality and quantity of ample, plush cushions nested within the shells of the chair.

Kirkham provides a brief discussion of the chair, styled as a relaxing refuge, as a masculine object—a concept furthered by Herman Miller advertising with images typically showing a male sitter reading or napping. As an informal domestic "throne" and in its particular emphasis on natural materials, one might expect the discussion to suggest it is more of a descendant of the richly grained oak and leather Morris chair of the arts and crafts movement than of the European modernist constructs of the 1920s. In any regard, Kirkham's essay provides a well-focused and useful addition to the understanding of the development of the chair within the Eameses's oeuvre.

The extended series of images of the chair, advertising, and related works that follows occupies the core of the book and, however interesting to peruse, is diminished in usefulness by its lack of accompanying page numbers or any identifying captions; awkwardly, the latter are provided in a key to the pictures by means of repeated thumbnail images.

The concluding texts feature brief interviews by David Hanks with Don Albinson, responsible for the fabrication of numerous Eames prototypes including the lounge chair; Max Depree of Herman Miller; textile designer Jack Lenor Larsen; former design curator Mildred Friedman; author and architect Stanley Abercrombie; and Lucia Eames, daughter of Charles

Eames; as well as an essay by C. Ford Peatross discussing the connection, through archives and exhibitions, of the Eameses to the Library of Congress. In these two sections one finds some of the most interesting new information about the creation of the chair and perspectives on its legacy and the repeated issues of cost, comfort, and Ray's involvement in its design. Although prepared primarily as a means to promote further research and sketch the breadth of the voluminous Eames archives at the Library of Congress, Peatross's essay reveals a significant discovery within the files of an illustrated 1955 letter by Ray to Charles describing the further refinement of the chair's arm positions as well as the section of the metal back connectors. This single document vividly captures the idea of the Eames office as working under Charles's orchestration rather than his specific aesthetic or mechanical dictates, echoing Albinson's comment about Charles's apparently vague descriptive approach to developing a preliminary design, noting "he would tell me what he wanted, and he expected me to figure out how to do it" (p. 150).

The work of Charles and Ray Eames will undoubtedly continue to be a source of interest for scholars interested in twentieth-century design. This celebratory effort, published on the fiftieth anniversary of the Eames lounge chair, provides intriguing perspectives on a design not necessarily acclaimed for any technical or aesthetic revelations, yet that nonetheless stands as an enduring object of desire. It has securely captured the imaginations of both design-conscious consumers and critics who revel in the degree of comfort, familiarity, and balance offered in a singular modernist work. Perhaps this is why it is both of its time and of our own, and through its continued fame and recognition, indeed, an icon.

Kevin W. Tucker
Dallas Museum of Art

Philip D. Zimmerman. *Delaware Clocks*. Dover, Del.: Biggs Museum of American Art, 2006. 62 pp.; numerous color and bw illus., bibliography, index. $24.95 pb.

There is a view of American clockmaking that has more to do with ideas about what it means to be American than it has to do with clockmaking. It is a frontier vision, whereby the hardy individual with limited means but unlimited freedom thrives by canniness, thrift, perseverance, and genius. A variation of this view (compounded with a somewhat overawed filiopietism) was put forward in the first monograph on the most famous of American clockmakers, Simon Willard. Published in 1911, its oddly distorted image of Willard came to be applied to American clockmakers generally, and still persists. This view fails to explain a great deal that ought to be of current interest about the clockmaking experience, including the sudden failure without issue of whole branches of the industry.

An alternative view of clockmaking proposes that successful clockmakers were more like Sam Walton than they were like the conflation of Daniel

Boone and Geppetto that Simon Willard's grandson seems to have imagined. In this view, the labor of making clocks can be almost infinitely divided, and the clockmaker can be seen to behave somewhat like an upholsterer, assembling the products of a number of different shops.

More and more studies are revealing the remarkable multiplicity of hands at work on the archetypal antique, the eight-day clock. *Delaware Clocks* very successfully compiles a great deal of the existing evidence on clocks of that region and examines numerous outstanding examples in admirable detail, revealing much of the complexity that underlies these esteemed objects.

Delaware Clocks was produced to accompany a temporary exhibition on the subject of clockmaking in Delaware, organized by the Biggs Museum of American Art in Dover, Delaware, and exhibited there and at the National Watch and Clock Museum in Columbia, Pennsylvania. Two pages list the nineteen clocks included in the exhibition, but the text, written by Philip D. Zimmerman as a continuous narrative across separate entries, expands generously beyond the common bounds of exhibition catalogues.

As Ryan D. Grover, curator of the Biggs Museum of American Art, points out in his introduction, *Delaware Clocks* is intended to "bring into focus actual communities of artisans" (p. 4). Examining communities of artisans is, as Mr. Grover points out, a useful alternative to "reinventing the standard lists of Delaware craftsmen involved in clockmaking."

The artisan community responsible for a clock can be said to be synchronous when a case maker, clock finisher, dial painter, and so forth each contribute to its production. The synchronous community can be narrowly local or extensive over wide geographic ranges, and typically is both. The artisan community is also asynchronous; clockmaking is complicated enough that a significant period of training is required, with apprentices learning the traditions of a particular shop from one or more artisans (who had themselves been trained in a shop), and perhaps themselves going on to train apprentices. A productive clock shop exemplifies, at any given moment, both kinds of artisan community. The evidence for these communities, generally only sparsely documented in the written record, is to be found in the clocks themselves, and *Delaware Clocks* takes ample advantage of it.

The text addresses "three identifiable schools of clockmaking" (p. 4): colonial Delaware clockmaking; clockmaking from the Odessa, Delaware, area; and post-Revolutionary Wilmington clockmaking.

The section on colonial Delaware clockmaking intersperses comments on clockmaking in general with a discussion of specific makers and clocks. The general discussion helpfully separates dials from movements and both from cases. This separation reflects a real distinction between disparate shop traditions. The shops that merge these functions—like the Dominys' on Long Island or the Blasdels' in Essex County, Massachusetts—are few and idiosyncratic, and no such shops appear to have operated in Delaware in the period under consideration, about 1741–1815.

With the exception of an impressively early (1658) reference to a New Amstel resident capable of clock repair, the story of clockmaking in colonial Delaware effectively begins in the 1740s with the little-known William

Furniss (active 1739–1749) and George Crow (active 1740–1762), who "left the first substantial body of work representing a single Delaware clockmaker" (p. 12). The discussion of Crow includes some interesting observations that are generally applicable to clockmakers, in Delaware and elsewhere, such as the presence of unfinished clock cases in a clockmaker's shop and finished clock movements in a cabinetmaker's shop. This, Zimmerman points out (p. 15), ought be interpreted, not as evidence of a clockmaker-cum-cabinetmaker (or the reverse), but as evidence that clockmakers sometimes provided shop space for cabinetmakers, and cabinetmakers sometimes took payment in clock movements, which they would case up and sell. Additionally, Zimmerman finds in the printed label pasted into one of Crow's clocks early (1761) evidence of a widening distance between clockmaker and customer (pp. 16–17, fig. 5b).

George Crow's sons George and Thomas both became clockmakers, and the section on colonial clockmaking continues with them (Thomas Crow, by virtue of his long career, reappears in the final section of *Delaware Clocks*). The younger George's clocks are few; he died young and seems to have worked only part-time as a clockmaker. Thomas was more prolific, and Zimmerman extracts a good deal of information from the cases that house his movements, notably in a closely reasoned examination of a very interesting clock case that harkens right back to clock central: Lancashire, England (pp. 23–24).

In contrast to the variety evident in the cases that house Thomas Crow movements, section two, "The Odessa Clocks," reveals a consistent regional preference for clock cases that is associated with the shop of John Janvier Sr. (1749–1801). Nine examples of cases labeled by, signed by, or attributed to Janvier or one of his sons, John Jr. (1777–1850) or Thomas (1772–1852), are included. The distinctive attributes of Odessa cases are examined in detail and summarized concisely (pp. 37–38).

The final section, "Wilmington Clocks of the Post-Revolution Era," examines the work of clockmakers and cabinetmakers at work in Wilmington in the last decade of the eighteenth century and the first of the nineteenth. The products of clockmaker Jonas Alrichs (1759–1802) and cabinetmaker John Erwin (1727–1797) feature prominently in this section, and Zimmerman is able to relate both to the shop of Thomas Crow. This section includes the last makers to produce the large eight-day clocks that are the principal subject of *Delaware Clocks*; in Delaware, as in New (and Old) England, these clocks and the shops that produced them disappeared quite suddenly in the second and third decades of the nineteenth century.

The last two clocks in *Delaware Clocks* are table clocks. One is signed by Thomas Crow as maker. Thomas Crow, "the most prolific and well-known clockmaker in late-eighteenth-century Wilmington" (p. 45), is well worth revisiting. His output, as illustrated in the first section of *Delaware Clocks*, is distinctly varied. The clocks are housed in cases with differing levels of ornament, including elaborate cases made in Philadelphia and plainer cases made in Wilmington. This sense of variety is augmented by an ornate, architectural case unlike any other made in America (see p. 23). Movements by many American makers can be found in cases from disparate cabinetmakers, and clockmakers were similarly free to patronize a variety of dial makers, particularly if their careers extended over a long period as Crow's did. Makers can be found that used both Boston-made and Birmingham painted iron dials, or both sheet brass and painted iron dials, and, occasionally, like Crow, both painted iron (figs. 8, 10) and composite brass dials (figs. 9, 11).

Adding to the perceived variety of Crow's output is a table clock (fig. 32), which employs several technologies distinctly different from those found in the eight-day clocks that make up the majority of his output. The table clock is spring-driven rather than weight-driven; it employs a fusee, a specialized tapered drum added to compensate for the decreasing tension of the relaxing spring; and its pace is governed by a crown-wheel and verge escapement. Good springs are very hard to make, and the vast clock tool industry of Lancashire effectively dominated their production worldwide until well into the nineteenth century. Fusees are also tricky and require a specialized engine (in addition to specialized skills) to be turned. Crown wheels, which have teeth parallel to the arbor (rather than perpendicular as in an anchor or deadbeat escapement), also require a specialized tool to be milled. As Zimmerman points out, "Many table clocks with American clockmaker's names on them were English movements, some of which were signed by their London makers" (p. 55), and the need for highly specialized tools and skills accounts for that fact.

This variety suggests Crow might be a good candidate for further investigation in light of the alternative interpretation of clockmaking mentioned above. Given the variety of craftsmen at work on his cases and dials, it is reasonable to wonder about the variety of craftsmen at work on his movements. Did one foundry provide his clock sets? How many calipers (templates for laying out the movement) were employed? How many clock finishers were at work? A particular advantage to this alternative approach is that it is readily falsifiable; on detailed examination, Crow's movements will reveal how they were produced.

Delaware Clocks illustrates two areas where clock studies in general might be profitably improved. The first is a matter of nomenclature. The terms "works" and "movement" are often used interchangeably, in this as in other studies, as are the terms "gear" and "wheel." The latter terms, "movement" and "wheel," were used by clockmakers from the seventeenth century onward; the terms "clockwork" and "gear" both acquired connotations in the nineteenth century that persist in the present and are not generally relevant to clockmaking.

The second has to do with illustrations. *Delaware Clocks* includes numerous pictures of movements that serve as reminders that there is something of interest behind the dial, but they tend to be, as is often the case when movements are illustrated, three-quarter views from the back. Far more useful would be views of the front plate with the dial and moon-phase trip wheel (if present) removed. This view would show at a glance whether one movement was made with the same caliper as another and whether the respective clock sets issued from the same source, revealing a good deal about the manufacturing methodology of the shop in question.

Philip Zimmerman does not disappoint as a writer; his research is fiercely accurate, his interpretations often both valid and provocative, and his lively interest in the topic is always evident. *Delaware Clocks* organizes, footnotes, and indexes a great deal of the information available on the topic, making it a valuable resource for any who see fit to pursue the many avenues of study its text suggests.[1]

David F. Wood
Concord Museum

1. I thank Robert Cheney for reading this review and providing several helpful suggestions.

Compiled by Gerald W. R. Ward

Recent Writing on American Furniture: A Bibliography

▼ THIS YEAR'S LIST includes works published in 2006 and roughly through August 2007. As always, a few earlier publications that had escaped notice are also included. The short title *American Furniture 2006* is used in citations for articles and reviews published in last year's edition of this journal, which is also cited in full under Luke Beckerdite's name.

As always, many people have assisted in helping to compile this list. I am particularly grateful to Jonathan Fairbanks, Luke Beckerdite, Kelly L'Ecuyer, Julie Muñiz, Dennis Carr, Jay Stiefel, Angela Segalla Breeden, David Wood, Steven M. Lash, Cheryl Robertson, and Barbara McLean Ward, as well as to the scholars who have written reviews for this issue.

Once again, I would be glad to receive citations for titles that have been inadvertently omitted from this or previous lists, as well as information about new publications. Review copies of significant works would also be much appreciated.

Adamson, Glenn, with Gary Michael Dault, David Dorenbaum, and Gord Peteran. *Gord Peteran: Furniture Meets Its Maker.* Milwaukee, Wis.: Milwaukee Art Museum and Chipstone Foundation, 2006. 192 pp.; numerous color and bw illus., checklist.

Ajmar-Wollheim, Marta, Flora Dennis, and Elizabeth Miller, eds. *At Home in Renaissance Italy.* London: V&A Publications, 2006. 420 pp.; numerous color and bw illus., summary catalogue, bibliography, index. (Comparative material.)

Albert, Gary. "The Museum of Early Southern Decorative Arts: An Introduction." *Antiques* 171, no. 1 (January 2007): 147–49. 7 color and bw illus.

Aleksa, Peter. "Hands On: Portsmouth Lolling Chair." *Antiques and Fine Art* 8, no. 1 (summer/autumn 2007): 206–7. Color illus.

American Period Furniture: Journal of the Society of American Period Furniture Makers 6 (2006): 1–80. Numerous color and bw illus., line drawings.

[Anderson, Jennifer]. "Portfolio: Jennifer Anderson." *American Craft* 66, no. 5 (October–November 2006): 63. 2 color illus.

Arnold, Mark. "The Best of the Old Is New: Period Furnituremakers Mount a Major Show in Savannah." *Woodwork,* no. 102 (December 2006): 60–64. Color illus.

———. "Contemporary Classics: Telfair Museum of Art Hosts First SAPFM Member Exhibitions." *American Period Furniture: Journal of the Society of American Period Furniture Makers* 6 (2006): 26–35. Color illus.

Asensio, Oscar. *DesignDesign: Furniture and Lights.* New York: Harry N. Abrams, 2007. 320 pp.; numerous color illus.

Aynsley, Jeremy, and Charlotte Grant, eds., with assistance from Harriet McKay *Imagined Interiors: Representing the Domestic Interior since the Renaissance.* London: V&A Publications, 2006. 304 pp.; numerous color and bw illus., bibliography, index.

Ayres, Linda. "Mount Vernon Ushers in a New Era." *Antiques and Fine Art* 7, no. 3 (autumn/winter 2006): 199–203. Color illus.

Barghini, Sandra. *Aspects of America: The American Museum in Britain.* London: Scala, 2007. 64 pp.; color illus.

Beach, Laura. "Abby Aldrich Museum Celebrates 50th Birthday." *Antiques and the Arts Weekly,* February 2, 2007, 1, 40–41. bw illus.

———. "Bayou Bend Turns Fifty." *Antiques and the Arts Weekly,* August 3, 2007, 1, 63–65. bw illus.

———. "Delaware Clocks." *Antiques and the Arts Weekly,* January 12, 2007, 1, 40–42. bw illus.

———. "Expressions of Innocence and Eloquence." *Antiques and the Arts Weekly,* January 19, 2007, 1, 62–65. bw illus.

———. "Shaker at Shelburne." *Antiques and the Arts Weekly,* June 29, 2007, 1, 44–45. 16 bw illus.

———. "'A Splash of Blue' at the Concord Museum." *Antiques and the Arts Weekly,* March 16, 2007, 1, 68–69. bw illus.

Beal, Suzanne. "Gary Knox Bennett's Melting-Pot Aesthetic." *American Craft* 66, no. 6 (December 2006–January 2007): 38–41. Color illus.

Beckerdite, Luke. *American Furniture 2006.* Milwaukee, Wis.: Chipstone Foundation, 2006. vii + 255 pp.; numerous color and bw illus., bibliography, index. Distributed by Antique Collectors' Club.

———. "The Life and Legacy of Frank L. Horton: A Personal Recollection." In *American Furniture 2006,* 2–27. 45 color and bw illus.

Bellion, Wendy. "American Fancy: Exuberance in the Arts, 1790–1820: An Exhibition Review." *Winterthur Portfolio* 40, no. 4 (winter 2005): 249–57. 5 bw illus.

Benes, Peter, ed. *New England Collectors and Collections.* Dublin Seminar for New England Folklife Annual Proceedings, 2004. Boston: Boston University Scholarly Publications, 2006. 224 pp.; 84 bw illus., bibliography. (See, in particular, essays by Jane C. Nylander, William N. Hosley, and Robert P. Emlen.)

Berlin, Carswell Rush. "Classical Furniture in Federal Philadelphia." *Antiques and Fine Art* 7, no. 5 (spring 2007): 192–99. Color illus.

Berliner, Nancy, and Edward S. Cooke Jr. *Inspired by China: Contemporary Furnituremakers Explore Chinese Traditions.* Salem, Mass.: Peabody Essex Museum, 2006. 160 pp.; numerous color and bw illus., biographies, checklist.

Binzen, Jonathan. *Judy Kensley McKie.* Boston: Gallery NAGA, 2006. 24 pp.; color illus., appendix. (See also Arthur Dion, "Treasure," p. 21.)

———. "Material Dexterity." In John Kelsey, ed., *Furniture Studio 4: Focus on Materials,* 6–15. Asheville, N.C.: Furniture Society, 2006. Color illus.

———. "Stacks and Stacks of Unusual Stuff." In John Kelsey, ed., *Furniture Studio 4: Focus on Materials,* 16–17. Asheville, N.C.: Furniture Society, 2006. Color illus.

Blackburn, Jean. "Furniture as Prop in the Social Theater of Life." In John Kelsey, ed., *Furniture Studio 4: Focus on Materials,* 79–91. Asheville, N.C.: Furniture Society, 2006. Color illus.

Boor, Allison, Jonathan A. Boor, Christopher Boor, Peter Boor, and John William Boor. *Philadelphia Empire Furniture.* West Chester, Pa.: Boor Management LLC, 2007. 596 pp.; 495 color and 126 bw illus., bibliography, index. Distributed by University Press of New England, Hanover and London.

Bourgeault, Ronald. "Fifty Years of Antiquing in the Piscataqua Area." In *Piscataqua Decorative Arts Society: Volume 2, 2004–2006 Lecture Series,* 31–44. Portsmouth, N.H.:

Portsmouth Decorative Arts Society, [2007]. 17 bw illus.

Bowe, Stephen, and Peter Richmond. *Selling Shaker: The Commodification of Shaker Design in the Twentieth Century*. Liverpool, Eng.: Liverpool University Press, 2007. x + 404 pp.; 56 bw illus., bibliography, index.

Boyd, Alisa. "'The Decoration of Houses': The American Homes of Edith Wharton." *The Decorative Arts Society: 1850 to the Present* 30 (2006): 75–91. 14 color and bw illus.

Brown, Jane Roy. "Manitoga Modern." *Preservation*, November–December 2006, 24–31. Color illus.

Brown, Johanna Metzger. "'A Laudable Example of Industry': North Carolina Moravian Furniture." *Antiques* 171, no. 1 (January 2007): 185–96. 15 color illus.

———. "A Southern Backcountry Perspective." *Antiques and Fine Art* 7, no. 4 (January–February 2007): 256–63. 9 color illus.

Brown, Michael K. "Bayou Bend: Celebrating Fifty Years." *Antiques and Fine Art* 8, no. 1 (summer/autumn 2007): 174–81. Color illus.

———. "An Essex County Wainscot Chair's Odyssey to Bayou Bend." *The Intelligencer* (spring 2007): 4–7. 1 color and 2 bw illus.

———. "A Newport Bureau Table's Odyssey to Bayou Bend." *The Intelligencer* (winter 2006–2007): 2–5. 1 color and 1 bw illus.

Burks, Jean M. "Out of This World: Shaker Design, Past, Present, and Future." *Antiques* 172, no. 2 (August 2007): 58–67. 18 color illus.

Byars, Mel. *New Chairs: Innovations in Design, Technology, and Materials*. San Francisco: Chronicle Books, 2006. 160 pp.; numerous color illus., index.

Cadou, Carol Borchert. *The George Washington Collection: Fine and Decorative Arts at Mount Vernon*. Manchester, Vt., and New York: Hudson Hills Press in association with Mount Vernon Ladies' Association, 2006. 303 pp.; 200 color and 54 bw illus., bibliography, index.

Campbell, Gordon, ed. *The Grove Encyclopedia of Decorative Arts*. 2 vols. New York: Oxford University Press, 2006. 1,290 pp.; numerous illus.

Carlano, Annie, and Bobbie Sumberg. *Sleeping Around: The Bed from Antiquity to Now*. Santa Fe: Museum of International Folk Art; Seattle and London: University of Washington Press, 2006. xi + 164 pp.; 138 color and bw illus., index.

Carr, Dennis. *American Colonial Furniture*. Guides to the Collection. New Haven: Yale University Art Gallery, 2004. 16 pp.; illus.

———. "Furniture." In Paul Finkelman, ed., *The Encyclopedia of the New American Nation*. 3 vols. New York: Charles Scribner's Sons, 2005.

———. "Going Dutch: The Mott/Willis Family Kast." *Yale University Art Gallery Bulletin* (2003): 100–103. Illus.

———. Review of Thomas Andrew Denenberg, *Wallace Nutting and the Invention of Old America*. In *Connecticut History* 43, no. 2 (fall 2004): 197–98.

Chicirda, Tara Gleason. "The Furniture of Fredericksburg, Virginia, 1740–1820." In *American Furniture 2006*. 96–137. 57 color and bw illus.

Child, Deborah M. "An Unbroken Chain of Custody: Pendant Portraits of Enoch and Susan Parker Parrot of Portsmouth, New Hampshire." In *Piscataqua Decorative Arts Society: Volume 2, 2004–2006 Lecture Series*. 104–13. Portsmouth, N.H.: Portsmouth Decorative Arts Society, [2007]. 19 bw illus.

Cohen, Deborah. *Household Gods: The British and Their Possessions*. New Haven and London: Yale University Press, 2006. 296 pp.; 153 color and bw illus., bibliography, index.

Coleman, Brian. "Focus on . . . Firescreens." *Nineteenth Century* 27, no. 1 (spring 2007): 36–38. Color and bw illus., bibliography.

———. Review of Karen Zukowski, *Creating the Artful Home: The Aesthetic Movement*. In *Nineteenth Century* 27, no. 1 (spring 2007): 43–44.

Connors, Michael. *French Island Elegance*. New York: Harry N. Abrams, 2006. 176 pp.; illus., bibliography, index.

———. "French Island Elegance." *Antiques and Fine Art* 7, no. 3 (autumn/winter 2006): 166–73. Color illus.

"Consensus Collecting." *Antiques and Fine Art* 7, no. 5 (spring 2007): 152–60. Color illus. (Re collection of Stephen and Dinah Lefkowitz, Old Saybrook, Connecticut, of eighteenth-century New England furniture and other objects.)

Davis, Deborah. "The Lure of Antique Frames." *Antiques and Fine Art* 7, no. 4 (January–February 2007): 268–73. 7 color illus.

———. *The Secret Lives of Frames: One Hundred Years of Art and Artistry*. New York: Filipacchi, 2007. 223 pp.; numerous color illus., bibliography.

De Dampierre, Florence. *Chairs: A History*. New York: Harry N. Abrams, 2006. 430 pp.; numerous color and bw illus., index.

Denker, Ellen Paul. "A Gracious Way of Life." *Antiques* 172, no. 1 (July 2007): 100–107. 16 color illus.

"Discoveries: Cabinetmaker's Account Books." *Antiques and Fine Art* 8, no. 1 (summer/autumn 2007): 24. 1 color illus. (Re account books covering the years 1815–1848 of Joseph Murphey [1796–1872] of South Berwick, Maine, owned by the Portsmouth Athenaeum.)

"Discoveries: 'Fully Elastic Armchair.'" *Antiques and Fine Art* 7, no. 6 (summer 2007): 18. 1 color illus. (Re bentwood chair by Samuel Gragg of Boston recently acquired by the Carnegie Museum of Art, Pittsburgh, Pennsylvania.)

Donnelly, Max. "Inside One of New York's 'Artistic Houses.'" *The Decorative Arts Society: 1850 to the Present* 30 (2006): 59–73. 24 color illus.

Edwards, Clive, et al. *The Intelligent Layman's Book of British Furniture, 1600–2000.* Edinburgh: SITA Technology, 2006. 352 pp.; numerous color illus., line drawings, maps, index.

Eisenbarth, Erin E. "Made for Love: Selections from the Jane Katcher Collection of Americana." *Antiques and Fine Art* 7, no. 5 (spring 2007): 205–9. Color illus.

Ellis, John. "The Craft Master." *Metropolis* 26, no. 8 (March 2007): 224–32, 243–45. 13 color illus. (Re Sam Maloof.)

Erbes, Scott. "Living with Antiques: A Kentucky Couple Collects." *Antiques* 171, no. 5 (May 2007): 100–109. 14 color illus.

Fayen, Sarah. *Going Out of Style: 400 Years of Changing Tastes in Furniture.* Milwaukee, Wis.: Milwaukee Art Museum, 2007. 13 pp.; color illus., bibliography.

———. "Historic Opinions: How Critics Shaped American Taste in Furniture." *Antiques and Fine Art* 8, no. 1 (summer/autumn 2007): 155–61. Color illus.

Feld, Elizabeth, and Stuart P. Feld. "Classical Decorative Arts of Philadelphia." *Antiques and Fine Art* 7, no. 5 (spring 2007): 185–91. Color illus.

———. *For Work and for Play: A Selection of American Neo-Classical Furniture.* New York: Hirschl & Adler Galleries, 2007. 12 pp.; color illus.

Fiske, John. "Speculative Carving: An Undocumented Practice of Seventeenth-Century Workshops." *Antiques* 170, no. 4 (October 2006): 126–31. 6 color illus.

FitzGerald, Dennis. "Blurring the Boundaries by Maintaining a Tradition of Alternatives" (review). In John Kelsey, ed., *Furniture Studio 4: Focus on Materials,* 46–55. Asheville, N.C.: Furniture Society, 2006. Color illus.

Fleming, John, and Michael Rowan. "Folk Furniture of Canada's Doukhobors." *Antiques* 171, no. 3 (March 2007): 78–87. 14 color illus.

[Fogarty, Kate]. "Bill Stumpf, 1936–2006." *Modernism* 9, no. 4 (winter 2006–2007): 44. 1 color and 1 bw illus.

Follansbee, Peter. "Connecting a London-Trained Joiner to 1630s Plymouth Colony." *Antiques and Fine Art* 8, no. 1 (summer/autumn 2007): 200–205. 7 color and bw illus.

Fredell, Gail. "Hitting the Design Wall, and Climbing Over." In John Kelsey, ed., *Furniture Studio 4: Focus on Materials,* 56–65. Asheville, N.C.: Furniture Society, 2006. Color illus., bibliography.

Friedman, Marilyn F. "Defining Modernism at the American Designers' Gallery, New York." *Studies in the Decorative Arts* 14, no. 2 (spring/summer 2007): 79–116. 17 color and bw illus.

Frelinghuysen, Alice Cooney, et al. *Louis Comfort Tiffany and Laurelton Hall: An Artist's Country Residence.* New York: Metropolitan Museum of Art, 2006. xiii + 262 pp.; 348 color and bw illus., chronology, bibliography, checklist, index. Distributed by Yale University Press, New Haven and London.

Friedman, Barry, et al. *Ron Arad.* New York: Barry Friedman Gallery, 2005. 105 pp.; numerous color illus.

Furniture Matters: A Periodic Forum of the Furniture Society (summer 2006): 1–10. bw illus.

Furniture Matters: A Periodic Forum of the Furniture Society (fall 2006): 1–12. bw illus.

"Gallery." *Woodwork,* no. 102 (December 2006): 43–49. Color illus.

"Gallery." *Woodwork,* no. 103 (February 2007): 39–46. Color illus.

"Gallery." *Woodwork,* no. 104 (April 2007): 38–45. Color illus.

"Gallery." *Woodwork,* no. 106 (August 2007): 37–40. Color illus.

"Gallery." *Woodwork,* no. 107 (October 2007): 40–49. Color illus.

Gant, Sally. "Seeking the Treasures of the Chesapeake: The Museum of Early Southern Decorative Arts." In [Catalogue of] *52nd Washington Antiques Show: Treasures of the Chesapeake,* 79–85. Washington, D.C., 2007. 9 color illus.

Gates, Jo Elam, and John "Jay" A. Gates III. *Antique Furniture 101.* Midlothian, Va.: Gates Antiques Ltd. 142 pp. and 11 DVDs.

Gibson, Scott. "Jon Brooks: Working Where Art and Function Collide." *Woodwork,* no. 102 (December 2006): 22–29. Color illus. (See also "Improving on Nature's Curves," p. 29.)

Gorman, Carma R. "The Changing Status of Design in *Art in Every Day Life. 1925–1940.*" *Studies in the Decorative Arts* 14, no. 2 (spring/summer 2007): 145–65. 11 bw illus.

Goss, Nancy Douthat, and Alexandra West Rollins. "The National Society of the Colonial Dames of America: The First 116 Years." *Antiques* 172, no. 1 (July 2007): 58–63. 9 color illus.

Green, Harvey. Review of Thomas Andrew Denenberg, *Wallace Nutting and the Invention of Old America.* In *Journal of American History* 91, no. 1 (June 2004): 282.

———. *Wood: Craft, Culture, History.* New York: Viking, 2006. xxxii + 464 pp.; 108 bw illus., bibliography, index.

Greenberg, Alan. *Architecture of Democracy: American Architecture and the Legacy of the Revolution.* New York: Rizzoli, 2006. 204 pp.; numerous color and bw illus., index.

Greenfield, Brian G. Review of *Wallace Nutting and the Invention of Old America.* In *Journal of American History* 91, no. 3 (December 2004): 973–76. 2 bw illus.

Gronning, Erik, Joshua W. Lane, and Robert F. Trent. "Dutch Joinery in 17th-Century Windsor, Connecticut." *Maine Antique Digest* 35, no. 8 (August 2007): 8D–13D. 29 bw illus.

Guidot, Raymond, et al. *Industrial Design: Techniques and Materials.* Paris: Editions Flammarion, 2006. 351 pp.; numerous color and bw illus.

Gustafson, Eleanor H. "Collectors' Notes: Cabinetmakers Edward Holmes and Simeon Haines Revisited." *Antiques* 171, no. 5 (May 2007): 76, 78. 5 color illus.

———. "Museum Accessions." *Antiques* 171, no. 2 (February 2007): 24. 3 color illus. (Includes side chair designed by Frank Lloyd Wright and recently acquired by the Museum of Fine Arts, Boston.)

Hamler, A. J. "Joe Cress: Bringing History to Life, One Desk at a Time." *Woodwork*, no. 104 (April 2007): 20–26. Color illus.

Hardiman, Tom. "Theodore Atkinson's Journal and Conspicuous Consumption in 1730s Portsmouth." In *Piscataqua Decorative Arts Society: Volume 2, 2004–2006 Lecture Series*, 23–30. Portsmouth, N.H.: Portsmouth Decorative Arts Society, [2007]. 10 bw illus.

———. Review of Nancy Goyne Evans, *Windsor-Chair Making in America: From Craft Shop to Consumer.* In *American Furniture 2006.* 229–30.

[Hewitt, Benjamin A., Collection]. *Fall New Hampshire Weekend.* Portsmouth, N.H.: Northeast Auctions, October 28–29, 2006. 226 pp.; numerous color illus. (See lots 697–893, and Patricia E. Kane, "Benjamin Attmore Hewitt, 1921–2006," p. 97.)

Haygood, Paul M., and Matthew A. Thurlow. "New York Furniture for the Stirlings of Wakefield, Saint Francisville, Louisiana." *Antiques* 171, no. 5 (May 2007): 126–35. 14 color illus.

[Hirschl & Adler Galleries]. *American Masterworks from the Munson-Williams-Proctor Arts Institute Celebrating an Educational Alliance with Pratt Institute.* New York: Hirschl & Adler Galleries, 2006. 12 pp.; color illus.

Hirshler, Erica E. Review of Harvey L. Jones, with a contribution by Kenneth R. Trapp, *The Art of Arthur and Lucia Mathews.* In *American Furniture 2006.* 231–34.

Holtzman, David. "John Friel and the Rise of Pocahontas Woods." *Woodwork*, no. 107 (October 2007): 18–25. Color illus.

Hosley, William. "Extraordinary Furniture Discoveries." *Antiques* 172, no. 1 (July 2007): 92–99. 12 color illus.

———. "A Precious Legacy of Furniture." *Antiques* 172, no. 1 (July 2007): 84–91. 14 color illus.

Howard, Hugh. *Dr. Kimball and Mr. Jefferson: Rediscovering the Founding Fathers of American Architecture.* New York: Bloomsbury, 2006. xii + 305 pp.; bw illus., appendixes, glossary, notes on sources, index.

Hulme, F. Edward. *Victorian Fret-Work and Wood Carving: Patterns and Instructions.* London: Marcus Wood and Co.; Belfast: Royal Ulster Works, 1877. Reprint. Mineola, N.Y.: Dover Publications, 2005. (Published originally as *Examples for Fret-Cutting and Wood-Carving.*)

Hurst, Ronald L. "Great American Folk Art at the Abby Aldrich Rockefeller Folk Art Museum, Part II." *Antiques and Fine Art* 8, no. 1 (summer/autumn 2007): 168–73. Color illus.

———. "Peter Scott, Cabinetmaker of Williamsburg: A Reappraisal." In *American Furniture 2006.* 28–53. 35 color and bw illus.

Hurwitz, Michael, Judy Kensley McKie, and Amy Forysth. "Judy Kensley McKie: Work That Stands as if It Always Was." In John Kelsey, ed., *Furniture Studio 4: Focus on Materials*, 112–21. Asheville, N.C.: Furniture Society, 2006. Color illus.

Iovine, Julie V. "Plastic Fantastic: Wendell Castle's Red, Yellow, and Blue Period." *New York Times Style Magazine: Design*, spring 2007, 40. Color and bw illus.

Jobe, Brock. "Two Case Studies: The Furniture of Portsmouth, New Hampshire, and Southeastern Massachusetts." In *Piscataqua Decorative Arts Society: Volume 2, 2004–2006 Lecture Series.* 62–64. Portsmouth, N.H.: Portsmouth Decorative Arts Society, [2007]. 4 bw illus.

Johnson, Bebe Pritam. "What Is the Award of Distinction? How Can You Win One?" In John Kelsey, ed., *Furniture Studio 4: Focus on Materials*, 122–26. Asheville, N.C.: Furniture Society, 2006. Color illus.

Johnson, James Hunter, and Christine Minter-Dowd. "Treasures of the Chesapeake: The 52nd Washington Antiques Show Loan Exhibition." In [Catalogue of] *52nd Washington Antiques Show: Treasures of the Chesapeake*, 52–57. Washington, D.C., 2007.

Johnston, Nancy N. "All Things Being Equal: Traditional and Modern Furniture." *Antiques and Fine Art* 7, no. 5 (spring 2007): 150–51. 2 color illus.

Kagan, Dick. "Tailoring Nature." *Art & Antiques* 29, no. 4 (April 2006): 46, 48–49. 6 color illus. (Re contemporary furniture maker Silas Kopf.)

Kane, Patricia E. "A Recently Rediscovered Rhode Island Furniture Maker: Icahbod Cole." *Antiques* 171, no. 5 (May 2007): 110–17. 12 color illus.

Katcher, Jane, David A. Schorsch, and Ruth Wolfe, eds. *Expressions of Innocence and Eloquence: Selections from the Jane Katcher Collection of Americana.* Seattle, Wash: Marquand Books in association with Yale University Press, New Haven and London, 2006. 428 pp.; 510 color illus., catalogue, indexes. (Includes essays on furniture by Charles Santore, Patricia E. Kane, Jean M. Burks, Scott T. Swank, and Philip Zea; catalogue by David A. Schorsch and Eileen M. Smiles.)

Kelly, James C., Barbara Clark Smith, et al. *Jamestown, Québec, Santa Fe: Three North American Beginnings.* Washington, D.C., and New York: Smithsonian Books, 2007. 191 pp.;

numerous color and bw illus., checklist, index.

Kelsey, John, ed. *Furniture Studio 4: Focus on Materials*. Asheville, N.C.: Furniture Society, 2006. 128 pp.; numerous color illus., index.

Kenny, Peter M. "The New Classical Galleries in the American Wing at the Metropolitan Museum of Art." *Antiques* 171, no. 2 (February 2007): 50–57. 19 color illus.

King, Stuart. "An Introduction to Marquetry." *Woodwork*, no. 107 (October 2007): 64–71. 25 color illus., glossary.

Kirtley, Alexandra Alevizatos. "Philadelphia Furniture in the Empire Style." *Antiques* 171, no. 4 (April 2007): 92–101. 13 color illus.

———. Review of Nancy Goyne Evans, *Windsor-Chair Making in America: From Craft Shop to Consumer*. In *Winterthur Portfolio* 41, no. 1 (spring 2007): 86–89.

Kirtley, Alexandra Alevizatos, and David Demuzio. "A Hollingsworth Family Sofa and Its Upholstery Revealed." *Antiques and Fine Art* 7, no. 5 (spring 2007): 216–19. 7 color illus.

Kisluk-Grosheide, Danielle O., Wolfram Koeppe, and William Rieder. *European Furniture in the Metropolitan Museum of Art: Highlights of the Collection*. New York: Metropolitan Museum of Art, 2006. viii + 282 pp.; numerous color and bw illus., index. Distributed by Yale University Press, New Haven and London.

Klaric, Arlette. "Gustav Stickley's Designs for the Home: An Activist Aesthetic for the Upwardly Mobile." In *Seeing High and Low: Representing Social Conflict in American Visual Culture*, 177–93. Berkeley: University of California Press, 2006.

Knight of Glen, The, and James Peill. *Irish Furniture: Woodwork and Carving in Ireland from the Earliest Times to the Act of Union*. New Haven and London: Yale University Press for the Paul Mellon Centre for Studies in British Art, 2007. xi + 323 pp.; 400 color and 100 bw illus., catalogue, appendixes, bibliography, index. (Includes "A Dictionary of Eighteenth-Century Irish Furniture Makers" compiled by John Rogers.)

Koda, Harold, and Andrew Bolton, with an introduction by Mimi Hellman. *Dangerous Liaisons: Fashion and Furniture in the Eighteenth Century*. New York: Metropolitan Museum of Art, 2006. 128 pp.; 68 color illus., catalogue, bibliography. Distributed by Yale University Press, New Haven and London.

Lavine, John. "Inspired by China: An Interview with Clifton Monteith." *Woodwork*, no. 102 (December 2006): 72–76. Color illus.

———. "Inspired by China: An Interview with Joe Tracy." *Woodwork*, no. 103 (February 2007): 60–65. Color illus.

———. "Inspired by China: An Interview with Michael Puryear." *Woodwork*, no. 104 (April 2007): 72–76. Color illus.

Leath, Robert A. "Many Hands, Many Voices: Southern Furniture at MESDA." *Antiques* 171, no. 1 (January 2007): 151–59. 14 color illus.

———. "Robert and William Walker and the 'Ne Plus Ultra': Scottish Design and Colonial Virginia Furniture, 1730–1775." In *American Furniture 2006*. 54–95. 54 color and bw illus.

———. "Southern Perspective: The Museum of Early Southern Decorative Arts at Old Salem." [Catalogue of] *53rd Annual Winter Antiques Show*, 115–21. Bronx, N.Y.: East Side Settlement House, 2007. 13 color illus.

L'Ecuyer, Kelly H. Review of Nancy E. Green, ed., *Byrdcliffe: An American Arts and Crafts Colony*; Maureen Meister, *Architecture and the Arts and Crafts Movement in Boston: Harvard's H. Langdon Warren*; and Eileen Maning Michels, *Reconfiguring Harvey Ellis*. In *Journal of the Society of Architectural Historians* 66, no. 1 (March 2007): 119–21.

Lesher, Pete, Melissa McLoud, and William Thompson. "The Chesapeake's Distinctive Heritage." In [Catalogue of] *52nd Washington Antiques Show: Treasures of the Chesapeake*, 58–67. Washington, D.C., 2007. 14 color illus.

Levitties, John. "Cotswold School Furniture." *Antiques and Fine Art* 7, no. 3 (autumn/winter 2006): 188–91. Color illus.

Loar, Steve. "The Adirondack Chair: A Recent Student Show Reinterprets an American Classic." *Woodwork*, no. 106 (August 2007): 41–47. Color illus.

———. "A Brief History of Adirondack Chairs." *Woodwork*, no. 106 (August 2007): 80. 3 bw illus.

Long, Christopher. *Paul T. Frankl and Modern American Design*. New Haven and London: Yale University Press, 2007. xi + 225 pp.; 42 color and 120 bw illus., bibliography, index.

———. "Paul T. Frankl: Pioneer of Modern American Design." *Modernism* 10, no. 2 (summer 2007): 74–83. Color and bw illus.

———. "The Viennese *Secessionsstil* and Modern American Design." *Studies in the Decorative Arts* 14, no. 2 (spring/summer 2007): 6–44. 35 color and bw illus.

Lourie, Alexander. "'To Superintend the Necessary Repairs': The Careers and Work of William and Washington Tuck." In *American Furniture 2006*. 138–83. 55 color and bw illus.

Lovell, Sophie, et al. *Furnish: Furniture and Interior Design for the 21st Century*. Berlin: Die Gestalten Verlag, 2007. 271 pp.; numerous color illus., index.

Lucchesi, Roxanne, and Jennifer M. Tiernan. "From Function to Fantasy: Dunbar's Legendary Ad Campaign." *Modernism* 9, no. 3 (fall 2006): 72–81. Color illus.

Marcoux, John. *The Elegant Triangle.* Providence, R.I.: South Dorset Press, 2007. 152 pp.; 80 color and 40 bw illus., appendix, bibliography.

Marling, Karal Ann. "America Inside Out: The View from the Parlor." In *Frederic Church, Winslow Homer, and Thomas Moran: Tourism and the American Landscape,* 132–45. New York: Bulfinch Press, 2006.

Martin, Terry. "Neil Scobie: The Complete Woodworker." *Woodwork,* no. 106 (August 2007): 19–24. Color illus.

Mascolo, Frances McQueeney-Jones. "Lifestyle: American Folk Art in a Classical Setting." *Antiques and Fine Art* 7, no. 4 (January–February 2007): 220–30. Color illus.

———. "Lifestyle: A Bit of New England in Pennsylvania." *Antiques and Fine Art* 7, no. 6 (summer 2007): 102–11. Color illus.

———. "Lifestyle: The History Within." *Antiques and Fine Art* 7, no. 4 (January–February 2007): 236–49. Color illus.

———. "Lifestyle: A Time Capsule with Heart." *Antiques and Fine Art* 8, no. 1 (summer/autumn 2007): 126–35. Color illus.

McBrien, Johanna. "A Taunton Chest Revisited." *Antiques and Fine Art* 7, no. 5 (spring 2007): 235–37. Color illus.

McGuire, Laura M. "A Movie House in Space and Time: Frederick Kiesler's Film Arts Guild Cinema, New York, 1929." *Studies in the Decorative Arts* 14, no. 2 (spring/summer 2007): 45–78. 20 color and bw illus.

Meikle, Jeffrey. *Design in the USA.* New York: Oxford University Press, 2005. 252 pp.; numerous color and bw illus., timeline, bibliography, index.

Meister, Maureen. "Two Arts and Crafts Houses: Paradigms in Pasadena and Boston." *Antiques* 172, no. 3 (September 2007): 112–19.

Miller, Don R. "The Tension between Design and Art." In John Kelsey, ed., *Furniture Studio 4: Focus on Materials,* 92–94. Asheville, N.C.: Furniture Society, 2006. Color illus.

Minardi, Lisa. "A Timely Discovery: The Story of Winterthur's Jacob Graff Clock." *Antiques and Fine Art* 7, no. 5 (spring 2007): 238–39. 4 color illus.

Mingen, Gerald C., and John B. Vander Sande. "Attributing a Vernacular Six-Board Chest." *Antiques* 171, no. 5 (May 2007): 136–37. 2 color and 1 bw illus.

Minter-Dowd, Christine. "Treasures of the Chesapeake." *Antiques and Fine Art* 7, no. 4 (January–February 2007): 305–9. 9 color illus.

Moline, Julia. "Norman Cherner Deconstructed." *Modernism* 9, no. 4 (winter 2006–2007): 78–91. Color and bw illus.

Montgomery, Gladys. "A Houseful of Friends." *Antiques and Fine Art* 7, no. 3 (autumn/winter 2006): 152–65. Color illus. (Re private collection including some furniture.)

Moore, J. Roderick, and Marshall Goodman. "Painted Boxes and Miniature Chests from Shenandoah County, Virginia: The Stirewalt Group." *Antiques* 172, no. 3 (September 2007): 76–83. 19 color illus.

Moscou, Margo Preston. "New Orleans's Freemen of Color: A Forgotten Generation of Cabinetmakers Rediscovered." *Antiques* 171, no. 5 (May 2007): 146–53. 12 color illus.

Murtha, Hillary. "The Reuben Bliss Bedchamber at the Brooklyn Museum of Art: A Case Study in the History of Museum Period Room Installation." *Winterthur Portfolio* 40, no. 4 (winter 2005): 205–17. 6 bw illus.

[Museum of Early Southern Decorative Arts]. "Southern Perspective." *Old Salem Museum and Gardens* 1, no. 1 (fall/winter 2006–2007): 18–31. Color illus.

[Nakashima, George]. *New Life for the Noble Tree: The Dr. Arthur and Evelyn Krosnick Collection of Masterworks by George Nakashima.* Sale N08275. New York: Sotheby's, December 15, 2006. 120 pp.; numerous color illus. (Contains essays by Derek E. Ostergard, Pamela Hersh, Mira Nakashima, and others.)

[National Society of the Colonial Dames of America, The]. Special issue. *Antiques* 172, no. 1 (July 2007): 56–121. Numerous color illus. (See specific articles cited elsewhere.)

Nelson, Louis P. "Architecture as Artifact: Period Rooms at MESDA." *Antiques* 171, no. 1 (January 2007): 171–75. 10 color and bw illus.

"N.H. Furniture Masters' Auction on Oct. 22." *Antiques and the Arts Weekly,* October 6, 2006, 21. 3 bw illus.

Nylander, Jane C. "Treasure Houses of the Colonial Dames." *Antiques* 172, no. 1 (July 2007): 70–77. 12 color illus.

Nylander, Richard C. "A Visit with Bert and Nina Little." *Historic New England* 7, no. 3 (winter/spring 2007): 2–7. Color illus.

Obbard, John W. *Early American Furniture: A Guide to Who, When, and Where.* Paducah, Ken.: Collector Books, 2006. 464 pp.; 700+ line drawings, bibliography.

O'Brien, Jack. "A New Bedford Masterpiece." *Antiques* 171, no. 5 (May 2007): 138–45. 14 color and bw illus.

Peill, James. "Knights and Castles: A History of Irish Furniture." *Antiques and Fine Art* 7, no. 4 (January–February 2007): 294–99. 6 color illus.

Phaidon Design Classics. 3 vols. New York: Phaidon Press, 2006. Numerous illus., indexes.

Podmaniczky, Michael. "The Baking of Preconceived Notions: Another Take on Roy McMakin." In John Kelsey, ed., *Furniture Studio 4: Focus on Materials,* 95–103. Asheville, N.C.: Furniture Society, 2006. Color illus., line drawings.

———. "Old Brown Furniture: John Townsend Lights Up the Metropolitan" (review). In John Kelsey, ed., *Furniture Studio 4: Focus on*

Materials, 104–11. Asheville, N.C.: Furniture Society, 2006. Color illus.

Porges, Maria. "The Sensuous Curve: Scandinavian Modernists and Their Influence on Contemporary California Design." *American Craft* 66, no. 5 (October–November 2006): 74–75. 6 color illus.

[Porset, Clara]. *Clara Porset's Design: Creating a Modern Mexico.* N.p.: Museo Frank Mayer; Difusión Cultural, Centro de Investigaciones de Diseño Industrial, Universidad Nacional Autónomede México; Turner, 2006. 181 pp.; numerous color and bw illus., catalogue, bibliography.

Priddy, Sumpter. "Early Furniture of the Chesapeake." In [Catalogue of] *52nd Washington Antiques Show: Treasures of the Chesapeake,* 104–11. Washington, D.C., 2007. 11 color illus.

Richardson, Louise. "The Shopping Experience in 18th-Century Portsmouth." In *Piscataqua Decorative Arts Society: Volume 2, 2004–2006 Lecture Series.* 4–11. Portsmouth, N.H.: Portsmouth Decorative Arts Society, [2007]. 7 bw illus.

Rieman, Timothy D. *Shaker Furniture: A Craftsman's Journal.* Atglen, Pa.: Schiffer, 2006. 300 pp.; illus.

Rishel, Joseph J., and Suzanne Stratton-Pruitt, et al. *The Arts in Latin America, 1492–1820.* New Haven and London: Yale University Press in association with Philadelphia Museum of Art, Antiguo Colegio de San Ildefonso, Mexico City, and Los Angeles County Museum of Art, 2006. xxiii + 568 pp.; 431 color and 45 bw illus., chronology, biographies of artists, bibliographies. (See especially chapter 7, "Observations on the Origin, Development, and Manufacture of Latin American Furniture," by Jorge F. Rivas P.)

Rivas P., Jorge F. *El Repertorio Clásico en el Mobiliario Venezolano Siglos XVIII y XIX / The Classical Repertoire in Eighteenth- and Nineteenth-Century Venezuelan Furniture. Cuaderno 9 / Notebook 9.* Colección Patricia Phelps de Cisneros. Caracas, Venezuela: Fundación Cisneros, 2007. 80 pp.; 46 color illus., checklist, bibliography, index.

Robertson, Cheryl. "Related Objects: The Family Stuff of Victorian Interiors." *New-York Journal of American History* 66, no. 3 (spring/summer 2006): 56–63. bw illus.

Rosenberg, Alan. "Victoriana 1930." *Nineteenth Century* 27, no. 1 (spring 2007): 15–23. Color and bw illus.

Sammons, Tania Jane. "Pioneers in Historic Preservation." *Antiques* 172, no. 1 (July 2007): 64–69. 9 color illus.

Sanders, Beverly. "The G.I. Bill and the American Studio Craft Movement." *American Craft* 67, no. 4 (September 2007): 54–62. Color illus. (See profile of furniture maker Arthur Espenet Carpenter, p. 57.)

[Schindler, Rudolph M.]. *R. M. Schindler: The Gingold Commissions.* West Hollywood, Calif.: Los Angeles Modern Auctions, December 3, 2006. 88 pp.; color and bw illus. (Includes essays by Thomas M. Hines, Gerard O'Brien, Michael Boyd, and Mark Lee.)

Schinto, Jeanne. "Israel Sack and the Lost Traders of Lowell Street." *Maine Antique Digest* 35, no. 4 (April 2007): 32C–33C. 11 bw illus.

[Shelly Collection]. *The Pioneer Americana Collection of Dr. and Mrs. Donald A. Shelley.* Downingtown, Pa.: Pook & Pook, April 20–21, 2007. 219 pp.; numerous color illus.

Sherrer, John, and Russell Buskirk. "Discoveries from the Field: A Charleston Linen Press?" *Antiques and Fine Art* 8, no. 1 (summer/autumn 2007): 125. Color illus.

Silander, Lisa. "Not a Lot of Bunk, but Just Enough." In John Kelsey, ed., *Furniture Studio 4: Focus on Materials,* 40–45. Asheville, N.C.: Furniture Society, 2006. Color illus.

Smith, David S. "Made in Pennsylvania." *Antiques and the Arts Weekly,* July 6, 2007, 1, 40–42. 17 bw illus.

Smith, John, Penny Smith, and Oscar Fitzgerald. "The View from Beyond the Edge." In John Kelsey, ed., *Furniture Studio 4: Focus on Materials,* 29–39. Asheville, N.C.: Furniture Society, 2006. Color illus.

Sperling, David A. "John Scudder and Family: From Skilled Craftsmen to Leaders of Men." *Maine Antique Digest* 35, no. 7 (July 2007): 8B–9B. 13 bw illus.

Stiefel, Jay Robert. "'A Clock for the Rooms': The Horological Legacy of the Library Company of Philadelphia." *Antiquarian Horology* 29, no. 6 (December 2004): 804–26. 26 color and 1 bw illus.

———. Review of Morrison H. Heckscher, *John Townsend: Newport Cabinetmaker.* In *Journal of the Early Republic* 26, no. 4 (winter 2006): 670–76.

Stone, Stephanie. "Chris Buchanan: A Study in Passion and Practicality." *Woodwork,* no. 103 (February 2007): 20–27. Color illus.

Strauss, Cindi. *Crafting a Collection: Contemporary Craft in the Museum of Fine Arts, Houston.* Houston: Museum of Fine Arts, Houston, 2006. 63 pp.; color illus., checklist.

Stuart, Susan. "Furniture by Gillows of Lancaster for Thomas English of Boston." *Antiques* 171, no. 6 (June 2007): 96–102. 16 color and bw illus.

Styles, John, and Amanda Vickery, eds. *Gender, Taste, and Material Culture in Britain and North America, 1700–1830.* Studies in British Art, vol. 17. New Haven and London: Yale Center for British Art and the Paul Mellon Centre for Studies in British Art, 2006. viii + 358 pp.; 84 color and bw illus., index. Distributed by Yale University Press, New Haven and London.

Temin, Christine. "Dale Broholm: Commissioning Studio Furniture:

A Client's Tale." *American Craft* 67, no. 4 (September 2007): 48–53. 5 color illus.

———. "Gallery Focus: Inspired by China; Traditional Furniture and Contemporary Inspiration." *Antiques and Fine Art* 7, no. 4 (January–February 2007): 315. 4 color illus.

———. "Inspired by China." *American Craft* 67, no. 2 (April–May 2007): 54–57. 6 color illus.

Thurlow, Matthew A. "Aesthetics, Politics, and Power in Early-Nineteenth-Century Washington: Thomas Constantine & Co.'s Furniture for the United States Capitol, 1818–1819." In *American Furniture 2006*. 184–228. 50 bw illus.

Tudge, Colin. *The Tree: A Natural History of What Trees Are, How They Live, and Why They Matter*. New York: Crown, 2006. xix + 459 pp.; line drawings, notes and further reading, glossary, index.

Van Hinte, Ed., ed. *Under Cover: Evolution of Upholstered Furniture*. Rotterdam: 010 Publisher, 2006. 121 pp.; numerous color and bw illus.

Volk, Joyce Geary. "Re-creating Jonathan Warner's Bed Hangings." *Antiques and Fine Art* 8, no. 1 (summer/autumn 2007): 198–99. 1 color illus.

Volk, Joyce Geary, and Jeannette Hopkins, eds. *The Warner House: A Rich and Colorful History*. Portsmouth, N.H.: Warner House Association, 2006. 169 pp.; numerous color and bw illus., bibliography, index.

Ward, Barbara McLean, ed. *The Moffatt-Ladd House: From Mansion to Museum*. Portsmouth, N.H.: Moffatt-Ladd House and Garden, 2007. 80 pp.; color and bw illus. (With contributions by Jane C. Nylander, Cheryl E. Cullimore, Stephanie R. Rohwer, Carolyn Parsons Roy, and Gerald W. R. Ward.)

Ward, Gerald W. R. "A Taunton Chest *redivivus*." *Antiques and Fine Art* 7, no. 5 (spring 2007): 232–34. 6 color and bw illus.

Ward, Gerald W. R., comp. "Recent Writing on American Furniture: A Bibliography." In *American Furniture 2006*. 235–41.

Ward, Gerald W. R., and Julie Muñiz, with contributions by Kelly H. L'Ecuyer and Nonie Gadsden and an essay by Matthew Kangas. *Shy Boy, She Devil, and Isis: The Art of Conceptual Craft, Selections from the Wornck Collection*. Boston: Museum of Fine Arts, Boston, 2007. 183 pp.; numerous color illus., bibliography, index.

Ward, Gerald W. R., Nonie Gadsden, Kelly H. L'Ecuyer, and Melinda Talbot Nasardinov. *MFA Highlights: American Decorative Arts and Sculpture*. Boston: Museum of Fine Arts, Boston, 2006. 224 pp.; numerous color illus., bibliography, index.

[Wheatcroft, David]. *The Authentic Eye: Revisiting Folk Art Masterworks*. Westborough, Mass.: David Wheatcroft Antiques, 2005. Unpaged; 68 color illus., checklist.

White, Betsy K. *Great Road Style: The Decorative Arts Legacy of Southwest Virginia and Northeast Tennessee*. Charlottesville: University of Virginia Press, 2007. xxi + 212 pp.; 197 color illus., bibliography, index. (See especially chapters 1–2, pp. 21–97, on furniture and chairs.)

Wiggers, John. "The Legacy of the Golden Spruce." In John Kelsey, ed., *Furniture Studio 4: Focus on Materials* (Asheville, N.C.: The Furniture Society, 2006), 18–26. Color illus.

———. "Materials: What Is Sustainably Harvested Timber?" In John Kelsey, ed., *Furniture Studio 4: Focus on Materials*, 18–26. Asheville, N.C.: Furniture Society, 2006. Color illus.

———. "What Can Anyone Do?" In John Kelsey, ed., *Furniture Studio 4: Focus on Materials*, 28. Asheville, N.C.: Furniture Society, 2006. 1 color illus.

Wilk, Christopher, and Nick Humphrey, eds. *Creating the British Galleries at the V&A: A Study in Museology*. London: V&A Publications/Laboratorio Museotecnico Goppion, 2004. xii + 283 pp.; numerous color and bw illus., 13 appendixes, bibliography, index.

Williams, Gareth. *The Furniture Machine: Furniture since 1990*. London: V&A Publications, 2006. 176 pp.; numerous color and bw illus., bibliography, index.

Williams, Stephen Guion, and Gerard C. Watkins. *A Place in Time: The Shakers at Sabbathday Lake, Maine*. Boston: David R. Godine, 2006. 96 pp.; illus.

Wilson, Dean. "Lead Toward the Future." In John Kelsey, ed., *Furniture Studio 4: Focus on Materials*, 66–78. Asheville, N.C.: Furniture Society, 2006. Color illus.

Wilson, Kristina. "The Avant-Garde and the Conservative in Lighting Design: The Modernism of Walter W. Kantack." *Studies in the Decorative Arts* 14, no. 2 (spring/summer 2007): 117–44. 16 bw illus.

———. "Rethinking American Modernist Design, 1920–1940: Guest Editor's Introduction." *Studies in the Decorative Arts* 14, no. 2 (spring/summer 2007): 2–5.

Winters, Laurie, et al. *Biedermeier: The Invention of Simplicity*. Milwaukee, Wis.: Milwaukee Art Museum, 2006. 399 pp.; numerous color illus., bibliography, index.

Wolf, Ruth. "Expressions of Innocence and Eloquence: Selections from the Janer Katcher Collection of Americana." *Antiques and Fine Art* 7, no. 3 (autumn/winter 2006): 192–98. Color illus.

Wood, David F. *An Observant Eye: The Thoreau Collection at the Concord Museum*. Concord, Mass.: Concord Museum, 2006. 159 pp.; numerous color illus., index.

Wood, Ghislaine, ed. *Surreal Things: Surrealism and Design*. London: V&A Publications, 2007. 362 pp.; numerous color and bw illus., bibliography, index. Distributed by Harry N. Abrams, New York.

Woods, Claudia. "Famous Clock a Gift to the Society." *New England Ancestors* 8, no. 1 (winter 2007): 13. 3 bw illus. (Re tall-case clock, ca. 1788, by Joseph Mulliken of Concord, Massachusetts, recently acquired by the New England Historic Genealogical Society, Boston.)

"The *Woodwork* Index." *Woodwork*, no. 102 (December 2006): 80–96. (Comprehensive index covering first one hundred issues of this magazine.)

Zimmerman, Philip D. *Delaware Clocks*. Dover, Del.: Biggs Museum of American Art, 2006. 62 pp.; numerous color and bw illus., bibliography, index.

———. "Living with Antiques: Charming Forge Mansion near Womelsdorf, Pennsylvania." *Antiques* 172, no. 3 (September 2007): 94–103. 18 color illus.

———. "Mystery Solved: Identifying an Early Philadelphia Federal Side Chair." *Antiques* 171, no. 5 (May 2007): 118–25. 15 color illus.

Zukowski, Karen. *Creating the Artful Home: The Aesthetic Movement*. Layton, Utah: Gibbs Smith, 2006. 176 pp.; numerous color and bw illus., bibliography, list of resources, index.

Index

Aalto, Alvar, 262
Abercrombie, Stanley, 264
Adams, Lemuel, 141
Adams, Nehemiah, 211, 213, 219
"Advice to an Author" (Earl of Shaftesbury), 182
Aesop's fables, as design motif, 6, 7(fig. 6), 41n7
Affleck, Lewis G., 112
Affleck, Thomas, 6, 33, 40n2, 40n4, 40n5, 43n28, 45, 75, 112, 165n6, 209, 237–38
Aitken, John, 111(fig.), 113, 128, 130n4
Akin, James, 131n10, 141
Albinson, Don, 264, 265
Alexander, Richard, 199, 210, 232, 236
Allen, Amos Denison, 192, 233
Allen, Nathaniel, 225
Allentown (Pa.) Call, 252
Alling, David: chair repair by, 196, 197, 199, 200; child's chair repair by, 208; settee repair by, 205–6; stool repair by, 202–3
Allison, Mark, 162(figs. 53 & 54)
Allison, Michael, 121(fig. 17), 140, 161–62(&fig. 52)
Alrichs, Jonas, 156, 267
Alston, Joseph, Jr., 75
Alston, Joseph, Sr., 75
Andalusia, 256
Anderson, Andrew, 141
Anderson, Elbert, 141
Anderson, Henry, 75
"Anhing," 173(fig. 5), 174
Antiques, 260
Appendix to the Cabinet-Maker and Upholsterer's Drawing-Book (Sheraton), 131n10
Appliqué: frieze, 8(fig. 8), 9(figs.), 119(fig. 13); tympanum, 24, 26(fig. 39)
Apprentices, signature of, 145–47 (&fig. 25)
Aprons, of card tables, 122(&fig. 19), 124, 126(fig. 28), 128(fig. 31)
Argo, 10, 41n10, 82
Armchairs, 89; child's, 207(fig.); Eames, 261–65; mahogany, 12(fig. 12); maple, 201(fig.); sack-back Windsor, 155(fig. 41); Speed, 251, 254; Springleaf, 262; walnut, 198(fig.)
Art of Japanning Published at the Request of Several Ladies...The, 182
Arts and crafts, Frankl and, 252

Arts and Crafts in Philadelphia, Maryland and South Carolina, 1721–85 (Prime), 75, 76, 77, 78, 79, 80, 81
Ash: bedstead, 219(fig.); great chairs, 90(fig.), 93(fig. 19), 95(fig. 22), 96(fig. 23), 97(figs.), 98(fig. 27), 98(fig. 28), 99(figs.), 100(figs.), 102(fig.), 103(fig.), 104(fig.), 107(fig.); high chair, 105(fig.)
Ashton, Isaac, 232
Asian coastline, depicted on japanned furniture, 174–77(&figs.)
Aurora General Advertiser, 113
Avery, Jeduthern, 223
Avery, Oliver, 215, 223

Backgammon tables, 233
Badlam, Stephen, 156–57, 161, 199
Bagnal, Samuel, 75
Baily, Joel, 134, 136
Baize, 233
Baker, Benjamin, 215, 216
Baker, William, 75
Ball, John T., 216
Baltimore: dining table, 229(fig. 11); side chair, 195(fig.)
Banister backs, 195
Barcelona Exhibition, 264
Barclay, Andrew, 188n16
Barker, William, 194, 234
Barnard, Samuel, 158
Barnes, Elizur: bedstead altera?tion by, 219; bedstead repair by, 212, 213; bench painting by, 206; chair repair by, 192, 196–97, 199, 208; cradle repair by, 210; crib repair by, 210; dressing table repair by, 232; stool repair by, 202, 203; table alteration by, 225; tea table repair by, 227; worktable repair by, 236
Barnes, J., 113
Barnet, Isaac, 14, 42n14, 46, 61, 75
Barnhill, Robert and Elizabeth, 125(fig. 26)
Barnwell, George, 183
Barry, Joseph, Jr., 119
Barry, Joseph B. *See also* Joseph B. Barry & Son: George Wright and, 112–13, 120, 128–29, 131n9, 131n10; G. W. Pickering and, 259; label of, 142, 143(figs.), 163; shop location, 111(fig.)
Basin stands: mahogany, 237(fig.); repairing, 237–38
Baskerville, John, 188n16

Basswood, cabinet-on-stand, 169(fig.); Windsor armchair, 155(fig. 41)
Bathsheba, David and, 172–73(&fig. 3)
Bayley, Moses: high chest, 147(fig. 26); signature of, 147–48(&fig. 27)
Beake, William, 164n3; chest of ?drawers, 135(fig. 4); mark of, 134, 135(fig. 5)
Beale, Pennell, 205, 224, 230, 232
Beckerdite, Luke, 16, 33
Beckford, Benjamin, Jr., 200
Bed screws, installing, 213–14
Bedsteads: alterations to, 218; assembly and disassembly of, 217–18; cot, 219–20; field, 218; maple, 212(fig.); press/turn-up, 219(&fig.); repairing, 210–20
Beech, great chair, 88(fig. 9)
Beesley, William, 238
Bench, repair of, 206
Benge, Samuel, 200
Benjamin, Miles, 215, 228, 238
Benjamin Randolph (Peale), 2(fig.)
Bentley, William, 205
Berger, Jean, 187n4
Bernard, Nicholas, 39, 40n5
Betagh, William, 173
Betsy, 82
Biddle, Clement, 27, 43n23, 46
Biddle, John, 227, 232
Biddle family, 125(fig. 25)
Biggs Museum (Dover, Delaware), 257, 266
Biomorphic coffee table, 251, 254
Biomorphic lounge chair, 264
Birch: bedsteads, 211; dressing table, 231(fig.); high chest of drawers, 171(fig.)
Birch veneer: breakfast table, 123 (fig. 22); card table, 121(fig. 15)
Birdsey, Joseph, Jr.: armchair, 155 (&figs.); label of, 155(fig. 42)
Bird's-eye maple, 259
Bishop Ridley chair, 86–87(&fig. 6), 99
Blacking, for bedsteads, 214
Black walnut: bedsteads, 211; dressing table, 231(fig.); high chair, 105(fig. 42)
Blasdel's, 266
Blow, Richard, 205
Blue Book Philadelphia Furniture (Hornor), 40n4, 75, 79
Boardman, Langley, 220, 236

Board-seated turned chairs, 83–109; American, 96–107(&figs. 24–30, 37–41, 43); Boston tradition, 103–7 (&figs. 38–41, 43); early British chairs, 84–87(&figs. 1–6); early Dutch chairs, 87–91(&figs. 7, 9); later British chairs, 88(fig. 9), 90(fig. 12), 93(fig. 19), 96(fig. 23), 100–101(figs.); Plymouth ?tradition, 98–103(&figs. 28–30, 37); Welsh tradition, 91–96(&figs. 15–18, 20–22)
Bookbinding, japanned furniture and, 189n16
Bookcases, skyscraper, 251, 252–53
Booker, Richard, 201
Boone, Daniel, 265–66
Boor, Allison, 255
Boor, Christopher, 255
Boor, John William, 255
Boor, Jonathan A., 255
Boor, Peter, 255
Boston: board-seated turned chairs, 103–7(&figs. 38–41, 43); card table, 151(fig. 34); high chair, 105(fig.); japanned furniture in, 169; japanned high chest of drawers, 171(fig.), 179(fig.), 184(fig.); japanned looking glass, 177(figs.); side chairs, 136(fig. 6), 157(fig. 44)
Boston furniture makers, struck marks of, 156–57
Bottoming, repairing seat, 192–94, 208
Bouvier, Michael, 205, 236
Bowdoin, James, 187n1
Boynton, Thomas, furniture repair by, 194, 203, 208, 212, 228
Bracket clocks, 21
Bradford, William, great chair and, 98(&fig. 28), 101, 102, 108n2
Branding irons, 152–53(&fig. 37)
Branning, John, 76
Breakfast tables: cost of, 230; George Wright, 123–24(&fig. 22); mahog?any, 229(fig. 12); repair of, 229–31
Brewster, Benjamin, 102(fig.)
Brewster, William, great chair and, 98, 99(fig. 29), 101, 108n2
Brice, James, 197, 227
Bridport, George, 113, 130n6
Brinckerhoof, James L., 199–200, 202, 216
British board-seated turned chairs: early, 84–87(&figs. 1–6); later,

88(fig. 9), 90(fig. 12), 93(fig. 19), 96(fig. 23), 100–101(figs.)
Bromwich, Anna, 3
Bronson, Isaac, 200
Bronzing, 197
Brouwer, Jacob: bedstead repair by, 216, 218; bench repair by, 206; breakfast table repair by, 230; card table repair by, 233; crib repair by, 210; table repair by, 220, 222; tabletop cleaning by, 224
Brown, Joseph, Jr., 206, 225
Bryant, Nathaniel, 229
Bunratty Castle, 109n12
Bureau table, of commode form, 21
Burgis, William, 177–78(&fig. 13)
Burling, Thomas, 141, 199
Burl veneer: breakfast table, 123 (fig. 22); card table, 121(fig. 15); pier table, 117(fig.)
Button, George, 236
Butts, Richard, 6, 41n5, 47, 76
Byrnes, Caleb, 142, 145; chest-on-chest, 144(figs.)

C. L. Prickett and Sons, 42n13
Cabinet Dictionary (Sheraton), 193, 238
Cabinet-Maker and Upholsterer's Drawing-Book, The (Sheraton), 119(&fig. 13), 131n10
Cabinet-Maker and Upholsterer's Drawing-Book and Appendix (Sheraton), 142
Cabinet-on-stand, japanned, 169(fig.), 186n1
Cadwalader, Elizabeth (Lloyd), 6, 33, 36, 43n27, 47
Cadwalader, John, 6, 11, 32–33, 36, 43n27, 43n28, 47, 165n6, 208, 238
Cadwalader, Lambert, 32–33, 34(fig.), 47
Cadwalader family side chair, 33(fig.), 35
Calder, Alexander, 112
Caldwell, Josiah, 148(fig. 30), 149
Camp, William, 130n4, 131n10, 141, 142(&fig.), 163
Candlestands: mahogany, 234(fig.); repair of, 234–36
Caned chairs, 136(&fig. 7)
Canopy top, 213
Card tables, 258; George Wright, 111. *See also* mechanical; swivel-top; mahogany, 14(fig. 17), 21, 24(figs.),

121(fig. 17), 151(fig. 34); mechanical, 120–23(&figs. 15–21), 124(&fig. 24); repair of, 232; satinwood, 128 (fig. 32), 129(fig.); swivel-top, 124–27(&figs. 25–31), 131*n*13; walnut, 232(fig.); yellow poplar, 116(fig.)
Carswell Rush Berlin, 256
Cartwright, Shackerly, 76
Casters: for bedsteads, 214; for card tables, 233; for chairs, 199; for tea tables, 227
Cedar, high chest, 15(fig. 20)
Cedrella, dining table, 229(fig. 11)
Celtic Fringe, 108*n*4
Chaffee, Reuben, 210
Chair casters, 199
Chair feet, modifying, 194–95
Chairs. *See also* Armchairs; Board-seated turned chairs; Side chairs: children's, repair of, 206–8(&fig.); club, 264; Eames lounge, 261–65; easy, 29(fig.), 194, 197, 205; empire, 259; fancy, 195–96(&fig.); lolling, 197, 205; mahogany, 199; repairs and alterations to, 192–202(&figs.); rocking, 194, 206, 207–9, 239*n*5; *Womb*, 264; *Men Shoveling Chairs (Scupstoel)*, 83
Champlin, Christopher, 202, 214, 224, 235
Chappel, William, 155
Charlestown (Massachusetts), washstand, 237(fig.)
Chase, James, 222
Cheever, Samuel, 227
Cheney, Silas: bedstead repair by, 214–15, 215; candlestand repair by, 235–36; chair repair by, 194, 196, 198, 199, 200; kitchen table repair by, 234; settee repair by, 205; table repair by, 222, 224; washstand repair by, 238
Cherry: candlestands, 235; chairs, 197; side chair, 101(&fig. 34); stands, 234; tables, 220, 222, 228
Cherub heads, 181–82, 188*n*16
Chestertown (Maryland), Ringgold House, 8(figs.)
Chestney, James, 195
Chestnut, great chair, 100(fig. 32)
Chest-on-chest, walnut, 144(fig. 21)
Chest-on-frame, walnut, 145(fig. 23)
Chests, empire, 255–56
Chests of drawers: empire, 259; walnut, 135(fig. 4)

Children's furniture, repair of, 206–10(&figs.)
Chimneypieces, 7–8(figs.), 9(fig. 9), 26(fig. 40), 27
"Chinese Men," 174(fig. 7)
Chinnery, Victor, 109*n*16, 166*n*21
Chippendale, Thomas, 32(&fig.), 229–30, 237; desk-and-bookcase, 18(&fig.), 19(figs.)
Chippendale furniture, in Philadelphia, 258
Chishold, Archibald, 197–98
"Chloe" (Pope), 182
Christie's, 256
Chrysler, Jacob, 6, 47
Churchill, Lemuel, 157
Clapier, Louis, 111, 118, 128
Clark, William, 165*n*13
Clarke, John, 82
Claypoole, George, 6, 41*n*5, 47, 209
Clocks: brackets, 21; Delaware, 265–69; table, 267–68
Close stools/close-stool chairs, 197, 201–2
Club chairs, 264
Coates, Samuel, 200, 205, 214, 217
Cocks, William, 112, 130*n*4
Coffee table, biomorphic, 251, 254
Cole, Solomon, 200, 210, 234
Collection de Meubles et Objets de Goût, 118–19(&fig. 11)
Collins, John, 205
Collins, Robert, 82
Collins, Stephen, 198–99, 209, 212, 215
Colonial Delaware clockmaking, 266–67
Coloring: for bedsteads, 215; for candle?stands, 236; for chairs, 197; for children's chairs, 208; for tables, 225
Commercial discovery, 183
Commode-seat chairs, 33(&fig.), 43–44*n*28
Compleat English Gentleman, The (Defoe), 180
Conant, Stephen, 203
Connecticut, great chairs, 97(fig. 24), 98(fig. 27)
Connelly, 131*n*16
Connelly, Henry, 113, 128(fig. 32), 129, 200, 203
Cook & Parkin, 259
Cork-topped coffee table, 251, 254
Cornell, Rebekah, 43*n*23
Cornwall, great chair, 93(fig. 19), 96(fig. 23)

Cot bedstead, 219–20
Couch, 204(&fig.)
Courtenay, Hercules, 5–7(&figs. 5–6), 14(&figs.), 29, 40*n*5, 48, 63, 76
Cowan, Robert, 231
Cowdrey, Jonathan, 228
Cox, Joseph, 138(&fig. 11)
Cradles: repair of, 206, 208, 209–10; walnut, 209(fig.)
Crage, David, 234
Crage, Robert, 214, 222
Cranbrook Academy, 262, 263
Crane, Elisha, 212
Cranmer, Thomas, 87
Cresson, Jeremiah, 76
Cribs, repair of, 210
Cricket, 203
Croghan, George, 11, 20–21(&fig. 30), 30, 38, 41*n*10, 42*n*13, 48, 233
Crossbanding, 123–24(&fig. 23)
Crow, George, 267
Crow, George (II), 267
Crow, Thomas, 267–68
"Crowne and Looking Glasse in Long Acre," 136
Crusoe, Robinson, 183
Curled maple, worktable, 236(fig.)
Curled maple veneer, worktable, 236(fig.)
Currier, True, 194, 203, 219, 222, 224, 235

Dampier, William, 174–75, 177, 178, 180, 188*n*7
Dancaster, H., 202
Danforth, Job, 199, 210, 212, 227, 234
Danforth, John, 216
Dauterman, Carl, 173
David, Abraham, 234
David, Bathsheba and, 172–73(&fig. 3)
Davidson, William, 76, 77
Davis, David, 221
Davis, William, 82
Davison, Samuel, 194
Deakin, John, 82
Deakin, Robert, 81
Defoe, Daniel, 180, 183, 189*n*20
Deland, Philip, 235
Delaplaine, Joseph, 227
Delaplaine, Joshua, 202, 224, 231
Delaware Clocks (Zimmerman), 265–69
Del Vecchio, Charles, 139(&fig. 14)
Depree, Max, 262, 264

Derby, Elias Hasket, 157, 199, 232
Derby, John, 200, 231
Derry, John, 11, 41*n*12
Deschler, David, 40*n*4
Design: industrial, 253; modern, 251–55
Desk-and-bookcases: Chippendale and, 18–20(&figs. 26–28); mahogany, 19(fig. 28), 21–24 (&figs. 31–34), 160(fig. 50); maple, 149(figs.)
Desks: lap, 40*n*1; tambour, 158 (&fig. 46), 167*n*26
Devon, great chair, 93(fig. 19)
Dewey, Daniel, 238
Dewey, Henry F., 208
Diana, 78, 82
Dining tables: mahogany, 229(fig. 11); repair of, 227–29
Director (Chippendale), 230, 237
Disbrowe, Nicholas, 164*n*2
"Dog and the Meat, The" (Aesop), 6, 7(fig. 6), 41*n*7
Dominy, Nathaniel, V, tea table, 226(fig.)
Dominy's, 266
Donnell, Nathaniel, 76
Door frieze, 38(fig. 60)
Douglas, Samuel, 214, 235
Doz, Andrew, 40*n*5, 49, 80
Drawers, replacement of, 223
Drawing-Book (Sheraton), 230, 236
Dressing box, 232
Dressing tables: black walnut, 231(fig.); repairing, 231–32
Drinker, Daniel, 198–99, 209
Duck, for sacking, 215
Dunham, Daniel, 208
Dunlap, John, 146
Dunlap, Samuel, 146–47
du Pont, Eleuthère Irénée, 130*n*7
du Pont, Henry Francis, 43*n*22
Durand, John, 192, 193(fig.), 210, 216, 221
Durand, Samuel, 192, 193(fig.)
Durand, Samuel, Jr., 192, 193(fig.)
Dyer, Elisha, 199

Eames, Charles, 254, 261, 262, 263, 264–65
Eames, Lucia, 264
Eames, Ray Kaiser, 254, 261, 262, 265
Eames Lounge Chair, The (Eidelberg et al.), 261–65
East Hampton (Long Island), tea table, 226(fig.)
Easton, Robert, 76
Easy chairs, 194, 197, 205; mahogany, 29(fig.)
Edes, Edmund, 136
Edsall, Thomas, 104, 109*n*19
Egerton, Abraham S., 213, 215
Eidelberg, Martin, 261
Elfreth, Jeremiah, Sr., 204, 205
Eliot, John, great chair and, 83, 105, 108*n*2, 109*n*20
Ellery, Benjamin, Jr., 233
Elliott, John, Jr., 149
Elliott, John, label of, 136, 137–38(&fig. 10), 139
Elliott, John, Sr., 228
Elm, great chairs, 86(fig. 6), 93(fig. 18), 94(fig.), 95(fig. 21)
Elmendorf, Peter, II, 152(fig. 37)
Elmendorf, Peter E., 195
Embassy from the East India Company (Nieuhof), 173(fig. 5), 174(&fig. 7), 177, 178, 180(&fig. 16), 188*n*7
Emerson, Peter, 214, 227
Emlen, George, Jr., 24, 42*n*21
Emlen, Nancy, 24, 49
Emlen, Sally, 24, 49
Emlen, Sarah, 42*n*21, 49
Empire furniture, Philadelphian, 255–61
England: great chairs, 84(figs.), 85–87 (&figs. 5 & 6), 88(fig. 9), 90(fig.), 100(figs.); side chair, 153(fig. 38); use of paper labels in, 136
Engravers: paper labels and, 141–42; use of cherub heads, 181
Erasmus, Desiderius, great chair and, 99–100, 109*n*16
Erwin, James, 156
Erwin, John, 156, 267
"ES" mark, 158(&fig. 47), 159
Evans, David: bedstead alteration by, 218; bedstead assembly by, 217; bedstead painting by, 214; bedstead repair by, 211; card table repair by, 232, 233; close-stool repair by, 202; dining table repair by, 227–28; sofa repair by, 205
Evans, Edward, 164*n*2; mark of, 133–34(&fig. 3); scrutoire, 134(figs.)
Evans, J. M., 260
Evans, Nancy Goyne, 154
Eyre, John, 217

Fancy chair, 195–96(&fig.)
Fauntleroy family of Virginia, 83

Feet: modifying chair, 194–95; ogee-bracket, 21, 23(figs. 32 & 33)
Fenimore, Mary Wilkinson, 29
Fennimore, Don, 257, 260
Fiddle backs, 195
Field bedstead, 218
Finials, 101(fig. 35), 103; urn-and-flame, 103(&fig. 38)
Finley brothers, 130*n*6
Fisk, Samuel: mark of, 156, 157 (&fig. 45); side chair, 157(fig. 44)
Fisk, William: card table, 151(fig. 34); mark of, 151–52(&fig. 36), 157(&fig. 45); side chair, 157(fig. 44)
Fitch, Thomas, 150
Fitz-Randolph, Benjamin, 40*n*2
Flag (*Juncus*), 192
Fleeson, Plunkett, 30, 43*n*28, 49, 204–5, *see also* Flesson
Fleetwood, David, 259
Flesson, Plunkett, 76–77
Fling, John, 77, 80
Flock, Philip, 77
Footboards, 212–13
Foote chair, 96(&fig.), 109*n*14, 109*n*15
Foote family, 96
Footman, Peter, 77
Footstool, 203
Ford, Daniel, 194
Ford, Henry, 263
Forman, Benno, 136
Form and Re-Form (Frankl), 251
Forster, Jacob: label of, 140–41; washstand, 237(fig.)
Foulk, Adam, 82
Fowell, John, 77
Francis, John, 232
Francis, Mrs. John, 210
Francis, Simon, 157
Frankl, Paul T., 251–55
Franklin, Benjamin, 215
Freeborn, Henry, 230
Frelinghuysen, Frederick T., Jr., 199
Fridsberg, Olof, 182
Friedman, Mildred, 264
Frieze appliqué, 8(fig. 8), 9(figs.), 119(fig. 13)
Frothingham, Benjamin, 138–39 (&fig. 12), 165*n*8
Fruitwood, great chair, 88(fig. 9)
Furniss, William, 266–67
Furniture: empire, 255–61; japanned. *See* Japanned furniture; Peasant, 252
Furniture makers' marks, 133–67; first, 133–34; "I" mark, 136(&fig.

7); paper labels, 133, 136–42(&figs. 9–16, 18); shipping marks and, 149–50; signatures, 142–52(&figs. 22, 24–25, 27–29, 32–33, 35); stamp marks, 152–61(&figs. 37, 39–40, 43, 45, 47, 51); stenciled, 161–63(&fig. 52); stencil makers, 152(fig. 36)

Furniture repairs and alterations, written evidence of, 191–249; bedsteads, 210–20(&figs.); breakfast, or Pembroke, tables, 229–31(&fig. 12); candlestands and light stands, 234–36(&fig. 15); card tables, 232–33(&fig.); chairs, 192–202 (&figs.); children's furniture, 206–10(&figs.); dining tables, 227–29(&fig. 11); dressing tables, 231–32(&fig. 13); kitchen tables, 233–34; long seats, 204–6(&fig.); stands and stand tables, 234; stools, 202–3; tables, 220–25; tables of ?special note, 234; tea tables, 226–27 (&fig.); terminology, 192, 220, 237; washstands and basin stands, 237–38(&fig.); work?tables and work stands, 236(&fig.)

Fussell, Solomon, 136, 194, 204, 215, 232

Gaines, John, II, 203, 204
Gansevoort, Peter, 212
Garvan, Beatrice, 40*n*1, 40*n*2, 75, 77
Garvan high chest carver, 16(&fig. 22), 20(&fig. 29)
Gentleman and Cabinet-Maker's Director (Chippendale), 18(&fig.), 19(figs.), 32(&fig.)
George Seddon and Son, 205
Gere, James, 196, 223, 235, 236
Gilbert, Alexander H., 238
Gilbert, Christopher, 164*n*2
Gilbert, Jane, 231
Gilding, 197, 206
Gillingham, James, 28
"Gilmanton," 149(fig. 32), 150
Gilt table, 234
Girard, Stephen, 118, 128; bedstead repair for, 213, 214, 220; chair repair for, 199, 200; couch repair for, 205; stool repair for, 203; worktable repair for, 236
Go-carts, repairing, 210
Goddard, Stephen, 224
Goddard, Thomas, 224
Goddard, Townsend, 202, 214, 235

Godwin, Abraham, 141
Gould, Nath, 150–51(&fig. 33)
Gould, Nathaniel, 232
Goût antique, le, 118–19, 131*n*9
Grand Rapids Art Museum, 261
Granger, Henry, 77
Grasbury, Joseph, 6, 50
Gratz, Michael, 209, 226
Graves, Leroy, 33
Great chairs: American, 96–107(&figs.); Boston, 103–7(&figs. 38–41, 43); British, 84(figs.), 85–87(&figs. 5 & 6), 88(fig. 9), 90(fig. 12), 100(figs.); Cornwall, 93(fig. 19), 96(fig. 23); Dutch, 88(fig. 9); New York City, 97(figs.); Plymouth, 98–103(&figs. 28–30, 37); South African, 89(figs.); Welsh, 91–96(&figs. 16–18, 20–22); Wethersfield (Connecticut), 97 (fig. 24)
Greene, Albert C., 205
Greene, Richard W., 211, 214, 216, 234
Greene, Samuel W., 205
Greene, William, 224
Greenough, David S., 200
Gregg, George, 146(&fig.), 166*n*14
Grigsby, Leslie, 173
Griswold, Joseph, 210, 211, 214, 233
Grover, Ryan D., 266
Guide (Hepplewhite), 230
Guilbaud, John, 136
Gulliver, Lemuel, 183
Gumley, John, 164*n*2

Haines, Ephraim, 220
Haines, Jonathan, 77
Haircloth, 200
Hamilton, James, 3
Hamilton, William, 77
Hancock, Thomas, 188*n*16
Hand, Jesse, 216
Hanks, David, 261, 264
Hanlin, John, 77
Hathorne (Hawthorne), ?Benjamin, 214
Hatton, Edward, 183–84
Haughton, George, 77
Haughton, John, 77
Haven, Abner, 208
Haven, David, 233–34
Hawley, Elisha, 197
Hawthorne, John, 227
Hays, Thomas, 154
Headboards, 212–13

Heckscher, Morrison, 133, 150, 187*n*2
Hepplewhite, George, 230, 237, 238
Herman Miller, 254, 263, 264
Herrick, Jonathan, 221
Hertrog, Andrew, 76, 77
Hewes, Ezekian, 154(&fig.)
Hewett, John, membership certificate, 141(fig.)
Hewitt, John, 120
Heyl, Mary, 118
"Heytamon," 180(fig. 16)
Hickory: side chair, 193(fig.); for splint, 194; Windsor armchair, 155(fig. 41)
High chairs, 105(&figs.); mending, 208
High chest base, mahogany, 17(fig. 24)
High chests: japanned, 171(fig.), 173(fig.), 174(fig. 6), 175(figs.), 176(fig.), 179(fig.), 180(fig. 15), 184(fig.), 184(fig. 18), 185(fig.), 186*n*1; mahogany, 14–17(&fig. 20), 25(fig. 37); maple, 147(fig. 26)
High stools, 203
Hine, Thomas, 261, 262, 263
Hinsdale, Jacob, 206
Hirschl & Adler, 256
Historic Deerfield, 109*n*17
Hobby horses, repairing, 210
Hockaday, John, 211, 214, 215, 227
Hockenbull, John, 77–78
Holcomb, Allen, 194, 218, 223–24, 232, 235, 238
Hollingsworth, Levi, 209
Holmes, Elisha Harlow, 209, 224, 225, 228
Holmes, Hartwell, 219, 221, 236
Home show, 262
Hook, William, 214
Hopkins, John G., 205
Hopkinson, Mr. and Mrs. Oliver, 130*n*6
Hornington, Catermon, 76
Hornor, William Macpherson, Jr., 40*n*4, 75
Houghton, Luke, 235
Houston, William, 146
How, Samuel, 30, 51
Howard, John, 78, 82
Hummingbird, 82
Humphrey, James, 40*n*2, 51
Humphreys, James, Jr., 20
Humphrey's price book, 42*n*18
Humphries, Joshua, 204, 222
Huntington (Connecticut), Windsor

285   INDEX

armchair, 155(fig. 41)
Hurd, Nathaniel, 138(fig. 12), 139
Hurley, Thomas, 205
Huston, William, 11
Hyland, Charles, 223, 225

"I" mark, 136(&fig. 7), 153
Imitation finishes, 196
Indianapolis News, 252
Industrial design, 253
Initials, as makers' marks, 152–53 (&figs. 39, 43, 45, 47, 49, 51)
Interest of City and Country to Lay No Duties, The, 181(fig.)
Ionic scroll capitals, 259
"I + S" mark, 158, 160

J. B. Barry & Son, 112
Jackson, Stephen, 199
James, Edward, 156(&fig.)
Janvier, John, Jr., 267
Janvier, John, Sr., 267
Janvier, Peregrine, 156
Janvier, Thomas, 267
Japanned furniture, 168–90; audience for, 182–86; cabinet-on-stand, 168(fig.); first-person experience and, 180–81; furniture as literature and, 170–82; high chests of drawers, 171(fig.), 173(fig.), 174(fig. 6), 175(figs.), 176(fig.), 179(fig.), 180(fig. 15), 184(fig.), 185(fig.); looking glass, 177(figs.); mercantile sensibility and, 182–86; ship's-eye perspective and, 177–78(&figs. 11, 12); as sign of wealth and status, 170; taste for chinoiserie and, 170
Japanners, 169, 187n4
Jefferson, Thomas, 40n1, 113
Jenkins, Paul, 206, 211, 213, 222, 236
Johns, Richard, 197, 202
Johnson, Thomas, 5–6, 9(fig. 10), 52
Johnson Company, 254
Johnston, Thomas, 52, 170, 181, 187n2, 188n16
Jones, Gershom, 212
Jones, John, 3, 52, 78
Joselyn, Joel, 146–47
Joseph B. Barry & Son, 111, 117(&fig.), 118(&fig. 10), 119, 120(fig.), 130n7
Josiah, Emanuel, 82
Journeyman Cabinet and Chair Makers' Pennsylvania Book of Prices, The, 120, 125(fig. 26)
Journeymen, two-initial stamps and, 153
"JS" mark, 160–61(&fig. 51)
Jugiez, Martin, 39, 40n5
Juncus, 192

Keith, James, 105
Kendall, Benjamin, 78
Kennedy, Robert, 42n13, 52, 78
Kennett Square (Pennsylvania), 146; chest-on-frame, 145(fig. 23)
Kern, A. C., 114(fig.)
Ketches, 227
Kimball, Edmund, 192
King, Daniel, 153
King, Joseph, 82
King, Mary, 24, 43n22
King, Sarah, 43n22
King Stephen's throne, 85–86(&fig. 5), 108n6
Kinsman, Nathaniel, 202, 222
Kirk, John, 256
Kirkham, Pat, 261, 262, 263
Kirtley, Alexandra Alevizatos, 257
Kitchen tables, repairing, 233–34
Klismos chairs, 259
Knee carving, 12(figs. 13 & 14), 13(&fig. 16), 14(fig. 18), 16(fig. 23), 24(fig. 36), 25(fig. 38), 28(fig. 43), 35(fig. 50), 36(fig. 55), 37(fig. 57), 38(fig. 59)
Kneeland, Samuel, 141
Knoll, 254
Knox, Henry, 199, 205, 212, 224, 230, 232

Labels: function of, 139–42; ?furniture illustrations on, 141–42(&figs. 17, 18); furniture makers' marks, 136–42(&figs. 9–16, 18); of Joseph B. Barry & Son, 120(fig.); placement on furniture, 142; on Windsor chairs, 155(&fig. 42)
"Lady's Dressing Room, The" (Swift), 185
Lambert Cadwalader (Peale), 34(fig.)
Lander, Benjamin, 200
Landon, George, 194, 207, 214, 235
Lane, Isaac, 78
Lannuier, Charles Honoré, 119
Lap desk, 40n1
Larned, Samuel, 202
Larson, Jack Lenor, 264
Lasley, Peter, 76, 78
Latimer, Hugh, 87
Latrobe, Benjamin Henry, 113, 130n6; card table, 116(fig.); pier table, 115(fig. 6); side chair, 115(fig. 5)
Lawrence, Thomas, 30, 52, 78, 215
Lawrence, Thomas, Jr., 78
Layback, in board-seated chairs, 93–94, 96, 100
Leaming, Aaron, 216
Leather, for seat upholstery, 200
Leaves, dining table, 228
Lee, Chapman, 194, 222, 234
Lee, Hancock, 105(fig. 42)
Lee family great chair, 83, 108n2
Leverett, William, 228
Levy, Bernard, 165n9
Levy, S. Dean, 165n9
Library of Congress, 265
Lightfoot, James, 78
Light stands, 234–36
Lillo, George, 183
Linacre, James, 221
Livingston, Robert R., 199, 228, 234
Lolling chairs, 197, 205
London. *See also* England: cabinet-on-stand, 169(fig.); japanned furniture in, 169
London Merchant, The (Lillo), 183
Long, Christopher, 251
Long, Melchor, 78
Long seats, repair of, 204–6(&fig.)
Loockerman, Vincent, 39–40, 44n31, 79
Looking glass, japanned, 177(figs.)
Loomis, Reuben, 222, 230
Loring, Joshua, 187n1
Lovell, Margaretta, 133
Lovett, Elizabeth, 202
Low, Alexander, 213, 233
Low, Henrietta, 213, 215–16
Low, Nicholas: bedstead assembly for, 218; bedstead repair for, 213, 216; bench repair for, 206; card table repair for, 233; crib repair for, 210; dining table repair for, 228; table repair for, 220, 222, 223, 224
Low stool, 203
Lyell, Fenwick: bedstead repair by, 213–14; card table repair by, 233; cradle repair by, 209; dining table repair by, 228; sofa repair by, 205; stool repair by, 203; table alteration by, 225; tabletop cleaning by, 224; washstand repair by, 238; ?worktable repair by, 236

Lyon family, 125(fig. 25)
Lyre platform, 258
MacBride, Walter, 154
Mackay, Robert, 131*n*10
Maddock, Abraham, 78
Madison, James and Dolley, 130*n*6
Maggs, John, 77, 78–79, 80
Magill, Arthur, 192
Magrath, Richard, 200
Mags, John, 79
Mahogany, 10; armchair, 12(fig. 12); bedsteads, 211; breakfast tables, 123(fig. 22), 229(fig. 12); candlestands, 234(fig.), 235; card tables, 14(fig. 17), 24(fig. 35), 121(figs. 15, 17), 124(fig. 24), 125(figs.), 127(fig.), 151(fig. 34); chairs, 197, 199; for close stools, 201; desk-and-bookcases, 19(fig. 28), 22(fig.), 160(fig. 50); dining table, 229(fig. 11); easy chair, 29(fig.); high chest base, 17(fig. 24); high chests, 15(fig. 20), 25(fig. 37); pier table, 117(fig.); sideboard table, 30(fig.); side chairs, 10(fig.), 33(fig.), 35(fig. 51), 36(fig. 54), 37(fig. 56), 38(fig. 58), 39(fig.); stands, 234; tables, 220, 228; tambour desk, 158(fig. 46); tea tables, 13(fig. 15), 27(fig. 41), 226–27(&fig.); washstand, 237(fig.)
Mahogany veneer: breakfast table, 123(fig. 22); card tables, 124(fig. 24), 125(figs.), 127(fig.), 128(fig. 32); dining table, 229(fig. 11); empire chests, 256; pier table, 117(fig.)
Mantle truss, 15(fig. 19)
Maple: armchair, 201(fig.); bedsteads, 212(fig.), 219(fig.); card table, 116(fig.); chairs, 197; child's armchair, 207(fig.); couch, 204(fig.); curled, 236(fig.); desk-and-bookcase, 149(fig. 31); great chairs, 98(fig. 27), 99(fig. 29), 102(fig.), 104(fig.), 107(fig.); high chair, 105(fig.); high chests, 147(fig. 26), 171(fig.), 179(fig.), 184(fig.); side chairs, 115(fig. 5), 136(fig. 6), 137(fig. 8), 193(fig.), 195(fig.); tables, 220, 222; Windsor armchair, 155(fig. 41)
Marble, Mary Ann, 211
Marble tables, 234
Martin, William, 30, 53, 79
Massachusetts: bedstead, 212(fig.); couch, 204(fig.); desk-and-bookcase, 149(figs.); dressing table, 231(fig.)
Mather, Cotton, 83, 108*n*2
Mather, Increase, 105
Mather, William, 235
Matthews, Samuel, 79, 204, 209, 210, 227
Matting, 192
McCall, Samuel, Sr., 223
McConachy, Robert, 228
McDonald, Elizabeth Bleecker, 217, 233
McElroy, Cathryn, 134
McGuffin, Robert, 128(fig. 32), 129(&fig.), 131*n*16
McPherson, John, 11, 53, 77
Mears, John, 79
Mechanical card tables, 120–23 (&figs. 15–21), 124(&fig. 24)
Mechanical table, 131*n*11
Men Shoveling Chairs (Scupstoel) (van der Weyden), 83, 87(&fig.), 93
Mercantile sensibility, japanned furniture and, 182–86
Merchant's Magazine, The, 183–84
Merchant's Map of Commerce, The (Roberts), 184
Meredeth, Rebecca Cadwalader, 44*n*28
Meredeth, Samuel, 44*n*28
Meredith, Samuel, 209
Merrifield, George, 213, 219, 220
Mésangère, Pierre de La, 118, 119(fig. 11), 131*n*9
Metropolitan Museum of Art, 256
Milford (Connecticut), side chair, 193(fig.)
Miller, Alan, 16, 33
Milnor, William, 3
Minis, Isaac, 130*n*7
Mitchell, David, 182
Mitchell, Edward Craig, 42*n*18
Mitchell, Henry, 40*n*3
Mix, Joseph, 222
Montgomery, Charles, 130*n*4, 255
Moody, John, 79
Moody, Thomas, 192
Moore, Joshua, 79
Moore, Oliver, 220, 224, 235
More, Thomas, 99
Moreen, 200
Morris, Deborah, 197
Morris, Paul, 79
Morris, Samuel, 217
Morse, Benjamin, 225
Morss, Joshua: high chest, 147(fig. 26); signature of, 147–48(&fig. 28)
Moyers, Thomas J., 207
Moyers and Rich, 224
Moyse, John, 79
Mullony, John, 82
Museum of Modern Art, 263
Museum of Welsh Life, 109*n*12
Music stool, 202

Narrative(s): furniture as, 173–82; sea, 173–82; through images, 172–73
National Watch and Clock Museum (Columbia, Pennsylvania), 266
Neate, William, 197
Nestell, Christian M., 234
Netherlands: board-seated turned chairs, 87–91(&figs. 7 & 9); side chairs, 100, 101(fig. 34)
Neville, Thomas, 11, 41*n*11, 42*n*13, 43*n*26, 54, 79
New Book of Ornaments, A (Johnson), 5, 6, 9(fig. 10)
Newburyport (Massachusetts): ?candlestand, 234(fig.); high chest, 147(fig. 26)
New Dimensions (Frankl), 251
New England: bedstead, 219(fig.); child's armchair, 207(fig.)
New England Primer, 172
New Jersey, cradle, 209(fig.)
New Map of the City of Philadelphia for the use of Firemen and others, The (Paxton), 111(fig.)
Newton, Aaron, 215
Newton, Phineas, Jr., 235
New Voyage Round the World, A (Dampier), 174–75, 177, 178, 180
New Voyage to the East Indies (Symson), 173
New York: great chairs, 97(figs.), 98(fig. 27); worktable, 236(fig.)
New York City: great chairs, 97(figs.); mechanical card table, 121(fig. 17)
New-York Revised Prices for Manufacturing and Cabinet and Chair Work, 127
Nichols, Walter, 198, 221, 222
Nieuhof, Johan, 173(fig. 5), 174(&fig. 7), 178, 180(&fig. 16), 188*n*7
Night cabinet/pot, 201
Night chairs, 201–2
Noguchi, Isamu, 254
Norris, Charles, 138, 204, 209, 210,

287   INDEX

227
Norris, Mary, 209
Noyes, Elizabeth, 148(fig. 29), 150, 166*n*16

Oak: cabinet-on-stand, 169(fig.); card tables, 124(fig. 24), 128(fig. 32); great chairs, 92(fig. 17), 93(fig. 18), 95(fig. 22), 97(figs.), 103(fig.), 104(fig.); side chair, 115(fig. 5); Windsor armchair, 155(fig. 41)
Object, conception of, 185–86, 189–90*n*24
Odessa (Delaware) clockmaking, 266, 267
Ogee-bracket feet, 21, 23(figs. 32, 33)
Oil: for bedsteads, 214; for breakfast tables, 230–31; for stands, 234; for tables, 225; for tabletops, 224
Oldfield, John, 204
One Hundred and Fifty New Designs (Johnson), 5, 6
Ornamental furniture painting, 196
Owners, marks of, 166*n*22

Paine, John, 216, 221, 222, 234
Paint: for bedsteads, 214–15; for breakfast tables, 231; for chairs, 196–97; for cradles, 210; for dressing tables, 232; for kitchen tables, 234; for rush seating, 193; for stands, 234; for tables, 225; for washstands, 238
Panels, narrative and, 172, 188*n*6
Parker, George, 170, 181
Parkhurst, Moses, 221
Partridge, A., 221
Partridge, E. G., 221
Paul T. Frankl and Modern American Design (Long), 251–55
Paxton, John A., 111(fig.)
Peale, Charles Willson, 2(fig.), 33, 34(fig.)
Peasant furniture, 252
Pease, Judith, 150
Peatross, C. Ford, 261, 265
Pemberton, James, 200
Pemberton, Joseph, 208, 209, 210, 213, 217–18, 231
Pembroke tables: cost of, 230; mahogany, 229(fig. 12); repairing, 229–31
Penciling, 197
Penn, John, 40*n*1, 40*n*2, 55
Penn, William, 164*n*2

Penn's Paquet, 82
Pennsylvania, cradle, 209(fig.)
Pennsylvania Book of Prices, 120, 122–23
Pennsylvania Gazette, 6
Pennsylvania Journal, 137
Pennsylvania Packett, 40*n*3, 42*n*16, 77
Perkins, Simon, 194
Philadelphia: armchairs, 12(fig. 12), 198(fig.), 201(fig.); breakfast table, 123(fig. 22); card tables, 14(fig. 17), 24(fig. 35), 116(fig.), 121(fig. 15), 125(figs.), 127(fig.), 128(fig. 32), 232(fig.); chest of drawers, 135(fig. 4); chimney?piece, 7(figs.); Chippendale furniture in, 258; desk-and-bookcases, 19(fig. 28), 22(fig.); easy chair, 29(fig.); empire furniture, 255–61; French immigrants in, 118–19; high chest base, 17(fig. 24); high chests, 15(fig. 20), 25(fig. 37); mechanical card table, 124(fig. 24); pier tables, 115(fig. 6), 117(fig.); scrutoire, 134(fig. 2); sideboard, 110(fig.); sideboard table, 30(fig.); side chairs, 10(fig.), 33(fig.), 35(fig. 51), 36(fig. 54), 37(fig. 56), 38(fig. 58), 39(fig.), 115(fig. 5), 137(fig. 8); tea tables, 13(fig. 15), 27(fig.)
Philadelphia: Three Centuries of American Art (Garvan), 75, 77
Philadelphia Cabinet and Chair Makers' Union Book of Prices for Manufacturing Cabinet Work, 127
Philadelphia Empire Furniture (Boor et al.), 255–61
Philadelphia Museum of Art, 39, 44*n*30, 130*n*6, 131*n*16, 256
Philadelphia Packett, 76
Phyfe, Duncan, 199, 202, 216
Piano stool, 202
Pickering, G. W., 259
Pickman, Benjamin, 169, 187*n*1, 187*n*2, 189*n*19
Pier tables, 43*n*27, 258; George Wright, 111; glass, 32(fig.); mahogany, 117(fig.); yellow poplar, 115(fig. 6)
Pilgrim Hall, 108*n*2
Pillar, mending, 235
Pine: armchair, 201(fig.); cabinet-on-stand, 169(fig.); chest of drawers, 135(fig. 4); great chairs, 98(fig. 28), 100(fig. 31)
Pinking, 125(fig. 26)

Pins, in bedsteads, 216
Pintles, 213
Pitman, Mark, 148(fig. 30), 149
Pittsburgh Furniture Project, 130*n*3
Planing: breakfast tables, 230–31; tabletops, 223–24
Plant material, cradles from, 210
Plates, narrative and, 172, 188*n*6
Pleasant and Profitable Companion, The, 183
Plinth, of card tables, 122(&fig. 18), 124, 125, 126(fig. 29), 127
Plymouth (Massachusetts) board-seated turned chairs, 98–103(&figs. 28–30, 37)
Plywood Group, 262, 263–64
Polish: for cradles, 209; for dining tables, 228; for stands, 234; for tables, 225
Pollard, John: Benjamin Randolph and, 5–6, 16, 24, 25(fig. 38), 28(&fig. 43), 40*n*5, 41*n*5, 41*n*8, 42–43*n*21, 55, 70, 76, 79; desk-and-bookcase, 21, 22(fig.); easy chairs, 29(&fig.), 31(fig.); high chest base, 17(figs.); pier table, 43*n*27; sideboard table, 30(fig.); side chair, 37, 38(fig. 58)
Pope, Alexander, 182
Poplar: card table, 24(fig. 35); desk-and-bookcase, 19(fig. 28); high chests, 15(fig. 20), 25(fig. 37); pier table, 117(fig.)
Porter, Moses, 229
Portsmouth (New Hampshire), bedstead, 212(fig.)
Posts, for bedsteads, 211
Powel, Samuel, 6, 14, 35, 217
Power, Thomas, 79
Prankhard, John, 79
Pratt, Jesse, 214
Press bedstead, 219(&fig.)
Preston, Titus, 194, 196, 214, 221–22, 227
Price, of Pembroke tables, 230
Prices: Humphrey's, 20, 42*n*18; New York City, 127; Philadelphia, 20, 28, 42*n*20, 43*n*26, 120, 122–23, 127
Prices of Cabinet and Chair Work (Humphrey), 20, 40*n*2
Priestley family, 125(fig. 25)
Prime, Alfred Coxe, 75
Prince, Samuel, 141
Prindle, Eliakim, 233
Pritchard, John, 77

Proud, Daniel, 192, 208
Proud, John, 192
Proud, Samuel, 192, 208
Proud family, 195

Querville, Anthony Gabriel, 260

Ranck, Peter, 206
Randall, Reuben S., 220, 236
Randolph, Benjamin, 2(fig.), 233; account book, 4–6(&figs.), 28(fig. 42); account book, index to, 45–60; advanced style of, 29–40(&figs.); armchair, 12(fig. 12); attributions to, 11–28(&figs.); biography of, 3, 40n2; business success of, 6, 10–11; card table, 24(figs.); craftsmen, 75–81; desk-and-bookcases, 19(fig. 28), 21–24(&figs. 31–34); easy chair, 29(fig.), 31(fig.); employees of, 5–6; goods at vendue and, 6, 10; high chest, 14–17(&fig. 20), 25(fig. 37), 42n15; lumber trading and, 10–11; receipt book, 4; receipt book, index to, 61–74; ship, captain, and port references, 82; sideboard table, 30(fig.), 32–33; side chairs, 10(fig.), 35(&fig. 51), 36(fig. 54), 37(fig. 56), 38(fig. 58), 39(fig.); tea tables, 13–14(&fig. 15), 27–28(&fig. 41); trade cards, 18(&fig.), 163(&fig. 55)
Ranken, William, 214, 217
Rantoul, Robert, 211, 221
Rawson, Joseph, 205
Rawson, Samuel, 205
Read, John, 30, 56, 80
Recovery, 82
Red cedar, bedstead, 211
Redfield, Elias, 225
Redman, John, 81
Red oak, child's armchair, 207(fig.)
Reed, Elias, 145
Reeve, Tapping, 198, 199, 236
Reger, William, 230
Reifsnyder, Howard, 43n22
Reynolds, James, 40n5, 56, 80
Rhea, Robert, 133
Rhode Island, couch, 204(fig.)
Rich, Fleming W., 207
Richmond, John, 216
Richmond, William, 216
Ridley, Nicholas, 87
Ridley chair, 108n8
Ringgold, Thomas, 41n9, 56
Ringgold House (Chestertown, Maryland), 6, 29; chimneypiece, 8(fig. 7), 9(fig. 9); frieze, 8(fig. 8)
Rittenhouse, David, 77
Rivera, Jacob Rodriguez, 215, 216
Robbins, Philemon, 199, 224, 233, 238
Roberts, Lewes, 184, 185–86
Roberts, Rookesby, 210, 230
Roberts, S., 154
Roberts, William, 212
Robins, Elizabeth, 111
Robinson, Charles C., 216
Rocking chairs, repairing or converting, 194, 239n5; children's, 206, 207–9
Rococo style. *See* Randolph, ?Benjamin
Rodgers, John, 229
Rogerson, John, 82
Rollinson, William, 141
Roseman, Joseph, 130n3
Rosewood veneer, card table, 128(fig. 32)
Ross, James, 82
Ross, John, 82
Roundabout chairs, 197
Rule joint bedstead, 219
Rush chairs, 137(fig. 8); repairing, 192–94(&fig. 1), 196
Rushton & Beachcroft, 43n28

Saarinen, Eero, 263, 264
Sack, Israel, 166n16, 166n17
Sacking bottom, 215–16
Sager, John, 196, 205, 214, 220, 228, 231
Saixes, Benjamin, 202
Salem furniture makers, marks of, 157–58
Salem (Massachusetts): breakfast table, 229(fig. 12); desk-and-bookcase, 160(fig. 50); tambour desk, 158(fig. 46)
Salix, 210
Samuel Powel House (Philadelphia), chimneypiece, 7(fig. 5)
Sanderson, Elijah: breakfast table, 229(fig. 12); label of, 159(fig. 48); mark of, 158–59(&figs. 47 & 49), 161; painted initials of, 159(fig. 49); repairs by, 199, 231; tambour desk, 158(fig. 46)
Sanderson, Jacob: breakfast table, 229(fig. 12); label/mark of, 158–61(&figs. 48 & 51); repairs by, 199, 231
Sass, Jacob, 228
Satinwood: breakfast table, 123(fig. 22); card table, 121(fig. 15), 128(fig. 32), 129(fig.); in mechanical card tables, 120; pier table, 117(fig.)
Satinwood veneer: breakfast table, 123(fig. 22); card tables, 121(fig. 15), 128(fig. 32)
Saunders, Peter, 80
Savadge, Thomas, 80
Savery, William: bedstead assembly/disassembly by, 217–18; bedstead repair by, 213; chair repair by, 200, 208; cradle repair by, 209; crib painting by, 210; paper labels of, 136–37(&fig. 9); side chair, 137(fig. 8); toilet table repair by, 231
Scadin, Robert C., 232, 233
Scrutoire, walnut, 133, 134(figs.)
Sea narratives, japanned furniture and, 173–82(&figs.)
Seat casings, repairing, 195–96
Seating, 192
Seat rail construction, 85(fig. 4)
Segar, Benona, 221
Senter, Isaac, 198
Settees, repair of, 205–6
Seymour, John, 161
Seymour, Thomas, 152
"SF" mark, 157, 167n24
Shaftesbury, Earl of, 182, 188n7
Shaw, Alexander, 202
Shaw, John, 197
Shaw and Chisholm, 221, 227
Shepard, Bettey, 196
Shepper, John, 80
Sheraton, Thomas, 119(&fig. 13), 131n10, 142, 193, 230, 236, 237, 238
Sherman, William, 234
Shipley, George, 140(&figs.)
Shippen, Edward, 138
Shippen, Edward, Jr., 228
Shipping instructions, 149–50
Shipping marks, 149–50(&fig. 32)
Shoemaker, Jonathan, 80
Shoemaker, Thomas, 3, 57, 80
Short, George, 233
Short, Joseph, 161, 211; candlestand, 234(fig.)
Shute, Mary, 6
Sideboards: empire, 256, 259–60; white pine, 110(fig.)
Sideboard tables: Benjamin Randolph, 6, 30(fig.); mahogany, 30(fig.)

Side chairs, 157(fig. 44), 193(fig.); caned, 136(fig. 6); cherry, 100, 101(fig. 34); mahogany, 10(fig.), 33(fig.), 35(fig. 51), 36(fig. 54), 37(fig. 56), 38(fig. 58), 39(fig.); maple, 137(fig. 8), 195(fig.); walnut, 153(fig. 38); yellow poplar, 115(fig. 5)
Signatures, as makers' marks, 142–52 (&figs. 22, 24–25, 27–29, 32–33, 35), 165n13; multiple, 147–49
Sign of the Chinese Shield, 6
Sign of the Easy Chair, 30
Sign of the Golden Ball, 42n13
Sign of the Golden Eagle, 3
Silberg, Nicholas, 238
Simpkins, John, 161
Simpson, Joseph, 161
Skyscraper bookcases, 251, 252–53
Slat-backs, 195
Slats for bedsteads, 216
Slead, Edward, 222, 236
Smith, Benedict, 230
Smith, Ebenezer, Jr., 202, 211
Smith, Elizabeth Noyes, 150, 166n16
Smith, Ezekiel, 223
Smith, Howard, 223
Smith, James, III, 166n16
Smith, John, 161
Smith, Robert C., 260–61
Smither, James, 18(fig.), 80
Smith & Hitchings, 161
Snowden, Isaac, 80
Snowden, Jedediah, 80
Society of Journey-men Cabinet-makers, membership certificate, 141(fig.)
Sofas, empire, 259
South Africa, great chairs, 89(figs.)
South East View of the Great Town of Boston (Burgis), 177–78(&fig. 13)
Southmayd, John B., 213
Speed armchair, 251, 254
Speedwell, 10
Spindle, 101(fig. 35)
Spinet stool, 202
Splint, for seating, 194
Springleaf armchair, 262
St. Méry, Moreau de, 217
Stain: for bedsteads, 214, 215; for ?dining tables, 228; for kitchen table, 234; for stands, 234; for tables, 223–24, 225
Stalker, John, 170, 181
Stamper-Blackwell House, 6, 29
Stamp marks, 152–61(&figs. 37, 39–40, 43, 45, 47, 51)
Standing stool, 210
Standish, Myles, great chair and, 98, 99(fig. 30), 101, 108n2
Stands, 234; light, 234–36
Stanton (Delaware), chest-on-chest, 144(fig. 21)
Stenciled marks, 152(fig. 36), 161–63(&fig. 52)
Stephens, David, 232
Stephenson, William, 11, 41m12
Stile carving, 36(figs. 52 & 53)
Stinkwood, great chairs, 89(figs.)
Stools: close, 201–2; repair of, 202–3; standing, 210
Straw matting, 194
Stretchers, repairing, 195
Striping, 197, 206, 208, 238
Strycker, Jacob, 96
Stuyvesant, Peter, 233
Sugar, Thomas, 215
Surface coating, for chairs, 199
Swaim, William, 130n6
Swan, Daniel, 223
Sweet gum, high chest base, 17(fig. 24)
Swift, Jonathan, 183, 185, 189n20
Swivel-top card tables, 124–27(&figs. 25–31), 131m13
Symonds, Joseph, 223
Symson, William, 173

Table clocks, 267–68
Table leaves, work on, 221–22
Table legs: repairing, 221, 228; replacing, 222–23
Tables: backgammon, 233; breakfast, 123–24(&fig. 22), 229–31(&fig. 12); card. *See* Card tables; dining, 227–29 (&fig. 11); dressing, 231–32(&fig. 13); gilt, 234; kitchen, 233–34; marble, 234; pier. *See* Pier tables; repair of, 220–25; stand, 234; tea. *See* Tea tables; work-, 236(&fig.), 258–59
Talcott, George, 234
Taliaferro, Lawrence, 199
Tambour desk, 158(&fig. 46), 167n26
Tardy, Mathurin, 234
Taylor, Abner, 223
Taylor, George, 218
Taylor, Hiram, 218, 220
Taylor, John, 202, 223
Tea table lock, 227
Tea tables, 39; mahogany, 13(fig. 15), 27–28(&fig. 41), 226(fig.); repairing, 226–27

Tenon system, of great chair, 90–91(&figs. 13–15)
Thomas, John W.: chest-on-frame, 145(fig. 23); signature, 145–46(&fig. 24)
Thrones, 108n5, 108n6; King Stephen's, 85–86(&fig. 5), 108n6
Tiffany, Isaiah, 207, 220–21
Till, William, 134
Tinkham, Ephriam, 103, 109n18
Tipping, 197, 208
Tobey, Lemuel, 225, 227
Toilet table, 231
Townsend, Edmund, 139, 165n8
Townsend, Job, 139, 165n8
Townsend, Job, Jr.: backgammon table repair by, 233; sacking bottom installation by, 216; table repair by, 221, 223
Townsend, Job E.: backgammon table repair by, 233; bedstead repair by, 211, 215; breakfast table repair by, 230; candlestand repair by, 235; chair repair by, 200, 202; children's chair repair by, 206–7; couch repair by, 204; cradle repair by, 209; dining table repair by, 228–29; dressing table repair by, 232; go-cart repairs by, 210; table repair by, 221, 222, 223, 224; tea table repair by, 227
Townsend, John, 133, 139(&fig. 13)
Trade cards, 18(fig.), 142(fig. 18), 163(fig. 55)
Treatise on Japanning and Varnishing (Stalker & Parker), 170, 181, 187n5
Tristin, John, 79, 80
Tristin, Thomas, 80
Trollope, Frances M., 217
Trotter, Daniel, 199, 200, 205, 213, 214, 218, 235
Trumble, Francis, 80–81, 209, 225
Trundles, 214
Tryon, David, 11, 82
Tuck, Samuel J., 196
Tucker, Mrs. St. George, 216
Tucker, St. George, 210, 214, 215, 223, 225, 227
Tucker, W. and R., 206
Tufft, Thomas, 209, 218
Tufts family chair, 103–4(&fig. 38), 109n19
Tulip poplar: chest-on-chest, 144(fig. 21); chest-on-frame, 145(fig. 23); desk-and-bookcase, 22(fig.); side

chair, 36(fig. 54)
Turner, Abby Ann, 43*n*22
Turner, Abby Ann King, 43*n*22
Turner, William, 24, 43*n*22, 58, 228
Turning, for replacement bedstead posts, 211
Turn-up bedstead, 219(&fig.)
Two-initial stamps, 153
Tybout, Andrew, 81
Tyler, Ebenezer, 82
Tympanum appliqué, 24, 26(fig. 39)

Upholstering: chairs, 200; couches, 205
"Upper Edge" mark, 149(&fig. 32)
Urn-and-flame finials, 103(&fig.)

Vail, Joseph, 141
Vallance, Robert, 77, 81
van der Rohe, Mies, 264
van der Weyden, Rogier, 87(fig.)
Van Pelt, Edward, 43*n*22
Van Pelt, Ellen, 43*n*22
Van Pelt, Peter, 43*n*22
Van Vechten, Solomon, 152(fig. 37)
Varnish: for bedsteads, 214, 215; for breakfast tables, 230–31; for candlestands, 236; for children's chairs, 208; for cradles, 209–10; for dining tables, 228; for kitchen table, 234; to protect coloring, 197; for rush seating, 193; for settees, 206; for stands, 234; for stools, 203; for tabletops, 224, 225; for washstands, 238
Vases, narrative and, 172, 188*n*6
Vaughn, Samuel, 228
Virginia, high chair, 105(fig. 42)
Vose, Isaac, 235
Vose and Coates, 211
Voyage Round the World (Betagh), 173

Wadsworth, Daniel, 238
Wales. *See under* Welsh
Wallace, William, 85, 86
Waln, Mary (Wilcocks), 111, 113, 128
Waln, Richard, 128
Waln, William, 111, 112, 113
Waln House, The (Kern), 114(fig.)
Walnut: armchairs, 198(fig.); card table, 232(fig.); chairs, 197; chest of drawers, 135(fig. 4); chest-on-chest, 144(fig. 21); chest-on-frame, 145(fig. 23); couch, 204(fig.); cradle, 209(fig.); scrutoire, 134(fig. 2);

sideboard table, 30(fig.); side chairs, 153(fig. 38); tables, 228
Walsh and Egerton, 223
Walton, Sam, 265
Walton, Samuel, 81, 204, 222
Wanton, William, 216
Ward, Joshua, 200
Ward, Miles, 202
Washington, George, 40*n*1, 59
Washington, Martha, 40*n*1
Washstands: mahogany, 237(fig.); repairing, 237–38
"Watering," 200
Wax, for stands, 234
Wayne, Samuel, 222
Wayne, William, 212
Webb, Benjamin, 211, 213
Webster, John, 30, 43*n*28, 59
Welch, John, 82
Welsh board-seated turned chairs, 91–96(&figs. 16–18, 20–22)
Wetherill, Samuel, 115(fig. 6)
Wetherill, Thomas, 113, 115(fig. 6), 117
Wethersfield (Connecticut), great chair, 97(fig. 24)
"WF" mark, 157
Wharton, Thomas, 209
Whipple, Stephen, 194
White, C. H., 259
White, Donald P., III, 103
White, J. F., 259
White, Joseph, 149
White cedar: card table, 125(fig. 26); chest of drawers, 135(fig. 4); chest-on-chest, 144(fig. 21); desk-and-bookcase, 19(fig. 28), 22(fig.); high chest, 25(fig. 37); high chest base, 17(fig. 24); scrutoire, 134(fig. 2); side chairs, 33(fig.), 39(fig.)
Whitehead, William, 141
White oak: card table, 24(fig. 35); desk-and-bookcase, 19(fig. 28); dining table, 229(fig. 11); easy chair, 29(fig.); high chest, 25(fig. 37); side chair, 38(fig. 58)
White pine: bedstead, 212(fig.); breakfast table, 123(fig. 22), 229 (fig. 12); card tables, 116(fig.), 121(fig. 15), 124(fig. 24), 125(fig. 26), 128(fig. 32), 151(fig. 34); desk-and-bookcases, 149(fig. 31), 160(fig. 50); dressing table, 231(fig.); high chests, 147(fig. 26), 171(fig.), 179(fig.), 184(fig.); japanned looking glass, 177(figs.);

pier table, 115(fig. 6); scrutoire, 134(fig. 2); sideboard, 110(fig.); side chair, 115(fig. 5); tambour desk, 158(fig. 46); washstand, 237(fig.)
"WH" mark, 153(fig. 39)
Wightman, Thomas, 151; card table, 151(fig. 34); inscription, 151(fig. 35)
Wilder, Billy, 264
Wilder, Josiah P., 212–13, 215
Wilkinson, Bryan, 41*n*5, 59, 81, 82
Willard, Simon, 265, 266
Williams, Jacob, 203
Williams, John, 81
Williams, Samuel, 81, 209, 226–27
Willing and Morris, 11, 82
Willow cradle, 210
Willow *(Salix)*, 210
Wilmington (Delaware) clockmaking, 266, 267
Wilson, James, 41*n*5, 59, 81
Wilson, William, 197
Windsor chairs: paper labels on, 155(&fig. 42); repairing, 195; stamped, 154–55(&fig. 40)
Windsor settees, 205–6
Winterthur Museum, 44*n*30, 145, 256
Wistar, Charles, 230
Wolcott, Oliver, 215, 236
Womb chair, 264
Women: chinoiserie and, 182, 189*n*17; reading and, 182, 189*n*17
Woodbury, Abigail, 211
Woodhouse, Samuel, 36
Workman's Guide, The, 214
Worktables/work stands: curled maple, 236(fig.); empire, 258–59; repairing, 236
Workwoman's Guide, The, 216, 220
Wright, Elizabeth (Robins), 111–12
Wright, George G., 110–31; apprenticeship and stylistic development of, 112; biography of, 111–12, 129–30*n*2; breakfast table, 123–24(&fig. 22); card table, 111; furniture attributed to shop of, 124–29(&figs.); furniture documented to shop of, 120–24(&figs.); journeyman years of, 112–19; mechanical card tables, 120–23(&figs. 15–21), 124(&fig. 24); move to Pittsburgh and Ohio, 111–12, 130*n*3; pier table, 111, 117–18(&figs.), 119(fig. 12); shop locations, 111(fig.); sideboard, 110(fig.), 111, 112, 113(&fig.); swivel-top card tables, 124–27(&figs. 25–31)

Wright, John, 111
Wright, Sarah (Fleming), 111
Yellow pine: breakfast table, 123(fig. 22); card table, 232(fig.); chest-on-chest, 144(fig. 21); desk-and-bookcase, 19(fig. 28); high chest base, 17(fig. 24); high chests, 15(fig. 20), 25(fig. 37); sideboard table, 30(fig.)
Yellow poplar: card table, 116(fig.); cradle, 209(fig.); pier table, 115(fig. 6); sideboard, 110(fig.); side chairs, 115(fig. 5), 195(fig.); worktable, 236(fig.)
Yew, great chairs, 90(fig.), 92(fig. 17)
Young, Nathan, 81

Zane, Isaac, 42*n*15, 60
Zimmerman, Philip D., 37, 265, 266

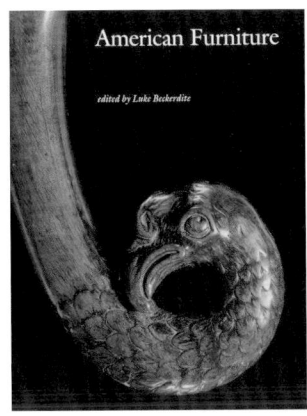   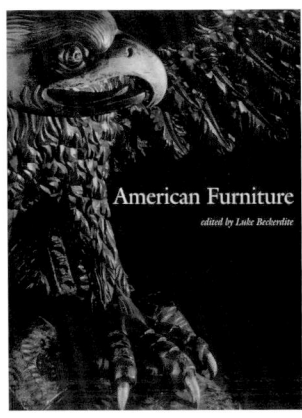

   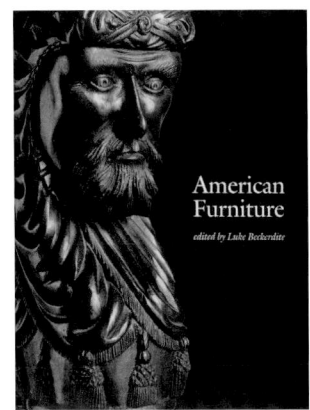

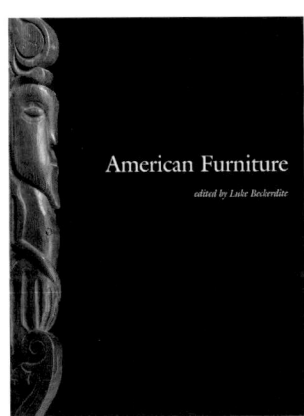  

Published Annually
by the
CHIPSTONE
Foundation

Distributed by
Antique Collectors' Club Ltd.
Eastworks
116 Pleasant Street
Easthampton, MA 01027
USA
info@antiquecc.com
800-252-5231